'If I Had a Son'

JACK CASHILL

If I Had a Son

RACE, GUNS, AND THE RAILROADING
OF GEORGE ZIMMERMAN

 WND Books

'IF I HAD A SON'

WND Books, Inc.
Washington, D.C.

Book Designed by Mark Karis

WND Books are distributed to the trade by:
Midpoint Trade Books
27 West 20th Street, Suite 1102
New York, NY 10011

WND Books are available at special discounts for bulk purchases. WND Books, Inc.,
also publishes books in electronic formats. For more information call (541) 474-1776
or visit www.wndbooks.com.

First Edition

ISBN 13 Digit: 978-1-938067-21-1 (Hardcover)
978-1-938067-33-4 (eBook)

Library of Congress information available.

Printed in the United States of America.

Dedication

To Ytz4mee, Sharon, StellaP, Finch, WeeWeed, Bijou, Garnette, Ad Rem, DiWataman, Chip Bennett, and especially, Sundance

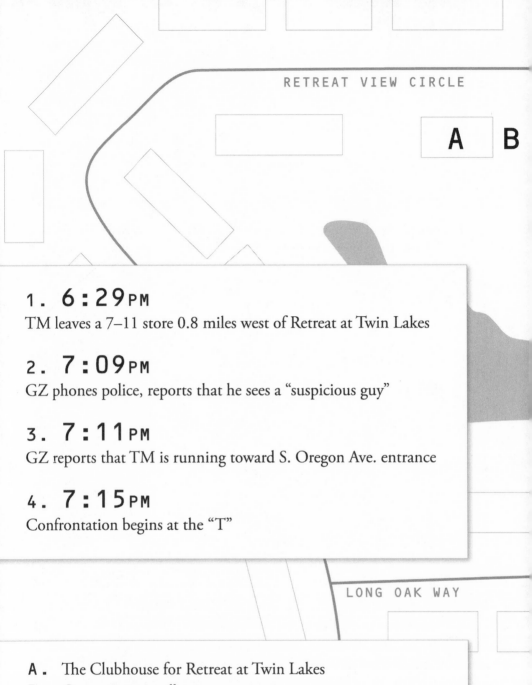

RETREAT VIEW CIRCLE

A | B

1. **6:29**PM
TM leaves a 7–11 store 0.8 miles west of Retreat at Twin Lakes

2. **7:09**PM
GZ phones police, reports that he sees a "suspicious guy"

3. **7:11**PM
GZ reports that TM is running toward S. Oregon Ave. entrance

4. **7:15**PM
Confrontation begins at the "T"

LONG OAK WAY

A. The Clubhouse for Retreat at Twin Lakes
B. Community mailboxes
C. Where GZ parked his truck
D. Brandy Green's townhouse, where TM was staying
E. GZ stopped and completed his 9-1-1 call
F. The confrontation begins here
G. The altercation ends here
H. Eyewitness 6's townhouse

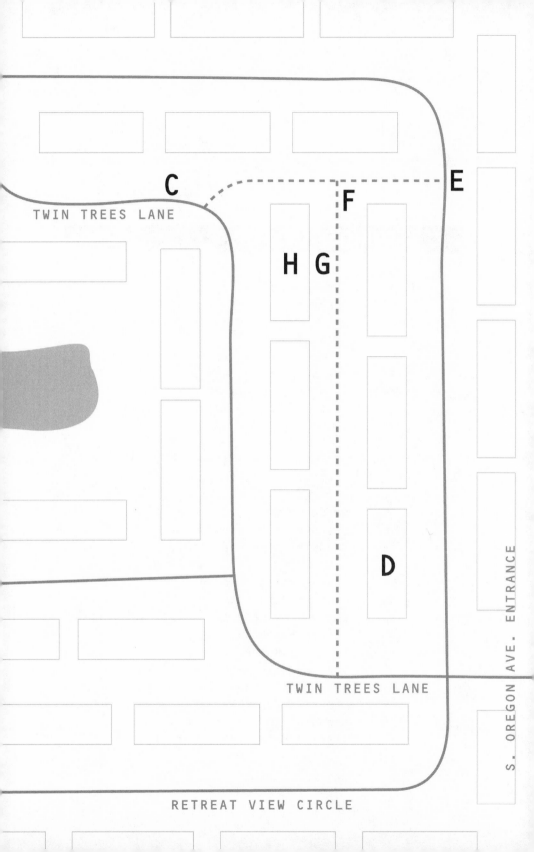

TWIN TREES LANE

C

E

F

H G

D

TWIN TREES LANE

S. OREGON AVE. ENTRANCE

RETREAT VIEW CIRCLE

Contents

PART 2: THE TRIAL

Acknowledgments

KUDOS TO THOSE GOOD SOULS in the blogosphere—
TalkLeft, Legal Insurrection, Daily Caller, and the *Conservative Treehouse*—who did the serious reporting on this case
that the major media failed to do. Their reporting helped
secure George Zimmerman his acquittal and make this book possible.
I would also like to commend those publishers, Joseph Farah at WND
Books and Thomas Lifson at *American Thinker*, who allowed me to
contribute to the conversation.

Thanks also to my agent, Alex Hoyt, for knocking on many a door
until the folks at WND Books had the courage to open theirs. All the
folks at WND Books—Michael Thompson, Albert Thompson, Aryana
Hendrawan, Amanda Prevette, Meredith Johnson—have been prompt
and helpful. Geoffrey Stone's editing was patient and thoughtful. Mark
Karis's cover art was inspired, and Joseph Farah was intrepid as always in
shepherding this project through. Thanks, too, to my webmaster, Debra
Blackstone, and my one insightful reader who has chosen understandably
to remain anonymous. And, of course, I am always grateful to my wife,
Joan, for encouraging me in projects that inevitably prompt my friends
to say, "Watch your back."

A final word of thanks to Bob Zimmerman and his son, Robert Jr.,
for their insights. In America, no family should have to endure what theirs
has gone through. I am hopeful that this book will shame at least a few
people into understanding that.

Part 1

THE SHOOTING

1

BRAVING THE TANK

O N JUNE 5, 1989, a lone young man in a white shirt stood defiantly in front of a column of Type 59 tanks heading east on Beijing's Avenue of Eternal Peace. The tanks stopped. They had to. Too many people around the world were watching for the tanks to just run the man down.

Among those following events in Tiananmen Square was a fellow now known to friends as "Sundance," a recent college grad then back at home in Florida.[1] The outrageous bravery of the unknown Chinese man fascinated him. Although not at all political at the time, and an insignificant witness to the tragedy, Sundance found himself drawn deeply to Tank Man and the other young dissidents under fire. For the first time, Sundance watched the news intently, Ted Koppel's *Nightline* in particular, and tuned in to talk radio as well.

Sundance remembers listening to a radio show in his car on which a panel of guests weighed in on "the right-wing crackdown" in China. The oppressors were communists, thought Sundance. How could they be right wing? When he got home—this was before cell phones or the Internet—Sundance turned on the show, got the call-in number, and dialed. He had never done anything like this before. "I just need to correct the host," he told the producer. "The oppressors in China are hard-line communists. They're on the far *left*."

Next thing Sundance knew, he was on the air. He repeated his assertion to the panelists about the misinformation they were spreading. For a few excruciating seconds, no one quite knew what to say—dead air weighs heavily on radio. Finally, one panelist spoke up. "You're right," he conceded. With that admission, he made Sundance aware that the individual citizen can sometimes see the world more clearly than his supposed betters in the media.

Slowly, tentatively, Sundance began his transition from passive bystander to intellectually engaged participant in American democracy. That much said, life kept him on the political sidelines. He returned to the grocery chain where he had bagged his way through his adolescence and worked his way up to very near the top. He also started a family. In the meantime, the Internet was opening doors for activists that had never been opened before. By the 2008 election, Sundance was a regular on a few key blogs. He had found his voice in their "comments" sections and met people with similar views and who also wanted a voice. The readers of these blogs were creating a genuine community "downstairs." Often, they would direct their comments to the posts of others rather than the article itself. Alliances formed. Friendships grew out of the alliances.

By 2009 Sundance felt most at home at HillBuzz, an unorthodox and oddly conservative blog overseen by eccentric Hillary Clinton supporter and openly gay Kevin Dujan. For HillBuzz regular "StellaP," a Detroit-area grandma and IT professional, Dujan's site proved to be a hospitable "watering hole" until that "terrible Saturday in November 2010." Explains "Sharon," a sixty-something farmer's daughter from Montana and a fellow HillBuzz devotee, "Dujan went weird on us." He started insulting guests, many of whom had been supportive. After some harsh words, visitors like Sharon and StellaP found themselves being driven away or even formally "banned." StellaP remembers being "horrified at the real possibility that [she] would be separated from [her] friends forever."[2]

By that time, though, the collective had made enough e-mail contacts to regroup at a side room called the Connection. There they talked among themselves—Sundance, Ytz4mee, Sharon, StellaP, Finch, Wee-Weed, Bijou, Garnette, Ad Rem—and concluded they were ready for something more. "I was tired of being nice," says "Ytz4mee," a military spouse and full-time mother of four. "We needed a space where we could be ourselves and teach others how to deconstruct the mainstream media narrative." And so, in February 2011, the blogging collective known as the *Conservative Treehouse* found a cyber home all its own.

Like Sundance, all the "Treepers," as the *Treehouse* participants called themselves, can define with some precision the moment when they switched from passive witness to active participant in the life of the republic. For a few, the transition was even more dramatic as they morphed, like Ytz4mee, from "raving socialist" to stalwart constitutionalist. But none of the eight "admins" who run the site, Sundance included, ever expected that one day they would be standing, metaphorically at least, where Tank Man stood.

They have stared down a powerful hydra-headed force that the mainstream media, out of fear or ideological complicity, refuse even to acknowledge. "We Ain't Backing Down," Sundance headlined a post in bold red letters after the opposition began to pound them. "Get That Through Your Thick Skulls."[3] It was Ytz4mee who first labeled this force "the Black Grievance Industry," or just BGI. The BGI is not as scary as the Chinese army, but if the Treepers are just about all that stands between you and it, the BGI can be pretty damn frightening. Those with doubts need only ask the family of the man whose rights the Treepers have spent more than a year defending, the besieged "white Hispanic," George Michael Zimmerman. George and his family will put those doubts to rest.

2

GATHERING THE FACTS

ON SUNDAY NIGHT, February 26, 2012, George Zimmerman sat down with Sanford Police Department (SPD) detectives and wrote out in longhand his account of the shocking incident that had just left him rattled and bloody. Zimmerman, who writes well, began with background information. In August 2011 his neighbor's house had been broken into while his neighbor was home with her infant son. She barricaded herself and her child in an upstairs bedroom and called 9-1-1. The SPD quickly responded, and the intruders fled. Zimmerman's wife, Shellie, saw them fleeing and "became scared of the rising crime."[1] Zimmerman promised that he would do what he could to keep her safe. One result was that he and some of his Retreat at Twin Lakes neighbors formed a Neighborhood Watch Program. The SPD gave them a nonemergency number to call if they saw anything suspicious.

At 7:09 p.m. on that Sunday evening, Zimmerman followed through on the advice the police had given him. Upon driving to the neighborhood Target to do some grocery shopping, he spotted "a male approximately 5'11" to 6' 2" casually walking in the rain and looking into homes." Zimmerman was driving slowly behind the suspect when he called the number he had been given:[2]

SPD: Sanford Police Department [*garbled recording*], this is Sean.

GZ: Hey, we've had some break-ins in my neighborhood and there's a real suspicious guy, uh [near] Retreat View Circle. The best address I can give you is 111 Retreat View Circle. This guy looks like he's up to no good or he's on drugs or something. It's raining and he's just walking around, looking about. [00:25]

SPD: Okay, and this guy, is he white, black, or Hispanic?

GZ: He looks black.

SPD: Did you see what he was wearing?

GZ: Yeah, a dark hoodie, like a gray hoodie, and either jeans or sweat pants and white tennis shoes. He's here now. He's just staring. [00:43]

SPD: Okay, he's just walking around the area . . .

GZ: Looking at all the houses.

SPD: Okay . . .

GZ: Now he's staring at me. [00:48]

SPD: Okay, you said that's 1111 Retreat View or 111?

GZ: That's the clubhouse.

SPD: That's the clubhouse. Do you know what the . . . he's near the clubhouse right now?

GZ: Yeah, now he's coming toward me.

SPD: Okay.

GZ: He's got his hands in his waistband. And he's a black male. [1:09]

SPD: How old would you say he looks?

GZ: He's got a button on his shirt, late teens.

SPD: Late teens, okay.

GZ: Uh-huh. Something's wrong with him. Yep, he's coming to check me out. He's got something in his hands. I don't know what his deal is. [01:26]

SPD: Let me know if he does anything, okay?

GZ: [anxiously] See if you can get an officer over here.

SPD: Yeah, we've got 'em on the way. Just let me know if this guy does anything else.

GZ: Okay. These a**holes. They always get away.

Zimmerman was driving from a point near the clubhouse to a spot farther east on Twin Trees to keep an eye on Martin. The sounds suggest that Zimmerman got out of the truck at this point, but had not yet begun to follow Martin on foot.

GZ: When you come to the clubhouse, you come straight in and you go left. Actually, you would go past the clubhouse. [1:53]

SPD: Okay, so it's on the left-hand side from the clubhouse?

GZ: Nah, you go in straight through the entrance and then you would go left. You go straight in; don't turn and make a left. Shit, he's running. [2:08]

Martin meanwhile headed east along an east-west cut-through between the two streets Twin Trees Lane, where Zimmerman was parked, and Retreat View Circle. He then turned south on a dog walk that intersects the cut-through and runs between the backs of the buildings on either street. The town house where he had been staying was only a few hundred feet down that dog walk.[3]

SPD: He's running? Which way is he running?

GZ: Down toward the other entrance of the neighborhood. [2:14]

SPD: OK, which entrance is that he's headed towards?

Zimmerman knew the general direction in which Martin was headed but could no longer maintain a visual from the area of the truck. Ambient wind sounds suggest he started walking swiftly, roughly in the same direction Martin was running.

GZ: The back entrance. It's f***ing cold. [*garbled, much disputed*]

The dispatcher obviously heard the wind sounds.

SPD: Are you following him? [2:24]

GZ: Yeah.

SPD: Okay. We don't need you to do that. [2:26]

GZ: Okay.

SPD: All right, sir, what is your name? [2:34]

GZ: George. He ran.

At this point, Zimmerman's breathing relaxed, and the sound of wind abated.

SPD: All right, George, what's your last name?

GZ: Zimmerman.

SPD: And George, what's the phone number you're calling from?

GZ: 407-435-2400.

SPD: All right, George, we do have them on the way. Do you want to meet with the officer when they get out there?

GZ: Yeah.

SPD: All right, where are you going to meet with them at?

GZ: Um, if they come in through the gate, tell them to go straight past the clubhouse and, uh, straight past the clubhouse and make a left and then they go past the mailboxes; they'll see my truck. [3:10]

SPD: All right, what address are you parked in front of? [3:21]

GZ: Um, I don't know. It's a cut-through so I don't know the address. [3:25]

SPD: Okay, do you live in the area?

GZ: Yeah, yeah, I live here.

SPD: Okay, what's your apartment number?

GZ: It's a home. It's 1950—oh, crap, I don't want to give it out—I don't know where this kid is [*inaudible*] [3:40]

SPD: Okay, do you just want to meet with them at the mailboxes then? [3:42]

GZ: Yeah, that's fine. [3:43]

SPD: All right, George, I'll let them know you'll meet them at—

GZ: Could you have them call me and I'll tell them where I'm at? [3:51]

SPD: Okay, that's no problem.

GZ: My number . . . you've got it?

SPD: Yeah, I've got it. 407-435-2400?

GZ: Yeah, you got it.

SPD: Okay, no problem. I'll let them know to call you when they're in the area. [4:02]

GZ: Thanks.

SPD: You're welcome.

The call ended four minutes and change after it started. "The dispatcher told me not to follow the suspect & that an officer was on the way," Zimmerman picked up the narrative. "As I headed back to my vehicle the suspect emerged from the darkness and said, 'You got a problem?'" When Zimmerman answered "No," the suspect said, "You do now."

> As I looked and tried to find my phone to dial 9-1-1 the suspect punched me in the face. I fell backwards onto my back. The suspect got on top of me. I yelled "Help" several times. The suspect told me, "Shut the f*** up." As I tried to sit upright, the suspect grabbed my head and slammed it into the concrete sidewalk several times. I continued to yell "Help." Each time I attempted to sit up, the suspect slammed my head into the sidewalk. My head felt like it was going to explode. I tried to slide out from under the suspect and continue to yell "Help."
>
> As I slid the suspect covered my mouth and nose and stopped my breathing. At this point I felt the suspect reach for my now exposed firearm and say, "Your [*sic*] gonna die tonight Mother F***er." I unhol-

stered my firearm in fear for my life as he had assured me he was going to kill me and I fired one shot into his torso. The suspect sat back allowing me to sit up and said "You got me."

At this point I slid out from underneath him and got on top of the suspect holding his hands away from his body. An onlooker appeared and asked me if I was ok. I said "No." He said "I am calling 9-1-1." I said "I don't need you to call 9-1-1. I already called them. I need you to help me restrain this guy." At this point a SPD officer arrived and asked "Who shot him." I said I did and placed my hands on top of my head and told the officer where on my persons [sic] my firearm was holstered. The officer handcuffed me and disarmed me. The officer then placed me in the back of his vehicle.[4]

Zimmerman's own account ended here. Officer Timothy Smith arrived at roughly 7:17 p.m. and reported finding Zimmerman standing near Martin, who was lying facedown in the grass. Officer Smith noted that Zimmerman's back was wet and covered with grass and that he was bleeding from the nose and the back of his head.[5] As Officer Smith would tell the state attorney's office, Zimmerman volunteered that he had shot Martin. "I was yelling for help but no one would help me," he told Smith and complained that his head was hurting. The officer handcuffed Zimmerman "for safety reasons."[6] Officer Jordan Broderick arrived shortly afterwards and saw "that the back of Zimmerman's head was cut and he was bloodied."[7] Officer Jonathan Mead also saw Zimmerman in custody and "noted his injured nose and bleeding head."[8] As Mead told the state attorney's office in April 2012, he had "dealt with Zimmerman before at the complex when Zimmerman had found open doors and houses. Zimmerman had reported suspicious persons that he had lost sight of when they (the suspicious person) went around a building. Zimmerman had been on foot when [he] met him on prior occasions."[9]

Officer Richard Ayala arrived at the scene soon after Officer Smith. When he got there, Smith had Zimmerman at gunpoint, so he tended to Martin, who was then lying facedown with his hands under his body. He rolled Martin over and "felt a large cold can in the center pocket."[10] Martin had forty dollars and change in his pants pockets as well as "one (1) red '711' brand name lighter, photo button, Skittles, and headphones"[11] When Ayala and a fellow officer attempted CPR and other first aid, the can came loose and was misidentified as an "Arizona brand name tea can."[12]

The officers located Martin's cell phone in the grass away from the body.

Before Officer Smith drove Zimmerman to the Sanford police station, he asked Zimmerman if he wanted to go to the hospital. Zimmerman declined. On the way to the police station, though, Zimmerman complained "that his head hurt and he felt a little light headed."[13] Asked once again if he wanted to go to the hospital, Zimmerman hesitated and then declined again. Once at the station Officer Smith took Zimmerman to the interview room and kept an eye on him for health reasons. Soon after, Sanford police fingerprinted him, removed his clothes as evidence, conducted forensic tests on his hands for gunpowder residue, and kept his handgun for examination. Zimmerman signed a Miranda warning waiver, forgoing his rights to having an attorney present. Then, beginning at 8:15 p.m. on Sunday, the police questioned him at length.

The first officer to interview Zimmerman was Investigator Doris Singleton. Zimmerman accurately described Martin to her as "early twenties to late teens" and "six-footish, slender build." The story he told Singleton tracked closely with his written account, but it was more detailed. He related, for instance, how Martin saw him in his truck, lights on, engine running, and walked completely around the car. Apprehensive, Zimmerman rolled up his windows. After Martin circled the car, he disappeared in the direction of the north-south dog walk, and this was when Zimmerman exited the car to keep an eye on him. At the end of this initial interview, Singleton told Zimmerman he "did the right thing" by calling the police.

"Is that what you guys normally do when you see someone suspicious, you just call?" When he answered yes, she asked, "You don't try to make contact with them?"

"No," he said.[14]

In a second session Singleton tried to determine exactly where Zimmerman was when he saw Martin and where Martin went when he disappeared. Singleton, however, had not been to the site, and their communication on this subject was imprecise.

Just after midnight lead investigator Chris Serino took over. He had been to the site and interviewed a number of eyewitnesses. He walked Zimmerman through the scenario once more and noted, among other details, "no defense wounds on his arms or hands." Serino was impressed by "the consistency between Zimmerman's account of events and those provided by the witnesses." He observed, too, that Zimmerman's injuries "appeared generally consistent" with the known facts. As a result, "Zimmerman was released from police custody." Serino cautioned, however, that the initial encounter between Zimmerman and Martin had "no known eyewitnesses."[15] None would come forward. No new facts of substance would emerge, but as it turned out, the case was far from closed.

While Zimmerman was being interrogated, Martin's father, Tracy Martin, was dining out in nearby Orlando with his girlfriend, Brandy Green.[16] Martin, forty-five, a truck driver, had divorced Trayvon's mother, Sybrina Fulton, in 1999 when Trayvon was just a toddler. Martin subsequently married Alicia Stanley, whom he had been seeing before the divorce. According to Stanley, the couple formally separated just weeks before the shooting, but Tracy had been courting Green for more than two years.[17]

It was at Green's Twin Lakes condo that Trayvon had been staying. He had arrived in Sanford by bus on February 21. Although he had stayed at Green's several times before, this was the first time he'd stayed without his father. The last time Tracy Martin saw his son was Saturday, the night before the shooting. He and Green spent that night in an Orlando hotel, but he gave Trayvon some money "to eat and go to the movies." When he and Green returned to the town house on Sunday night after dinner, Green's fourteen-year-old son, Chad Joseph, told his mother that Trayvon had walked to the store hours earlier and not returned. Figuring Trayvon must have gone to a late movie with his cousin, Stephen "Boobie" Martin, Tracy turned off his phone and went to bed. When Trayvon had still not returned by the next morning, Martin checked with his nephew Stephen and learned that he had not seen Trayvon either. He then had Brandy "call Juvenile Justice . . . to see if anyone by the name Trayvon Martin had been picked up."[18] Finally, Tracy called the Sanford Police Department and asked to file a missing persons report. He told the police that he had not seen Trayvon since 8:00 or 8:30 on Saturday night.[19] After a few phone calls back and forth, the police told him a car was on the way. Martin waited outside Green's house to greet the police. Knowing something of his son's recent problems, he likely expected to see him in their custody.

Three cars arrived, not just one. In the third car was the chaplain, never a good sign. Based on the earlier phone conservations with Martin, the police had to suspect that Trayvon was the victim in question, but he had no identification on him when shot. To confirm his suspicions, investigator Chris Serino asked Martin if he had any recent pictures, and Martin showed an image of Trayvon captured on his smartphone. Serino sighed and shook his head. He then went to his car, returned with a folder, and asked Martin if they could go inside. Once seated, he pulled out a photo of Trayvon taken at the scene of the shooting. There was no mistaking who it was. Serino explained the circumstances surrounding Trayvon's death and summoned for a victim's advocate to assist.[20] From that moment on, Tracy Martin's life would move in a direction utterly surreal even for the father of a slain youth.

That morning, Shiping Bao, the associate medical examiner in Volusia County, performed an autopsy on Trayvon. He concluded that Martin was killed by a single gunshot to the chest at very close range. The autopsy also revealed an abrasion on Martin's left ring finger that could have come from a thrown punch. Underreported at the time of the autopsy's release nearly three months after the shooting was one critical fact about the living Martin: he stood five feet eleven inches tall and weighed 158 pounds.

That morning Serino had reviewed the 9-1-1 calls. He noted that on one call a male's voice could be heard yelling, "help" or "help me" fourteen times in approximately forty seconds. "The voice was determined to be that of George Zimmerman, who was apparently yelling for help as he was being battered by Trayvon Martin."[21]

That afternoon Tracy Martin and Brandy Green visited the site of the shooting. Keith Landry, a reporter for local Fox 35 TV, just happened to be there at the same time. "Was that a friend of yours?" he asked Martin naively. "That was my son," answered a grim, stone-faced Martin. Green was much more emotional and forthcoming. "He don't know anybody here," she cried. "He just came down here. He was bored. So he walked to the store. He was on his way back home. I'm living down here. He was sitting on the porch and this man killed him. Are you serious?"[22]

Later that day, at 5:20 p.m., Zimmerman accompanied Serino, Singleton, and Sgt. Randy Smith on a walk-through of the crime scene. A Sanford Police Department (SPD) technician taped the reenactment.[23] The twelve-minute video shows a remarkably unguarded and respectful Zimmerman driving and walking the officers through the estate and explaining what happened where and why. Zimmerman looks nothing like the hulking brute in the mug shot taken seven years earlier and posted everywhere in the weeks to come. Trimmer and benignly suburban in a white Lacoste polo shirt, the short, well-spoken twenty-eight-year-old seems altogether unthreatening. Only the two butterfly bandages on the back of his head and a nose, still swollen from the encounter, mark him as a man in a jam.

In the video Zimmerman elaborates on what he told the dispatcher the night before. He says he was on his way to Target to do his weekly grocery shopping when he first saw Martin standing on the grass in the rain in front of a house at 1460 Retreat View Circle that had a history of break-ins. "I felt there was something off about him," he casually tells the Sanford police. He drove past Martin, parked in front of the clubhouse, and called the nonemergency dispatcher. Martin walked past him, looking at his truck, and then walked right on Twin Trees Lane and out of Zimmerman's sight. Zimmerman backed out of his spot, drove in the direction Martin had walked, and parked on Twin Trees Lane. He then saw Martin heading east toward the cut-through between Twin Trees Lane and the next street over, Retreat View Circle. Then, however, he came back and circled Zimmerman's truck menacingly, his hand in the pocket of his hoodie faking a gun, before heading down the cut-through again.

The dispatcher asked for an address. Zimmerman could not remember the name of the street in this small subdivision where streets circle about and zigzag after the fashion of subdivisions everywhere. So he got out of his car to look for an address. Not seeing one on Twin Trees Lane, he headed across the cut-through toward Retreat View Circle. To this point, Zimmerman's testimony tracks almost perfectly with his call to the dispatcher the night before. The deviations are minor, and on the video Zimmerman does not appear deceptive.

The video shows Zimmerman and the police investigators walking across the concrete cut-through nearing Retreat View Circle when Zimmerman remembers a key detail: he had been halfway across that sidewalk, at the point where it intersects the north-south dog walk, when the dispatcher asked if he was following Martin. Zimmerman tells the SPD:

And I said yes because I was, you know, in the area. They said, "We don't need you to do that," and I said "Okay." That's when I walked straight through here to get the address.[24]

At the time, Zimmerman could not have begun to imagine how critical this detail was. He tells the police that he walked through to Retreat View Circle and started walking back to his truck. He reached the point where the cut-through intersected the north-south dog walk, the "T" intersection. Here he heard Martin yell out to him from behind him to his left, "Yo, you got a problem." When Zimmerman fumbled for his phone, Martin punched him in the nose, breaking it on that first punch. He pushed Zimmerman down as he stumbled to regain his footing and got on top of him.

"I started screaming, 'Help, help' as loud as I could," Zimmerman tells the investigators, and to silence him Martin covered his mouth and nose with his hands and said, "Shut the f*** up." When he struggled to get up, Martin slammed his head against the concrete. "It felt like my head was going to explode, and I thought I was going to lose consciousness," Zimmerman says emphatically. He also offered very specific detail about his exchanges with a witness before the shooting. Someone stepped out and offered to call 9-1-1, Zimmerman told him, "No, help me. I need help." He did not get it.

Fox 35's Keith Landry interviewed that witness earlier in the afternoon, an interview that aired about twenty minutes before Zimmerman and the police revisited the scene. "The guy on bottom who I believe had a red sweater on was yelling to me, 'help, help,'" the witness told Landry. "I told them to stop and I was calling 9-1-1." As he headed upstairs to call, he heard a gunshot. The witness continued, "When I got upstairs and looked down the person that was on top beating up the other guy was the one laying in the grass. I believe he was dead at that point."[25]

Zimmerman and the officers arrived at that same spot a half hour after Landry's live broadcast. In the video, he shows the officers how and roughly where the shooting took place. As Zimmerman tells it, when he squirmed to get his head off the concrete, his jacket lifted up. Martin saw the gun and said, "You're going to die tonight, mother f***er." Martin then reached for the gun. Zimmerman restrained Martin's hand and pulled the gun from the holster with his free hand. He fired one shot at close range. Martin sat upright.

Zimmerman tells the investigators, "He said, 'you got me, you got it, you got me, you got it,' something like that." Zimmerman explains to the officers that he thought Martin had been scared but not hit, so he pushed Martin off, rolled him over, and got on top of him. Police arrived soon thereafter, saw the body, and asked who did the shooting. Zimmerman tells the officers that he said, "I did," and without prompting put his hands over his head and acknowledged his firearm, now holstered. The police handcuffed Zimmerman, seized his gun, and took him away. As the video concludes, one officer asks the other if he has any more questions. Neither one does.

From the crime scene, the officers took Zimmerman back to the station. There investigator William Ervin introduced Zimmerman to a fairly simple voice stress test to determine whether he had been truthful. Before beginning, Ervin asked him a few questions about his experience the night before, and Zimmerman confirmed what he had written, namely, that he was looking for an address to give the dispatcher when Martin appeared "out of nowhere," asking, "You got a problem?"

"Looks like you got banged up pretty good," said Ervin. He then asked Zimmerman to rate his current stress level on a scale of one to ten. Although uncertain, Zimmerman suggested a "seven."[26] Erwin then led him through nine basic questions:[27]

1. "Is your name George?"

2. "Is the color of this other wall green?"

3. "Is today Monday?"

4. "Did you confront the guy you shot?"

5. "Is this the month of February?"

6. "Were you in fear for your life when you shot the guy?"

7. "Are we in the city of Sanford?"

8. "Have you ever driven over the posted speed limit?"

9. "Am I wearing a watch?"

To establish controls, the technician asked Zimmerman to lie on questions two and eight. On the relevant questions, four and six, he answered no, he did not confront Martin, and yes, he did fear for his life. He passed the test. At that point, Zimmerman seemed relaxed, and the police seemed trusting. He could be forgiven for thinking that the worst was behind him.

It was not, not by a long shot.

3

BRACING FOR THE STORM

TWO DAYS AFTER THE SHOOTING, Tracy Martin and Brandy Green made their first trip to Sanford Police Department headquarters. Trayvon's mother, Sybrina Fulton, would not come to Sanford until the story exploded in the media. Tracy Martin needed to see the body and get some answers as to how and why his son died. While at the station, police played Zimmerman's call and some of the 9-1-1 recordings from neighbors who had reported the shooting. On one of these recordings, desperate cries of help are clearly audible for roughly forty seconds until a gun is fired, at which time the cries promptly stop. Reuters, which did a comprehensive report on the first few days, failed to report a key detail about this particular audio. Martin told the police that the screams for help were *not* those of his son. The *Orlando Sentinel* reported this fact on March 17. "It was Zimmerman, [Investigator] Serino said. He said he is certain of that because he played a recording of that voice for Trayvon's father, Tracy Martin, and the Miami man said the voice was not his son's."[1] Serino's comments have added weight in that he was openly sympathetic to Martin's plight.

Unfortunately, the *Sentinel* edited Serino's comment out of its online version,[2] but it was captured as reported by any number of blogs, including ones sympathetic to Martin, like the *Democratic Underground*. Other police officers also confirmed they overheard Martin's admission. The

Reuters article in question was written five weeks after the shooting. By that time Martin had a vested interest in keeping his initial observations about the screams to himself. In fact, on April 2 of that year, he told the State prosecutors who were interviewing him that he was "emotionally upset" when the police played the 9-1-1 call, and he "didn't give his full attention to the recording." Martin denied ever saying that the voice yelling for help was not his son's. He went on to say that he listened to the tape many times subsequently and was sure that it was Trayvon yelling for help.[3] It was not the only time he misled prosecutors during that interview.

After playing the 9-1-1 calls for Tracy Martin two days after the shooting, Serino escorted him to another room, where they reviewed Zimmerman's version of events. He also questioned Tracy Martin about Trayvon. As will become evident soon enough, the sympathetic Serino seems to have believed what Tracy Martin told him about his son. According to Martin, Serino told him, "I want to interview [Zimmerman] again to catch him in a lie."[4]

Intentionally or otherwise, Serino raised enough suspicion about Zimmerman's actions to provoke Tracy Martin. Ignoring the details of the beating, Martin came to believe that Zimmerman had stalked his son because he was black. Outraged that the Sanford police had bought Zimmerman's self-defense claim, Martin turned to attorney Patricia Jones. Although reportedly Martin's sister-in-law, she is certainly a friend. They share a Masonic bond, Martin being a district grand master for the International Free and Modern Masons, and Jones being the chairman of trustees for the Order of Eastern Star. Jones contacted a relative, who contacted a friend, and all calls led finally to Benjamin Crump, a high-profile, Tallahassee-based civil rights attorney.

This was a made-to-order case for Crump, who had a history of intervening on behalf of black victims of white injustice, real and otherwise. He and law partner Daryl Parks had successfully represented the family of fourteen-year-old Martin Lee Anderson, who died in a boot camp–style youth detention center in 2006. While running in a required exercise, Anderson stopped and complained of fatigue. This being a boot camp, guards prompted him to continue his run, but he soon collapsed and died. Parks and Crump promptly—and perversely—turned the case into a racial issue. Under pressure from the Black Grievance Industry, a special prosecution team led by future attorney general Pam Bondi tried seven guards and a nurse for manslaughter. The prosecution witnesses could not agree on what actually caused Anderson's death. Given that the eight defendants were looking at thirty years in prison if convicted, it mattered whether they had improperly used force, accidentally suffocated Anderson trying to revive him, or simply failed to act in a timely matter. The defense meanwhile argued consistently and convincingly that Anderson died of complications from sickle-cell anemia. A jury took fewer than ninety minutes to acquit all eight of the accused. Nevertheless, hoping to buy racial peace, the Florida legislature shut down the otherwise successful boot camp program and compensated Anderson's family $4.8 million for his death.[5]

Two days after the shooting, when Crump got the call on the Trayvon Martin case, he was in Jacksonville, litigating the case of a black bail bondsman who had been shot and killed by a white sheriff's officer. Jones soon put Crump in touch with Tracy Martin. According to Crump, he signed on to represent Martin's parents "approximately two days" after the shooting "to pursue any wrongful death and other claims they or Trayvon's estate may have."[6] "I told [Tracy Martin] to believe in the system," Crump would later relate. He was sure that Zimmerman would soon be arrested. To press the Trayvon Martin case, Crump proceeded to use what Marc Caputo of the *Miami Herald* called the "boot camp playbook."[7]

On that same Tuesday, February 28, Sanford investigator Trekelle Perkins received a telephone call from an anonymous female who claimed Zimmerman had "racist ideologies" and that he was capable of instigating a lethal confrontation.[8] To this point, Zimmerman's name had not been mentioned in the media. The caller would leave no identifying information. When later speaking to the FBI, Serino identified Perkins, who is black, as one of several people pressuring him to file charges against Zimmerman. He also complained about leaks within the department. The call would seem to have been prompted by one of them.[9]

The following day, Wednesday, February 29, Fort Lauderdale funeral director Richard Kurtz transported Martin's body back to Miami for a Friday viewing and a Saturday funeral. Kurtz should not have been a relevant player in this drama, but he made himself one soon enough. Later that same day Serino called Zimmerman back in for an extensive interview. Unlike the earlier interviews, which had been fairly straightfor-ward, this was a "challenge" interview, straight out of the police handbook. Throughout it, Serino introduced some conspicuous bits of disinformation designed to rattle Zimmerman and prompt him to reveal any details he might have been hiding.[10]

"This person was not doing anything bad," Serino said of Martin. "He was 17 years old, an athlete, um, probably somewhere [*sic*], somebody who was gonna be in avionautics, a kid with a future. A kid with folks that care. In his possession we found a, uh, can of, uh, iced tea and a bag of Skittles. And about $40 in cash. Not a goon." Serino presented the information not as speculation but as a result of his own quasi-scientific investigation. "Part of what I've been doing the last couple days is trying to get into his head, a psychological profile, and find out what his likes are, dislikes are, his hobbies, all the rest of that stuff." He concluded, "This child has no criminal record whatsoever, ah, good kid. A mild-mannered kid."[11]

In that one session alone, Serino referred to Martin as a child ten times, the word emerging as code for "defenseless victim." And yet Serino later admitted to Zimmerman that this "child" was "about 6 foot, about 150 pounds." To put this in perspective, legendary boxer Tommy "The Hitman" Hearns was six foot one, 145 pounds, when he first won the world welterweight title as a twenty-one-year-old. He won his first pro-fessional fight at nineteen and had won 155 amateur fights before that. Martin, of course, was no Tommy Hearns. For one thing, he weighed 158 pounds, thirteen pounds more than Hearns. For another, at least in Serino's retelling, he was not a fighter. "The child has no record at all, no violent tendencies, none of this, that I can, that I know of. That anybody else knows of," he assured Zimmerman. "His folks would've told me."[12]

Zimmerman clearly knew more about the true nature of Trayvon Martin than Martin's folks did. He had the wounds to show for it. If Serino had made merely a cursory review of Martin's ample social media pages, he would have known enough not to tell Zimmerman what he did. That is, of course, unless Serino were intentionally bluffing. At one point, for instance, he told Zimmerman that one of Martin's hobbies was videotaping "everything he does." As a result, claimed Serino, Martin had a "very impressive" library of images trapped in his phone. Serino claimed he would have reviewed them all by then, "but the battery died," and the

SPD is "working on that." This buildup led to Serino's ultimate tease: "There's a possibility that whatever happened between you and him is caught on videotape." The gambit did not work. Said Zimmerman simply, "I prayed to God that someone videotaped it."[13]

In reporting on this interview, Serino made an observation that was lost to almost every observer in the media and in the law enforcement establishment. When he asked Zimmerman why he had not engaged Martin in conversation when he approached his truck, Zimmerman claimed to be "afraid for his safety." He also denied that he was "chasing" Martin, a denial that rings true if he was indeed fearful. According to Zimmerman, he was following Martin only to keep him in sight.

By this time, too, Serino had become aware that there were rumblings in Sanford's black community. "Court of public opinion is going to beat up on you a lot, OK?" he said to Zimmerman as though there were a good response to that question. Serino then added the unsettling observation, "A lot of people don't think that your injuries are consistent with getting in a life-threatening type thing." A lot of people? Zimmerman had to be asking himself who these people were and how they knew about his injuries. The story had yet to make the newspaper.[14]

That was about to happen. Two hours after Serino began the interview, the *Orlando Sentinel* posted its first article about the shooting online, "Boy, 17, shot to death in Sanford during 'altercation,' police say." The article said nothing about the race of either Trayvon Martin or George Zimmerman. Martin was identified as a Miami high school student who was visiting a relative. Citing FOX 35 News as her source, the *Sentinel*'s Susan Jacobson reported that the shooter and Martin had "been in a fist-fight right before the killing." The police did not release Zimmerman's name because he had not been charged. He had, however, "told officers he shot the boy." The police understood the shooting had to be "very disturbing" for the residents of the Retreat at Twin Lakes and promised to investigate thoroughly.[15] Although many of the facts in the article were wrong, the errors were innocent. That would change in a hurry.

By Thursday, March 1, the word had spread that a white man had shot a black teen and gone free. The rumor was that Serino's superiors, particularly Seminole County state attorney Norman Wolfinger, had suppressed his effort to charge Zimmerman with manslaughter. The local president of the NAACP, Turner Clayton Jr., sent Sanford police chief Bill Lee an e-mail asking to meet and discuss Martin's shooting. It's unclear when or whether Clayton met with Lee, but Velma Williams, the only black member of the five-person Sanford city commission, met with Lee on March 1, four days after the shooting. "I can see a train coming down the track at 50 miles an hour, and you better get a handle on this," she told Lee. He reassured her that the investigation was objective and fair, but she wasn't exactly buying it. "People were getting suspicious, saying we knew that was going to happen based on history," she later told Reuters.[16]

On Friday, March 2, a public viewing was held for Martin at the Richardson Funeral Home in Miami Gardens, Florida, a largely black Miami suburb where Martin had been living on and off with either an uncle or his mother, Sybrina Fulton. The funeral was held the next morning at the Antioch Missionary Baptist Church nearby. At the time of the "Home Going Ceremony," as the funeral was called, the death of Trayvon "Slimm" Martin seemed to the world beyond his family just another unfortunate statistic. Over the previous thirty years, as the US Justice Department reported, "Blacks were disproportionately represented as both homicide victims and offenders." The victimization rate for blacks was six times higher than the rate for whites. The offending rate for blacks was almost eight times higher than the rate for whites. Males represented 77 percent of homicide victims and nearly 90 percent of offenders. More than a third of murder victims were under twenty-five, as were nearly half of all offenders.[17] Like Martin, the great majority of homicide victims, usually more than 70 percent, are killed by perpetrators using handguns.

At the time of his funeral, Martin's death seemed much too ordinary. It attracted no media attention. The only controversy that emerged from the funeral was the presence there—or, more likely, the absence—of a mystery girl who would come to be known as Witness 8, or Dee Dee. Although the authorities were not yet aware of her role in Martin's death, they soon would be.

As of March 5, a week and a day after the shooting, the story remained a back-page affair. The *Orlando Sentinel* ran its second story on the case, this one just a few paragraphs long. The news hook was that the still-unidentified man who shot Martin was a member of the gated community's neighborhood watch. There was no mention of his race or Martin's.

The Zimmermans, the Sanford Police Department, and the Sanford community at large may have been feeling the rumbles, but they had no idea of the media tsunami that was building momentum just offshore.

4

MOBILIZING THE PLAYERS

*B*Y THE WEEKEND OF THE FUNERAL, Benjamin Crump was fully engaged. "[Forty-eight] hours passed and they still hadn't arrested him," Crump said of Zimmerman. "After that we just had to do what we had to do."[1] Among the first things he did was enlist the help of Sanford attorney Natalie Jackson, a former naval intelligence officer and a board member of the local NAACP. On Monday, March 5, Jackson reached out to Ryan Julison, an Orlando-based media strategist and the one white member of what was rapidly becoming Team Trayvon.

Although Julison protested that he involved himself in the Martin case simply to help the grieving parents "get justice for their son,"[2] he had worked with Jackson on other race-based legal cases, including, coincidentally, the Sherman Ware case that Zimmerman had spearheaded—more on this later. Of greater consequence, on the same he day signed on with Team Trayvon, Julison proudly announced on his Facebook page that his firm "led the communications and PR effort" on behalf of the "$1.25 billion Black Farmers Settlement."[3] That's right, "billion."

This landmark class action case usually goes by the name of *Pigford* and/or *Pigford II*. Pigford deserves a book of its own, but suffice it to say that claims were filed on behalf of more than ninety-four thousand black farmers even though the US Census Bureau never counted more than thirty-three thousand such farmers during the period in question. The fear of a "racism" charge scared the major media away from reporting, so that task was left to Andrew Breitbart's *BigGovernment* on the right and the *Huffington Post* on the left. "The fraud of Pigford is real," confirmed the *Huffington Post*'s Lee Stranahan. "It's tens of millions of dollars, at least. The USDA knows about it. They aren't telling the truth and unfortunately, if we're going to get to the truth it's going to have to come from Republican-led hearings."[4] In December 2010 *BigGovernment* described the case as one of "mind-boggling government malfeasance and corruption," but even that does not quite capture the magnitude of the scam.[5]

It was not until April 2013 that the *New York Times* chose to cover the scandal. It did so with a major front-page story that blamed the "Obama administration's political appointees at the Justice and Agriculture Departments" for a massive misdirection of funds, at least $1.33 billion that became "a runaway train, driven by racial politics."[6] In March 2012, though, Julison could still boast of a Pigford notch on his belt. If nothing else, that seeming triumph showed he knew his away around what Treepers called "the BGI," the Black Grievance Industry.

Given his experience with the Martin Lee Anderson case, Crump understood that the national media were suckers for a story with a racial angle, specifically one that featured a black victim of white injustice. He also suspected that if enough national pressure could be brought to bear, the local authorities would crack. After meeting with Crump and Jackson, Julison immediately began pitching the Trayvon saga to the larger world. "I am happy to share the initial media pitch and subsequent pitches with you," a defensive Julison would later write to the *Treehouse*, "but there is no reference made to race in them."[7] Given the media response to the pitch, it is hard to take Julison at his word. Reuters bit first. On March 7, just two days after Julison was contacted, the London-based international news agency posted an article by Barbara Liston headlined "Family of Florida boy killed by Neighborhood Watch seeks arrest."[8]

Beyond the headline, the article is almost entirely about race. The oversized opening sentence establishes a thesis that has proved irresistible to the major media for the last half century: "The family of a 17-year-old African American boy shot to death last month in his gated Florida community by a white Neighborhood Watch captain wants to see the captain arrested, the family's lawyer said."[9] To this point, the *Orlando Sentinel* had not mentioned the race of either Martin or Zimmerman. In an article the following day, the *Sentinel* mentioned the respective race of each of the parties only in the fourteenth paragraph.

Not Reuters. Reuters was writing press releases for Team Trayvon. Zimmerman was a "loose cannon." Liston quoted Julison as saying, "If the 9-1-1 protocol across the country held to form here, they told him not to get involved. He disobeyed that order." Martin, by contrast, was a "good kid." He hoped to be a pilot. He was carrying the soon-to-be-iconic iced tea and Skittles, the latter for Brandy's "thirteen-year-old" son, Chad, now elevated to the role of Martin's "brother" and made a year younger than he actually was. Said Crump, "Trayvon only has Skittles. He has the gun." Crump told Liston that race was "the 600 pound elephant in the room," but he abused the metaphor. Race was only the unspoken elephant if no one was talking about it. Crump wanted to talk about nothing else. Liston concluded her article with a quote from Crump, "Why is this kid suspicious in the first place? I think a stereotype must have been placed on the kid."[10] In this one article, Team Trayvon had established exactly the narrative it wanted. In the weeks to come, the major media—facts be damned—would work overtime to reinforce that narrative.

On March 8, Current TV's the *Young Turks*, reportedly the most-watched online TV show in America, took up Martin's cause. Cohost Ana Kasparian, an impressively self-righteous twenty-five-year old, made no fewer than a dozen errors in her five-minute presentation: Martin's father lived in the gated community with Martin's stepmother; Martin went for snacks at halftime of the NBA game; he was walking to the store when shot; Zimmerman called 9-1-1. Unfortunately, not all of her misstatements were this forgivable. Consider, for instance, her claim, "There was no self-defense in this situation." As she envisioned the action, Zimmerman called 9-1-1 and said "there was someone in the gated community who looks very suspicious, i.e. a young black man who makes me uncomfortable." Apparently to ease his discomfort, "George Zimmerman decides to go ahead and shoot the seventeen-year-old black boy in the chest, which led to his death."

"Oh, my God," gasped her cohost, Cenk Uygur. "He just shot him?"

"He just shot him," affirmed Kasparian, who then pontificated, "I get so angry when people deny there is racism in this country."[11]

The black girl that Zimmerman took to his high school prom would not have been quite so quick to smear her date with the racism brush. In fact, Zimmerman made about as unlikely a racist poster child as America could produce. In December 2010 a police lieutenant's son, Justin Collison, sucker punched a black homeless man named Sherman Ware outside a bar. Although Ware suffered a concussion and there was video evidence of Collison's attack, no action was taken against Collison, who is white, for nearly a month. Reuters's reporter Daniel Trotta talked about the incident in his April 3 analysis of the early days of the Trayvon phenomenon; he made no mention of Zimmerman's role in that controversy.[12]

That role was a significant one. Upset at the lack of media attention the Ware case was getting, Zimmerman and his wife, Shellie, printed fliers demanding that the community hold accountable the officers responsible for misconduct. They then passed the fliers out to area churches. At a public meeting in January 2011, Zimmerman took the floor and said, "I would just like to state that the law is written in black and white. It should not and cannot be enforced in the gray for those that are in the thin blue line." The meeting was recorded on video. As a result of the publicity, police chief Brian Tooley, whom Zimmerman blasted for his "illegal cover-up and corruption," was forced to resign, and Collison was arrested.[13] Zimmerman headlined his fliers with a famous quote from Anglo-Irish statesman Edmund Burke: "The only thing necessary for the triumph of evil is for good men to do nothing."[14] He might more accurately have quoted Oscar Wilde, another Anglo-Irishman: "No good deed goes unpunished."

Zimmerman's involvement in the Ware case was not out of character. George grew up in Manassas, Virginia, the son of Bob and Gladys Zimmerman. Bob was a magistrate judge and Vietnam vet; Gladys was a Peruvian immigrant and deputy court clerk. As the New York Times would fairly report only after the thuggish vigilante meme had burrowed into the nation's consciousness, the Zimmermans "ran a disciplined household that emphasized service, responsibility and the Roman Catholic faith." George was an altar boy who served Mass in both English and Spanish and remained committed to the faith as an adult. "They were so polite," a Manassas neighbor said of the Zimmermans. "They always looked after you before themselves."[15]

In 2001, the senior Zimmermans bought a small retirement home in Lake Mary, Florida, for future use, and they trusted George enough to move in by himself soon after graduating from high school. He started his career as an insurance agent and then prospered as a mortgage broker in the halcyon days of the real estate bubble. When the bubble burst, his company folded, and he worked a variety of jobs while talking seriously of becoming a police officer. At the time of his confrontation with Martin, Zimmerman was attending college part-time and working full-time as a loan underwriter and forensic review analyst at Digital Risk, a fraud detection company that contracted with financial institutions.

Among the various documents the FBI collected was a printout of Zimmerman's MySpace page from 2005. The agents may well have gotten it from his ex-fiancée, who strongly objected to the fact that George listed himself as "single" despite the fact they were living together. Twenty-one at the time he posted this information, Zimmerman came across as a pretty typical guy of his time and place. He listed his religion as Catholic, his ethnicity as Latino/Hispanic, and his height as a very generous five ten. Implicit in his self-description was his ambition. He acknowledged on his MySpace page that some of his friends resented him for leaving Manassas, but he asked rhetorically, "Can you really hate on someone for improving thier [sic] life?"[16] He told his friends he had opened his own insurance agency and was making forty-five to sixty thousand dollars a year, a claim likely as inflated as his height.

In November 2007, Zimmerman married Shellie Nicole Dean, a local girl from Longwood, an Orlando suburb. He had just turned twenty-four. She was a twenty-year-old cosmetologist who specialized in facials. At the time of the shooting, Shellie was studying to be a nurse and had as humble a public profile as any woman her age in America. That would change.[17] Despite Zimmerman's father's protests about the high rate of crime in Sanford, the couple moved to the Retreat at Twin Lakes in 2009.

The *New York Times* put in context what many other media had been busily sensationalizing: namely, Zimmerman's earlier contretemps with the law. In his annus horribilis of 2005, he had been arrested for pushing an undercover alcohol agent, whose official status Zimmerman was not aware of. The charge was dropped when Zimmerman agreed to a pretrial diversion program, which allowed him to avoid prosecution in favor of probation. About a month later, he and his then fiancée traded petitions for injunctions after each claimed to be a victim of the other's temper. The injunctions expired a year later without further ado. For all that, as the *Times* noted, "Mr. Zimmerman seemed to have a protective streak—a sense of right and wrong—that others admired." The reporters cited several examples of Zimmerman going out of his way to help struggling adolescents, including two black teenagers he and his wife, Shellie, had been mentoring through the Big Brother/Big Sister organization.[18]

In early 2012, though, it was Zimmerman who was struggling and needed help, but there was no George Zimmerman to help him. The mother of the two teens volunteered to speak out, but Zimmerman urged her to remain silent for her own safety.[19] Tonetta Foster, the sister of Sherman Ware, joined the mob demanding Zimmerman's arrest. "I stand for justice," she insisted at a Trayvon rally on March 19 at the Seminole Criminal courthouse, "for Trayvon, for Sherman Ware."[20] The local NAACP, with whom Zimmerman worked on the Ware case, turned its back on him as well. On March 26, George's brother Robert sent an impassioned letter to local NAACP head Turner Clayton, asking him to "call off the dogs. Period. Publicly and swiftly." As Robert reminded Clayton, Zimmerman's "was the only nonblack face in the meetings for justice" in the Ware case. "It's time for you to end the race issue in this matter and call for cooler heads to prevail," Robert pleaded, but without success or much expectation of the same.[21]

Ware's attorney, in fact, was Natalie Jackson, a key player on Team Trayvon. In early April 2012, when the Zimmerman family talked publicly about George's involvement in the Ware case, Jackson denied that he had handed out any fliers and dismissed the family's attempt to establish Zimmerman's commitment to racial justice. "It's a PR strategy, a propaganda campaign," said Jackson. "His friends and family are doing him a big disservice by race-baiting." Jackson made the impressively disingenuous point that racism is "not what we're talking about. We're talking about whether he was justified in taking Trayvon Martin's life."[22]

Even before the media ramped up the pressure, George Zimmerman sensed at least some of the trouble to come. Hysterical at the news of the shooting, his wife, Shellie, called George's best friend and mentor, Mark Osterman, and he met her at the scene. An air marshal with the Department of Homeland Security and a former sheriff's deputy, Osterman had taught Zimmerman how to shoot. He accompanied Shellie to the police station that night, and when George was released early the next morning, the Zimmermans went back to Osterman's home in nearby Lake Mary. After a sleepless night, George showed up at the breakfast table the next morning, his eyes now blackened, his nerves shot, his soul beginning its descent into mourning and guilt. "George's strong Catholic convictions were at play here," says Osterman. "He felt he had committed an 'unpardonable sin.'"[23]

Later that morning Zimmerman went into his office to meet with his liaison in human resources. A coworker who saw him that morning told the FBI that he looked "horrible," with bandages on the front and back of his head. She added that he seemed "physically and emotionally distraught and devastated."[24] Zimmerman left after he consulted with HR and never came back. He returned to Osterman's house, where he and Shellie stayed for the next four or so weeks.

By March 8, Zimmerman was in a world of hurt, and the emotional pain was growing more acute daily. Reuters had outed him by name, and Kasparian slandered that name to the best of her limited ability. "Although names are blacked out on the police report," wrote Barbara Liston in her Reuters article, "Crump and media reports at the time of the shooting identified the caller as George Zimmerman."[25] No, the media reports had not identified Zimmerman by name. Crump did, and he surely had help from within the Sanford Police Department. Liston also identified Zimmerman as white. She likely knew no better.

"People assume I was white because of my last name," the olive-skinned Zimmerman would tell Sean Hannity in a July 2012 interview, but as he explained, he identified himself "first as an American and then an Hispanic-American."[26] Reuters would later acknowledge that Zimmerman "was raised in a racially integrated household and himself has black roots through an Afro-Peruvian great grandfather—the father of the maternal grandmother who helped raise him."[27] His mother was dark enough, in fact, that she was on at least one occasion denied restaurant service in preintegration Virginia.[28] Zimmerman told Hannity he learned to speak Spanish from his Peruvian mother and grandmother before he learned to speak English. The pair largely raised him during his early years as his father, Bob Zimmerman, a career Army officer and Vietnam veteran, moved from post to post, including two tours in Korea. Given his upbringing, Zimmerman has more claim to being "Hispanic" than white-raised President Barack Obama has to being "black."

Historically, the media are as shy about highlighting Hispanic injustice toward blacks as they are keen on exploiting stories of white injustice toward blacks. Consider, for example, an August 2007 incident that also involved the killing of black youth by a man of Peruvian origin. That evening, Jose Carranza and five of his buddies were drinking and smoking marijuana in a Newark, New Jersey, schoolyard when they spied four young, black students, two male and two female, playing music, and judged them easy prey.

Unlike with Trayvon Martin, there were no complicating factors in the victims' biographies. Twenty-year-old Dashon Harvey was entering his junior year at Delaware State University. Eighteen-year-old Terrence Aeriel was to begin at Delaware State the following month. Nineteen-year-old Natasha Aeriel also attended Delaware State. Twenty-year-old Iofemi Hightower was holding down two jobs while she saved to attend college.

Carranza and his pals pulled guns on the four and robbed them. Then they forced them to lie facedown while they sexually assaulted the girls. "All I could keep doing was saying, 'Jesus, Jesus, Jesus,'" testified Natasha Aeriel, who survived the attack. "It probably was a little too loud because somebody told me to shut the f*** up." One of the gang members put his knee in Aeriel's back and slashed her throat with a machete. Upon seeing her own blood, Aeriel willed herself to push off her attacker and started to run. It was then that Carranza's crew opened fire, killing Aeriel's three friends with gunshots to the back of the head and wounding Aeriel. She survived to finger the attackers and has since graduated from Delaware State.[29]

At the time, this story received a fair amount of attention locally but almost none nationally. After the attack, the late Terry Anderson, an iconoclastic Los Angeles–based black talk show host, challenged black leaders to speak out. "If you make one simple change, and change Jose Carranza to a white man, I will guarantee you that [Sharpton and Jackson] would be screaming and marching in the streets." They did not, and as a result the story quickly faded.[30]

In his valuable memoir, *Radical Son*, David Horowitz tells a story that answers the question of why the Carranza killings attracted so little attention. While still a leftist, Horowitz had recommended his friend, an unassuming forty-two-year-old mom named Betty Van Patter, to help the Black Panthers manage their business affairs. When she proved too honest, these much-fawned-over Marxists fired her then murdered her. "In my entire life, I had never experienced a blacker night," wrote Horowitz.

Worse was yet to come. When Horowitz sought justice for Van Patter, he found, much to his dismay, that no one cared. "There was only silence," said Horowitz of his allies on the left. "The incident had no usable political meaning and was therefore best forgotten."[31] In a similar vein, the schoolyard killings, however grotesque, had no usable political meaning for the BGI and the media. Carranza, like Zimmerman, had Peruvian roots. But unlike Zimmerman, he was an illegal alien, a member of the violent Central American gang MS-13. He had been previously arrested on charges of aggravated assault and rape, and at the time of the murders was still in the country, free on bail.

The BGI has long had a symbiotic relationship with the Democratic Party. Although illegal immigration would seem to work against the best interests of its natural constituency, the BGI has proven unwilling to challenge the amnesty-friendly Democrat position. Carranza was to that position what Willie Horton had been to Michael Dukakis's position on prison furloughs—a living, breathing embarrassment. Were the media to give the Carranza case the attention it deserved, they would not only highlight the self-defeating nature of the Democratic posture, but they would also stir dissension between blacks and Hispanics. If one googles Jesse Jackson or Al Sharpton and Jose Carranza, all that can be found are blog postings along the lines of "Where were Al Sharpton and Jesse Jackson?" The fact that Zimmerman is a household name and Carranza is not, testifies to the power of the BGI to create the news it likes and suppress the news it doesn't.

This is not a new phenomenon. Those who doubt the ability of the BGI-Democrat-media complex to control the flow of racially oriented news might inquire about the human abattoir that abortionist Kermit Gosnell ran in Philadelphia or the twenty-seven blacks killed in President Bill Clinton's 1993 tank assault at Waco. If still not satisfied, they might ask about the 250 or so black children whose bodies were dumped into a mass grave in Oakland's Evergreen Cemetery during the Jimmy Carter presidency. They would learn that the man who ordered their murder in Guyana was a Carter supporter, a Democratic vote harvester and BGI accomplice by the name of Jim Jones. The Guyana dead, like the Waco dead, like the Philadelphia dead, like the Newark dead, have gone unmourned because, unlike Trayvon Martin, they had no usable political meaning.

If George Zimmerman had been named George Carranza or even Jorge Zimmerman, it is unlikely that Crump and his allies would have taken the case. Nor would the media or the Democratic establishment have wanted any part of it. As it happened, though, the original police reports identified Zimmerman as a white man. Whoever leaked that information to "the community" looked no further. Purposefully or not, Team Trayvon took that seeming fact and ran with it, fully indifferent to Zimmerman's background either as a native Spanish speaker or a civil rights activist. The major Latino groups in the Democratic media complex fell quickly into line and were unmoved by the realization that Zimmerman was one of their own.

On March 22, La Raza president Janet Murguía wrote that her organization was joining "allies in the civil rights community in calling for a real investigation for this grievous failure of justice."[32] Harsher still, Roberto Lovato, cofounder of the Latino advocacy organization Presente. org, passed judgment on Zimmerman as recklessly as an Alabama judge on the Scottsboro Boys: "The Latino community joins the African American community and other communities in condemning George Zimmerman as what he is—a murderer and a racist." Lovato felt free to condemn Zimmerman because his ethnic bona fides were suspect. "His background is not clear," said Lovato. "Is he Latino? Is he white? Is he both? Who knows? It's irrelevant. What's relevant are his actions, his racist comments, and his cold-blooded killing of an innocent young man."[33] As Lovato's ignorant diatribe made clear, Team Trayvon and its media friends had convinced even Zimmerman's potential ethnic allies that he was a racist.

On that fateful March 7 day, either through a reckless indifference to facts or a conscious effort to suppress them, Team Trayvon chose to introduce George Zimmerman to the world as a thuggish white man, a loose cannon, an armed vigilante who preyed on undersized black children. To make this story line work, Crump and his associates also had to scrub Martin's background and package him as something that he was not, an innocent little boy. They would have remarkable success in doing both.

5

MANAGING THE HYSTERIA

ANDREW BEAUJON REPORTS on the media for the Poynter Institute, a self-described "international leader in journalism education."[1] On April 17, 2012, with the Trayvon Martin story "relatively quiet," he took the opportunity to applaud the media that broke the story. In a sloppy bit of reporting, Beaujon overlooked Reuters, which published its story on March 7, and singled out Mark Strassmann of CBS News's Atlanta bureau, who went public on March 8. Beaujon cited the *New York Times* as his source.[2]

According to the *Times*, Strassmann was "tipped off," presumably on March 7 by Julison, and he promptly contacted Crump. Strassmann then sent an e-mail to the producers of *CBS This Morning*. Within forty minutes they wrote back to him, "We can interview the victims' parents tomorrow." The *Times* headlined its story, "In Slain Teenager's Case, a Long Route to National Attention."[3] Long route? It took Julison a day or two of phone calls before Martin's parents were on national TV. The media love these kinds of stories, true or otherwise, verified or not.

By the time Beaujon wrote his laudatory article, he had to know how badly major media reporting had distorted the case. He chose not to mention any of it. The first reader to post a comment, "Gary," noticed the oversight. "Ah, so that's where all the misinformation began," he wrote. "An amazing level of incompetence from the legacy media. Just a bunch of sock puppets controlled by Crump."[4] Twenty years earlier, the major media could have blown off Gary and people like him. In the age of the Internet, it was possible, but no longer easy.

On Thursday, March 8, *CBS This Morning* aired Strassmann's piece. For three-plus minutes Tracy Martin expressed his grief over his son's death and his outrage that Zimmerman had not been arrested. Getting the parents in front of the cameras was at the heart of Julison's strategy. No one dared challenge a parent who buried a child. Later that morning, Crump staged a press conference in Orlando that featured Tracy Martin, proxy mom Brandy Green, and Martin's cousin Stephen. Throughout the photo op, Stephen held a five-year-old picture of Martin from his Pop Warner football days.

That day's coverage on Orlando's *Eyewitness News 9* uncritically captured the message that Crump and Julison had framed. Reporting on the story was a young black reporter named Daralene Jones. "Since he was a boy seventeen year-old Trayvon Martin wanted to play football and become a pilot," she told the viewers, who repeatedly saw the Pop Warner picture from the press conference. As Jones told the story, Martin was returning through this predominantly white, gated community with Skittles and iced tea when Zimmerman spotted him. He promptly called the police to report a "suspicious black man." He then ignored the dispatcher's command to not confront Martin. A scuffle resulted, and Zimmerman fatally shot "the boy." Said Tracy Martin at the press conference, "We just don't understand why the Sanford Police Department is really sitting on their hands." Added Crump, "Trayvon Martin, a seventeen-year-old kid, has Skittles. No way you can say self-defense."[5]

When confronted by Jones on the self-defense issue, police chief Bill Lee talked about "facts and circumstances" but seemed to concede that Zimmerman's call to the Sanford police dispatcher would prove he had disobeyed police orders to not confront Martin. "If your son had been white do you think he would have been shot and killed that day?" Jones asked Tracy Martin provocatively. Martin, of course, answered no. Jones then concluded with a summary statement about Zimmerman: "We wanted to know if the neighborhood watch leader is getting special treatment because he is white."[6] In a half hour of research, Jones could have discovered that this privileged "white" person was actually a Hispanic civil rights activist who helped get the last police chief fired, but that would have undone the preferred story line. And what Jones was saying locally was precisely what the major media were about to say nationally.

The search for truth was left almost exclusively to the blogosphere, but that search did not begin until at least three weeks after the incident. Early on, social media were used almost exclusively to promote Team Trayvon's message. On April 13, 2012, Texas blogger Christian Yazdanpanah provided a useful summary of the social media's accomplishments during the previous month, titled approvingly "How Marketers Brought George Zimmerman to Jail."[7]

The social media efforts began on March 8, the day CBS News ran its first piece, with a social media coordinator named Kevin Cunningham, a redheaded "super Irish" son of political activists. Cunningham, who had attended law school at the historically black Howard University, read the story on a Howard fraternity e-mail list and created a petition on Change. org called "Prosecute the killer of our son, 17-year-old Trayvon Martin." He shared that petition with other members on the fraternity list, who then shared it with their contacts on other social networks. Cunningham collected more than ten thousand signatures in just a few days and then transferred administrative rights to the Martin family. Once celebrities as diverse as Spike Lee, Deepak Chopra, and Mia Farrow caught on, the signings took off, with more than one hundred thousand received within the first week. And that was just the beginning.

Despite his pious claims of pro bono good-deed-doing, Ryan Julison felt the need to brag about his successes. "Check this story out from Reuters running on Yahoo! News on the Trayvon Martin murder," Julison Communications posted on its Facebook page March 10. "More than 18,000 comments so far. This has certainly struck a nerve around the country." ABC News had also picked up the story. "Coordinated interviews with *Good Morning America* and the family of Trayvon Martin," Julison boasted that same morning.[8]

The *Good Morning America* piece added a new wrinkle or two, but it only reinforced the narrative established by Team Trayvon. ABC News Atlanta's Yunji de Nies reported that Trayvon was an unarmed teenager carrying Skittles. He had always wanted to be a pilot or a football player. The viewer saw an innocent child smiling on the screen as a montage of preadolescent photos was shown. The reporter talked about the 9-1-1 call to establish that Zimmerman ignored the dispatcher's order not to confront Martin, but said the police were not releasing it. There was no reference to Zimmerman's race. In the one photo shown of him, a mug shot from 2005, the scruffy, overweight thug did look ethnic, but the name Zimmerman was left to carry the message of racist white man. Having done a little research, ABC added one more damning note: Zimmerman had once been arrested for battery on a law enforcement officer and resisting arrest, but the charges were later dropped. For the first time, Tracy Martin and Sybrina Fulton were interviewed together. Sybrina got the last word. "This clearly was murder. It was not an accident," she cried, "and it hurts. It hurts as a mother."[9]

6

MANNING THE GATES

*I*N THE FALL OF 2009, three years before the incident, George Zimmerman's wife, Shellie, had an encounter that would eventually and irrevocably change both her life and her husband's. The offending party was a pit bull named Big Boi. The first time the dog ran wild and cornered Shellie, Zimmerman called the dog's owner to complain. It did little good. Soon afterward, Big Boi intimidated Shellie's mother and her dog. That time, George called Seminole County Animal Services and, as recommended, went out and bought pepper spray. That did no good.

The third time the dog got loose, Zimmerman called Animal Services again. Finally, Animal Services sent one of its agents. According to a lengthy and fair-minded April 25 Reuters article, Animal Services confirmed the visit. Unconfirmed, but entirely believable given the sequence of events, is that the agent suggested George should get a gun. Pepper spray, George learned, would offer no useful defense against a raging pit bull. George and Shellie both did what the agent suggested. They took a firearms training course, got their concealed-carry permits, and bought a pair of guns. George got a Kel-Tec PF-9 9mm handgun.[1] For the next two years, he and his friend Mark Osterman went to a nearby shooting range about once a month for practice. There, the experienced Osterman schooled Zimmerman in maintenance, safety, and weapon retention among other subjects.[2]

If it seems unlikely that a pit bull would be running wild in a gated community, that is because the Retreat at Twin Lakes is not what one might think upon hearing the term "gated community." In the sales brochures, the Retreat seems the model of modern Florida community: swimming pool, clubhouse, and plenty of green space to boot. The earliest buildings in the 263-townhome community date back only to 2004. The initial cost of one of the 1,400-square-foot townhomes was $240,000.[3] In the beginning, Twin Lakes had "middle class" stamped all over it. The walled, nicely landscaped exterior lent the appearance of prosperity just as the iron gates at each entrance lent the illusion of security.

By 2012, however, the community was neither prosperous nor secure. When the Florida real estate market collapsed in 2008, real estate at Twin Lakes cratered. By the time of Martin's death, units were selling for less than $100,000, forty of them were vacant, and more than half were being rented, including Brandy Green's.[4] Some of the newer renters were being subsidized through the Section 8 program, and strangers wandered through the Retreat's exposed western flank, which the developers had never quite gotten around to fencing. The community "got bad," one resident told the FBI.[5] At the time of the shooting, despite what the media were telling America, less than half the occupants at Twin Lakes were white.

In fact, the city of Sanford itself was 30 percent black, twice the Florida average and three times that of the surrounding and more prosperous Seminole County. Nearly 20 percent of the city's residents lived below the poverty line, and poverty historically breeds criminals. According to *CityRating.com*, the violent crime rate for Sanford in 2010 was higher than the national average by nearly 70 percent, and the city's property crime rate topped the national average by more than 115 percent.[6] In Sanford, at least, there was a reason developers built walls around their communities.

When the FBI descended on the Retreat in April 2012 to assess Zimmerman's state of mind, the agents got an earful on the state of the neighborhood. Frank Taaffe, whom the FBI identified by name, offered a brief history of its rapid decline. As he told the agents, when real estate was hot, several people had bought into the community hoping to "flip" the town houses quickly. When the market tanked, they were unable to sell and forced to rent, often without conducting proper background or credit checks. He saw more trash, more speeders, and more flagrant violations of the homeowners' association rules. He described the community now as "transient" and "not stable." New renters included an unmarried black woman and her three children, one of whom would later be arrested for the sale of cocaine. According to Taaffe, the family was openly selling marijuana out of the house. In another case, as Taaffe related, a search warrant was served on a Hispanic family for selling drugs out of their home.[7]

FBI Witness 47 described Zimmerman as "always friendly and a very nice guy." She and Zimmerman had talked because there had been "some break-ins in the neighborhood." On one occasion, she told Zimmerman that she had observed "a young black male going door to door attempting to see who was home." Zimmerman gave her his card and told her to call him if she saw anything suspicious.[8]

Witness 46, "a stay at home mom," had moved from the Retreat before the Martin incident. She had good reason to move. In August 2011, two months after moving in, three young black men broke into her house while she was home. She retreated with her infant son to his room and made a desperate 911 call.[9]

Given the Retreat's transient population, crime increased. The Zimmermans themselves had two grills and a bicycle stolen off their back porch. After a series of break-ins in summer 2011, the Sanford police helped Twin Lakes start a neighborhood watch program. The volunteer coordinator for the Sanford Police Department, civilian staffer Wendy Dorival, called the first meeting. By her account, about twenty-five of the neighbors showed up, and they were enthusiastic. There seemed an obvious need for a coordinated watch. She told the Florida Department of Law Enforcement (FDLE) investigators during an interview on March 19, 2012, that the group needed to pick a coordinator. The homeowners' association asked Zimmerman, and he agreed. Dorival met with him, explained the responsibilities, and gave him a coordinator's handbook.[10] Although wary of the Sanford Police Department, Zimmerman had nothing but praise for Dorival. In September 2011, he sent a letter to police chief Bill Lee, commending her performance and thanking her for restoring his faith in the local police, which been tested by the Sherman Ware incident.[11]

The next month, the homeowners' association sent out its newsletter with an appeal for help. Illustrated with the cartoon of a man looking through a magnifying glass in the style of Sherlock Holmes, the appeal read:

We have recently experienced an increased incidence of crime within the community, including three break-ins in the past month, which is why having residents committed to being members of the Neighborhood Watch and reporting suspicious activities is so important. We must send a message that we will not tolerate this in our community![12]

According to the *Tampa Bay Times*, in the first two months of 2012, the Sanford police received fifty-one calls for service from Twin Lakes. Although most calls did not involve an active crime, the callers reported eight burglaries, two bike thefts, and three simple assaults.[13] It could have been worse. On February 12, the homeowners' association sent out an explanatory tweet: "Our Neighborhood Watch leads to four arrests in burglaries in the RTL. Great job!"[14]

George Zimmerman deserved more than a little credit. He took the role of neighborhood watch coordinator seriously. A few weeks before his encounter with Martin, Zimmerman sent an e-mail to his neighbors, alerting them to an attempted break-in and warning them to be on the lookout for an African American teenage male approximately five foot ten inches who was not believed to be a resident of the neighborhood. Three days later, Zimmerman sent another e-mail to his neighbors, alerting them to a successfully executed daytime robbery. He implored them to "report any suspicious persons, vehicles, or activities."[15] On February 20, Zimmerman sent out another e-mail announcing the apprehension of a man who "allegedly" broke into several homes in the neighborhood. Zimmerman did not mention his race, but his driver's license listed an address from within the Retreat.[16]

Prior to the shooting, what Zimmerman did on the night of February 26 was not extraordinary. He and other residents had done it before. No one told them not to. Sanford police officer Jonathan Mead confirmed that he had on one or more occasions responded to calls and found Zimmerman "on foot" after Zimmerman "lost sight" of "suspicious persons" he had been monitoring.[17] Other neighbors were as vigilant as Zimmerman. Witness 46 told the FBI that after that break-in at her house, her husband called the nonemergency dispatcher about once a week to report "suspicious looking kids." On one occasion he reported seeing "young black males" walking around the community, playing with screen doors. "If [Frank] Taaffe would have seen Trayvon Martin," the FBI reported, "he would have kept a visual on him." According to Taaffe, the Sanford police had instructed neighborhood watch volunteers to do just that.[18]

Despite the evidence to the contrary, the media tried to portray Zimmerman as a paranoid vigilante. "From January 2011 until the night of the shooting," wrote Andrew Cohen in *The Atlantic*, "a period of roughly 13 months, Zimmerman called 9-1-1 for one reason or another an astounding 46 times." This information came from a sloppy Sanford police report that listed the date range of those calls as 2011–2012. When the Sanford Police Department corrected the record to read 2001–2012, a ten-year difference, it didn't matter to Cohen. As he figured it, even if Zimmerman had made the calls over eleven years instead of one year, they still showed "his frustration/obsession with people he deemed 'suspicious.'"[19] What they also showed, if the media cared to look, was Zimmerman's reluctance to take the law into his own hands. There was no record of his ever having done so before. Nor was there any record of his volunteering the race of a suspect unless asked.

In 2012 none of this mattered. It was a presidential election year. Florida was the ultimate battleground state. And gun control was a potentially winning issue. This gave the Democrats and their media allies the incentive to draw a stark distinction between the unarmed boy with his Skittles and iced tea and the brooding vigilante George Zimmerman with, in the words of a *US News & World Report* op-ed, "his arrest record and history of violence."[20] And draw they did.

7

WASHING ONE'S HANDS

O N MONDAY, MARCH 12, Sanford police chief Bill Lee must have felt as though he had been caught in a twenty-fifth anniversary reenactment of Tom Wolfe's prescient 1987 novel, *Bonfire of the Vanities*. This book details the pressure brought to bear upon the judicial system by the BGI and the media to arrest a "great white defendant" for the death, however unintentional, of a young black man who may or may not have deserved his fate. Lee was definitely feeling the pressure, but in real life, there was nothing remotely comic about it.

Police Chief Lee knew something his critics did not: George Zimmerman had made an excellent case that he'd acted in self-defense. "Until we can establish probable cause to dispute that," Lee told a small crowd of reporters and black activists outside Sanford City Hall that morning, "we don't have the grounds to arrest him."[1] Lee later told the *Orlando Sentinel* that he did not believe the Sanford Police Department had sufficient evidence to charge Zimmerman. Serino told the FBI much the same, namely that he "did not believe he had enough evidence at the time to file charges."[2]

Despite his reservations, Lee "had Serino fill out the probable cause affidavit because without it, the State Attorney's Office would not take over the investigation."[3] Lee wanted no part of this case and, in fact, Serino did fill out a capias request on a negligent manslaughter charge a day later.

A capias request is the equivalent of an arrest warrant. In this case, it represented little more than a hot potato–passing formality. However, the summary statement of the capias request Officer Serino filled out seemed to war against the evidence that preceded it. Although Serino had his misgivings about Zimmerman's performance—why, for instance, did he not attempt meaningful dialogue with Martin when he had the chance?—he conceded that Zimmerman followed Martin "to maintain surveillance."[4] This was what a watch captain was supposed to do. In pointing out the obvious, Serino countered the many claims that Zimmerman stalked, chased, or even hunted Martin down, in the immortal words of one Florida congresswoman, "like a rabid dog."[5]

Lee staged a March 12 press conference to ease racial tensions. He did not exactly succeed. "The black community sees your department protecting the shooter," shouted one man over Lee's protestations. "A little black boy is dead."[6] As Lee was learning, justice didn't stand a chance against the beyond-the-grave appeal of a "little black boy," even one who towered over his killer.

That afternoon Lee's department turned the case over to the Seminole-Brevard State Attorney's Office. As Bianca Prieto of the *Orlando Sentinel* reported, the state attorney would now decide "whether to file charges against 28-year-old George Zimmerman, a white man, who shot and killed Trayvon Martin, an unarmed black 17-year-old who was walking in a gated neighborhood last month."[7] This was the first *Sentinel* article to make race the focal point of the discussion, even though Prieto, the paper's criminal justice reporter, had not yet learned of Zimmerman's ethnicity. No matter, Lee had passed the buck to State Attorney Norm Wolfinger, and now it was his turn to experience what Tom Wolfe described in the title of another comic tour de force as "mau-mauing the flak catchers."[8]

That same day the *Sentinel* documented what form the flak would take. A prominent Baltimore evangelist was holding a rally that very evening at a Sanford church. College students were organizing a rally for Monday outside the Seminole County Courthouse. Team Trayvon was demanding that Zimmerman be charged with murder. This, the *Sentinel* reporters had cause to suspect, was just the pregame warm-up. And as Wolfinger, too, would discover, there was nothing funny about any of it.

The Trayvon Martin shooting case was certainly hot and getting hotter. On Tuesday, March 13, Wolfinger announced his receipt of the case, and two days later he sent a letter to Gerald Bailey, commissioner of the Florida Department of Law Enforcement (FDLE), asking for assistance. On March 19, seemingly unaware that Wolfinger had already asked for help, Florida governor Rick Scott asked the FDLE to intervene. If that were not pressure enough, on that same Monday the US Department of Justice also threatened to wade in. At this stage, there was no countervailing pressure. Everything the local authorities heard must have sounded to them a whole lot like "Give us Barabbas!"

On March 16, under pressure from Team Trayvon, the Sanford Police Department released the 9-1-1 calls, as well as Zimmerman's initial non-emergency call. Later that day, the SPD turned copies of the calls over to the media. Tracy Martin had listened to at least some of these calls two days after the shooting, including the call by Zimmerman. At the time, he made a mental note of the dispatcher's request that Zimmerman not follow Martin. His lawyers seemed convinced that this request would help them make their case that Zimmerman was a rogue stalker. What they heard on March 16 was not nearly as convincing as they had hoped. No matter. They had their agenda set and the media in their corner.

This was a critical moment in the life of the Trayvon phenomenon. Despite a national piece here and there and a surging social media groundswell, no national celebrity had descended on Sanford as of mid-March. The Twitter hashtag #Trayvon had not trended. And the story had barely broken out of Florida. This all changed with the release of the 9-1-1 calls. If the content of these calls would eventually help Zimmerman, the reporting on them did quite the opposite.

Enter ABC correspondent Matt Gutman stage left. Blogger Antoine Reid described Gutman's TV appeal, at least to the low-information slice of the news audience. "Where the heck did ABC recruit this guy from?" gushed Reid. "It's like Christmas when this guy comes on to report about something—he has that stereotypical immaculate dark news anchor hair, a nice build to him, wears the tightest shirts he can find. Wooh, heat wave!"[9] Gutman grew up in the affluent New Jersey suburb of Westfield, graduated from Williams College in 2000, and had been rapidly climbing the ABC News ladder ever since. Based in Miami, he had the opportunity to own the Martin story and the ambition to do just that.

A century ago, shortly after founding the University of Missouri School of Journalism, pioneering editor Walter Williams penned the timeless Journalist's Creed. Successful journalism, Williams insisted, is "tolerant but never careless, self-controlled, patient, always respectful of its readers but always unafraid, is quickly indignant at injustice; is unswayed by the appeal of the privilege or the clamor of the mob; seeks to give every man a chance."[10] They apparently failed to teach Williams's creed at Williams College or reinforce it at ABC. On March 13, Gutman violated just about every one of its cautions, tweeting that Zimmerman "shot 17yr old teen bc he was black, wore hoodie walking slowly." From day one, he worked under the elitist assumption that the Sanford police were either corrupt, incompetent, or both, and discounted whatever information led them to refrain from arresting Zimmerman, "likely not 2 be arrested."[11]

Late on March 16 Gutman posted a piece on the ABC News website that helped set the tone of the coverage to come. He based its inflammatory headline, "Trayvon Martin Neighborhood Watch Shooting: 911 Tapes Send Mom Crying From Room," fully on the word of PR maestro Ryan Julison and admitted as much. The article implied, although it did not say so specifically, that Sybrina Fulton left the room in tears because she heard her son scream for help on the 911 calls. Attorney Natalie Jackson was busy making this point. "You hear a shot, a clear shot, then you hear a 17-year-old boy begging for his life," she was widely quoted as saying. "Then you hear a second shot."[12]

In the accompanying video piece for *Good Morning America*, Gutman reinforced this insinuation. In the process, he may have set a new national record for most mistakes of consequence in a two-minute news bite:[13]

GUTMAN: It was February 25.

TRUTH: It was February 26.

GUTMAN: Trayvon was staying at his stepmother's.

TRUTH: Martin was staying with Brandy Green, a girlfriend of his father's. His mother as well as his stepmother, Alicia Stanley, lived in greater Miami.

GUTMAN: He left for the store at halftime of the NBA All-Star Game.

TRUTH: He left hours earlier. He was dead before the game started.

GUTMAN: The "gunshots" are triggering outrage.

TRUTH: There was only one gunshot. The media coverage was triggering the outrage.

GUTMAN: Trayvon was "100 pounds lighter."

TRUTH: He was less than fifty pounds lighter. The autopsy recorded Trayvon as weighing 158 pounds. Zimmerman weighed in at the police station at 207, fully clothed.

GUTMAN: "You can hear him stalk Martin."

TRUTH: He did not stalk Martin. When the dispatcher realized Zimmerman was following Martin and said, "We don't need you to do that," Zimmerman said, "Okay" and stopped. Gutman edited out Zimmerman's "Okay" and followed immediately with his own comment, "But then came the gunshots."

GUTMAN: Zimmerman had a record—"battery on a police officer and resisting arrest."

TRUTH: The charges had been dropped. Gutman did not mention that fact.

GUTMAN: Police have been accused of "correcting one eyewitness, while ignoring another."

TRUTH: Yes, but the Sanford police did so for good reason. Several eyewitnesses had seen very little. Others had seen a lot. Witness 11 called 9-1-1, and one can hear desperate cries of "Help!" for roughly forty seconds until they promptly stop with a gunshot. The investigators knew it was Zimmerman who was crying out. An hour after the shooting, the best eyewitness, Witness 6, told the Sanford police that he saw a "black man in a black hoodie on top of either a white guy . . . or an Hispanic guy in a red sweater on the ground yelling out help." According to Witness 6, the black man on top was "throwing down blows on the guy MMA [mixed martial arts] style."[14] Witness 13 waited until the fighting ended, went outside, and saw Zimmerman walking towards him. "Am I bleeding?" Zimmerman asked. Witness 13 answered yes. He also noticed "blood on the back of his head" and took a picture of it.[15]

Gutman may not have heard the audio of these interviews, but Witness 6—"Jon," as he identified himself on camera—had spoken on camera to a local TV station the day after the shooting. "The guy on bottom who I believe had a red sweater on was yelling to me, 'Help, help,'" the witness said. "I told them to stop and I was calling 911." As both Zimmerman and the witness confirmed, Zimmerman appealed directly to this man for help.[16]

The one witness Gutman presented on camera was the one all the media wanted, Mary Cutcher, a thirty-one-year-old massage therapist. Cutcher appeared in Gutman's piece at a Team Trayvon press conference, where she said confidently, "We know it's not self-defense." As Gutman suggested, Cutcher was one of the witnesses the Sanford police corrected or ignored, but he did not say why. In fact, on her 9-1-1 call Cutcher insisted that there was "a black guy standing up over [the shooting victim]."[17] The SPD could not take this information seriously.

In an interview with the Sanford police four days after the shooting, Cutcher claimed, "I didn't pay much attention to [the altercation]. I didn't hear any words. It sounded like someone was struggling or hurt or something." She clarified that to say, "I heard nothing but a little kid scared to death or crying."[18] In her defense, it is understandable that Cutcher came to believe that Martin was the "little kid" she thought she heard. Team Trayvon had been feeding the media old images of Martin as a boy, and the media had been showing them uncritically. Gutman used a half dozen of them in his *Good Morning America* piece. When he talked about the struggle between Martin and Zimmerman, the viewer saw the photo of a thuggish, heavyset Zimmerman from 2005 countered by an *Onion*-worthy photo of an innocent young Martin actually hugging a baby. In fact, however, Martin was an all-but-full-grown young man with fully mature vocal cords. As one old girlfriend posted on a memorial site, "I loved his deep voice."[19] Cutcher did not hear a "little kid."

Over the next few days, Gutman's reporting grew more reckless and inflammatory. The FBI was now investigating the case as a hate crime. Why? Zimmerman, in his call to the dispatcher, had used a "possible racist remark."[20] Gutman never specified what that remark was. According to Gutman, even more damning evidence had emerged that the police had inexplicably ignored, and, better still, Gutman was exclusively allowed to hear it. As he related, Team Trayvon had interviewed a sixteen-year-old girl who had been on the phone with Martin in his last minutes and promised to blow the case wide open—but more on Dee Dee in the chapters to come.

If a controversy erupts outside New York and the *New York Times* does not notice it, is it really a controversy? In the media world, the answer is no. And so it was that on March 16, 2012, Trayvon Martin's death took on new life when the *Times* recognized it. In the initial article, Miami bureau chief Lizette Alvarez made a shocking number of errors for a story that was already three weeks old. The only error that the *Times* corrected—and not until three weeks later—was among the least consequential, namely, that Zimmerman's forty-six calls to the Sanford Police Department came over a period of years, not months. The two shots and the hundred-pound differential went uncorrected. Ignoring the stylebook, Alvarez did what many others in the media had begun to do: call Zimmerman by his last name and Martin by his first.

Worse was that Alvarez reported as fact fictions about which even Gutman had only speculated. One was that "the dispatcher told [Zimmerman] to stay in his car," but that he disregarded the order. In fact, the dispatcher, who was not a police officer, had no authority to tell Zimmerman to do or not do anything. His request not to follow Martin came after Zimmerman had already left his truck. In any case, Zimmerman honored the request, but Alvarez failed to report this. More damaging still, Alvarez elevated Mary Cutcher's ramblings to the level of genuine evidence. "Mary Cutcher and her roommate said they heard Trayvon pleading," Alvarez wrote. "Then they heard a gunshot. They rushed outside and saw Mr. Zimmerman standing over the teenager." The fact that the Sanford police took only a "brief statement" from Cutcher and showed no interest in following up with her led Alvarez to imply that they were ignoring Cutcher to protect Zimmerman.

Alvarez earned a minor place in journalism history when she labored to identify Zimmerman's ethnicity. Until this point, given his name, it was widely reported that Zimmerman was white. In her March 16 article, Alvarez introduced the notion that Zimmerman was "white and Hispanic."[21] In a March 22 article, she famously refined that categorization to "white Hispanic," an ethnic designation uniquely Zimmerman's.[22] As an exasperated father, Bob Zimmerman observed, "George MUST be kept white . . . . somehow."[23] Although no one at the *Times* would ever admit it, the "white" part of the designation served to prevent the shooting from igniting black-Hispanic tensions, especially in Florida, especially in an election year. If nothing else, Alvarez's reporting helped undermine the self-serving notion of Hispanics as "La Raza," or a race apart.

IF I HAD A SON'

been kidnapped, raped, sodomized. "KKK" and "nigger" were inscribed on her body.[2] Brawley accused six white men, one of them a police officer, of attacking her. As with the Martin case, the Brawley story exploded in the media all but unfiltered by common sense.

Sharpton assumed the role of Brawley's publicist. When Tawana refused to cooperate with prosecutors, including New York State's attorney general Robert Abrams, Sharpton contended that doing so would be like "asking someone who watched someone killed in the gas chamber to sit down with Mr. Hitler."[3] Along with Brawley's lawyers, Sharpton asserted that a local prosecutor named Steven Pagones was among those who had kidnapped and raped Brawley. Pagones endured nearly the hell that George Zimmerman has had to experience. Incapable of being shamed, Sharpton shifted blame to a local police cult affiliated with the Irish Republican Army. The case collapsed, according to *Slate*, "when a security guard for Brawley's lawyers testified that the lawyers and Sharpton knew Brawley was lying." Pagones later sued Sharpton and was awarded a sixty-five-thousand-dollar judgment, eventually paid by Johnnie Cochran and other Sharpton benefactors.[4]

Despite several other equally egregious adventures in race-baiting—the Crown Heights Riot and the Freddie's Fashion Mart massacre come quickly to mind—Al Sharpton had sufficiently rehabilitated himself by 2004 to seek the Democratic nomination for president. The left-leaning *Slate*, by the way, revisited the Brawley story when evaluating his candidacy. By 2011, the still-unrepentant Sharpton had acquired respectability enough to get his own nightly show on MSNBC. It was from this pulpit that he began to proselytize about America's racist legacy as manifested anew by the killing of Trayvon Martin.

In a vacuum the March 19 episode of Sharpton's Politics Nation seemed an exemplar of reckless race-baiting, but it was only marginally less responsible than what Matt Gutman had been serving up at ABC. The half-hour format allowed Sharpton to pound home the message that the case was "a national outrage to many of us." The critical word of that phrase was not "outrage" but "us," meaning, of course, black America. Nothing if not politically savvy, Sharpton made no reference at all to Zimmerman as being Hispanic. He was focusing black animus against a more traditional target, the presumably white police. "How can they not make an arrest in this case?" asked Sharpton. "What is going on there

8

HOGGING THE STAGE

*A*L SHARPTON JUMPED INTO THE MESS mouth first. He knew Benjamin Crump from previous escapades and had been in touch with Team Trayvon from the beginning. The release of the 9-1-1 calls revealed, he claimed on the March 19, 2012, episode of his MSNBC show *Politics Nation*, the "shocking heart-breaking picture of what happened that rainy night."[1] It also gave him the ammunition to fill the entire half hour of his show. That Sharpton has a show at all is testimony to the fact that politically cooperative black Democrats have more lives than the proverbial cat.

Sharpton got his start as a teen when Jesse Jackson appointed him as youth director of his all-purpose nonprofit, Operation Breadbasket. By the time he was eighteen, the ambitious Sharpton had formed his own organization, the National Youth Movement, and was embarking on a "civil rights" career so thoroughly rococo it made Jackson's seem a model of restraint and decorum.

The case that first thrust Sharpton into the national spotlight mirrored the Martin case, at least in its media strategy. In November 1987, fifteen-year-old Tawana Brawley stepped off the bus after a long day at school. She headed to her upstate New York home a mile down a country road and then disappeared into the night. She was found four days later, dazed, confused, and covered in feces. According to her attorneys, Brawley had locally, and why does it seem like they're allowing probable cause to be dismissed and they're trying this in the secrecy of the police department?"[5]

In the course of the March 19 show, Sharpton orchestrated a remote interview with Benjamin Crump and Tracy Martin. To this point, the senior Martin had been a model of decorum for someone whose son was killed under ambiguous circumstances. He had allied himself, however, with people more interested in a payday than in justice. "His father, his mother, his family have heard them," Crump told Sharpton of the many cries for help on the 9-1-1 tapes, "and they all know that is Trayvon Martin."[6] Based on a Crump interview, the *Huffington Post* reported that Tracy Martin "broke down crying as he listened to the audio." Said Martin allegedly, "My son was crying for help, and he still shot him."[7] In fact, Tracy Martin knew otherwise, and he said as much in the presence of several police officers during his first day at the station. That said, the momentum of the case no longer allowed, if it ever did, for minor concerns like the truth.

Back in Sanford on March 19, George's father Bob Zimmerman was pleading with the FDLE investigators that they discover the truth quickly and declare it publicly. "Everything I hear in the news is absolutely wrong," he told them.[8] For Zimmerman, the most significant untruth was the declaration by the Martin family and the media that the voice heard crying on the 9-1-1 tapes was Martin's. He could understand the stress Martin's mother was under. When he first heard her declaration, he assumed the quality of the tapes led to her confusion. But when he heard the tapes himself, all doubt vanished. The tapes were clear. There was no confusion. His voice quivering with emotion, Zimmerman swore under oath, "That is absolutely, positively George Zimmerman. Myself, my wife, family members, and friends know that is George Zimmerman. There is no doubt who is yelling for help."[9]

The senior Zimmerman had gotten out of the hospital just four days before the shooting. He had suffered a heart attack. Earlier in the month of February, his mother-in-law, Christina, who had lived with her daughter and Bob Zimmerman for thirty years, had to be hospitalized when her Alzheimer's medicine caused debilitating side effects. Once the atmosphere turned ominous, the three had to change their phone number and seek refuge in a hotel. "All of us are getting death threats," Bob Zimmerman told the investigators.[10] George's brother Robert traced the start of "the terror" to March 7, the day the "false narrative" took hold. "We would all essentially become homeless," said Robert, "on the run in and out of hotels."[11] Before the month was through, comedienne manqué Roseanne Barr would tweet their home address to her 110,000 followers. "I thought it was good to let ppl know that no one can hide anymore," said the ever-helpful Barr.

That same week film director Spike Lee re-tweeted the supposed home address of George Zimmerman to his 250,000 followers. In his eagerness to make life even more hellish for the neighborhood watch coordinator, Lee sent out the address of the wrong George. The other George Zimmerman and his wife had to leave their home because of the harassment and hate mail. On that same day, improbably enough, the National Basketball Players Association (NBPA) demanded "the prompt arrest of George Zimmerman," given his "callous disregard for Mr. Martin's young life." If that demand were not intrusive enough, the NBPA also insisted that police chief Bill Lee be canned for "dereliction of duty and racial bias."[12]

Meanwhile, the New Black Panther Party was openly offering a ten-thousand-dollar bounty for the capture of "child killer" George Zimmerman and passing out "Wanted Dead or Alive" posters.[13] Not to be out-menaced, the New Black Liberation Militia promised to head to Florida and attempt a citizen's arrest on George. "We'll find him. We've got his mug shot and everything," Najee Muhammad, a leader of the militia group, told the Associated Press. In perfectly nonjudgmental prose, the AP inquired as to whether such an arrest would be legal. The authorities they consulted seemed to think that the militia would "face a high legal hurdle in taking such action since they didn't witness a crime."[14] These legal niceties offered Zimmerman no assurance. Fearing for his life, George left Florida to hide out with relatives in the Washington, D.C., area.

On March 20 Daniel Maree, a young, black digital strategist then with the ad agency McCann Erickson, launched what he called the Million-Hoodie March to pressure Florida authorities to arrest Zimmerman. Within three days, Maree had gotten more than a million signatures, a glowing article in *Ad Age*, and an enthusiastic letter of support from McCann North America president Hank Summy. "This is an extraordinary story and a brilliant example of how one person's idea, combined with the power of social media, and built by collaboration, can change the world," wrote Summy.[15] Yes, it was brilliant if, in fact, Zimmerman targeted Martin because he was black, killed him in cold blood, and skated because of police favoritism toward white, or at least whitish, citizens. Otherwise, it was a terrifying example of the mindless power of the social media.

On March 21 Maree hosted the first of the Million Hoodie Marches in New York. Although only a few hundred people showed up, the idea was potent enough to attract the media as well as Martin's parents, who were in town for a media tour. Maree, still a day or two away from being a celebrity, called the timing "incredible." According to CBS News, the crowd greeted Tracy Martin and Sybrina Fulton with chants of "We want arrests." Why the plural "arrests," and who else might be in the line of fire, no one troubled to explain. "This is not a black and white thing," Fulton told the crowd. "This is about a right or wrong thing." She may have been sincere, but for the media and the crowd, including Maree, it was all about black and white. "I was outraged and wanted to do something about it," he told CBS. He also shared the fact that he first learned about the case "earlier this week."[16]

It was still just Wednesday.

9

CHASING THE TRUTH

N EARLY FOUR WEEKS AFTER THE SHOOTING, Team Trayvon fully owned the narrative. They faced very close to no media or political pushback at all, not in Florida, not in the nation at large. An Obama supporter and civil rights activist himself, Zimmerman had to feel as friendless as a human being possibly could. He surely sensed no relief on that late March day, and Team Trayvon likely felt no threat, when an obscure blog called the *Conservative Treehouse* began to do what it did best, as blogger Ytz4mee put it, "to deconstruct the narrative, to find out who all the people were behind the curtain."[1] On this case, as was typical, the Treepers pulled back the curtain as a team. One Treeper would post, and the other members and their allies would comment. Unlike most such sites, however, the goal was not just to air gripes. The goal at the *Treehouse* was to analyze existing data, add information, and, finally, to solve problems. In late March 2012, there was no messier problem to solve than the Trayvon story.

Sundance launched the inquiry on Thursday morning, March 23. His headline expressed his uncertainty about what had happened in Florida and his uneasiness about its airing in the world's media. (I first heard of the case on Irish TV). "Look, I'm as concerned at Trayvon Martin's shooting as anyone," Sundance observed, "but 'A Million Hoodie March'? Really? C'mon . . ." He was particularly concerned about the "optics," the obvious imbalance in visual imagery, "the 12-year-old pictures of a pee wee football playing choir boy." This struck him as excessive and unfair. "Young Mr. Martin was visiting his father after getting suspended from school," wrote Sundance. "Trayvon was 17 years old when this occurred. Seventeen."[2]

Others shared Sundance's misgivings. "Apparently the police have written statements from eye witnesses who saw Trayvon on top of Zimmerman, punching him," commented Ytz4mee. She added another bit of useful information: "When the family retained legal counsel, the FIRST action of the attorney was to have Trayvon's school records sealed. I find this a curious response for the family of a 'model' student who 'majored in cheerfulness.'"[3] She was alluding here to a March 17 article in the *Orlando Sentinel* that uncritically quoted a teacher of Martin's.[4] "If [Martin] was visiting his father," asked the Treeper barnslayer, "why was he out alone? Why was there a struggle? Why didn't the 'kid' just run? The security guard is hispanic/black. Where's the racism?"[5] Treeper Patriot Dreamer linked to a source that claimed Bob Zimmerman said his son was a "Spanish-speaking minority with many black family members and friends."[6] To be sure, all of these were bits and pieces, and not every fact was correct. Nevertheless, within hour one on day one of collective *Treehouse* engagement, the average Treeper had a better handle on the case than did the editorial board of the *New York Times*.

Of course, the folks at the *Times* and other mainstream citadels would never admit this. Going on a half century, they had consistently misreported racial issues and willfully misunderstood those who would challenge them. The *Times* proved particularly resistant to the lessons of experience. In their insightful book *Until Proven Innocent: Political Correctness and the Shameful Injustices of the Duke Lacrosse Rape Case*, authors Stuart Taylor and KC Johnson document how the *Times* woefully misreported the Duke story just six years before.

As the authors relate, the *Times* initially resisted the general media impulse to convict the accused lacrosse players of raping a black stripper before the evidence was established. Taking the lead for the *Times* was sportswriter Joe Drape. In a series of articles shortly after the story first broke in March 2006, Drape was among the very few reporters to present the defense's case thoroughly and fairly. In fact, there was no other case. Durham County district attorney Michael Nifong built his prosecution of the three accused players on a foundation of suppressed evidence and outright lies. Nifong's handling of the affair ended up costing him his job, his law license, his fortune, and even his freedom—at least for the day he served in the Durham County Jail on a contempt of court charge.

Early on, Drape sniffed a hoax and told his editors as much. His reporting encouraged the defenders of the accused, and they fed him more inside information, hoping he would set the story straight. Drape never got the chance. He told the Duke people that he was "having problems with his editors." Problems, indeed; they replaced him with reporters Rick Lyman and Duff Wilson, whose "politically correct politics," according to Taylor and Johnson, routinely trumped the facts. Sports columnist Serena Roberts complemented the reporting with opinions righteously indifferent to the truth. "The message was clear," wrote Taylor and Johnson. "Lynch the privileged white boys and due process be damned." Unfortunately for the *Times*, the case blew up in Nifong's face and its reporting was remembered as a "journalistic laughingstock."[7]

For all their public failures, especially on matters of race, the guardians of the mainstream media still felt free to trash those like the Treepers who would challenge their stranglehold on the news. A classic exchange along these lines occurred more than two years before the Trayvon shooting on the mainstream's punditry showcase, *Meet the Press*. Host David Gregory and his heavy-hitter guests—Tom Friedman of the *New York Times* and NBC's anchorman emeritus Tom Brokaw—were fretting openly about the fate of Barack Obama's recently deposed "Green Jobs Czar" Van Jones.[8]

An attorney and "civil rights activist," Jones had been fast-tracking his way through the Black Grievance Industry by cleverly fusing racial and environmental issues.[9] In the way of background, Jones had come of age as a committed Marxist-Leninist-Maoist with a serious grudge against the police. As a leading member of STORM, Standing Together to Organize a Revolutionary Movement, he showed his contempt for justice and common sense by organizing the Bay Area campaign to free Mumia Abu Jamal, the most conspicuously guilty cop killer ever to muster up a movement on his behalf.

It was with the terrorist attacks on September 11, 2001, that Jones truly showed his colors. Within hours of the attack, he and his fellow STORM troopers were denouncing American imperialists for having invited disaster by mistreating the Muslim world. The very next day he helped stage a vigil protesting "anti-Arab hostility." In 2006, as WND first reported, the unrepentant Jones signed a petition calling for nationwide "resistance" to the police, whom he accused of using the 9/11 attacks as a pretext to justify torture.[10] In 2009, when Obama appointed Jones as special adviser for green jobs, bloggers noticed his past. The chattering classes took offense that they had.

"You can be a target real fast," Gregory worried out loud about Jones. "A lot of people will repeat back to me and take it as face value something that they read on the Internet," cautioned Brokaw. "And my line to them is you have to vet information." The ever-pious Friedman added, "The Internet is an open sewer of untreated, unfiltered information, left, right, center, up, down, and requires that kind of filtering by anyone."[11] The fact that Friedman's employer championed the disgraced Nifong long after the blogosphere turned him into a human piñata did not seem to prick his hauteur.

As the Trayvon story developed, once again the stench was coming from the mainstream. All the serious filtering that was being done was taking place at sites like the *Treehouse*. Each post would spawn a "thread," and the thread was unkind to misinformation. "The thread is where things happen," said Treeper Sharon. "People contribute out of nowhere." She should know. A natural writer who grew up on a farm and now lives in rural Oregon, Sharon came out of nowhere herself to find a home at the *Treehouse*. She often spends six or seven hours a day tending to the *Treehouse*'s cyber garden.[12]

Of the three hundred or so regular contributors to the Martin thread, the most prolific was DiWataman. Sundance, in fact, was convinced that DiWataman knew more about the case than anyone in America, including the defense attorneys and the prosecutor. Troubled by the media's handling of the story, the fortyish blogger first got engaged with the site in April 2012. "What interested me about the Treehouse was the collective effort to get at the truth," said DiWataman. "I saw something there I saw nowhere else: the urge to find the facts and get them out there." Libertarian by instinct, DiWataman did not quite share Brokaw and Friedman's trust in the major media's editorial probity. In fact, the media coverage of the Martin case appalled him. "On subjects dealing with race and sex," he added, "they deny facts, lie, hyperbolize, distort. I cannot believe how institutionalized the deception is." A stay-at-home dad in a Midwestern suburb, DiWataman thought nothing of spending a dozen or more consecutive hours on research, and no one paid him the first dime to do this. "From everything I have seen," DiWataman said months before the trial, "there is a ton of reasonable doubt about murder."[13]

DiWataman, Sundance, and their fellow Treepers made a point of not cozying up to the Zimmermans or sharing their information with the defense team. "Sometimes you have got to call the baby ugly," said Sundance. "If I found one iota of information contra the Zimmerman story, I would post it. I support the truth. It's not all about defending George."[14] That much said, the Zimmermans let him know how much they appreciated what the *Treehouse* was doing. Bob Zimmerman would later write, "The research that was being conducted by contributors to this site was astonishing."[15] Sundance described the family members as parched wanderers in a desert of disinformation who finally found someplace they could get a drink. He chose not to talk about the conversations he has had with the family, but they inevitably saddened him. As he and the Zimmermans recognized from the beginning, there could be no good outcome to this case. By the time the *Treehouse* got involved, the damage done was irreparable. For the three or four weeks after the story broke, Zimmerman had not felt free to leave Osterman's house save for after-dark walks with his dog, and each night the atmosphere only grew more ominous.[16]

"What fresh hell is this?" pundit Dorothy Parker is reported to have famously said upon seeing new and more disturbing news. In the month of March 2012, George Zimmerman could surely identify.

10

RUNNING OF THE BULLS

*I*F AL SHARPTON SEEMS BUFFOONISH from a distance, up close he can intimidate. When he descended on Sanford, Florida, for an evening rally on March 22, 2012, he reminded the overwhelmingly black crowd just why Bishop F. D. Washington ordained him a Pentecostal minister before he turned ten. He had the fire in his belly. After leading the crowd in a chant of "No justice, no peace," Sharpton powerfully reinforced the BGI narrative. "Twenty-six days ago, this young man, Trayvon Martin did nothin' criminal, did nothin' unethical," said Sharpton in his preacher's cadence. "He went to the store for his brother. He came back and lost his life. Trayvon could have been any one of our sons. Trayvon could've been any one of us."[1]

It had to pain the very reverend Jesse Jackson that when the Trayvon Martin story began to break nationally in mid-March 2012, he was on a pointless glad-handing tour of Europe. The evening of March 19, the night rival Al Sharpton dedicated his own TV show on MSNBC fully to the Trayvon story, Jackson was giving "his perspective on the fight against discrimination" at a 120-euro-a-head dinner in a swank Brussels hotel. The event was sponsored by Democrats Abroad Belgium.[2] The party's relentless vote harvesters were using the event to troll for votes and dough among the ex-pats, and Jackson was the best they could serve up.

As Jackson has long understood, the BGI derives its power from its symbiotic relationship with the Democratic-media complex. There was no clearer demonstration of this than Jackson's decision to embrace President Clinton after the Monica Lewinsky revelations. In an unintentionally comic saga, Jackson emerged as Bill Clinton's spiritual advisor and, with the aid of his attractive young assistant, Karin Stanford, comforted the repentant president in the midst of his moral crisis.

In August 1998, after the president's grudging TV apology, Chelsea Clinton reportedly asked that Jackson come to the White House to counsel her and her mom. Hillary, breathless, had presumably just found out the truth. The three were said to have prayed together for two hours. Jackson then praised Hillary for her strength and her love of her husband, and Hillary's poll numbers shot up. Jackson wasn't through. In December of that same year, he led an anti-impeachment rally at the Capitol. As expected, Jackson's support for the president did not come without a price. A *Business Week Online* article unconsciously suggests the nature of the likely payoff.

> As House impeachment managers began laying out their case in the Senate for the conviction of Bill Clinton, the president sought solace in a favorite, if unusual, haven: Wall Street. . . . [Clinton] is scheduled to speak on Jan. 15 to a Wall Street conference organized by Jesse L. Jackson. Jackson's meeting was designed to prod the financial industry both to hire more minority employees and to invest more money in economically distressed areas. Clinton plans to outline a series of steps to leverage billions of dollars in investment in inner cities and poor rural communities, sources tell Business Week Online.[3]

For years, the relentlessly clever Jackson was the public face of the BGI. In fact, he all but invented the industry. If pressed, historians could plausibly trace its birth to a specific time and place, namely the *Today Show* on the morning of April 5, 1968. The night before, in Memphis, an escaped convict by the name of James Earl Ray brought the idealistic phase of the civil rights movement to a sickening halt when he shot and killed Martin Luther King Jr. When hit, King was standing on the second-floor balcony of the Lorraine Motel in Memphis. His colleagues Ralph Abernathy and Andrew Young rushed to his side, but King never regained consciousness. An hour after the shooting, he was pronounced dead at nearby St. Joseph's Hospital.

With King's entourage in Memphis was an ambitious, young divinity school dropout who went by the self-anointed name the "Reverend" Jesse Jackson. By all accounts, King distrusted Jackson's ambition and did not much like the man. When the shot was fired, Jackson ducked for cover on the lower level of the motel. He had little contact with King before he was shot and none after. That did not stop Jackson from appearing on the *Today Show* the following morning, wearing an olive turtleneck that allegedly bore the stains of King's blood. "He died in my arms," said Jackson shamelessly of King.[4] That same day, still wearing the turtleneck, Jackson rushed back to Chicago and began a lifelong career cashing in on the legacy of his would-be mentor. As mentioned earlier, with King's death the idealistic phase of the civil rights movement had come to an end. With Jackson ascendant, the opportunistic phase had just begun.

As social philosopher Eric Hoffer once observed, "Every great cause begins as a movement, becomes a business and eventually degenerates into a racket."[5] Although the major media chose not to notice, the civil rights movement was following Hoffer's formula with Jackson as racketeer-in-chief. On the occasion of the second anniversary of King's death, *Time* magazine put Jackson on the cover and repeated the canard that Jackson "was the last man King spoke to" and that he "ran to the balcony and held King's head."[6] For more than forty years, Jackson has parlayed his spurious role as King's "heir apparent" into a series of financial scams, one bolder than the next.

Speaking of bold, Jackson's "assistant," Karin Stanford, was four months pregnant when Jackson brought her to the White House to counsel the president about his lustful ways. Five months later, she gave birth to Jackson's now famous "love child," Ashley. Given the awkwardness of the timing, Jackson's Rainbow/PUSH reportedly offered Stanford a forty-thousand-dollar moving fee and a ten-thousand-dollar-a-month retainer to help keep the young Jackson child out of the news. As *Tonight Show* host Jay Leno phrased it, Stanford had "found the pot of gold at the end of the Rainbow Coalition."[7]

When the story broke in 2001, Jackson promised to take "time off to revive my spirit and reconnect with my family before I return to my public ministry."[8] Al Sharpton, however, went right to work. He made a public show of supporting Jackson, but as the *Village Voice* reported, his allies were busily pushing the love child story forward. One black millionaire told the *Voice*: "I said to Sharpton, 'I'm going to bring Jesse down and make you the man.' Al said, 'I'm ready.'"[9] In any case, Sharpton climbed over his spiritually comatose mentor and seized the top spot in the BGI. Not one to yield gracefully, Jackson roused himself from his penitential siesta and made sure to show up wherever there was a grievance to be exploited. Going forward, the involvement of one of these aging showmen all but dictated the involvement of the other.

In September 2007, for instance, both Sharpton and Jackson had shown up in a Deep South pit stop of a town to demand justice for the so-called Jena 6. The march that the two old bulls led drew as many as twenty thousand would-be civil rights champions to an overwhelmed Jena, Louisiana—no porta-potties in sight—and captured the unskeptical attention of the national media. The "6," not surprisingly, were black, but they were not exactly the Scottsboro Boys. They made their way into the history books nearly a year earlier when their leader, Mychal Bell, punched a white fellow student from behind and knocked him cold. His friends then joined Bell in kicking and stomping the victim while he lay unconscious.

No one disputed the assault. What Jackson and Sharpton were protesting was the severity of the punishment. The six were originally charged with attempted second-degree murder and conspiracy, but by the time of the march, cooler heads had prevailed and only Bell remained in jail. He had been convicted of aggravated second-degree battery and conspiracy to do the same.

Indifferent to the facts and keen on reliving the glory days of the civil rights movement, the BGI and their media enablers portrayed this congenial town of three thousand as a vestigial remnant of the Jim Crow South. "White students hanging nooses barely punished, a schoolyard fight, excessive punishment for the six black attackers, racist local officials, public outrage and protests"—this, wrote journalist Craig Franklin in the generally liberal *Christian Science Monitor*, was the state of affairs in Jena as the media had America believe. The only problem, he continued, was that "[m]yths replaced facts, and journalists abdicated their solemn duty to investigate every claim because they were seduced by a powerfully appealing but false narrative of racial injustice." Having covered the case up close and from the beginning, Franklin could barely contain his rage.

Said he in the way of assessment, "I have never before witnessed such a disgrace in professional journalism."[10]

For all the efforts of Jackson and Sharpton, the Jena 6 movement died aborning in no small part because Mychal Bell, what with his head-kicking assault and four priors for violent crimes, made such an unattractive poster boy. Trayvon Martin had much more potential. As Jackson told the marchers in Louisiana, "There's a Jena in every state." In Florida, the "Jena" would be Sanford. Surely to Jackson's chagrin, Sharpton had beaten him there by days and to the cause by weeks. Nor was Sharpton Jackson's only competitor. The ambitious young president of the NAACP, Ben Jealous, had bailed out of a conference in Geneva, Switzerland, and made his way to Sanford days before even Sharpton arrived.

On Tuesday, March 20, 2012, Jealous brought the power of the NAACP's well-known national brand to bear on the citizens of Sanford and their hapless flak catcher of a mayor, Jeff Triplett. In a profoundly rigged "town hall" meeting, Jealous made three "demands" of the mayor, the first two of which were specific to Martin's death. One was that the killer "be brought to justice." Jealous had a specific notion as to what form that justice should take. "He needs to be locked up," said Jealous of Zimmerman, "and he needs to be charged with murder." The second of the two demands, which logically should have been the first, was that the investigation "start at the very bottom."[11]

Jealous made his case for Zimmerman's guilt during an extensive interview on the Internet TV show *Democracy Now.* Like the show's hosts, Jealous casually asserted as fact the many fictions that sustained the Trayvon narrative. In demanding the removal of the police chief, Jealous described a police department not unlike the one Sidney Poitier's "Virgil Tibbs" visited in *In the Heat of the Night.* As Jealous recounted events, the officers were called to a scene "where a man has killed a boy." Once there, they made "no attempt to check the hands of the shooter," test the clothing for DNA evidence, or "otherwise gather evidence from that scene." Worse, said Jealous, no one attempted to contact Martin's parents.[12] He let stand the widely held belief that Martin's body went unclaimed for days.

Jealous had to know better. This California-bred, Columbia-educated Rhodes Scholar had spent the last few days in Sanford and spoken at length with the mayor. The cynic is tempted to say, "Follow the money."

No doubt the more the NAACP could play up the race factor, the more money they could raise in their appeal for a remedy.

For Jealous, though, one suspects a personal crusade. Like George Zimmerman, Jealous's father is white. Jealous was born in 1973, years after the last productive civil rights march, and raised in the leafy confines of suburban California. To preserve his own shaky hold on authenticity, he dared not undermine the grievance narrative embraced by Sharpton and Jackson. If anything, he had to reinforce that narrative. One subtle way he did so on the *Democracy Now* show was to overlook Zimmerman's ethnicity. The hosts did the same. Although Zimmerman has the same claim to the label "Hispanic" as Jealous does to "black," the audience was left thinking that Zimmerman had to be white. Needless to say, Jealous made no reference to Zimmerman's work with the local NAACP on the Sherman Ware case. If he were to secure the NAACP president's rightful place at the head of the march with Sharpton and Jackson, he could be no less bold in his bluster.

No sooner did Jesse Jackson return from Belgium than he commandeered the press and tried to make up lost ground. "There was this feeling that we were kind of beyond racism," he told the *Los Angeles Times* on March 23. "That's not true. [Obama's] victory has triggered tremendous backlash." This was pure BGI BS: if things had changed for African Americans post-Obama, they had only gotten worse. "Blacks are under attack," Jackson assured the media, which phrase the *Times* used in its absurdly provocative headline.[13]

Three days later, Jackson made his way to Sanford, where his presence was still capable of generating headlines like "Jackson, Sharpton to Lead March for Trayvon Martin," and getting top billing in the process.[14] Although social media played a major role in generating interest in the case, the presence of these old bulls and their NAACP protégé gave the case its legitimacy. Despite their preposterous misadventures over the years, the media still treated them like the rightful heirs to King's legacy.

Fortunately for Jackson, his own history as a neighborhood watchman and racial profiler had been eased on down the memory hole. In 1991 Jackson bought a red brick mansion in a Washington, D.C., neighborhood as vulnerable as Sanford's Retreat at Twin Lakes. Months after the Jacksons moved in, a burglar broke into the house and made off with some valuables while Jesse's mother-in-law was home alone. She heard the burglar and then saw him run away. As with Shellie Zimmerman, the sight of a fleeing home invader unnerved her. "When somebody breaks into your house and robs it," Jackson remarked at the time, "you just feel as if everything has been breathed on."[15]

It got worse. Eight months later, Jackson's wife, Jacqueline, was taking out the garbage when she saw a black woman urging her male companion to shoot another black fellow, which he promptly did. As Jacqueline watched, the second man staggered down the street and died. Not too long afterwards, a robber shot a grocer in a small store across the street. This was soon followed by a nasty incident right down the block in which two young men in the front seat of a car shot and killed their three seatmates in the back.

The triple homicide prodded Jackson to action. Much as Zimmerman did following the home invasion in his subdivision, Jackson called for a "victim-led revolution."[16] This campaign involved appointing block captains, recording the license plate numbers of drug dealers, and notifying the police of suspicious activity. At the time, Jackson acknowledged where the crime was coming from.

"There is nothing more painful for me at this stage in my life," he admitted in November 1993, "than to walk down the street and hear footsteps and start to think about robbery and then look around and see it's somebody white and feel relieved."[17] In this rare honest moment, Jackson declared black-on-black crime to be "the premier issue of the civil rights movement today."[18] It may have been, and may still be, but protesting black crime did not pay nearly as well as shaking down white Wall Street. In the twenty years that followed, roughly 150,000 American blacks were killed by other blacks, and Jackson elevated none of their deaths to the level of "cause." He might have ignored the death of Trayvon Martin as well, if that damnable Al Sharpton had not shown up in Florida and forced his hand.

11

OBLIGING THE MOB

HE PRESSURE THE OLD BULLS and their young media-savvy allies brought to bear on Florida officialdom worked scarily well. As government officials from Roman prefect Pontius Pilate to Florida governor Rick Scott can attest, mobs have a way of intimidating. To ease the pressure and appease the mob, the city of Sanford and the State of Florida started sacrificing their own. On March 21, the day after Ben Jealous's town hall meeting, the Sanford City Commission stoked the bonfire by voting no-confidence in police chief Bill Lee. Although the commissioners did not have the authority to fire the chief, they did not need it. On March 22, the day of Sharpton's rally, the rattled Lee stepped down, temporarily at least, from the job, after less than a year as chief.

Claiming that he had been a "distraction," Lee declared, "I do this in the hopes of restoring some semblance of calm to a city which has been in turmoil for several weeks." That calm was not forthcoming. As the *Orlando Sentinel* observed, "His announcement did little to appease protesters furious that he did not arrest the shooter, crime-watch volunteer George Zimmerman." Lee was the initial target, but he was not the ultimate one. If Lee had been savvier about the power game being played, he might have seen himself as the pawn he was. Indeed, upon hearing the news of his resignation, Tracy Martin told a cheering crowd in Sanford that it meant "nothing." Said Martin, "We want an arrest."[1]

Later that same day, Seminole County state attorney Norm Wolfinger removed himself from the case as well. This could not have been voluntary. Just two days earlier he'd called a grand jury for April 10 to "collect and evaluate all the facts" of the case. By March 22, though, he was citing the "public safety" of the citizens of Seminole County as one reason for his withdrawal.[2] In other words, he was informed, directly or otherwise, that if he did not step down, there could be mayhem in the streets. In his prepared statement he asked that another state attorney be appointed to manage the case. He did not have to ask. Earlier that day, Governor Scott had met with Team Trayvon and assured them that Wolfinger was history.[3] Attorney general Pam Bondi was signaling her submissiveness as well. On March 20, while verging on tears, the well-meaning Bondi described Martin to the press as an "innocent young boy."[4]

On the evening of March 22, Governor Scott announced his appointment of Jacksonville state attorney Angela Corey, a Bondi ally, to take over the investigation. Corey, an Arab-American, had been elected to that position in 2012, the first woman so elected. Like Governor Scott, she was a Republican. Unlike Scott, she was up for reelection in 2012. Corey, in turn, appointed as lead prosecutor for her team an aggressive assistant state's attorney from her jurisdiction, named Bernie de la Rionda. In his twenty-seven years on the job, de la Rionda had tried 250 cases, 67 of which were homicides.[5]

In the course of her career as a prosecutor, Corey herself had tried fifty-four murder cases. She had a reputation for being particularly tough when it came to gun crimes. In 2009, for instance, a sixty-five-year-old Army veteran with fourteen years of service and a concealed carry permit, Ronald Thompson, fired two shots into the ground to scare off four young thugs who were harassing an elderly neighbor. Thompson rejected a three-year plea deal and went to trial. There, he was convicted of aggravated assault and handed a twenty-year term as required by Florida's mandatory minimum law, this despite the fact that his only crime in the past was a DUI. When a judge commuted the sentence to three years, Corey appealed and successfully restored the sentence to twenty years. The fact that Thompson was diabetic and had already had several open-heart surgeries softened Corey's heart not a whit.[6]

In a case that played out after Corey had been selected to investigate the Zimmerman shooting, she secured a twenty-year sentence for a woman named Marissa Alexander, who, like Thompson, merely fired a warning shot. In this case, according to Alexander, her husband attempted to strangle her after he read some cell phone text messages she had sent to her ex-husband. She tried to flee, but when she got to the garage, she realized she had forgotten her car keys. With good reason to be fearful, she grabbed a handgun and went back in to get her keys. Once inside the house, her husband started menacing her anew, and she fired a shot into the ceiling to warn him off. "I believe when he threatened to kill me, that's what he was absolutely going to do," she said at trial. "Had I not discharged my weapon at that point, I would not be here."[7]

As with Thompson, Corey offered Alexander a three-year plea deal, and she, too, rejected it. Feeling she had done nothing wrong, Alexander took her chances on a trial. Her attorneys tried to use the Florida Stand Your Ground law as defense, but a judge rejected that gambit, claiming that Alexander's return to the home showed insufficient fear for her safety.

CNN contributor and syndicated columnist Roland Martin protested the prosecution and the twenty-year sentence mightily. "Why was she charged, convicted and sentenced?" Martin asked. "Because State Attorney Angela Corey, the same prosecutor leading the Trayvon Martin case, said that the gun was fired near a bedroom where two children were and that they could have been injured."[8] Florida congresswoman Corrine Brown attended the sentencing hearing and confronted Corey. "There is no justification for 20 years," Brown protested. "All the community was asking for was mercy and justice."[9]

In the case of George Zimmerman, Brown asked for neither mercy nor justice. From the beginning, she just wanted his head. On a website posting dated April 11, the congresswoman claimed to have sat down with various Sanford city officials, including the police chief, in a meeting that lasted exactly five and a half hours. Her conclusion: "There was sufficient evidence for an arrest." To validate her position, she added, "Millions of people around the world came to the same conclusion."[10] That those millions did not include the Sanford police who actually saw the evidence scarcely troubled Brown.

Roland Martin had no use for Zimmerman either. A year after the incident, he was comparing Zimmerman's shooting of Martin to the brutal 1955 lynching of Emmett Till, a fourteen-year-old Chicago boy who made the mistake of whistling at a white woman in Mississippi.[11]

It should not surprise anyone that race has played a major role in the perception of justice and mercy. Alexander was black. Thompson was white. Corinne Brown and Roland Martin expressed no more sympathy for Thompson than they did for Zimmerman. Unlike either Alexander or Thompson, though, Zimmerman faced a clear and present threat on the night of February 26. His broken nose, his bloodied head, and his screams for help attested to that. In the months that followed, however, the real threat, the deeper threat, came from the pressure of the "millions" who shared Representative Brown's empty sentiments. Although no Emmett Till, if anyone had cause to fear mob justice at this stage, it was Zimmerman.

On the same day that Governor Scott relieved Wolfinger and appointed Corey, he announced his intent to appoint a Stand Your Ground task force. In a press release from that same day, Scott euphemized his capitulation as "listening to many concerned citizens in recent days."[12] In just the six days since the *New York Times* reported on the case, Scott persuaded then lieutenant governor Jennifer Carroll to lead the task force and Tallahassee pastor R. B. Holmes to be the vice chair. He also "reached out" to a half dozen other prominent Floridians who agreed that a task force needed to be assembled on a law that passed the Florida Senate unanimously just a few years earlier. Rarely does government act so swiftly. Even Team Trayvon had to be shocked at how quickly events were moving.

12

BEGETTING A SON

ILLIONS OF AMERICANS VOTED for Barack Obama for president in 2008 thinking that he could address the problems that vexed Jesse Jackson's D.C. neighborhood and others like it in ways that no white political leader could. George Zimmerman was one of those millions. Ironically, it was Jesse Jackson who saw to it that Obama never really tried.

On Father's Day, June 15, 2008, Obama took his campaign to the twenty thousand–member Apostolic Church of God in Jackson's home turf, Chicago's South Side. Obama's message was unequivocal. The *New York Times* took a day off from worrying about the separation of church and state and headlined its article on the talk "Obama Sharply Assails Absent Black Fathers."[1] To murmurs of approval from the almost entirely black congregation, Obama preached, "If we are honest with ourselves, we'll admit that too many fathers are also missing." Lest the listeners think Obama was speaking in general, he added, "You and I know this is true everywhere, but nowhere is it more true than in the African American community." He then spelled out the consequences, including the fact that boys who grow up in fatherless homes are "twenty times more likely to end up in prison."[2]

Martin grew up in an on-and-off-again fatherless home. By 2012 he was trending toward inclusion in Obama's statistics. Obama had little good to say about the Tracy Martins of the world. "They have abandoned their responsibilities," said Obama of the fathers who had left their homes, "acting like boys instead of men."[3]

In most quarters, Obama's talk was well received. "He kept it real all of those other so called black leaders never touched this subject about fatherless homes reason why one jesse jackson was one of those fathers," wrote one woman, punctuation be damned, in the comment section of a YouTube posting of the speech.

Jesse Jackson was indeed one of those fathers. As late as 2012, Karin Stanford was still hectoring him for child support for Ashley, their celebrated love child. He took Obama's comments as a personal and professional insult. A few weeks later, awaiting a remote interview with Fox News, Jackson made his feelings known on a hot mic. "I want to cut his nuts out," Jackson whispered. "Barack, he is talking down to black people." This was all most people were allowed to hear, but there was more. Almost universally, the media edited out the participial phrase that followed—"telling niggers how to behave."[4] Sharpton, of course, heard the slur and made sure others did too. "I think this certainly does not reflect the Reverend Jackson that we all know and love," said Sharpton, meaning not a word of what he said.[5] More important, Obama heard it all, and he got the message.

Suzanne Goldenberg, reporting for Britain's left-leaning *Guardian*, did a better job than most in the American media of assessing the political ramifications of Jackson's remarks, not so much for Jackson as for Obama. She cited Jackson's various apologies and his plea that Obama "represents the redemption of our country," but her headline caught the dynamic behind the dust-up: "Jackson gaffe turns focus on Obama's move to the right." Goldenberg raised the question that many on the left had been asking, "What has happened to Obama since he won the Democratic nomination?"[6]

As she noted correctly, Obama's focus on individual responsibility upset those on the left who "hold government policies to account for the impoverishment of African American families," Jackson being chief among them. Although Goldenberg did not go into detail, she raised a secondary issue that most in the America media chose not to explore, specifically, "Obama's place in the African American community."[7] In his 1995 memoir, *Dreams from My Father*, Obama related his own quest to discover "a workable meaning for his life as a black American."[8] This did not come easy to him. When he left his white mother and grandparents behind in Hawaii for college in Los Angeles, he knew no more about African American culture than what he had seen on TV. He described himself accurately as "a would-be black man."[9] For all of his seeming gaffes, Jackson had hit Obama where he was most vulnerable—his shaky hold on authenticity. Obama never felt secure in his identity as an African American.

Jesse Jackson had no such issues. He may have oversold his contribution, but he did walk the walk, including the legendary 1965 Selma to Montgomery march. By contrast, when candidate Obama spoke in Selma in 2007, in order to connect with the civil rights legacy he concocted a story about his parents being so inspired by the march that "they got together and Barack Obama Jr. was born." For an added touch of "authenticity" he delivered the story in a preacher-like cadence. Said Obama in conclusion, "So don't tell me I don't have a claim on Selma, Alabama. Don't tell me I'm not coming home to Selma, Alabama."[10] He wasn't. In reality, by the time of the march, Obama's father had long since abandoned the family. While Jackson and other protestors were confronting angry white state troopers in Alabama, the three-year-old Obama was collecting seashells with his white grandfather in Waikiki.

This fantasy worked well enough on liberal white America, but Obama could not fool himself, and he certainly could not fool the old bulls and their allies. After Jackson punched back, Obama never again made as hard-hitting a jab at the heart of the problem afflicting black America as he did in his Father's Day 2008 speech. Four years later that Father's Day speech still had currency in black activist circles. As each March day passed in 2012, and one black leader after another stirred the Trayvon stew, Obama's continued silence provoked the activists to lash out. The clever among them knew Obama's stress point. "Obama is perfectly willing to give a sermon to black men on Father's Day about what they need to be doing," wrote Yvette Carnell, a blogger and former Capitol Hill staffer, "but totally incapable of advocating for a black boy who was murdered in the street while carrying only Skittles and iced tea."[11]

What piqued Carnell and many others was Obama's response to the controversy involving a white feminist by the name of Sandra Fluke. Broadcaster Rush Limbaugh insulted Fluke on February 29, three days after Martin's death. Two days later, Obama called Fluke on his own initiative to console her. However, nearly four weeks after the killing of Martin, there was no consolation for his family and no public acknowledgment of his death.

The pressure was mounting, and the language was intensifying. The head of the Congressional Black Caucus, a seeming moderate from Missouri named Emanuel Cleaver, struck the tone expected of a prominent black politician. In a formal statement, Cleaver argued that the Zimmerman case set a "horrific precedent of vigilante justice" and accused the Sanford Police Department of "a blatant disregard for justice." In urging the Department of Justice to investigate, Cleaver insisted that Martin's "only crime seems to be the color of his skin."[12]

Obama had to say something. On the morning of March 23, in the White House Rose Garden, he introduced Dartmouth president Jim Kim as next head of the World Bank. He then took just one question, almost assuredly prearranged, and it addressed Martin's death. "Obviously this is a tragedy," said Obama solemnly. "I can only imagine what these parents are going through. When I think about this boy I think about my own kids and I think every parent in America should be able to understand why it is absolutely imperative that we investigate every aspect of this and that everybody pulls together, federal, state and local to figure out exactly how this tragedy happened."[13]

Had the president stopped here, he would have said enough to appease at least the media, if not the hard core among the activists. He would have won no honors for political courage, but as he knew, courage led in another direction altogether. By that time, the White House had access to all the information the Sanford Police Department did. The courageous step for Obama would have been to defend the Sanford Police Department and to demand an end to the media lynching of George Zimmerman. As an African American, he had more latitude to do that than a white politician would have. He chose not to. Concluded Obama after some meaningless temporizing: "But my main message is to the parents of Trayvon—if I had a son, he would look like Trayvon."[14] Obama would not have known that Zimmerman openly supported him for president, but even if he had, that support would not have mattered more to him than Zimmerman's support for Sherman Ware mattered to Ware's sister or the Sanford NAACP. There were larger stakes involved.

Back at the *Treehouse*, the Treepers sensed the potency of Obama's remarks immediately. Within hours Sundance posted a piece calling Obama's intervention "staggeringly selfish opportunistic exploitation." He added, "Oh man, we are gonna be hearing about this story for weeks from every possible nuanced organization that relies on racism and special interest exploitation to provide their cause celeb." In her response Wee-Weed neatly summarized the crux of *Treehouse* thinking: "I think Mr. 'The Police Acted Stupidly' has just stuck a size 11-1/2 in his mouth."[15]

WeeWeed was referring, of course, to Obama's instinctive denunciation of the Cambridge, Massachusetts, police for arresting black scholar Henry Louis Gates in July 2009. Gates, a Harvard professor, had just returned to his house from an overseas trip. When the front door failed to open, he and his driver forced it open. A neighbor saw them do it and, not knowing Gates, called 9-1-1. When Sgt. James Crowley arrived and asked Gates to step outside, the professor exploded, accusing the officer of targeting him because "I'm a black man in America?" Gates continued to abuse and threaten Crowley, and after two warnings, Crowley arrested him on a disorderly conduct charge. Under pressure, the local district attorney dropped the charges, but Crowley refused to apologize, and the police brass backed him up.[16]

At a press conference six days after Gates was arrested, a reporter from the *Chicago Sun-Times* asked Obama what the incident said about race relations in America. Although admitting he did not know all the facts, Obama had confidence enough in America's "long history" of racial injustice to announce, "The Cambridge police acted stupidly."[17] Obama knew less about Crowley than he did about the incident itself. Like Zimmerman, Crowley defied the racist stereotype. He was not only a model officer, but also an Obama supporter. A black police commissioner had personally selected him to teach recruits about the pitfalls of racial profiling.[18] As these facts and others emerged, Obama was forced into an awkward "beer summit" to pacify the nation's police and the people who believe in them.

There would be no beer summit for George Zimmerman. Unlike Crowley, he had no allies with clout. Besides, too much was at stake in an election year in America's most vital battleground state for Obama to apologize or equivocate. He had just lent his imprimatur to the BGI narrative, and he would have to stand by it.

As Obama must have anticipated, few dared to criticize him. Former Speaker of the House Newt Gingrich was the exception. Still in the running for the Republican presidential nomination, Gingrich called Obama's message "disgraceful" and scolded the president for "trying to turn [Martin's death] into a racial issue." Gingrich elaborated, "Is the president suggesting that if it had been a white who had been shot, that would be OK because it didn't look like him?"[19] But Gingrich got little support from other Republicans and almost none from the media, including the conservative media. The *National Review* took the lead in misinforming the right. Heather Mac Donald called the shooting "a grossly disproportionate response to a fistfight, even leaving aside the fact that Zimmerman had initiated the encounter."[20] Robert VerBruggen insisted that "[s]upporters of pro-self-defense policies should roundly condemn Zimmerman's actions, and Florida should change its laws to prevent this incident from repeating itself."[21] And *National Review* editor Rich Lowry, writing in the *New York Post*, headlined his piece "Shocker! Sharpton is right for once."[22] Sharpton, of course, was not right. For all his boldness, Gingrich, too, missed the larger point. Martin's death had already been turned into a racial issue. That train had long since left the track. Now, with Obama fully on board, there was no way it could ever return to the station.

Zimmerman's friend Mark Osterman later identified that March 23 day as the low point in a long, depressing month. Said Osterman, "George was more hurt than angry about the negative reactions across the country."[23] Now with a ten-thousand-dollar bounty on his head and the president siding openly with the Martins, Zimmerman felt that he could no longer put the Ostermans; his wife, Shellie; and the Ostermans' ten-year-old daughter at risk by staying in Seminole County. Late that afternoon, he loaded a few necessities and his dog, Oso, into his truck, kissed his wife good-bye, and headed north to stay with relatives in the Washington, D.C. area. He felt freer with every mile he drove. That feeling did not last long.[24]

13

REMOVING THE SCALES

*D*URING THE MONTH OF MARCH 2012, as the story gained momentum, the editors of the *Miami Herald* thought it might be worthwhile to look into Trayvon Martin's background. Of course, all of the media should have been doing this, but no editor or producer other than those at the *Herald* made more than the most cursory inquiries into the why or how of Martin's evolution from the smiley innocence of his ubiquitous preteen photos into an eager and competent brawler.

Information on Martin bled slowly into the mainstream, in no small part because Team Trayvon had promptly sealed young Mr. Martin's school records. As often as not, the news that the media did report was either incomplete or inaccurate. The initial Reuters piece of March 7, for instance, had Martin visiting his father and "stepmother" for no cited reason. On March 9, NBC Miami added some clarification. Tracy Martin claimed that his son had been suspended from Dr. Michael M. Krop Senior High for a week for an unspecified cause, and he had come to Sanford "to disconnect and get his priorities straight."[1] In fact, Martin had been suspended for two weeks, not one, but the family refused to say why Martin was suspended, only that he "had violated some type of school policy."[2]

On March 17, the *Orlando Sentinel* apparently thought it necessary to solidify Martin's reputation. Now, his suspension was back to five days, and it was due to "tardiness." The *Sentinel* talked to Michelle Kypriss, Martin's English teacher, who assured *Sentinel* readers that Martin, a junior, was "an A and B student who majored in cheerfulness."[3] Martin, the *Sentinel* continued, was studying to be an engineer, with a particular interest in aviation. This interest was piqued by a plane ride he had taken two years earlier. That trip may have taken Martin to the ski slopes, where earlier photos shown on TV news had pictured him. He was, from the looks of things, not a deprived child. His parents, a truck driver and public housing official, respectively, earned more than a hundred thousand dollars a year between them.

On March 22 the *Herald* let it be known that Martin "had nonviolent behavioral issues in school" and confirmed that he had indeed been suspended for ten days. "He was not suspended for something dealing with violence or anything like that," said Tracy Martin. "It wasn't a crime he committed, but he was in an unauthorized area [on school property]." The article insisted, however, that the college-bound Martin was "a typical teen" and reinforced his status as a son of the middle class. It was not every black teen in Florida, after all, who had been to a Broadway musical and regularly went horseback riding with his mom.[4]

Understandably, Martin's extended family hung on to the sanitized version of the young man's life. By all accounts, up until the last two years of his life, Martin had been a typical teen. In an interview with *Esquire*'s John Richardson, Martin's aunt Miriam summed up the family's understanding of their nephew and son: "First thing you need to know about Trayvon, she says, is he loved his dad." As Tracy told the story, the then nine-year-old Trayvon dragged him from what could easily have been a fatal apartment fire. Trayvon reportedly got along with everyone. He was always smiling. He loved to eat. He loved football. He loved Nickelodeon. He loved his uncle Ronald, a quadriplegic, and helped him out. Ronald was the one who got him interested in planes. And he knew God. "He understood that man could not create the earth and the clouds and the water," said Miriam. She and her husband, Stephen Martin, a former Marine and Tracy's brother, were positive influences on young Martin's life, and, as Miriam noted, "he spent as much time at their house as he did anywhere else."[5] And therein lay the crux of the problem. In the last years of his young life, Martin was being shuttled between one house and another—his mother's, his father's, his uncle's, his father's girlfriend's.

The reason Trayvon ended up in limbo those last two years of his life was because he lost the one place he called home, the house where he had spent 90 percent of his time from age three until the age of fifteen, the home of Alicia Stanley, Tracy Martin's second wife and Trayvon's stepmother. When Tracy left Alicia for Brandy Green, Trayvon was fifteen. That was the time when Trayvon began to wander off track and there was no one readily available to redirect him. In his *Esquire* piece, Richardson did not so much as mention Stanley. Almost no one in the media did. "I'm here with you to let people know that I exist," Stanley would tell CNN's Anderson Cooper. "And I would not sit back anymore and take the lies that's out there being told. I'm the one that went to them football games. I'm the one that was there when he was sick."[6]

At the time of Trayvon's death, Martin was still married to Stanley, and yet, as Stanley told Cooper, Team Trayvon edited her life out of the narrative. "He hasn't told me why he stopped communicating with me and telling me anything that was going on," she said of Tracy Martin, "so everything that I was finding out, I was finding out on the TV or through friends. And I would call him and ask him why he's not calling me, and he said, well, I was busy, you know, stuff like that." Team Trayvon's relentless propaganda campaign worked much better with just one grieving mom and dad representing the fallen son. Alicia Stanley ceased to exist. So did Brandy Green. The presence of either would have muddied the visual. At the time of his death, everyone claimed to know Trayvon, but no one really did, not even Alicia Stanley. She thought it impossible Trayvon would start a fight. "He's not what the media make him out to be," Stanley told Cooper, "this thug."[7]

A Facebook exchange between Tracy Martin and Miriam from October 27, 2010, when Trayvon was just fifteen, spoke to the warning signs of a young life that had suddenly become unmoored:

TRACY: I need time to myself 2day!!!!!! my son think imma damn fool! this is the part i hate in our father to son relationship! when you start telling lies about nothing you gone walk you ass into an ass cuttin! be honest with your old boy [meaning, the father] and you wont have to get yelled at like a negro in the streets!

MIRIAM: That's right and when you finish cutting his ass send him to home to Auntie & Uncle house so we can get on him too. You know how we do it.[8]

In reality, Trayvon hadn't played football in years. His grades had tanked. His behavior had deteriorated. "He did hit some trouble in his teenage years. He skipped classes and got suspended a couple times," Richardson acknowledged. According to Tracy Martin, "It was just regular teenage stuff," but Sybrina regretted that her son had not passed the FCAT, Florida's major standardized test, that is required for graduation. "Trayvon was going to set that right, they know it," Richardson wrote. "One mistake doesn't mark you for life."[9]

On March 26, the Monday after Obama's Friday Rose Garden manifesto, the *Herald* dug a little deeper. It published a piece by Frances Robles whose very title, "Multiple suspensions paint complicated portrait of Trayvon Martin" should have caused the other media to put a brake on Martin's canonization. The A and B student who majored in cheerfulness had apparently been suspended three times within a year and "had a spotty school record."[10]

The most troubling of those suspensions was handed down in October 2011, four months before Martin's death. Yes, Robles reported, Martin was seen in an "unauthorized area," but that wasn't the half of it. A school police officer saw him in that area "hiding and being suspicious." There he had written "'WTF'—an acronym for 'what the f**k'"—on a locker. The next day the officer rifled through Martin's book bag, looking for the offending marker, and found something more interesting: twelve pieces of women's jewelry, a watch, and a large flathead screwdriver that the officer described as a "burglary tool." Martin reportedly told the officer that the jewelry wasn't his but that "a friend gave it to [him]." School police seized the jewelry and stored it.[11] All that came of this was a ten-day suspension for the graffiti. The stolen jewelry was stashed and the crime forgotten.

Four months later, Robles reported, Martin was suspended again after being "caught with an empty plastic bag with traces of marijuana in it" and a marijuana pipe. It was his third suspension within a year. He had earlier been suspended for tardiness and truancy. True to form, attorney Crump assured the *Herald* that Martin's school problems were "completely irrelevant to what happened Feb. 26."[12] This is the kind of thing an attorney says, but it is not the kind of thing a good reporter accepts uncritically. When Zimmerman first saw Martin, he told the dispatcher, "This guy looks like he's up to no good or he's on drugs or something. It's raining and he's just walking around looking about."[13] Given Martin's school record, Zimmerman could have been right on all counts.

Even after the *Herald* introduced this evidence, the major media still did not want to register it as an accepted part of the established narrative. In an April 1 article, for instance, the *New York Times* admitted Martin's three suspensions but claimed they were for "tardiness, for graffiti and, most recently, for having a baggie with a trace of marijuana in his backpack."[14] The *Times* was in good company. Up to that point, in just about every article that mentioned Martin's suspension, the reporter felt obliged to point out that Martin did not have a criminal record.

Sanford Police Department investigator Chris Serino early on said, "[Martin] has no criminal record whatsoever," calling him "a good kid. A mild-mannered kid."[15] The media almost universally sustained that tragically false narrative. Most took Team Trayvon's word for Martin's crime-free existence, but the Associated Press went the extra mile to prove it. On March 26, the AP reported that the State Department of Juvenile Justice had "confirmed that Martin does not have a juvenile offender record."[16] This information was said to have been obtained through a public records request, but juvenile records are confidential. As the Florida Bar has observed, however, the court uses a "good cause" standard to determine whether a given record should be released. In making this determination, "the court is to balance the privacy rights of those identified in the reports against the public interest."[17] Given the escalating political pressures, it is unlikely the court would have been as forthcoming if Martin did have a juvenile offender record.

Martin avoided the criminal justice system for one unlikely reason. He had the seeming good fortune of pursuing his education in the Miami-Dade County Public Schools, the fourth largest district in the country and one of the few with its own police department. The Miami-Dade Schools Police Department (M-DSPD) has more than 150 sworn personnel and, as the Martin case would reveal, problems unique to its peculiar mission. Through its diligent exploitation of the Freedom of Information Act, the

Conservative Treehouse was uniquely able to discover why the M-DSPD allowed Martin to skate. The exposure of the department's practices began inadvertently with the *Miami Herald* story on Martin's multiple suspensions. The article prompted M-DSPD Chief Charles Hurley to launch a major Internal Affairs (IA) investigation into the possible leak of this information to the *Herald*.[18]

As the investigation began, the officers realized immediately that they had a problem on their hands. "Oh, God, oh, my God, oh, God," one major reportedly said when first looking at Martin's data.[19] He could see that Martin had been suspended twice already that school year for offenses that should have gotten him arrested. In each case, however, the case file on Martin was fudged to make the crime less serious than it was.

To their credit, the officers, when questioned, told the truth about Martin and about the policies that kept him out of the justice system. From their statements, made under oath, it appears that Hurley instructed his officers to divert offending juveniles away from the criminal justice system and back to their respective schools for discipline. He did this subtly. As one sergeant told IA, the arrest statistics coming out of Martin's school had been very high, and the detectives were told that they "needed to cut back on any type of crime that was going on there."[20] This directive allegedly came from Hurley. At least a few officers confirmed that Hurley was particularly concerned with the arrest rates of black males in the Miami-Dade system. In a letter obtained by NBC 6 of South Florida, a senior detective wrote, "[Hurley] asked that I reduce the number of arrests I effect of all black juveniles. I told him regardless of the race of an individual; if probable cause existed for an arrest that individual would be arrested. He was not happy with my response to his request."[21]

"Chief Hurley, for the past year, has been telling his command staff to lower the arrest rates," volunteered another high-ranking detective. When asked by IA whether the M-DSPD was avoiding making arrests, that detective replied, "What Chief Hurley said on the record is that he commends the officer for using his discretion. What Chief Hurley really meant is that he's commended the officer for falsifying a police report."[22] The IA interrogators seemed stunned by what they were hearing. They asked one female supervisor incredulously if she was actually ordered to "falsify reports." She answered, "Pretty much, yes."[23]

In a purely statistical sense, Hurley's policies were working. On February 15, 2012, eleven days before Martin's death, the Miami-Dade County Public Schools put out a press release boasting of a 60 percent decline in school-based arrests, the largest decline by far in the state. "While our work is not completed, we are making tremendous progress in moving toward a pure prevention model," Hurley told the *Tampa Bay Times*, "with enforcement as a last resort and an emphasis on education."[24] In truth, however, the only "education" a diverted student like Martin was getting was to be sent home—or wherever—on an unmonitored suspension. As a result, his parents seemed genuinely oblivious of the kind of trouble he had been stumbling into. Nor was there any "prevention." With their previous crimes winked at, students felt empowered to commit more.

Martin's getting caught with the women's jewelry and a burglary tool should have been a wake-up call for everyone in his life. It was not. Given the directives from the top, the officer who apprehended Martin chose not to link him directly to the jewelry. He instead wrote a report about "found items" and traced those items to Martin only through the police report number. He did not do this of his own initiative. He had told a sergeant, as the sergeant later testified under oath, that the need to lower the crime stats "came up from his supervisor up the chain." The sergeant also acknowledged that "campus police records are not considered an educational record."[25] They cannot simply be sealed. Still, there was no further investigation. As far as Tracy Martin knew, his son had wandered into an "unauthorized area" and been suspended for writing graffiti. No big deal. Boys will be boys.

Within a year, Hurley was demoted and then forced out of the department. In his defense, school districts across the country had been feeling pressure to think twice before disciplining black students. In July 2012 the Obama administration formalized the pressure with an executive order warning school districts to avoid "methods that result in disparate use of disciplinary tools." The White House headlined the press release announcing this dubious stroke of reverse racism, "President Obama Signs New Initiative to Improve Educational Outcomes for African Americans."[26] Jesse Jackson brought this nonsense home to Sanford during a large April 1 rally. He implied that Martin would not have been killed if he had not been suspended from school, suspensions being just another form of "profiling" given that black students are more than three times as likely as their white peers to be suspended or expelled. "We must stop suspending our children," Jackson said, then told the crowd to repeat: "Invest in them. Educate them."[27] Days later, in Miami, Jackson would get more specific and more dishonest. "How did he leave Miami?" Jackson asked of Martin, "'cause he was suspended from school on some trivial notion that there was some marijuana dust in a bag."[28]

In a way, Jackson was right. Martin should not have been suspended. He should have been arrested on both occasions. Had he been, his parents and his teachers would have known how desperately far he had gone astray. Instead, Martin was "diverted" into nothing useful. Just days after his nonarrest, he was allowed to wander the Retreat at Twin Lakes, high and alone, looking, in Zimmerman's immortal words, "like he's up to no good or he's on drugs or something."[29]

Knowing that an established paper could get responses that a blog could not, the *Treehouse*'s Sundance tried to interest *Orlando Sentinel* reporter Rene Stutzman in the stolen jewelry case. He had taken the story about as far as a blogger could. Through some clever investigating, he had identified a home burglary in the neighborhood of Martin's high school on the same day that Martin had been busted for possessing stolen female jewelry. The latter jewelry was still in possession of the school police. He explained to the reporter that he needed to compare it to the jewelry stolen in the home burglary and needed the *Sentinel*'s help to do it.

"You want us to publish your stuff, right?" asked Stutzman. Sundance tried again to explain. "No," said Sundance. "I hold no proprietary ownership of the truth. I've just been digging holes trying to find it, and now, after months of digging, I have narrowed down the location to within inches." Sundance just wanted her to look at the documents he had acquired and make up her own mind.

At this point, Stutzman reverted to her institutional protection mode. "If [this information] pertains to Trayvon Martin's criminal behavior, or evidence of burglary, we are not interested," she told him. "Our editors and editorial board have decided that nothing about that has anything to do with the events in Sanford."[30] This is the same editorial board that green-lit the profoundly unsubstantiated and utterly irrelevant story that an eight-year-old George Zimmerman allegedly molested a six-year-old cousin. And the sad thing is that Sundance contacted Stutzman because he thought she was perhaps the most responsible reporter covering the case.

By March 26, the same day as the *Miami Herald* article about Trayvon's suspensions, the major media had to work overtime to preserve the BGI narrative of innocent black "child" murdered by racist armed vigilante. The blogs had gotten ahold of the story, and they dared to go where the paid press should have gone instantly, namely, into Martin's social media accounts. On Sunday, March 25, the *Treehouse* linked to a piece by blogger Dan Linehan, provocatively titled "Was Trayvon Martin a Drug Dealer?"

The Martin that the reader met on his twitpic account went by the name of "Slimm" and the unsavory handle "No_Limit_Nigga." Unlike the fresh-faced, innocent boy readers saw all over the news, this older, unsmiling Martin sported several gold teeth and numerous tattoos. Linehan also highlighted references to Martin's apparent drug use. After his death, several of his friends posted on Twitter pictures of rolled blunts (marijuana cigars) as a memorial to Martin. As shall be seen, Martin may have died in pursuit of one. From the postings on his Facebook account, it seems likely, too, that Martin not only consumed marijuana but also dealt it. On February 5, three weeks before his death, one friend told Martin, "We got business to talk." When Martin responded, "NO PHON," the exasperated friend posted back, "Damn were u at a nigga needa plant."[31]

Zimmerman attorney Mark O'Mara would later argue that the court had an interest in presenting Trayvon Martin as he appeared on the night of February 26, 2012, and that was not the "several-years-old photo of Trayvon Martin as a boy wearing a red shirt." Said O'Mara hopefully, "If the memory of Trayvon Martin is going to be a catalyst for a conversation about race relations in America then we should have an honest conversation."[32]

Unfortunately, he would find no one to converse with.

14

PICKING THE WRONG FIGHT

*W*HILE THE MEDIA were continuing to insist that Zimmerman had stalked Martin and that the cries for help from this "child" filled the night air, his friends had already come to another conclusion. Wrote Skee Dollah Nickus just two days after Martin's death, "Ima miss you till I die dog I know you whooped his ass doe."[1] Skee Dollah may have presumed this outcome given Martin's budding reputation for street fighting. As one of his cousins posted on Facebook, five days before his death, "Yu aint tell me you swung on a bus driver."[2] Blogger Dan Linehan wondered, as others have, whether this alleged attack may have contributed to Martin's most recent suspension. Given the M-DSPD's diversion policies, punishment, in fact, was more likely to come through the school than the courts. Only the major media had the resources to locate the bus driver and establish the truth of the story. They did not bother.

On April 1, Linehan posted a piece titled, "Did Trayvon Martin Referee School Fights?" Two of the five videos Martin posted on his You-Tube channel were of students street fighting at his high school. In one of the videos, Martin appears to be the referee. The cameraman on one video says, "Watch out, Trayvon, or I'll slap you nigga." The videos have since been removed from Martin's video channel. Gracing that site was a photo of Martin saluting the camera with both middle fingers raised.[3]

On Monday, March 26, the *Daily Caller* exposed the darker side of Martin's life to a broader audience in a story with the unsensational headline "The *Daily Caller* obtains Trayvon Martin's tweets." This Washington-based news and opinion website has a relatively high and respectable profile as a conservative/libertarian source. Its reporting on this controversial a subject would have been difficult for the major media to ignore, but ignore the media did the 152 pages of unedited tweets the *Daily Caller* culled from No_Limit_Nigga's Twitter account. Although most are innocuous, too many read like the one that follows: "f*** a bitch, any bitch, who you want? Take yo pick, but you gone have to take yo time." In their totality, they show Martin to be a vulgar, sexist, angry adolescent whose life was moving in no useful direction.[4]

More disturbing still for the keepers of the Trayvon flame was an article that same Monday in the Trayvon-friendly *Orlando Sentinel*. The article's lede was as straightforward as a hard right jab.

> With a single punch, Trayvon Martin decked the Neighborhood Watch volunteer who eventually shot and killed the unarmed 17-year-old, then Trayvon climbed on top of George Zimmerman and slammed his head into the sidewalk several times, leaving him bloody and battered, authorities have revealed to the *Orlando Sentinel*. That is the account Zimmerman gave police, and much of it has been corroborated by witnesses, authorities say.[5]

On Thursday of that same week, March 29, the *Daily Caller* revealed a second Martin Twitter feed, this one under the cryptic handle T33ZY_ Taught_M3. The accompanying photo showed a dead-eyed Martin staring into the camera with his middle finger extended. The photo was taken on June 17, 2010, when Martin was fifteen. His unease in the world would have been clear to anyone who chose to see. In the most provocative of the tweets, sent two months before he died, Martin urged an unknown friend, "Plzz shoot da #mf dat lied 2 u!" It is impossible to tell how literal he meant to be taken, but Martin's other tweets showed little gift for irony.[6]

That same week *New York Times* columnist Bob Mackey made a desperate attempt to shore up the Martin orthodoxy with an article titled "Bloggers Cherry-Pick from Social Media to Cast Trayvon Martin as a Menace." Mackey argued that the *Daily Caller* and others had ignored those communications that showed Martin in a more nuanced light, like his allegedly "poignant" comment that "You never notice da bad until all da good gone away." To give his argument teeth, however, Mackey first attempted to subvert the legitimacy of the social media posts that the *Daily Caller* and others had been running. He zeroed in on the photo of a menacing Martin making an obscene gesture at the camera. Mackey made the case that since Martin's social media sites were "reported" to have been hacked by an anonymous white supremacist, it was "possible" that photo could have been created through digital manipulation and "might not be genuine."[7]

Mackey linked to the reporting source, a Gotham-centric blog called *Gawker*, whose slogan—"Today's gossip is tomorrow's news"—neatly sums up the site's mission. A month before Martin's death, *Gawker* made a tactical change in editorial policy. Each day, a different staff writer was obliged to abandon his or her regular beat and post whatever item that writer felt would attract the largest audience, whether it be a "dancing cat" video or a Burger King bathroom fight. The editor described this strategy as "traffic-whoring."[8]

On March 29, *Gawker* headlined one of its posts "White Suprema-cist Hacks Trayvon Martin's Email Account, Leaks Messages Online." According to writer Adrian Chen, the hacker, Klanklannon, posted some of Martin's Facebook messages "Tuesday afternoon at around noon." That would have been March 27, two days after Linehan published his social media find and a day after the *Daily Caller* dropped its load. In reality, Klanklannon did not "hack" anything. He merely reported what was already in the news. The postings of an obscure white supremacist could matter only to someone eager to brand as "racist" anyone who engaged in what Chen called this "horrible quest to vet a dead teenager."[9]

More troubling still, a Google search reveals no other web presence for Klanklannon other than the Trayvon Martin post. Chen overlooked the very real possibility that "Klanklannon" was a one-off, pure false flag, a classic ruse de guerre employed to discredit any real reporting about Martin. This strategy would work, of course, only if someone like Bob Mackey at the *New York Times* fell for it, which is exactly what he did. Citing a traffic-whoring celebrity rag on a subject of national consequence without even confirming its source—Mackey's post followed *Gawker*'s by only six hours—showed just how little the *Times* learned from its Duke lacrosse debacle.

On Saturday, March 31, Al Sharpton and Ben Jealous led thousands through the streets of Sanford, Florida, in a media-stoked state of outrage. Sharpton saw an "American paradox" in that "we can put a black man in the White House but we can't walk a black child through a gated area in Sanford, Florida."[10] In his retelling, Martin was not a young man with a proven taste for violence, vulgar sex, and drugs, but a "child" whose death the march organizers compared to Jesus Christ's during a staged "benediction" in front of the police station.[11]

On that same day, the *Treehouse* went all in on the Trayvon story, posting a lengthy "soup to nuts deconstruction" of the case as it stood. "Throughout the past week," wrote Sundance all too accurately, "more new facts surrounding Trayvon Martin have been discovered thanks to the New Media doing the work the Institutional Lame Stream Legacy Media intentionally refuses to do."[12] Although on the Martin beat for only a week, the Treepers deciphered media hieroglyphics with impressive clarity. They presented a precise map and timeline, provided links to the various external information sources, carefully dissected the motives of the various players, and distinguished between what they knew for sure and what they believed. "Bravo, well done," wrote Dee in the comment section. "Not too many liberal media agenda stories have drawn my ire more than this one has. Intelligent analysis always wins over emotional reactions. I'm glad I'm on the right (correct, not political) side."[13] As time would tell, the wrong side was not about to yield.

15

NETWORKS BEHAVING BADLY

*I*N THE APRIL 9, 2012, issue of *People* magazine, more than a month after Trayvon Martin's death, the cover story was titled "An American Tragedy: Heartbreaking New Details." There, staring out from the magazine racks on just about every supermarket aisle in America, was a clean-cut Trayvon, age about thirteen. Those who read no deeper than the cover, and that is the great majority of those who saw the magazine, learned that the untimely death of this "unarmed" lad, as he was inevitably described, left "a family devastated and a country outraged."

In a thoughtful article published two days later at the news website for the Poynter Institute, reporter Alicia Shepard reviewed the ground rules for photo usage specifically in regard to the Trayvon controversy. "The standard is to use the most recent picture," Keith Jenkins, head of multimedia at NPR, told Shepard. He wondered why the media—*People* magazine most conspicuously—had consistently refused to honor that standard in its depiction of Trayvon Martin. As Shepard reported, the media consistently dipped well into Martin's past to show photos of him in a school football uniform, holding a snowboard, even kissing a baby. "He is the picture of innocence," she admitted.[1]

There was enough controversy surrounding photo selection, at least at the *Orlando Sentinel,* that photo editor Tom Burton posted a video explanation of the selection process online. According to Burton, the very first photo the *Sentinel* had access to was a relatively recent one of Martin in a gray hoodie that was provided to the newspaper by Team Trayvon on March 8, the day the Martin family held their first press conference.[2] When the Trayvon story first broke, Burton and his editors debated "whether the hoodie photo was making Trayvon look more like a criminal" but decided to run with it anyhow.[3] When twice asked by this author via e-mail whether the *Sentinel* air-brushed the photo to make it look less threatening, Burton evaded the question. Two versions of that photo circulated—a darker, rougher-looking one that appeared on Trayvon posters—and the refined one that appeared in the media. As to which was the original, that question remains unanswered.

To its credit, the *Sentinel* was the rare media outlet to run the "hoodie" photo in the first few weeks of coverage. Team Trayvon made sure that the world's media had other choices and flooded the market with precleared images of a youthful Martin. George Zimmerman, meanwhile, along with his wife and his parents, had been forced into hiding. Overwhelmed by the ordeal, they did not think to provide the media with photos of George. It was not until three weeks after the shooting that Mark Osterman evaded the media, snuck back into Zimmerman's town house, and secured a more recent photo. Excluding the *Sentinel*, the media made no effort to find a photo other than the one they had been running, the mug shot of a surly, overweight Zimmerman taken in 2005. Worse, more than a few outlets misidentified his orange polo shirt as a prison jump suit. Impressions set in. Corrections came slowly. The Zimmermans were up against BGI professionals like Ryan Julison, whose media tactics had been time tested. Before the shooting, Zimmerman identified with the civil rights movement. If he ever did, he could no longer.

As the Trayvon bandwagon picked up momentum, producers at several major networks jumped on board. In several astonishing instances, they moved from a biased presentation of evidence to outright manipulation. The mischief began at WJTV in Miami, an NBC affiliate. On March 19, three days after the Sanford Police Department released tapes of the relevant phone calls, Jeff Burnside, a station veteran with a shelf full of awards for environmental reporting, fronted a piece that featured a stunningly deceptive edit in George Zimmerman's initial call to the non-emergency dispatcher on February 26. The unedited tape ran as follows:

GZ: This guy looks like he's up to no good. Or he's on drugs or something. It's raining and he's just walking around, looking about.

SPD: OK, and this guy—is he black, white or Hispanic?

GZ: He looks black.

What the WJTV audience heard was something different: "This guy looks like he's up to no good. He looks black."[4] That was it. The dispatcher's question was edited out. With the issue of racial profiling being front and center, Burnside had to know how guilty the edit made Zimmerman appear. Martin's very blackness would seem to have caused Zimmerman to think him suspicious. The edit no doubt fueled the firestorm building against Zimmerman, especially in Florida, and, for the time being at least, it aired without pushback. Before he was through, Burnside would file nine stories on the case. One of those stories involved something of a coup for Burnside. He landed an interview with Al Sharpton in Sanford on March 22. "First interview upon arriving in Florida," Burnside boasted on his Facebook page. "And first to talk to him about the death of his mother just hours prior to sitting down with me." Two days later he would praise Sharpton to a Facebook friend, "I realized enormous respect for him during this week. Very smart guy."[5]

On March 20 and again on March 22, Lilia Luciano, reporting from Sanford for national NBC News, aired a news segment with a comparable edit, the second of these two occasions on the *Today Show*. Luciano set up the excerpted audio by describing Martin as the "the teen gunned down by Neighborhood Watchman George Zimmerman last month as he walked through this gated community wearing a hoodie." The edited phone exchange that followed fit the BGI narrative perfectly: Zimmerman targeted Martin not only because he looked black, but also because he wore the kind of clothing young black men distinctively wore, namely, the hoodie.

GZ: This guy looks like he's up to no good. He looks black.

SPD: Did you see what he was wearing?

GZ: Yeah, a dark hoodie.

To make this distortion work, NBC also edited out Zimmerman's complete response when asked what Martin was wearing. "Yeah, a dark hoodie like a gray hoodie," said Zimmerman, adding, "He wore jeans or sweat pants and white tennis shoes. He's here now."[6] After the editors at NBC got through with him, Zimmerman appeared to have focused exclusively on Martin's race and hoodie. Again, at the time, Luciano's report passed without much comment.

This stunning bit of agitprop went main stage on March 27 when NBC's Ron Allen, who is himself black, led his *Today Show* feature with the same abridged quote, both in audio and in text. Then, while explaining the case, Allen and his producer showed two innocent photos of Martin taken years earlier, this despite the availability of the more recent "hoodie photo." Allen then played a more subtly dismembered excerpt from Zimmerman's exchange with the SPD dispatcher, again with both text and audio:

SPD: Are you following him? [2:24]

GZ: Yeah.

SPD: Okay. We don't need you to do that. [2:26][7]

Left on the editing room floor was Zimmerman's response to the dispatcher's request, "Okay." Almost all the news features edited out Zimmerman's "okay." In fact, Zimmerman took the dispatcher's advice and stopped following Martin. Those who watched NBC would have thought otherwise. Wild-eyed partisans like pink-cowboy-hat-wearing Miami congresswoman Frederica Wilson certainly did when she famously ranted at a March 28 press conference in the Capitol that "Trayvon was hunted down like a rabid dog. He was shot in the street. He was racially profiled."[8] For all her hyperbole, everything Wilson said tracked with what she could have heard on NBC.

Little of what Allen reported was actually true. He claimed, for instance, that the case drew national attention only after the 9-1-1 tapes were released. In fact Reuters had reported on the story nearly two weeks earlier, and Sharpton was fully on board a week or so before the tapes were released. Allen then paraphrased Martin's parents as saying, "Police accepted Zimmerman's statements at the scene as fact and never gathered any more evidence that might reveal what really happened then." Allen had to know this was not even close to accurate. What persuaded the Sanford police to release Zimmerman were the key witness's statements that corroborated his own testimony. The audience was not allowed to know this. Allen let the parents' sentiments stand uncorrected. Curiously, the piece closed with Zimmerman's uncut audio—without text—airing over some crime scene video. The last thing the audience heard was Zimmerman saying, "He looks black."

By so obviously skewing the story to favor the BGI narrative, NBC woke the conservative watchdogs, none more prominent than Brent Bozell, head of the Media Research Center and *Newsbusters*. "This isn't distortion. This isn't bias," Bozell told Sean Hannity on March 30. "This is "an all-out falsehood." The usually reserved Bozell denounced the whole spectacle. "The radical left has already acted as judge, jury and executioner in this," he said emphatically. "This is another Tawana Brawley moment."[9]

NBC's reporting inspired Zimmerman to bring suit against the network, Ron Allen, Lilia Luciano, and Jeff Burnside in December 2012. The suit accused the defendants of manipulating the substance of the call, highlighting Martin's minority status but not Zimmerman's, and showing misleading photos of Martin all in an effort to create "a racial powder keg that would result in months, if not years, of topics for their failing news programs." The suit singled out the *Today Show* given its "plummeting ratings."[10] In fact, ABC's *Good Morning America* had just taken the high ground in the morning talk show wars, a source of very real anxiety at NBC. The suit did not help the network's reputation.

The mainstream media were nearly as upset as Zimmerman, in no small part because NBC's performance gave credence to the right's charge of a leftist bias. Reporting on March 31, Erik Wemple of the *Washington Post* described the NBC piece as "high editorial malpractice," but he thought it "great news" that the NBC brass was prepared to launch an internal investigation to determine how the network's reporting went awry.[11] On April 3, NBC News released a statement of findings. "During our investigation it became evident that there was an error made in the production process that we deeply regret," went the statement. "We will be taking the necessary steps to prevent this from happening in the future and apologize to our viewers."[12] On April 6, Brian Stelter of the *New York*

Times reported that NBC had fired an unnamed Miami-based producer involved in the editing of the March 27 *Today Show* piece. According to Stelter, throughout NBC there was "shock that the segment had been broadcast," especially since it had to clear a script editor, a senior producer, legal and standards department reviews, and the news judgment of the reporter, Ron Allen. Stelter concluded his piece with the ingenuous observation, "The people with direct knowledge of the firing characterized the misleading edit as a mistake, not a purposeful act."[13]

Although it might seem too unlikely to be true, it does appear that WJTV in Miami and national NBC News made the same "error" independent of each other. According to *Poynter*'s Andrew Beaujon, the WTVJ video was not the one that aired on NBC's *Today Show*. Beaujon's sources told him that the *Today Show* edit was traced to NBC's southeast headquarters, also based in South Florida, but not to WTVJ. Each of them received an unedited tape from the Sanford Police Department and performed comparable surgery on it.[14] For its part, WTJV fired Jeff Burnside, the reporter responsible for the misrepresentation, and NBC fired Luciano. "As anybody in the news business knows, something that seems very clear is often very, very complicated," Burnside told Beaujon, adding not a drop of clarity to the issue.[15]

Missed by the mainstream critics of NBC was why so many people at two different media outlets gave the green light to so flagrant a misrepresentation. These were not errors in any traditional sense of that word. These edits, whether consciously executed or not, had the effect of defaming George Zimmerman. The best-case scenario? Like wishful participants on a Ouija board, these reporters and producers allowed their minds to go where their hearts willed them, and too many pushed in the same direction as the BGI. The worst case, the more likely case, is that at least some among them set out to destroy Zimmerman and assumed that none of their peers would notice or care. If so, their assumptions almost bore out. It took outside pressure from the conservative media and the blogosphere to force the mainstream media to notice.

While NBC was clumsily subverting the record, CNN was doing the same, but much more imaginatively. Prodding CNN into action was the profane, upstart Current TV show *The Young Turks*. On the night of March 19, host Cenk Uygur played the unedited Zimmerman tape. No network had yet done that, in no small part because Zimmerman used the word "f**king" at one point and "assholes" at another. On an unenhanced tape, the first of those words is difficult to hear. The word that follows it is impossible to hear. Yet like those zealots who see images of the Blessed Virgin Mary in a grilled cheese sandwich, some in the *Young Turks'* viewing audience found racism in empty static and convinced themselves that Zimmerman said "f***ing coons."

The next evening Uygur thanked his audience for their perceptiveness. "No one picked up what you guys picked up," he congratulated them. He then played the unedited tape again, the key words of which are utterly incomprehensible, and declared, "That's unbelievable." Uygur continued, "It's possible he said 'goons.' It's possible he said something else." That much conceded, Uygur concluded, "but it certainly sounds like 'coons.'" He then explained how relevant was Zimmerman's use of that word given that it showed obvious bias and elevated the shooting to a hate crime.[16]

The next day, March 21, on Anderson Cooper's *AC360*, CNN reporter Gary Tuchman worked with audio design specialist Rick Sierra to isolate and enhance the audio from Zimmerman's call to the dispatcher. Even cleaned up, the audio was unintelligible, save, of course, to the true believers. Tuchman was one of them. "It certainly sounds like that word to me," said Tuchman, that word, of course, being "coons."[17] Media critic Tommy Christopher agreed. Said he, voicing the media consensus, "The result is, at the very least, more convincing than the raw audio."[18] At the time, no one at CNN was asking the most fundamental questions about Zimmerman's use of this word. Why, for instance, in 2012, would a young Hispanic civil rights activist think to use an archaic throwback word like "coons"? More basically, why would he begin a sentence with the pronoun "it" if he were to complete his thought with a plural noun, as in, "It's f***ing coons."

Not everyone was on board for this nonsense. Liberal media pundit Jon Stewart said on his show what most dispassionate observers were thinking, "That doesn't sound like a word at all!"[19] In the blogosphere, most everyone agreed with Stewart. At the *Treehouse*, where facts still mattered, StellaP posted Sanford's weather data for February 26, 2012, to assess whether the word "cold" made sense. For the record, it was sixty-three degrees at the time with a northeast wind from five to ten miles an hour.

One suspects that there were those within CNN's legal department who likewise had doubts about the network's reporting. Tuchman was sent back to the studio. This time, allegedly using an "even higher tech method" with the help of audio specialist Brian Stone, Tuchman admitted to CNN's Wolf Blitzer on April 4, "It does sound less like that racial slur." In fact, the word in question sounded a whole lot like "cold."[20] Again, though, Tuchman failed to mention the role the word "it's" should have played in interpreting what was said. "It's f**king cold" made sense, especially on a cool, damp Florida evening. "It's f**king coons" never made any sense either as a linguistic construct or as a reflection of Zimmerman's character. "I don't even believe George knew the derogatory meaning of the word 'Coons,'" said his father.[21] In the State's probable cause affidavit issued just a few days later, the investigators settled on "these f**king punks." Zimmerman told the SPD that he thought the word was "punks" when they interviewed him soon after the shooting.[22] That word, at least, was within his working vocabulary. Still, the damage had been done. Despite what should have been a complete exoneration, Tuchman concluded his broadcast saying, "But it's readily apparent there will still be controversy over what he really said."[23]

If all of this were not enough of a headache for Zimmerman, HLN legal harridan Nancy Grace started pounding her TV podium, demanding Zimmerman's arrest. Like so many of her media colleagues, the facts did not much interest her. On her March 26 show, she had Steve Helling of *People* magazine share his on-the-scene reporting with her audience. According to Helling, his three eyewitnesses saw neither a bloody nose nor any cuts on Zimmerman's head. "My sources are saying he was not injured," said Helling. He also claimed that "the original police report" confirmed the same. "At the outset, he is the aggressor," Grace concluded of Zimmerman. "That is what self-defense hinges on. You can't claim self-defense if you are the aggressor." In an unintentional bit of humor, she cautioned against allowing the investigation to become a "witch hunt."[24] As if!

16

DEFENDING THE DEFENSELESS

*T*HE PHRASE "POLITICALLY CORRECT" may sound benign, even amusing when used by late-night comedians, but it loses all its innocence when the forces driving a politically correct idea put their weight behind it. On no issue are those forces more intimidating than on the issue of race. In the face of those forces, most white Americans opt for silence, the consequences of which author Colin Flaherty dissects scarily well in his bestseller '*White Girl Bleed a Lot'*, a chronicle of the media's failure to talk about black-on-nonblack crime. George Zimmerman's friends learned the price of challenging the PC regime when they dared to speak out for him in public.

One Twin Lakes neighbor, Frank Taaffe, had the temerity to suggest why someone like Martin may have looked suspicious to George Zimmerman. Taaffe told CNN's Soledad O'Brien that earlier in February 2012 Zimmerman had spotted a young black male snooping around Taaffe's house and called the police. The Sanford police confirmed the call and the address. Zimmerman's complaint on the city's website reads, "Black male (leather jacket, black hat, printed PJ pants) keeps going to the residence which is owned by a white male. Black male subject in question was gone upon police arrival."[1]

Taaffe's town house was particularly vulnerable because he lived near the unauthorized shortcut into the community. He told the FBI that he saw about twenty-five people a week entering through that opening, the great majority being young black males, some of them smoking blunts. The few he approached blew him off.[2]

Taaffe truly provoked Martin supporters by claiming that black males had committed all of the eight recent burglaries in his neighborhood. The Sanford police again confirmed the burglaries but could account for suspects in only four cases, all four black males. In truth, it would not have mattered if the SPD had reported that all eight were black. So intense is the taboo against racial profiling on the left that citizens are expected to deny their own experiences or, at the very least, remain silent about them. The media have strengthened the taboo by failing to report comparable patterns in cities all across America. This self-imposed silence reached a new level of absurdity in April 2012 when the Norfolk, Virginia, newspaper *Virginian-Pilot* dithered two weeks before acknowledging that a mob of young black men gratuitously beat up two of its own reporters, one an Iranian-American female. "Do it for trayvon martin," an observer tweeted.[3]

At this stage, one would have thought the media had exhausted all possible ways of corrupting the case, but not quite. They attacked Taaffe and, in doing so, sent a message to all other witnesses whose accounts might help Zimmerman. Taking the lead in this bit of subversion was NBC's informational homeland for African Americans, the *Grio*. Ironically, NBC launched this, the first race-oriented "video-centric news community site," soon after Obama's election on the theme of "one people, one America." It goes without saying, of course, that a news community site providing European-Americans "with stories and perspectives that appeal to them" would have cost the career of any network exec who even floated the idea over the water cooler.

Grio founder David Wilson promised a site that would welcome all views, liberal and conservative, but the *Grio*'s exhaustive coverage of the Martin case moved almost exclusively in one direction, and God help the person who got in the way. All the way through to the trial, in fact, the *Grio* protested the "demonizing" of Martin by anyone who dared research his background. This criticism even extended to Zimmerman's attorneys, who had not just the right to do so, but the obligation.

Blacks who defended Zimmerman caught a distinctive brand of guff. Before taking on Taaffe, for instance, the *Grio* ran several pieces on

Joe Oliver, an African American who publicly and eloquently defended Zimmerman. A March 29, 2012, article by Kunbi Tinouye captured the puzzlement of the *Grio* staff as to why any self-respecting black man would do such a thing. "Could it be that he wants to 'elevate the conversation' and carve a niche for himself as a television contributor," wrote the suspicious Tinouye, "or perhaps even has aspirations for his own TV show?"[4] Tinouye apparently did not think it possible that Oliver, as a former broadcaster, just might have felt some obligation to report the truth.

The *Grio* went harder and deeper on Taaffe, who is white. Incredibly, the site produced a history of his encounters with the law—including a fifteen-year-old domestic battery case long since dismissed—that was far more exhaustive than any it had done on Martin. More than five months after the shooting, the *Grio* celebrated Taaffe's drunken driving arrest almost as enthusiastically as it did Zimmerman's arrest for second-degree murder. "George Zimmerman supporter Frank Taaffe arrested for DUI," shouted the *Grio* headline above a mug shot of "one of George Zimmerman's staunchest supporters."[5] If anyone at NBC thought it unseemly for one of its subsidiaries to undermine the judicial process by intimidating witnesses, that protest did not make it into the public record.

17

DECONSTRUCTING THE DECEIT

O N MARCH 28, one week after Anderson Cooper falsely accused Zimmerman of racial slurs on his CNN show and one day after Ron Allen falsely accused him of racial profiling on the *Today Show*, ABC News tried to regain its rightful place in the false accusation race. Leading the charge was ace fact-twister Matt Gutman. His online lede was a powerful one: "A police video taken the night that Trayvon Martin was shot dead shows no blood or bruises on George Zimmerman." As Gutman related, the initial police report claimed that Zimmerman was bleeding from the back of the head and the nose, but in the video, obtained exclusively by ABC, "No abrasions or blood can be seen."[1] Although Gutman did not say so, he surely implied that Zimmerman and the police conspired to exaggerate his injuries.

In his video presentation, Gutman edited in audio excerpts from mystery girlfriend Dee Dee to create a remarkably dishonest narrative given what was known by March 28. Like many of his media peers, Gutman edited out Zimmerman's "Okay" response to the dispatcher when asked not to pursue Martin. That detail buried, Gutman put this spin on events: "Zimmerman continues to pursue. Martin runs, then slows down just seventy feet from his back door. They fight. Then the black hole—no eyewitnesses, no videos." In this scenario, of course, Gutman described Martin with the obligatory "unarmed and carrying iced tea and Skittles" disclaimer. When finished with his own account, Gutman cut immediately to Martin's mother, who added, "We have no answers. He's a very good kid."[2]

The *Treehouse* wasted no time in dismantling Gutman's dumb show. The Treepers began by revealing how the ABC video strengthened Zimmerman's case. Yes, he wore a red jacket just as at least one key witness said the beating victim was wearing. Yes, when frozen and magnified, the video showed a wound on top of Zimmerman's head. Yes, Zimmerman had a bandage covering his nose. "But," as the March 29 post observed with some understatement, "there is a more visible issue with this video."[3]

That issue was a critical one. It had to do specifically with the police surveillance video, which, Gutman boasted, "was obtained exclusively by ABC News." As the Treepers noticed, the camera seemed to move as it shadowed the police and Zimmerman. CCTV surveillance video cameras do not move. They are fixed and stationary. Bottom line: this was not the original video or a digital copy of the original. It was video of a video, quite possibly taken by a Team Trayvon ally using an iPhone or something like it and given to Gutman. The *Treehouse* described the video as "stolen and intentionally leaked."[4] Likely suspects include a Sanford Police Department employee or a journalist working with someone in the SPD. In releasing this copy, Gutman failed to mention the obvious reason for the apparent lack of "blood or bruises"—namely, the loss of resolution from the original to the duplicate, not to mention the fact Zimmerman's wounds had been tended to at the scene.

The producers at CBS Evening News were apparently not reading the *Treehouse*. On that same day, March 29, they dragged out the surveillance video once again to make the absurd case that no violence occurred on the evening of February 26 except for the shooting of Martin. *CBS Evening News* anchor Scott Pelley introduced the segment with the improbable line, "The defense of George Zimmerman rests on a violent fight that he said occurred before he fired the shot that killed Trayvon Martin."[5] By this time, of course, there was abundant evidence in the public sphere that, at the very least, a violent altercation had taken place. Multiple eyewitnesses had called in to report it. The Sanford police had made their 9-1-1 calls public two weeks earlier. Pelley should never have led the CBS audience to believe that the fact of the "violent fight" hinged only on the testimony of George Zimmerman, but he did.

The folks in charge at *CBS Evening News* obviously had an agenda. To make their case, they showed the same discredited surveillance tape that ABC had shown the night before and reiterated the claim that Zimmerman "seemed to show no apparent injuries." Martin family attorney Benjamin Crump reinforced this claim. "Look at that video," he told the CBS faithful. "Do you see any blood on his head? He said he broke his nose. Look at that video. And look at how easy he walks out of the car."[6]

The video, of course, was day-old news. The real kicker was the "new evidence" introduced by CBS reporter Mark Strassmann. The source of this evidence was Crump crony Richard Kurtz, the Fort Lauderdale funeral director who prepared Martin for burial. "We could see no physical signs like there had been a scuffle [or] there had been a fight," Kurtz told the CBS faithful. "The hands—I didn't see any knuckles, bruises or what have you. And that is something we would have covered up if it would have been there."[7] CBS presented Kurtz to the public as a dispassionate observer. He was not. A longtime local NAACP president, he was routinely described in local media accounts as a "black activist." He was also an outspoken Democrat and a racial demagogue. "In 2002 we're going to get rid of that Bush in Tallahassee," Kurtz told an agitated crowd after the 2000 election debacle in Florida, "and in 2004 we're going to get rid of that Bush in Washington, D.C. Then we'll be free at last!"[8]

CBS should never have put a partisan like Kurtz on the air without checking to see whether his account matched that of the official autopsy report. It did not. Two weeks earlier, Shiping Bao, the associate medical examiner, had signed off on the medical examiner report's "Final Diagnoses and Findings." As the report made clear in agonizing detail, Martin had suffered only two injuries the night of February 26, one complex, one very simple. The complex one, the "penetrating gunshot wound of the chest," did lethal damage to Martin's heart and lungs. As to "other injuries," Bao lists only one, "an abrasion on the left fourth finger."[9]

Gawker headlined its story on the Kurtz revelation much as other media did, "New Evidence Contradicts Zimmerman's Claim of a Violent Fight with Trayvon Martin."[10] Implicit in the headline, however, was a false premise. Zimmerman never claimed to have been in anything like a fight. The word "fight" suggests a circumstance in which two combatants square off against one another. It was the media that introduced the concept of a fight or fistfight. By his own account, an account that the autopsy report supported, Zimmerman never threw a punch, never willfully entered into any kind of altercation. Both his wounds and Martin's tended to confirm the story that Zimmerman had been telling from the night of the shooting—Martin assaulted him, broke his nose on the first punch, jumped on top of him, and started wailing away.

From that point on, Zimmerman was just struggling to survive.

18

AWAITING THE NAZIS

*A*S A SUBSPECIES OF THE GENUS "media malpractice," the much-bruited threat of armed neo-Nazis patrolling the streets of Sanford deserves its own brief chapter. Responsibility for this bogus bombshell goes to Michael Miller, a reporter for the alternative publication the *Miami New Times*. In early April 2012, Miller sent a fresh jolt of fear into the already-troubled hearts of the Sanford citizenry. "Neo-Nazis are currently conducting heavily armed patrols in and around Sanford, Florida, and are 'prepared' for violence in the case of a race riot," wrote Miller in the original opening sentence, later modified. The article was peppered with photos of armed men with dogs, said to be members of the "National Socialist Movement" (NSM) then on patrol along the Mexican border in Arizona.[1]

For the left-leaning blogosphere, this story had simply too much sex appeal to bother verifying. It rocked for about twenty-four unmolested hours.[2] "Trayvon Martin Case: Armed Neo-Nazis Patrolling Sanford," read the headline of the *Huffington Post*. "CHILLING: Armed Neo-Nazis Patrol Sanford," shouted a headline on the *Daily Beast*. Charles Johnson of *Little Green Footballs*, like many of his peers, was keen to link the NSM to traditional conservatives. This was an election year, after all. "You know all that rhetoric about 'race war' that's showing up at Breitbart. com and many other right wing sites these days?" wrote Johnson. "It's not just rhetoric. There are some people in Sanford, Florida right now who are taking it very seriously indeed."[3] The mania even spread to the *New York Daily News,* which reported, "The Trayvon Martin case is getting even more heated as armed neo-Nazis are reportedly patrolling the streets of Sanford, Fla.—where the black, unarmed teen was shot and killed."[4]

In the midst of the hysteria, Jim Hoft of the conservative blog the *Gateway Pundit* finally asked the question that the media should have been asking all along. "Are Armed Nazi Socialists Really Patrolling the Streets of Sanford, Florida?" William Jacobson of *Legal Insurrection* took the trouble of answering Hoft's question, and the *Treehouse* published what Jacobson discovered. "None of the major publications spreading the rumors bothered to check with local law enforcement," wrote Jacobson on April 7. "I did." His e-mail exchange with the Sanford police went as follows:

> **JACOBSON:** There are a number of reports in the media that Neo-Nazis are conducting armed patrols in Sanford. Can you confirm or deny whether this is true, and provide any information you have on the subject?
>
> **SANFORD PD:** At this time the City of Sanford has not confirmed the presence of Neo-Nazis groups.
>
> **JACOBSON:** You say "not confirmed." Is there any indication of such patrols that the Department is aware of?
>
> **SANFORD PD:** We have no indication of any such patrols at this point in Sanford. The only large gathering was the children and their parents at the Easter egg hunt.

"I can't say this is the worst example of rumor mongering and irresponsible conduct by bloggers and the mainstream media I have ever seen, but it's a contender," wrote Jacobson in summary. "For *The Daily Beast, Huffington Post, Mediaite,* and *The Daily News* to spread such thinly-sourced claims without verification at a time when racial tensions already are high is irresponsible in the extreme."[5]

Jacobson was not quite accurate. The *Miami New Times* had, in a manner of speaking, verified the story. Their source, however, was NSM honcho Jeff Schoep, a character so absurd and irrelevant that even the race-baiting Southern Poverty Law Center (SPLC) has a hard time taking him seriously. In its so-called Intelligence Files, the SPLC warned that Schoep's Nationalist Socialist Movement was known, among other offenses, for "the violence it works hard to provoke."[6] Although Schoep was allegedly a "rising star on the neo-Nazi scene" for the past twenty years, the SPLC could not identify a single violent incident that he and his crew actually succeeded in provoking. There was a reason for his restraint. As Schoep explained to the *New Times*, "The Black Panthers have been offering bounties and all that. But if we called for a bounty on someone's head, I guarantee we'd be locked up as quick as I could walk out of my house."[7] It may not happen often, but Schoep here spoke the truth.

To be fair, most of the publications, the *Miami New Times* included, amended their online versions after Jacobson reached out to the Sanford police, but these minor changes did little to undo major damage. The *Huffington Post*, for instance, added the word "update" to the headline and acknowledged in the body copy that "the Sanford Police Department issued a statement, saying that there is no evidence of neo-Nazis in the area." Nevertheless, the editors left the incendiary headline in place, "Trayvon Martin Case: Armed Neo-Nazis Patrolling Sanford."[8] The patrols never exactly materialized.

Even the dependably hyperbolic SPLC had to concede there was no evidence of the twenty armed neo-Nazis that Schoep promised. "Instead, it seems that only three showed up," observed the SPLC. "They delivered some leaflets and posed for a photo-op with an NSM banner before leaving."[9] In Sanford, the Nazi incursion proved to be something less than a blitzkrieg.

19

GRABBING FOR THE GUNS

MALIGNING ZIMMERMAN AND HIS SUPPORTERS was a necessary part of the larger strategy to make gun rights a losing political issue, but it was not at all sufficient. Democrats and their media allies had to challenge the gun laws as well. Reason was not their weapon of choice. Emotion was. On March 22, as mentioned earlier, Florida governor Rick Scott yielded to BGI pressure and appointed a Stand Your Ground task force, but that was a local response, and little was expected of it.

Five days later, a month after the shooting, the antigun morality play moved to a bigger stage. On that day, Martin's parents attended an emotionally wrought forum on Capitol Hill. There, they heard Dan Gross, president of the Brady Campaign to Prevent Gun Violence, describe Florida as "the NRA's armed utopia." Zimmerman, according to Gross, was "the embodiment of the gun lobby and its dark vision for America."[1]

In truth, Florida did have relatively lenient gun laws as well as the most concealed carry permits in the country, with nearly 1.1 million active licenses at the time of Zimmerman's trial.[2] Gun control advocates routinely linked the prevalence of legitimate gun ownership to Florida's relatively high violent crime rate. "Since Florida enacted the NRA's concealed weapons law more than two decades ago," said Gross, "Florida has led the nation in violent crime—consistently ranking in the top five every year for states with the worst violent crime rates in America."[3] Gross pulled these numbers out of his posterior. In 2011, for instance, Florida's murder rate—a much more relevant statistic—was sixteenth highest in the nation but was less than every state in the Deep South other than Texas, another prominent gun rights state.[4]

In fact, the growth in the number of concealed carry permits represented, if anything, an effective response to crime rather than a cause of it. A review of the 2011 crime data by the Texas Department of Public Safety showed concealed carry permit holders to be dramatically more responsible than the average Texan. Although permit holders made up roughly 3 percent of the adult population, they committed only .2 percent of the crime, and their crimes tended to be less violent.[5] In Florida, in the four years preceding Martin's death, 2007–2011, firearm-related violent crimes dropped by one-third while concealed carry permits increased 90 percent. "We are at a 40-year low in our crime rate in our state," said Gov. Rick Scott emphatically. "From a public safety standpoint we are absolutely heading in the right direction."[6]

Nationwide, crime data had been working against gun control advocates for at least two decades. The Martin case was a seeming godsend. Yes, finally, a permit holder shot and killed someone, and not just anyone, but an innocent black child whose only sin was walking through a gated community while wearing a hoodie on his way back from getting Skittles and iced tea for his little brother. This narrative was essential not only for the BGI, but also for the antigun lobby and, by extension, the Democratic Party.

Gun control advocates took particular aim at Florida's so-called Stand Your Ground statute, which was signed into law by Governor Jeb Bush in 2005. At the time of passage, this law did not seem terribly controversial. It passed the Florida House by a vote of 94–20 and the Senate by a vote of 39-0. The law passed handily for good reason. While a resident has always had the right to defend himself in his own home—the so-called Castle Doctrine—the 2005 legislation expanded that right to any place where he (or she) was lawfully allowed to go. Before these laws were passed in Florida and elsewhere, victims were expected to retreat in the face of a serious threat. These statutes use a "reasonable person" standard to determine when and how a potential victim can respond to a serious threat. Florida law reads as follows:

A person who is not engaged in an unlawful activity and who is attacked in any other place where he or she has a right to be has no duty to retreat and has the right to stand his or her ground and meet force with force, including deadly force if he or she reasonably believes it is necessary to do so to prevent death or great bodily harm to himself or herself or another or to prevent the commission of a forcible felony.

Within weeks of Martin's shooting, liberal pundits were routinely referring to the Florida law as "shoot first, ask questions later." In its first article on the subject of Martin's death, the *New York Times* was already editorializing against the law. "Stand Your Ground is a law that has really created a Wild West type environment in Florida," criminal defense lawyer Brian Tannebaum was quoted as saying. "It allows people to kill people outside of their homes, if they are in reasonable fear for their lives. It's a very low standard."[7] A few days later the *Huffington Post* repeated the quote but removed Tannebaum's caveat, "if they are in reasonable fear for their lives."[8] For the media, certainly the left flank thereof, fearing for one's life was of little matter unless, of course, the potential victim was a female and a minority, as the Marissa Alexander case made clear.

John Lott, the nation's foremost gun law researcher, described the media discussion of the Stand Your Ground laws as "totally irresponsible caricature." He explained that the laws do not protect individuals who provoke an attack, use unnecessary force, or shoot a fleeing criminal in the back. Moreover, judges and jurors are the ones entrusted with determining what it was "necessary to do" to save one's life from a serious threat. As Lott also pointed out early in the Zimmerman investigation, "whether Zimmerman acted in self-defense with Trayvon on top of him and no place to retreat—or whether, in the other version of events, Zimmerman initiated the attack—the Stand Your Ground law isn't relevant."[9]

If Zimmerman's account were accurate, he did not need the protection of Stand Your Ground. The existing self-defense statutes in Florida or any other state would have sufficed. If Team Trayvon's account were true, no juror would find the behavior of an armed stalker who outweighed his child prey by a hundred pounds "reasonable." The Zimmerman attorneys agreed with Lott. "George did not have an ability to retreat because he was on the ground with Trayvon Martin mounting him, striking blows," they wrote on Zimmerman's legal website, "therefore the 'Stand Your

Ground' 'benefit' given by the statute simply does not apply to the facts of George's case: it is traditional self-defense."[10]

The point should have been moot from the beginning, but it was not. Florida was, after all, a battleground state in a presidential election year. As was well understood by the political operatives, the trial would come sometime after the November election. They did not need to convict Zimmerman in court. They merely needed to hammer this gun rights "poster child" in the court of public opinion, at least through November. Zimmerman the individual was irrelevant. Zimmerman the symbol was irresistible. These headlines, all from the first two months after the shooting, tell the tale:

MEET GEORGE ZIMMERMAN: HE IS THE NRA
—*Democratic Underground*, March 22; *Democrats for Progress*, March 24

WHAT THE NRA'S "FOUNDER" AND GEORGE ZIMMERMAN HAVE IN COMMON
—*Huffington Post*, March 29

SHAME ON THE NRA AND ITS NEWEST POSTER CHILD, GEORGE ZIMMERMAN
—*New York Daily News*, April 13

BRADY CAMPAIGN PRESIDENT: NRA PUT "THE GUN IN GEORGE ZIMMERMAN'S HANDS"
—*CNS*, April 16

As testament to the political appeal of the Martin case, on the forty-fourth anniversary of Martin Luther King's death, April 4, 2012, members of the Congressional Black Caucus introduced a resolution calling for further investigation into Trayvon's death and a repeal of Stand Your Ground laws in states around the country. Among those taking the lead was Rep. Frederica Wilson, a Democrat from Miami. As fate would have it, in 2005 Wilson was one of the thirty-nine Florida state senators who voted unanimously to pass Stand Your Ground.[11] Up for reelection in Martin's district in 2012, she was said to have regretted her earlier vote. Bob Zimmerman regretted the entire caucus, calling them "a pathetic, self-serving group of racists."[12]

In February 2013, with the November election no longer an issue, Governor Scott's nineteen-person Stand Your Ground task force came back with its findings. The allegedly "controversial" law proved not so controversial after all. "All persons who are conducting themselves in a lawful manner," the report began, "have a fundamental right to stand their ground and defend themselves from attack with proportionate force in every place they have a lawful right to be." The task force recommended some minor changes, particularly in regard to the mandatory sentencing laws that sent Thompson and Marissa Alexander to prison for a long duration, but otherwise left the law in place. Even the dissenting members of the task force—and there appeared to be only two—agreed with the general thrust of the law.[13]

20

CHANNELING ORWELL

ONCE THE NATIONAL MEDIA WERE ENGAGED, Team Trayvon had clout enough to have Zimmerman investigated and, ideally, arrested on federal civil rights charges. On March 18, ABC News reported that Crump had written a letter to Attorney General Eric Holder, asking him to assign the FBI to the case.[1] Crump's allies in Congress were circulating that same letter to keep the pressure on Holder. A notorious procrastinator on issues unfavorable to the White House, like "Fast and Furious," Holder did not take long to weigh the pros and cons of the Zimmerman case. On March 19, ABC reported that the FBI, the Justice Department's Civil Rights Division, and the US Attorney's Office for the Middle District of Florida would all investigate Martin's death.[2]

By Monday, April 2, FBI agents were already in Florida, questioning individuals in an Orwellian "parallel investigation" that focused less on Zimmerman's actions that fateful night than on his thoughts, past and present. Did he really say "coon" on his call to the dispatcher? Had he ever told a racial joke? Were the suspicious persons he reported to the police disproportionately black? In contemporary America words often matter more than actions. An L.A. jury set a double murderer free, in no small part because a detective on the Simpson case, Mark Fuhrman, used the word "nigger" ten years earlier. Team Trayvon and its allies in

Obama's Justice Department hoped the FBI would find some similar offense in Zimmerman's past.

By day two of the FBI investigation, agents Elizabeth Alexander and Matthew Oliver were grilling Sanford police investigator Chris Serino. The agents' first mistake was to get the date wrong on their report. They claimed to have interviewed Serino at the Sanford police station on "March 3, 2012," but this was only a week after the shooting and long before the FBI even knew of the case. More likely, the interview took place on April 3, as the transcription was produced on April 5.[3]

The agents' larger mistake—the Justice Department's, really—was their failure to understand that if anyone's civil rights were being abused, they were Zimmerman's. For starters, Serino viewed Zimmerman as "not a racist." Wrote the agents, "Serino believed that ZIMMERMAN'S actions were not based on MARTIN'S skin color rather based on his attire, the total circumstances of the encounter and the previous burglary suspects in the community."

Serino gave Zimmerman little credit for his actions and gave Martin too much for his. According to Serino, Zimmerman had a "little hero complex." He could have avoided the encounter altogether had he remained in his truck or if he had "identified himself to MARTIN as a concerned citizen and initiated dialog in an effort to dispel each party's concern." Serino it seems, was assuming that Martin had some interest in "dialog" and Zimmerman had time enough to initiate it.

Serino also worked under the assumption that Zimmerman had reached a "faulty conclusion" about Martin's activity at the time Zimmerman spotted him. As mentioned previously, Serino seemed blind to Trayvon's recent activities. He told Zimmerman early on that Martin didn't have a record and was a good kid. But by April 3, when the FBI interviewed him, Serino should have known Martin's troubled history with the Miami-Dade Schools Police Department. The M-DSPD had at least talked to the Sanford Police Department about Martin.

The paper trail on this is not hard to follow, at least not at first. On February 29, three days after the shooting, Sgt. Randy Smith of the Sanford police sent a request to Detective Steven Hadley of the M-DSPD, asking for information on Martin. This was to include information on his "arrest history/cases with you or local agencies."[4] Hadley searched the department's record management system, located the relevant eight-page report, faxed it to Sergeant Smith, and then called to confirm he had received it. A few weeks later, on March 26, the *Miami Herald* ran a story headlined "Multiple Suspensions Paint Complicated Portrait of Trayvon Martin," which detailed much of Martin's wayward behavior, including his apprehension with stolen jewelry and a burglary tool.

Given the political pressures on the Miami end, Hadley came under heavy fire from his chief for sending the report. He was appalled. "Currently, our department is functioning and operating out of fear," he told an Internal Affairs investigator. "It is tragic to see that I've been disciplined at the direction of Chief Hurley."[5] As it turned out, Hurley need not have worried about the Sanford Police Department. For reasons not fully established, the information sent by the M-DSPD never made it into the SPD's final victimology report.

One reason may have been that Sanford police sergeant Randy Smith, himself an African American and the liaison with Miami-Dade, showed little interest in learning about Martin's criminal behavior. In his sworn affidavit to the Internal Affairs division of M-DSPD, Smith conceded that he knew little about Martin's record "other than what I heard in the news." And what news he heard went no deeper than that of a "baggy or something" found in Martin's backpack. Smith, in fact, implied that the M-DSPD did not want him to know any more about Martin than he wanted to learn.[6]

Serino was feeling the heat on his end as well, and he said as much to the FBI. The officer who concerned him most was Arthur Barnes, who was "friendly" with Tracy Martin. For his part, Barnes told the FBI that the black community might well be "in an uproar" if Zimmerman were not charged. The FBI quoted Barnes as saying, "The community will be satisfied if an arrest takes place."[7] The need to pacify this community led the brass of two police departments, the State of Florida, and the US Department of Justice to conspire to arrest George Zimmerman, himself a minority. If that was not a civil rights violation, it would be hard to identify what was.

Team Trayvon members had reason to be optimistic. A week after the FBI launched its investigation, Attorney General Eric Holder addressed Al Sharpton's National Action Network in Washington, D.C. There, improbably, he thanked Sharpton "for your partnership, your friendship, and your tireless efforts to speak out for the voiceless, to stand up for the powerless, and to shine a light on the problems we must solve, and the promises we must fulfill."[8] This was the same Al Sharpton who had threatened to occupy Sanford if Zimmerman were not arrested immediately; the same Sharpton who perpetrated the Tawana Brawley hoax; the same Sharpton whose attacks on a "white interloper" in Harlem inspired a follower to kill seven of his employees; the same Sharpton who in the wake of anti-Semitic riots in Crown Heights boasted, "If the Jews want to get it on, tell them to pin their yarmulkes back and come over to my house."[9] Holder did have one thing right. Sharpton was tireless, but he was a solution to no known problem.

Sharpton and his Team Trayvon allies knew how well racial pressure could be brought to bear against the Justice Department. They were all of age to remember what happened in Los Angeles on March 3, 1991, and in the weeks and months that followed. In brief, a high-speed auto chase resulted in the forceful arrest of a 250-pound bruiser named Rodney King. The LAPD officers who subdued King, an African American then on parole for robbery, were either white or Hispanic. As much as Zimmerman wished someone had made a video of his incident, the officers in the King case wished someone had not.

Although the cops believed they had followed procedure, the video replay, especially as edited by KTLA in Los Angeles, looked brutal. Amateur videographer George Holliday picked up the action, slightly out of focus, when the six-foot-three, 250-pound King made his final charge at the officers. Holliday missed the earlier action: the peaceful submission of King's two black companions; the verbal commands for King to submit to arrest; his repeated refusals; a gang tackle in a vain effort to handcuff him; and King's almost superhuman immunity to the two shots from Sergeant Stacey Koon's stun gun. Only after King's last lunge did the officers use their batons. KTLA, and subsequently CNN, edited out that last lunge. Viewers saw only the baton blows. Rarely were they told of the events leading to the beating or of King's lengthy history of criminal mischief, much of it violent.

In 1991 there was no alternative media to correct the record, certainly not visually. Still, in April 1992, when exposed to the evidence, a Simi Valley jury found the four accused officers not guilty of using excessive force. The verdict did not sit well with certain residents of Los Angeles who had seen only the truncated version of King's arrest, and that a thousand times. That same day, the more lawless among them incited a riot that left fifty-three dead and caused billions of dollars in property damage. The fear that similar riots could break out all over America if Zimmerman were not arrested—or, if arrested, acquitted—colored every decision made by the prosecutors in this case. A headline in the social justice blog *Take Part* said out loud what others in the media and in the halls of justice were surely thinking: "On Trayvon Martin and the 20th Anniversary of the L.A. Riots: Could the trial of George Zimmerman spark violent civil unrest?"[10]

Under enormous pressure after the Los Angeles riots, the US Department of Justice promptly convened a federal grand jury. Not surprisingly, the jurors indicted the four officers on charges of violating King's civil rights, this just four months after their acquittal on criminal charges. The officers never had a chance. In the media, it was all but taboo to talk of concepts like "double jeopardy" or "innocent until proven guilty." The federal government put the officers on trial less than a year after the riots in downtown Los Angeles, an environment as agitated as Jerusalem circa AD 33. To no one's great surprise, the jury found two of the cops guilty of violating King's civil rights, and the court sentenced them to thirty months in a federal prison. Like Zimmerman, they received death threats. These threats were not idle. A black gunman tried to kill Sergeant Stacey Koon after he had been released to a halfway house. Not finding Koon there, the attacker took several hostages and killed one of them before police shot and killed him. And Koon did not have nearly the bull's-eye on his back that Zimmerman did.

As to Rodney King, he successfully sued the city of Los Angeles for $3.8 million. The federal court awarded his attorneys an additional $1.7 million in statutory attorney's fees. The money may have put a spring in the lawyers' steps, but it did little to improve the quality of King's life. For the next twenty years he committed one new and inventive act of self-destruction after another, interrupted only by a stint on the TV show *Celebrity Rehab*. After the Trayvon Martin case went public, someone, perhaps King himself, thought it would be a good idea for King to weigh in on the seeming parallels between Martin's fate and his own.

On April 11, 2012, King's "publicist" released a statement in which

King purportedly said, "The horrifying sound of a young black male screaming for his life on a 9-1-1 call reminded me of my horrifying scream on a videotape 20 years ago. At that time, I thought I was going to die. Very, very gratefully, I survived. Unfortunately, Trayvon Martin did not."[11]

King, alas, did not survive for long. Two months later, in his final act of self-destruction, he drowned in his fiancée's swimming pool after a daylong drinking and doping binge. As it happens, his fiancée had served on the jury that awarded King $3.8 million. Small world!

21

HOWLING FOR GEORGE'S HEAD

"**A**RREST ZIMMERMAN NOW!**"** shouted Al Sharpton at a March 22 rally in Sanford. The crowds responding enthusiastically to Sharpton's demand had a mix of motives. Those who accepted the orthodox version of events assumed the worst of the Sanford police. The media were painting the chief and his officers as spiritual descendants of Theophilus "Bull" Connor, the commissioner of public safety for the city of Birmingham, Alabama, during the head-banging phase of the civil rights movement. "The city claims that it is 'no Selma,'" read an all-too-typical snipe from the progressive media, but this *Daily Kos* blogger knew that it was. He claimed, in fact, that "Trayvon's shooting has brought to light a troubling pattern of racial injustice and prejudice." The article traced problems in Sanford as far back as 1947, when Jackie Robinson and his family "were run out of Sanford, Florida, with threats of violence."[1] Sixty-five years later it was the Zimmermans who were being run out of Sanford under threats of violence, but that irony was fully lost by those howling for Zimmerman's head. The left-leaning blogosphere had it all figured out. Michael Cohen, commenting in the *Opinion Zone* of the *Palm Beach Post* on the same day that Sharpton was demanding Zimmerman's arrest in Sanford, nicely captured the progressive zeitgeist:

The issue is this insane law and the corrupt and racist police dept. The police had "probable cause" to arrest Zimmerman just on what happened on those 9-1-1 tapes. But what did the racist police do? They come to crime site and they see a Black boy dead on the street with the murderer with a gun in his hand. Instead of taking the gun away from him and ARRESTING HIM FOR MURDER and testing him for drugs and alcohol or questioning witnesses, then LET HIM GO WITH HIS GUN because he said THE BOY THREATENED HIM. What right did this racist police dept act as a judge and jury to this murder?[2]

Trayvon's father, Tracy Martin, understandably demanded justice—or what he saw as justice—as did the family attorneys. "We want an arrest. We want a conviction, and we want him charged for the murder of our son," said Martin on the day of the March 22 Sanford rally. In his passion, however, Tracy Martin found himself slightly off message. Team Trayvon was not asking for a conviction. "All we're asking for is an arrest. We are saying arrest George Zimmerman," Natalie Jackson told Nancy Grace March 27 on her HLN show.[3] On that same day Benjamin Crump said much the same thing at a congressional hearing on racial profiling. "Simply arrest George Zimmerman," Crump demanded. "He'll have his day in court."[4] To just about everyone but the Zimmerman family and the Sanford police, the two attorneys sounded like the voice of moderation. They did not want to prejudge the case. They merely wanted justice.

On the same day Natalie Jackson called for Zimmerman's arrest on the *Nancy Grace Show*, ABC's ubiquitous Matt Gutman put his thumb on the "arrest" scale with a story that had lead SPD investigator Chris Serino at its center, "Trayvon Martin Cop Wanted Charge." According to Gutman, Serino had recommended that Zimmerman be charged with manslaughter on the very night of the shooting. Serino did not arrest him, according to Gutman, because the state attorney's office, headed by Norm Wolfinger, "determined there wasn't enough evidence to lead to a conviction." Gutman cited unnamed "multiple sources" for this bit of disinformation.[5]

A week later, Serino privately told the FBI something entirely different, namely that he "did not believe he had enough evidence at the time to file charges."[6] Serino named three Sanford police officers who "were pressuring him to file charges against Zimmerman after the incident." These were Sergeant Arthur Barnes and officers Rebecca Villalona and Trekelle

Perkins. According to the *Miami Herald*, Barnes and Perkins were black, and Villalona was married to an African American.[7] Serino implied that these officers were also leaking information about the case. He did not mention Gutman as the recipient of the leaks, but Gutman's agenda and that of the minority officers were fully simpatico.

An arrest, however, was no small matter. For Team Trayvon to demand one was to accuse Zimmerman of murder and the Sanford police of incompetence or racism or both. To demand an arrest knowing that a conviction was unlikely suggested motives other than the search for justice. Al Sharpton and Jesse Jackson had their own agenda. To maintain their power and relevance in what remained of the civil rights movement, they had to at least show up, not that they would have objected to a piece of the action. For Trayvon's mother, Sybrina Fulton, the love of money could not possibly outweigh the love of her son, but when she filed three weeks after the shooting to trademark the phrases "I Am Trayvon" and "Justice for Trayvon," she made skeptics wonder.[8] For Crump, money most surely came first. As a trial lawyer, his payday would come not with Zimmerman's criminal conviction but with a wrongful death lawsuit against deep-pocketed third parties like insurers of the Retreat at Twin Lakes Homeowners Association. To litigate such a case, however, it was essential that Zimmerman at least be arrested.

By early April 2012, the Treepers had come to suspect what was motivating Team Trayvon. Unlike their willfully blind peers in the major media, the Treepers knew how weak the case against Zimmerman was, and if they knew, Crump and Natalie Jackson had to know too. "The Trayvon family is not seeking justice in the form you would think," the *Treehouse* speculated on April 5. "No, they are seeking monetary justice, or more directly monetary gain. THAT is the motivation; and the absence of an 'arrest' is what stands between them and their ability to sue in civil court."[9] This was a reasonable speculation, but it was not one that the major media, given their fear of the BGI, chose to explore.

The *Treehouse* dared to do just that, citing the relevant Florida law to make its case. According to that law, an individual who uses force justifiably is "immune from criminal prosecution and civil action for the use of such force." As the law also makes clear, an arrest indicates "probable cause that the force that was used was unlawful."[10] In other words, if there is no arrest, the individual is presumed innocent and immune from civil action. If there is an arrest, all bets are off. To convict Zimmerman of a crime was another story. That required proof "beyond a reasonable doubt." To prevail in a civil trial required only "a preponderance of the existing evidence."

The most memorable example of this distinction, of course, involved former football great O. J. Simpson. In June 1994 his ex-wife, Nicole Brown, and her friend Ron Goldman were found stabbed to death in the entryway of Brown's Brentwood, California, home. The following October, a Los Angeles criminal jury found Simpson "not guilty." Just sixteen months after that, a Santa Monica civil jury, looking at the same evidence, unanimously awarded a $33.5 million judgment against Simpson for the wrongful death of Goldman and the battery of Brown. As Team Trayvon knew, the evidence against Zimmerman did not approach the evidence against Simpson. But if racial unease worked on Simpson's behalf, at least in the criminal trial, it would work against Zimmerman in both civil and criminal court. Securing a criminal conviction may not have been likely, but to secure a favorable verdict in civil court, with compensatory and punitive damages attached, would be possible, and to secure a pretrial settlement in the hothouse atmosphere of central Florida was likely.

The company that insured the Homeowners Association for the Retreat at Twin Lakes, Travelers Casualty and Surety Co. of America, knew the score. Likely expecting the price to go up with a conviction, Travelers reached an agreement with Tracy Martin and Sybrina Fulton in April 2013. Although the amount remained confidential, Martin's parents had earlier rejected a $1 million offer. The eventual payoff was rumored to be $2 million or close to it.[11] As to Crump, not only did he stand to get a slice of the parents' booty, but he also, according to the *New York Times*, "planned to file a separate lawsuit against Mr. Zimmerman at a later date."[12] The often-apropos phrase "follow the money" rarely explains behavior in cases involving the death of a child, but it would be naïve to deny its explanatory value in this case.

22

LOOKING FOR DEE DEE

WHILE WATCHING A PRELIMINARY HEARING online in late April 2013, Chip Bennett took satisfaction in seeing prosecutor Bernie de la Rionda flail away at the *Conservative Treehouse* by name. What troubled de la Rionda was what troubled many authority figures: bloggers had leveled the media playing field. The prosecutor could no longer control the narrative by feeding information to compliant media sources. De la Rionda worried, too, that the Zimmerman defense was taking its cues from the work done by the *Treehouse*, as though that somehow gave the defense an unfair advantage. In fact, though, the Treepers refused to communicate with the Zimmerman defense lest they be accused of doing what de la Rionda insinuated.

Bennett had been following Zimmerman's travails from the beginning and commenting on the *Treehouse* since June 2012. A chemical engineer by profession and a logician by avocation, the thirty-five-year-old Bennett believed "100 percent of the evidence in discovery supports Zimmerman. I don't think there's been a single bit of evidence that convicts."[1] As the June trial approached, he trusted that Zimmerman would be acquitted. On this point, he had more faith in the judicial system than many of his *Treehouse* colleagues.

Like all the Treepers, though, Bennett had real problems with Witness 8, the girl who had been on the phone with Trayvon Martin in the minutes leading up to his death. This mystery witness allegedly remained unknown even to Team Trayvon until March 18, 2012. On that Sunday, as Crump told the story, "Tracy Martin figured out his son's cellphone account password and gained access to his son's cellphone records."[2] Tracy Martin then found his way to the young woman to whom Crump would assign the pseudonym "Dee Dee." Months later, Natalie Jackson unwittingly undid this account of paternal devotion. "We hired an investigator that got the phone records," Jackson told a friendly interviewer from *Democracy Now*. "And once we saw Trayvon's phone record . . . [w]e contacted the person he was on the phone with. It was a young girl."[3]

Instead of contacting the police after discovering the young woman, Crump contacted ABC's always-pliable Matt Gutman, who was the only reporter allowed to listen to a phone interview with Dee Dee on March 19. The timing was fortuitous. To this point Team Trayvon had produced no new evidence that would prompt Zimmerman's arrest. "The best evidence we have is the testimony of George Zimmerman, and he says the decedent was the primary aggressor in the whole event," Sanford PD's Chris Serino told the *Orlando Sentinel* on March 16. "Everything I have is adding up to what he says."[4] And, if anything, Serino was sympathetic to the Martin family. The worm was about to turn.

On March 20, ABC ran footage of the ever-resourceful Gutman listening to the phone conversation with Dee Dee—an exclusive preview of what was to come later that day. Around lunchtime Crump shared what he learned in a press conference held for no obvious reason in the copy room of another law firm. CNN, among others, covered the press conference live. As studio anchor Kyra Phillips waited for the conference to begin, she enthused about the "chilling new perspective" added to the case by the testimony of this heartsick young woman who was on the phone with Martin when he was shot.[5]

Phillips then introduced CNN legal analyst Sunny Hostin. Hostin had spoken with Crump earlier and shared with the CNN audience exactly what Crump hoped she would share. "Trayvon Martin told his friend that someone was following him," said Hostin. "He was nervous. He was concerned. She explained to him that he should run. He told her he was not going to run, but he was going to walk quickly in an effort to get away from the person that he thought was pursuing him." Hostin summarized that this "was the last conversation that Martin had with anyone, and it also, in my view, dispels the notion of self-defense."[6]

A few minutes later, Phillips cut to the press conference. As Crump told the story, the young couple had been on the phone for an astonishing four hundred minutes that day, caught up as they were in "puppy love." So distraught was Dee Dee at Martin's death, said Crump, "[s]he couldn't even go to his wake she was so sick. Her mother had to take her to the hospital. She spent the night in the hospital." Lest the media try to exploit this romance, Crump asked them to "please respect her privacy. She is a minor."[7] As would be proven later, Dee Dee was neither hospitalized nor a minor, but those were the least troubling of the day's lies.

The extended phone calls took place during the time Martin walked to the neighborhood 7-Eleven and returned. According to Dee Dee, it started raining hard so Martin looked for shelter. It was then that Martin noticed that a man was "following him." As maintained by Crump, Dee Dee told Martin to "be careful. Just run home." At that point in Dee Dee's account, Zimmerman left the truck and pursued Martin, who could not quite seem to shake the plodding two-hundred-pounder. Lest the media rely only on his word, Crump played the actual recording for the press. Its climactic scene as described by Dee Dee was recorded as follows:

> He said this man was watching him so he put his hoodie on. Trayvon said, "What you following me for?" The man said, "What you doin' around here?" Then somebody pushed Trayvon because the headset just fell. . . . He didn't call back, so I was like okay he might have lost his phone in the grass cuz I thought it was a fight and then the next day . . .[8]

At this point, Crump abruptly shut off the recorder. The audio files later turned over to the defense reveal Crump asking Dee Dee a series of leading questions, and she providing him a series of inarticulate, barely audible answers. Throughout the interview, Crump tried to hammer her answers into a "He was just trying to get home and it started raining" (his words) template, and Dee Dee largely obliged.

"She connects the dots," Crump told his audience excitedly. "She completely blows Zimmerman's absurd defense claim out of the water." According to Crump, the twenty-eight-year-old "loose cannon" had no intention of going back to his truck. He pursued Martin and shot him down. Dee Dee heard it all. The witnesses confirmed her testimony. At the end of his presentation the outraged Crump demanded, "Arrest George Zimmerman for the killing of Trayvon Martin in cold blood today."[9]

Crump got his point across. Gutman headlined his piece on ABC. com, "Trayvon Martin's Last Phone Call Triggers Demand for Arrest Right Now." ABC's Diane Sawyer introduced Gutman's piece, which slammed the Sanford Police Department for its many presumed failings, by referring to Zimmerman as the "neighborhood *watchdog*." The piece closed with a photo of a younger Martin hugging a baby.[10]

In none of the contemporary reporting did anyone challenge Crump's account. No one asked why this girl failed to inquire about the fate of her presumed beau, who, when last heard from, was getting beaten by an unknown man. Why did she not call Martin's parents? Why did she not call the police after she learned of his death? How did she think the hulking Zimmerman managed to run down her younger, fitter friend?

These, however, were minor journalistic oversights compared to the most damning oversight of all: the failure to confirm who was crying out for help. By the end of March, the media had full access to the 9-1-1 calls from the eyewitnesses. As covered earlier, on the 9-1-1 call from Witness 11, one hears in the background roughly forty seconds of screaming. The man on the tape yells, "Help!" at least fourteen times. No one could deny the fear and desperation in his voice. The case hinged on that discovery, and yet not a single major media commentator thought to question Crump's concocted analysis of the screams.

"Logically, it makes sense that Trayvon Martin was the voice you heard crying on that tape," Crump insisted at the press conference. As to why those screams should be Martin's, Crump would have been better off saying nothing. Instead, he volunteered, in his reliably mangled syntax, "You can conclude who is the person crying out for help presumably when they see a gun."

Crump wanted the media to believe that Zimmerman chased Martin down, held him at gunpoint, caused him to wail like a banshee for forty seconds at the sight of the gun, and then shot him down in cold blood, knowing the police—whom Zimmerman himself had summoned— were minutes away.[11]

If that were not enough, Witness 6, the eyewitness with the best perspective on the incident, had talked on camera to the local TV station the day after the shooting and told the reporter what he told the Sanford police the night before, namely, that there was a "black man in a black hoodie on top of either a white guy . . . or an Hispanic guy in a red sweatshirt on the ground yelling out help," and that the black man on top was "throwing down blows on the guy kind of MMA [mixed martial arts] style."[12]

There was no excuse for the media not to incorporate this account into their reporting and not to connect it to Zimmerman's busted nose and bloodied head. Nor was there any excuse to overlook the timing of Dee Dee's emergence—just days after Team Trayvon got access to the audio of Zimmerman's call and could shape her testimony to fit it. But in the hysterical month of March 2012, the media were much too eager to convict the "white Hispanic" Zimmerman of an imagined hate crime to quibble with something as pedestrian as the truth.

23

LOOKING FOR CAUSE

*T*HE DEE DEE PRESS CONFERENCE added new energy to the case. Two days later the State of Florida took it over from the local prosecutor, and the day after that President Obama added his "If I had a son" imprimatur. The only problem was that what worked in the court of public opinion would not work in the court of law. Unless Team Trayvon could provide, as the song says, "a real live girl," there was still not much of a case.

On March 27 Florida state attorney general Pam Bondi offhandedly shared with CNN's Piers Morgan the challenges the State faced in this regard. Morgan, no friend of due process, asked the attorney general why she just did not say publicly, "You know what? This guy should be arrested." Bondi explained the delay, saying, "We need to get Trayvon's girlfriend to cooperate, which I don't know if it was happening previously." She added that the "wonderful lawyers" Crump and Parks, with whom she worked on the misbegotten Martin Lee Anderson case before her election as attorney general in 2010, may have had good reason for the delay. But, Bondi reassured Morgan, the girlfriend now seemed to be "cooperating."[1]

Finally, Team Trayvon promised the State that the girl would be available on April 2. That morning, state attorney Bernie de la Rionda and investigator T. C. O'Steen flew from Jacksonville to Miami for a series of interviews. At 3:40 p.m. they interviewed Sybrina Fulton and at 4:30 Tracy Martin, both at Sybrina's Miami apartment. Despite the fact that the Team Trayvon attorneys—Crump, Parks, and Jackson—were all present, the star witness did not show.

After some delay, a frustrated de la Rionda and two cars full of his allies drove to nearby Broward County, found the young woman known formally as Witness 8, and drove her back to Sybrina's apartment for the interview. There he interviewed 8, with Sybrina sitting next to her on the couch, and recorded the interview. Lacking a defense attorney to restrict him, he plied her with one leading question after another, for instance, "He was a good guy, right?" It was hard to answer questions like that in the negative. He also led her to repeat the canard about her falling ill upon hearing of Martin's death. "Okay did you end up going to the hospital or somewhere?" de la Rionda asked her. "Yeah. I had, like, um, high blood pressure," she answered. As to whether she and Martin were boyfriend and girlfriend, Witness 8 answered, "We were getting there."[2] Witness 8 proved a difficult interview. She was soft-spoken, reticent, and inarticulate. Even if he had not intended to, de la Rionda had to prod her for answers, and these were rarely clear even to de la Rionda.

The story Witness 8 told tracked with the story Crump played on March 20, with a few notable exceptions. In the April 2 interview, Witness 8 gave a more specific account of how Martin first became aware of Zimmerman. As she told it, a white man was watching Martin from a car while he spoke on the telephone. Then Martin approached the car. This corresponded with what Zimmerman had told the dispatcher on the night of February 26. After Martin walked past the car, Witness 8's account was inconsistent. Either the man was following Martin or he was "still watching, like, from the car."[3] In reality, Zimmerman stayed in the car for about forty-five seconds after Martin first approached. The closing of the car door on the dispatcher tape marked the time of Zimmerman's exit with some precision.

"I told him to run to that house," Witness 8 instructed Martin. "That house" was Brandy Green's condo, about four hundred feet away from Zimmerman's truck. Martin knew the way. He had been in Sanford for five days before the shooting and, according to Brandy Green's testimony, had visited Sanford seven or eight times before that. Green also noted that this was the first time Martin had stayed at her place without his father being present, further testament to the unanchored drift of his recent life.[4]

Martin told Witness 8 he was going in the back way—meaning up the dog walk behind the houses—because it was "more easier," which, in fact, it was. "You could tell he was running," Witness 8 told de la Rionda. She took her cues from the sound of the wind and from Martin's breathlessness. On the dispatcher tape, Zimmerman offered confirmation. "Shit, he's running," Zimmerman said at the 2:08 mark. Seconds later, he left the truck to maintain a visual on the suspect. Martin apparently headed east on the cut-through and south on the dog walk between the backs of the buildings, cutting off Zimmerman's line of sight. When the dispatcher asked Zimmerman which way Martin had gone, he replied, "Down towards the other entrance to the neighborhood." Green's town house was in that direction.

"He said he lost him," Witness 8 told de la Rionda. Martin should have lost Zimmerman easily. Even if he were jogging slowly, Martin would have reached Brandy Green's town house at about the 2:40 mark of Zimmerman's call to the police. At one point, according to Witness 8, Martin claimed to be "right by the house," presumably Green's.[5] This would have been just about the time Zimmerman yielded to the dispatcher's suggestion to stop following Martin. If Martin had reached the house, he did not stay there long. Zimmerman stayed on the line with the SPD for nearly two minutes after Martin took off for a destination about four hundred feet away. Zimmerman did not see him during that time, but he was concerned that Martin may have been lurking about. When the dispatcher asked for his home address, Zimmerman answered, "Oh crap! I don't want to give it all out. I don't know where this kid is." By this time, Martin should have been eating Skittles with Brandy's son, but he wasn't, and Zimmerman may have sensed it.

Witness 8's testimony about the sequence of events should have alerted de la Rionda to the possibility that Martin had no intention of going home. In one exchange, she tried to sum up what happened. "He said he lost the guy," she said patiently, "and then he ran for the back, said he lost him. He started walking back again. I told him, 'keep running.'" At this point, de la Rionda tried to interpret the witness's words to fit the State's preconceptions. If Trayvon were, in fact, "walking back" to confront Zimmerman, he would have no case against Zimmerman.

"So Trayvon said he started walking because he thought he lost the guy?" de la Rionda asked. The easily led witness answered yes.[6]

With the possibility of "walking back" dismissed, de la Rionda led the witness on in their shared attempt to portray Martin as the helpless victim of Zimmerman's relentless pursuit. As Witness 8 told de la Rionda, she kept urging Martin to run, but he couldn't "because he out of breath." Tired and scared, Trayvon told her that "the guy was getting real close to him."[7] The affidavit accommodated this fiction by claiming that Zimmerman "disregarded" the dispatcher's request that he stop following Martin. Instead, according to the affidavit, he "continued to follow Martin who was trying to return to his home."

If Martin were, in fact, trying to run to Green's town house, it is hard to imagine how Zimmerman could have caught him and "confronted" him as the prosecutors charged. He was four inches shorter than Martin and fifty pounds heavier. In the prosecution's most favorable scenario, Martin had a twenty-second head start to a destination no more than twenty seconds away. In reality, however, Martin had at least a two-minute head start to run the four hundred feet to Green's town house. That's how long Zimmerman was on the phone with the dispatcher *after* Martin started running. What is more, in separate interviews Brandy Green and Tracy Martin hinted that Trayvon had made it back to the town house. "He was sitting on the porch and this man killed him," Green had told a local reporter the day after the shooting. A few weeks later, after the story broke nationally, Tracy told a local reporter, "I don't know the exact path he took, but he did come in that back gate, and I knew he was going to the back of the house. He was sitting out there."[8]

Zimmerman's call to the dispatcher ended four minutes and change after it started at 7:13:39. According to Zimmerman's written narrative: "The dispatcher told me not to follow the suspect & that an officer was on the way. As I headed back to my vehicle the suspect emerged from the darkness and said, 'You got a problem?'" When Zimmerman answered, "No," the suspect said, "You do now."

As Witness 8 told the story, the pursuer was "getting real close" to Martin and apparently caught him. Martin said to him, "Why are you following me for?" Again, according to Witness 8, the "old man" answered, "What are you doing around here?" He then "bumped Trayvon." This exchange took place no more than a few feet from the T intersection of the dog walk and the cut-through, less than halfway to Brandy Green's town house from Zimmerman's truck. Zimmerman fired the fatal shot at 7:16:59, a little more than three minutes after he ended his call with the dispatcher. The first officer on the scene arrived less than a minute after that.

The prosecutors had to suspect that Martin circled back, but if so, they weren't about to air their suspicions. On April 11, Angela Corey's office drew up an affidavit of probable cause for second-degree murder. The affidavit was loaded. Martin was walking back to the town house "where he was living" when Zimmerman "profiled" him, this despite the fact that Martin was unarmed and "not committing a crime." Zimmerman "assumed Martin was a criminal." He called the police. The affidavit cited Martin's phone "friend" to attest, "Martin was scared because he was being followed by an unknown male and didn't know why."[9]

Again, according to the affidavit, and this was critical: "Zimmerman confronted Martin and a struggle ensued." Martin's mother then "identified the voice crying for help as Trayvon Martin's." Zimmerman admitted shooting Martin, and that apparently was good enough for the prosecutors. "The facts mentioned in this affidavit are not a complete recitation of all the pertinent facts and evidence in this case," the affidavit concluded, "but only are presented for determination of Probable Cause for Second Degree Murder."[10]

On the evening of April 11, Angela Corey took center stage at the Jacksonville state attorney's office to announce the outcome of that investigation.[11] A stocky, broad-shouldered woman in her late fifties, Corey compensated for her lack of height with the command presence of a pit bull. Like Zimmerman on his fateful night, Corey wore a red jacket, but as would soon become clear, that was hardly a signal of solidarity.

Zimmerman already knew his fate. Coincidentally, he was driving to Sanford that day to pick up Shellie and head back up north for a long weekend. When his friend Mark Osterman heard news of the impending arrest, he texted Shellie, who promptly called George. He got the call while about two hours north of Sanford, near Jacksonville. He called a contact with the FDLE and agreed to meet him at a McDonald's in Jacksonville. At that point Zimmerman did not have a lawyer. An Orlando defense attorney named Craig Sonner had claimed to be representing him, but

Zimmerman did not like the terms of the contract Sonner offered and never signed it. After arranging to meet with the FDLE agent, Zimmerman put in a call to another local attorney who came well recommended, Mark O'Mara, and O'Mara agreed to take the case.[12]

Zimmerman met the agent at the McDonald's and then followed him to the local FDLE office. Ten minutes before Corey began speaking, an officer placed Zimmerman in leg irons and told him he was under arrest for second-degree murder. At the same time Corey was speaking, special FDLE agents were transporting Zimmerman to the Seminole County Jail, where he would remain until his bond hearing a week later.[13]

If Zimmerman's supporters did not know initially where the presser was heading, they could have guessed by sentence three. After a quick introduction, Corey spoke of Tracy Martin and Sybrina Fulton as Martin's "sweet parents" and told of her promise to them that "we would get answers to [their] questions no matter where our search for the truth led us." Sometime between March 22 and March 26, Tracy had rendered himself sweeter by covering what appeared to be a "CaT" (Crippin all the Time) tattoo on the right side of his neck with a pair of praying hands.[14] Homage to God played better with the media than loyalty to a street gang, namely the Crips. As to Trayvon Martin, Corey classed him among those "precious victims" for whom her office was dedicated to seeking justice.

"We do not prosecute by public pressure or petition," Corey told the assembled media and seems to have convinced herself that she meant what she said. She repeated this point throughout the press conference in one variation or another. She and her team were "not only ministers of justice, but seekers of the truth," she assured the audience members, reminding the Hamlet fans among them of the player queen who did indeed "protest too much."[15]

Like a politician running for office, which she indeed was, Corey made every effort to compliment the Sanford Police Department and other agencies involved. And yet on the question as to whether the police investigation had been thorough, Corey gave the game away. "Before the investigation could be finished," she insisted, "there was a lot of outcry about this case, and then it changed course, and we got appointed to take over the investigation."[16] To the dispassionate observer, an "outcry" that changed the course of the investigation sounded very much like prosecuting "by public pressure or petition." The Treepers read politics into Corey's motivations. "One charge. Second Degree Murder," wrote Sundance. "She threw the book at him. Was this a smart decision? Legally, no. Politically, heck yeah." The *Treehouse* posted the second-degree murder statute:

> The unlawful killing of a human being, when perpetrated by any act imminently dangerous to another and evincing a depraved mind regardless of human life, although without any premeditated design to effect the death of any particular individual.[17]

The Treepers proceeded to analyze the case based on the available evidence. Was the killing "unlawful" or was Zimmerman acting in self-defense? What act of Zimmerman's was "imminently dangerous"? Was it getting out of his car in his own community to check on a suspicious person all the while staying in communication with the police? And most challenging of all, what did Zimmerman do to evince a "depraved mind regardless of human life"? After getting his head slammed against the concrete for at least forty seconds, his mind may have been a little fuzzy, but depraved? Despite their belief that the evidence was on Zimmerman's side, the Treepers, like that lone Chinese dissident, felt the weight of the machinery moving against them. Corey looked so confident. She had the Florida governor solidly on her side, the US attorney general as well, even the president. Almost to a person, the major media were cheering her on, and most important of all, the BGI had her back.

The opportunity to align oneself with the remnants of the civil rights movement has left many a Republican giddy. Corey was no exception. If her numbers reflected local norms, the great majority of the defendants she convicted in murder cases were black or Hispanic. Like the prosecutor Kramer in Tom Wolfe's *Bonfire of the Vanities*, she, too, must have thought "this eternal prosecution of blacks and Latins" was not immoral exactly, but in "bad taste." Now, however, she had a shot at what Wolfe called a "much-prized, ever-elusive . . . very nearly mythical creature, the Great White Defendant."[18] Zimmerman may not have been exactly white, but he was white enough, and she, Angela Corey, was on the side of the angels, the side of "sweet parents" and the "precious victims" and the Team Trayvon attorneys whom she chose to "especially thank."

"The first thing we did was pray with them," said Corey. By "them," she meant Martin's parents and their lawyers, Team Trayvon. In the rough-and-tumble of Florida racial politics, Angela Corey was finally the good guy. Natalie Jackson certainly thought so. "It's actually a very brave charge of Angela Corey, and it really shows that she conducted an independent, impartial, and fair investigation in this case," said Jackson. "She could have easily charged this as a manslaughter, to try to appease everyone, and she didn't. She did what prosecutors do. She charged it to the hilt."[19] Jonathan Capehart of the *Washington Post*, like many in the major media, was equally enthused. "I wondered if someone could take the life of another—an unarmed child—and not be judged in a court of law," he wrote immediately after Corey's press conference. "At 6:05, my faith was restored."[20]

The blogosphere was less impressed. At the *Treehouse*, one saw more and more references to a hybrid prosecutor named "Angela Nifong Corey" or "Angela Corey-Nifong." Mike Nifong, of course, was the district attorney of Durham County, who momentarily captivated the BGI and its media allies with his outrageous prosecution of three Duke University lacrosse players for the imagined rape of black stripper Crystal Mangum. Corey's newfound stature surely propelled her to press on in her prosecutorial folly even if it meant, in Sundance's words, igniting "the powder keg of racial division."[21]

24

DUELING WITH DERSHOWITZ

*O*N APRIL 12, THE AFFIDAVIT of probable cause was made public. On that same day George Zimmerman made his first court appearance, this time in gray jail coveralls. Relatively trim and mild mannered, he had to have surprised millions of Americans who had only seen the mug shot of a brooding, heavyset man taken seven years earlier. Seminole County Judge Mark Herr approved the affidavit and set Zimmerman's arraignment for May 29. With just one day on the job as Zimmerman's attorney, Mark O'Mara made no bones about his cluelessness. "I know so little about the evidence," he told a reporter from HLN.[1]

Later that morning, Zimmerman called his wife, Shellie, from jail. She told him, among other things, that his website was crashing from too much traffic. "People were just trying to give you, you know, words of support and kindness." Said Zimmerman, "Wow! That is awesome." Shellie added, "This, isn't that crazy how something like this just makes you, like, put everything in perspective in life?" Zimmerman agreed. "It's amazing how insignificant the things that we stress out over are," said Shellie, not yet sensing her own troubles to come.[2]

Unbeknownst to Angela Corey at the time, her moment of unalloyed glory would not last through the day. That evening America's preeminent celebrity defense lawyer, Harvard Law's Alan Dershowitz, appeared on

MSNBC's *Hardball*. Filling in for Chris Matthews was guest host Michael Smerconish. When Smerconish asked what he made of Corey's affidavit, Dershowitz did not dance around the answer. "It won't suffice," he replied. "Most affidavits of probable cause are very thin; this is so thin that it won't make it past a judge on a second degree murder charge."[3]

As Dershowitz explained, nothing about the affidavit "would justify second degree murder. The elements of the crime aren't established." From his perspective, almost everything in the affidavit was already in the public domain. Left out were all the exculpating factors—the stains on the back of Zimmerman's shirt, the blood on the back of his head, and his bloody nose. "It's irresponsible and unethical in not including the material that favors the defendant," he told an MSNBC audience that could not have been happy to hear this from a liberal jurist like Dershowitz.

Dershowitz would have been angrier still had he known of one other critical bit of information Corey had manipulated. The affidavit cited Martin's mother as the authority on whose screams the 9-1-1 calls recorded. Corey, however, ignored a more credible authority, Chris Serino. In the March 13 Capias Request he reported matter-of-factly, "Zimmerman can be heard in the background frantically yelling for help."[4] The fact that it was Serino who played the 9-1-1 call with the screams for Tracy Martin should have given added weight to his testimony. In fact, Serino hesitated to press charges against Zimmerman because those were his screams heard on the 9-1-1 call.

Dershowitz read politics into Corey's motives. "I think that what you have here," he continued, "is an elected public official who made a campaign speech last night for reelection when she gave her presentation, and over-charged, way over-charged." He expected a "good judge" to throw the case out and, if not, a jury to acquit.

Later that evening Smerconish put the same issue before another well-known defense attorney, Mark Geragos. He got the same answer. "I stated publicly when I saw the affidavit that this was about as bare-bones an affidavit as I have ever seen," he said, "and I would agree with [Dershowitz]."[5] Geragos suspected there had to be something more, that the prosecuting attorneys must have been holding back, but if they were, it was not obvious to any objective observer.

A week later, the State's case against Zimmerman took another public hit. Feeling the heat perhaps after pushing a doctored video weeks earlier, ABC's Matt Gutman produced a photo of Zimmerman's profoundly bloodied head on *Good Morning America*. A neighbor had taken the photo on his iPhone at the crime scene a provable three minutes after the shooting. As expected, Crump blew off the photo. "Prosecutors have seen all the evidence," Team Trayvon said in a release, "and still believe Zimmerman murdered Trayvon."[6]

Later that April 20 morning, at the bond hearing, Zimmerman surprised observers by taking the stand. He wore a dark suit and, underneath it, a bulletproof vest. His hands were shackled to a belt around his waist. His first words he addressed directly to Martin's parents. "I am sorry for the loss of your son," he said. "I did not know how old he was. I thought he was a little bit younger than I am. I did not know if he was armed or not." The court then heard from a number of character witnesses, including Zimmerman's father and mother, the latter of whom told how George had been mentoring two black youths, unusual behavior for a racist profiler.

The lanky, mild-mannered O'Mara scored some unexpected points on his first full day on the job as Zimmerman's defense attorney. The questions he posed to state investigator Dale Gilbreath at the bond hearing confirmed the weakness of the State's case. "Do you know who started the fight?" O'Mara asked Gilbreath. "Do I know? No," said Gilbreath.[7]

This was a shocking admission. The State was insisting Zimmerman was of sufficiently "depraved mind" to merit a second-degree murder charge, and yet its chief investigator had no evidence he started the fight. In fact, to the degree that there was evidence, that evidence supported Zimmerman's claim that Martin landed the first blow. Gilbreath's empty response suggested that the case was even flimsier than Dershowitz had imagined.

O'Mara also challenged Gilbreath on the word "profiled," a concept with obvious racial connotations. "Why did you use the word 'profiling' rather than 'noticed,' 'observed,' 'saw,' or anything besides the very precise word 'profiled?'" O'Mara asked him. Gilbreath had no good answer: the affidavit was a "collaborative" document, and he did not know who inserted the word "profiled." Nor did he know who decided to comb through Zimmerman's call to the dispatcher and put in quotes only the two sentences with expletives in them. Gilbreath's ignorance was particularly impressive in that he was one of only two people to sign the affidavit.[8] Judge Kenneth Lester heard enough to set the bond at a reasonable $150,000.

Angela Corey could not have been pleased with the way the case was shaping up. At some point during this period, she called the dean of Harvard Law School to complain about its star professor. As Dershowitz would tell the story, Corey was transferred to the Office of Communications and "proceeded to engage in a forty-minute rant." Again according to Dershowitz, Corey threatened to sue Harvard Law School, to have Dershowitz disciplined by the American Bar Association, and to file charges against him for libel and slander.[9]

To be fair to Corey, this account was filtered through Dershowitz and a Harvard functionary. "Her beef," as Dershowitz phrased it, was that he had criticized her for filing an affidavit that willfully omitted all information about Zimmerman's injuries. Corey reportedly denied that she had any obligation to include that kind of information in the affidavit as long as she later provided the defense with exculpatory evidence.

"She should go back to law school," said an unyielding Dershowitz, "where she will learn that it is never appropriate to submit an affidavit that contains a half truth, because a half truth is regarded by the law as a lie, and anyone who submits an affidavit swears to tell the truth, the whole truth and nothing but the truth." Dershowitz was not taking prisoners:

> Corey seems to believe that our criminal justice system is like a poker game in which the prosecution is entitled to show its cards only after the judge has decided to charge the defendant with second degree murder. That's not the way the system is supposed to work and that's not the way prosecutors are supposed to act. That a prosecutor would hide behind the claim that she did not have an obligation to tell the whole truth until after the judge ruled on probable cause displays a kind of gamesmanship in which prosecutors should not engage.[10]

Corey had waded into an argument she could not win, could not even publicly respond to, against a much too formidable foe. From then on she fixed her sights on more vulnerable prey, like George Zimmerman and his attorney Mark O'Mara. Although polished and well spoken, O'Mara failed to inspire confidence in Bob Zimmerman. As much as he admired O'Mara's legal skills, Bob felt that O'Mara was not the "strident advocate" his son needed. His "wait-and-see" attitude on the question of George's innocence clearly frustrated a father who had hoped to see a more forceful stand on his son's behalf.[11]

Sundance and many of the other Treepers shared Bob's concerns. It pained them to see O'Mara cozy up to Team Trayvon and their allies, to tear up about racial injustice on Black Entertainment Television, to concede that, were Zimmerman not his current client, he and Benjamin Crump would be on the same side.[12] On at least a few occasions, O'Mara gave the Treepers the impression that he cared more about protecting his career than he did his client. Career may have been part of the equation, but there was more. His personal safety and that of his family had to factor in. So, too, did his own social philosophy. This mix of motives led O'Mara to downplay the role that politics played in this case and to keep the issue of race more or less off the table. Whether this was strategically wise, neither he nor the Treepers would know until the verdict was in.

25

SHOOTING ONE'S FOOT

BY THE TIME DERSHOWITZ WROTE HIS JEREMIAD, June 5, 2012, George and Shellie Zimmerman had stumbled into a mess of their own making. On June 1, Bernie de la Rionda submitted a motion to Circuit Court to revoke George Zimmerman's relatively modest $150,000 bond. In the motion, de la Rionda contended that at the April 20 bond hearing, Zimmerman had "misrepresented" his family's finances and Shellie "lied" about the same. De la Rionda also contended that Zimmerman had claimed to have turned in his only passport when, in fact, he had a second one in a safe deposit box. Shellie reminded him of this while Zimmerman was still in custody before his bond hearing. The State had recorded their phone conversation and used it against them.

De la Rionda pounded the Zimmermans, Shellie in particular, for lying about what money they had available prior to the setting of the bond. Shellie had, in fact, testified under oath that the family had no money available. The prison calls, which the Zimmermans knew were being recorded, revealed that both were aware of substantial sums raised for their defense through PayPal. "Even though defendant was in jail at the time," de la Rionda argued, "he was intimately involved in the transfer of money into various accounts." He asked that the court revoke Zimmerman's bond or at least increase it substantially.[1]

De la Rionda's office had done considerable work putting the motion together. They had reviewed the phone calls, made transcripts, and produced copies of the Zimmermans' credit union accounts. The Zimmermans were guilty as charged. Circuit Judge Kenneth Lester revoked the bond and ordered Zimmerman returned to the Seminole County Jail. Zimmerman turned himself in two days later. "Refusing to accept this factually proven aspect of falsehood, under the guise of some kind of misguided deflection," warned Sundance on the *Treehouse* blog, "diminishes a Zimmerman advocate to the same level of naiveté as a Crump believer."[2]

On June 4 Team Zimmerman acknowledged the couple's deception on George's legal website and attempted to explain it. "The audio recordings of Mr. Zimmerman's phone conversations while in jail make it clear that Mr. Zimmerman knew a significant sum had been raised by his original fundraising website," read the brief. "We feel the failure to disclose these funds was caused by fear, mistrust, and confusion." In analyzing Zimmerman's state of mind at the time of the bond hearing, his attorneys reminded the reader that the Zimmermans had been driven from their home and their neighborhood. George had to quit his job. His mother and father had to leave their home. And George "had been thrust into the national spotlight as a racist murderer by factions acting with their own agendas."[3]

Indeed, one phone call from jail on April 16 had George and Shellie scheming as to how he could safely reenter the world once bonded. George suggested that they go to a hotel with a garage and tell management they would just stay for a few days. "Whoever picks me up can just go straight into the garage and go into the hotel through there," George volunteered. Shellie added a wrinkle, "Or transfer you into a different car. Have, like, my car waiting, in the garage."[4] They were not being paranoid. There was a bounty on George's head. In spite of his very real anxiety, Zimmerman never forgot to tell Shellie how much he loved her. On April 15, for instance, he recounted a "nice" dream he had in which he bought her a scarf for her birthday. "Oh, you're so cute," gushed Shellie. "I love you so much," said George. Their love was as real as their fear, but that did nothing to mitigate how badly they had erred. That same day, April 15, a post on their fundraising website conceded, the Zimmermans' financial scheming "undermined [George's] credibility."

It was the day after this posting that Dershowitz was prompted to weigh in on Corey's performance. "Ironically," he wrote, "Corey has now succeeded in putting Zimmerman back in prison for a comparably misleading omission in his testimony." If Zimmerman "intentionally deceived the court" as the motion argued, Corey also "misled and deceived the court" by submitting an incomplete affidavit for Zimmerman's arrest. Dershowitz described her behavior, both in filing a deceptive affidavit and in threatening him and his university, as the "the epitome of unprofessionalism."[5]

As heartening as Dershowitz's support must have been, it did nothing to get the Zimmermans out of their self-inflicted jam. On June 12 Corey tightened her headlock on the Zimmermans by charging Shellie with perjury. Shellie was promptly booked into the John E. Polk Correctional Facility, the same jail in which George had been festering since his initial bond was revoked. "The prosecutor sent a strong message that you have to tell the truth in court because it is the whole basis of the American judicial system," said an obviously pleased Benjamin Crump, whose less-than-truthful maneuverings had gotten Zimmerman arrested in the first place.[6]

A year later, as George prepared for his trial, Shellie prepared for hers. Shellie's attorney, Kelly Sims, argued that because Shellie's offense took place in Seminole County—not in Corey's Jacksonville—Corey did not have jurisdiction to charge Shellie, but Circuit judge Marlene Alva would not yield.[7] The State was playing hardball.

On July 5 Judge Lester returned his order setting bail. It was unforgiving. "Under any definition, the Defendant has flaunted the system," Lester wrote. In that "flaunt" means "show something off" Zimmerman "flaunted" the system under no known definition—Lester meant "flout"—but Lester's misuse of the language could not disguise his contempt for Zimmerman. He rejected O'Mara's attempt to portray his client as "a confused young man" who was fearful and resentful of a system that betrayed him. "This court finds the opposite," wrote Lester. The affidavit of probable cause that Dershowitz called "bare bones" to the point of irresponsibility, Lester now called "strong."

Lester described Zimmerman as manipulative, deceptive, and an obvious flight risk. He portrayed the community pressure Zimmerman faced as "non-violent and peaceful." With all this as background, he unapologetically set bail at $1 million and subjected Zimmerman, among other indignities, to electronic monitoring at his own expense, a twelve-hour nightly curfew, and a forced abstention from alcohol.[8]

On the night of February 26, 2012, George Zimmerman left home a hardworking, tax-paying citizen, and a good one at that. He had volunteered to serve as neighborhood watch coordinator in a crime-plagued community, a responsibility he took seriously. When, on the way to the store, he saw a suspicious-looking person, he did as instructed. He called the police. The prosecutors held this against him. As the affidavit read, Martin was walking back to the town house "where he was living" when he was "profiled" by Zimmerman.

Martin, of course, was not "living" at the Retreat. He was visiting. This distinction mattered in that Zimmerman did not recognize him. As to the profiling charge, Zimmerman did what any good neighbor should have done. That the word "profile" had become toxic in the Orwellian world of the politically correct did not make it criminal or even wrong. For his troubles, Zimmerman got his nose broken and his head bashed in. Finally, he shot and killed a seventeen-year-old, a traumatic event even for the shooter, even if in the right. In the days that followed, the nation's media and large, angry masses of people, most of them black, were demanding his arrest or worse. He was experiencing an existential horror few other Americans had ever suffered. There was a reason why he had to wear a bulletproof vest to court, and yet Lester, like Corey and de la Rionda, was treating him with no more respect than the burglars and home invaders that moved him to join the neighborhood watch in the first place.

A week after the second bond hearing, Corey released to O'Mara the results of the FBI's investigation into Zimmerman's racial bona fides. As the *Miami Herald* reported, the FBI had interviewed some thirty-five of Zimmerman's friends, neighbors, and coworkers, and, to a person, they "had never seen Zimmerman display any prejudice or racial bias."[9] The most revealing of the FBI interviews was with Zimmerman's onetime fiancée, herself Hispanic, with whom he lived for a period of time. The woman explained in detail the altercations she had had with Zimmerman, the most violent of which had them pushing each other. Although not at all hesitant to document his imperfections, the young woman thought Zimmerman to be "last person in the world" she would expect to be involved in the shooting of Trayvon Martin. He "never exhibited any biases or prejudices against anyone," she told the FBI, "and did not use racial epithets of any kind."[10]

His neighbors seemed most appreciative of Zimmerman. Witness 47, a Puerto Rican female, described Zimmerman as always friendly and a very nice guy. Despite the opportunity to comment on the race of suspicious people in the neighborhood, she never heard him say anything derogatory about any group or individual based on race or religion. Witness 45 likewise never heard Zimmerman making any derogatory racial remarks. He volunteered another wrinkle, namely, that he had heard the screams on the 9-1-1 tapes and was absolutely sure that it was Zimmerman's voice. He told of a neighbor who felt the same way. According to Witness 46, everyone liked Zimmerman, who was really nice. He never made any racist comments.

Not surprisingly, Corey's release of the FBI information made little dent in the news. In the online comment sections in the months that followed, even Zimmerman's supporters showed scant awareness that the FBI had cleared him of a civil rights offense.

Ignoring the FBI report, Team Trayvon worked relentlessly to keep the racial edge sharp. The last weekday before the trial began, Crump appeared on ABC's *The View* and assured the openly sympathetic Whoopi Goldberg that Martin's death was "certainly a civil rights case."[11] And while he and Sybrina Fulton talked about Martin, large photos of a cherubic preteen floated behind them.

The propaganda never stopped.

26

LOOKING FOR SOME LEAN

N MAY 25, 2012, the Treeper known as "DiWataman" posted the raw video of Martin's fateful visit to the 7-Eleven online and initiated arguably the best bit of blogging detective work since the busting of Dan Rather's Air National Guard scam eight years earlier. "I think Trayvon may know these three guys," DiWataman commented in reference to a posse of hooded young men who entered the store almost immediately after Martin left. For a variety of good reasons, DiWataman labeled the guys "The Three Stooges," and the name stuck.[1] What DiWataman discovered quickly is that the blogger "noneyobusiness" had already come to the same conclusion. Together, they and other Treepers reconstructed Martin's final hours in a way that was wildly at odds with the scenario advanced by the major media and much closer to the truth. In all versions, the iconic bag of Skittles loomed large.

In the first national news story on the case, Reuters led with the Skittles angle: "Trayvon Martin was shot dead after he took a break from watching NBA All-Star game television coverage to walk 10 minutes to a convenience store to buy snacks including Skittles candy requested by his 13-year-old brother, Chad." Reuters attributed this information to attorney Benjamin Crump. "What do the police find in his pocket? Skittles," Crump told Reuters. "A can of Arizona ice tea in his jacket pocket and Skittles in his front pocket for his brother Chad."[2]

Much of this information was wrong. The game had yet to start. Chad Joseph was fourteen. He was not Martin's brother. And the drink Martin was carrying was not iced tea—more on this later. The Skittles talking point was accurate, however, and it resonated. Two days later, the *Christian Post* elevated Martin's mission to the purely altruistic. "Seventeen-year-old Trayvon Martin simply wanted to get Skittles for his younger brother, Chad," read the opening sentence in the March 9 article.[3] In the weeks that followed, just about every media piece done on the shooting mentioned the Skittles, often as a symbol of Martin's innocence and thoughtfulness.

On April 2 Geraldo's brother Craig Rivera interviewed Chad Joseph and his mother, Brandy Green, for a segment of *Geraldo at Large*.[4] The Riveras treated the mother and son gingerly. A week earlier, Geraldo had offended Trayvon Nation, including his own son Gabriel, by blaming the hoodie for Martin's demise. "I am urging the parents of black and Latino youngsters particularly to not let their children go out wearing hoodies," Geraldo said on *Fox & Friends*. He had been walking the comment back ever since.[5]

Although Chad was far from fully grown, his voice had matured and deepened. Polite and soft-spoken, he described Martin as "nice to hang around with" and added a little nuance to the narrative. Martin did not go to the store just to get him Skittles. He went to the store because "he was bored" and "wanted something to snack on." As he was leaving, Martin asked Chad what he wanted, and Chad said, "Skittles." As far as Chad knew or was willing to say, Martin never came back. Martin also failed to buy himself anything "to snack on," the alleged motivation for him to walk two miles in the rain. Chad heard nothing of the altercation or the shooting.

A 7-Eleven security camera captured Martin outside the store walking east to west at 6:22 that evening (all times rounded to the minute). The Green townhome was roughly a mile away, which suggests that Martin left about 6:05, almost an hour before the NBA All-Star game, and walked north and west to the 7-Eleven. Inside the store, Martin grabbed an Arizona Watermelon Fruit Juice Cocktail from a row of glass-fronted refrigerators. The Skittles he picked up from a row of shelves perpendicular to the cash register. He then approached the clerk, over whom he towered, and put some bills and coins on the counter to pay for the snacks. At this point, he pulled out a couple more bills and appeared to negotiate unsuccessfully for something behind where the clerk was standing. Upon leaving at 6:25 he kept the bills in his hand.

Ninety seconds later, at 6:26, the three stooges entered. The clerk must have seen them before, as he did not seem alarmed by their appearance. All three had their heads covered with hats, wraps, sunglasses, and/ or hoodies as to be unrecognizable on a security camera. The head cover on one of them allowed just a little peephole for his eyes. Two of the three appeared to be black, and the third either white or Hispanic or, like Zimmerman, a "White Hispanic." DiWataman dubbed the white guy "Curly," as at one point he took off his knit cap and shook out his long, curly, dark hair.[6]

Of note, Curly walked into the store with a couple of bills visible in his hand, likely the bills Martin exited with. Curly took the bills to the counter and bought two cheap cigars, often used to roll blunts. The *Urban Dictionary* defines a "blunt" as a "cigar hollowed out and filled with marijuana." Its virtue was that it could be smoked in public "somewhat inconspicuously." The clerk kept the cigars behind the counter.

Curly then went into his wallet for more money and bought another cigar, probably for himself. He left the store at 6:28 while his buddy—Moe?—was still checking out. Fifty seconds later, at 6:29, the security camera picked up Martin walking back east toward the Retreat at Twin Lakes. He was turning as he walked as though he were making some parting remark to an unseen person. That person was almost assuredly Curly, who had just as assuredly bought Martin a cigar or two, since Martin was too young to buy them on his own and had no ID on him in any case. Earlier that morning, in fact, Martin had remained in the car while his cousin Stephen bought a cheap Black and Mild cigar from the same 7-Eleven. This much Stephen told the State investigators.[7] What he and Trayvon were doing up at 8:00 a.m.—or why he was even in Sanford—the State did not pursue. It seems likely they had been out all night and stopped at the 7-Eleven to cop one last blunt. Brandy Green told those same investigators that when she and Tracy came home later Sunday morning, they found Stephen and Trayvon sleeping.[8]

If his own communications were to be believed, Martin's drug use did not stop with marijuana. In July 2011 Martin began subscribing to the daily video log of a character named Andy Milonakis, whose life seems dedicated to drugs, specifically a concoction known by various street names, including "purple lean" or "purple drank." The *Urban Dictionary* describes purple drank as "a mixture of Promethazine/Codeine cough syrup and sprite, with a few jolly ranchers and/or skittles thrown in." In May 2012 the *Treehouse* posted a screen-capture of a revealing Facebook exchange from June 2011 between Martin and a character called "Mackenzie DumbRyte Baksh":

MARTIN:	unow a connect for codine?
MACKENZIE:	why nigga
MARTIN:	to make some more
MACKENZIE:	u tawkin bout the pill codeine
MARTIN:	no the liquid its meds. I had it b4
MACKENZIE:	hell naw u could just use some robitussin nd soda to make some fire ass lean
MARTIN:	codine is a higher dose of dxm
MACKENZIE:	I feel u but need a prescription to get it[9]

Martin obviously had some familiarity with this world. The reader will have noted, too, that a soft drink like Arizona Watermelon Fruit Juice Cocktail and some Skittles would get the user two-thirds of the way to some "fire ass lean."

On the night of the shooting, the Sanford police incorrectly identified Martin's drink of choice as "Arizona brand name tea." They did not do so on purpose, and the prosecutor followed their lead. "He said 'iced tea' right?" Bernie de la Rionda asked Witness 8 as to what Martin had gotten at the 7-Eleven. "Yeah," she answered, as though Martin had actually told her that. The media continued to refer to the drink as tea long after they should have known better. This was due in part to sloppiness, in part to racial sensitivity about the word "watermelon," and in part to the drug implications of a fruity soft drink.

Although the video quality of Martin outside the store was far from clear, he wore a distinctive black-and-white button that made it possible to identify him with some certainty. Even in the dark and the rain, Zimmerman noticed it and told the dispatcher, "He's got a button on his shirt." The button memorialized one "Cory Craig Johnson," a cousin of Martin with a long rap sheet and a short life span. In 2008 he died at age thirty-six. When Trayvon's mother, Sybrina Fulton, appeared on a local TV show sponsored by the *Miami Herald*, she visibly froze when the host said to her, "I'm aware [Trayvon] was wearing a button that night." After glancing uncomfortably at Trayvon's aunt, Stephanie Sands, Sybrina said abruptly, "That's a family member." Unaware she was treading on unwelcome ground, the host kept asking about the button before Sybrina switched topics to Trayvon's love for his grandmother.[10]

Martin left the store with the earbuds from his cell phone firmly planted. He did a lot of phoning that day. He had been on one call continuously from 5:09 to 6:30. He would either make or receive a half dozen more calls in the remaining forty-five minutes of his life. At roughly 7:05 Zimmerman spotted Martin on Retreat View Circle, the street nearest the shortcut that Martin likely took. That spot was no more than twelve minutes away from the 7-Eleven, which left some twenty-five minutes for Martin to smoke a blunt. An overgrown vacant lot between the store and the exposed western flank of the Retreat would have provided Martin all the cover he needed.

In her April 2012 interview, Witness 8 provided something of a time alibi. The relevant part of her deposition with Bernie de la Rionda went as follows:

8:    It started raining.

DLR: It started raining, and did he go somewhere?

8:    Yeah, he ran to the, um, mail thing.

DLR: Like, I'm sorry, what?

8:    Like a mail, like a shed.

DLR: Like a mail—like a shed, like a mail area?

8:    Yeah, yeah.

DLR: Like a covered area, because it was raining?

8: Yeah.

DLR: So did he tell you he was already inside, like, the gated place?

8: Yeah. He ran in there.

De la Rionda was leading Witness 8 to account for the time gap in a more innocuous way. Her memory of the mail shed, however, seemed much too convenient, especially since she had claimed in her initial interview with Crump that Martin sought relief from the rain "under the shade" of another apartment. Both she and Crump also insisted that Martin put his hood up because it started raining. In fact, Martin had the hood up in the store and when he left it. Despite the obvious inconsistencies, the State used Witness 8's testimony in charging Zimmerman with murder.

After the shooting, the police found Martin's body lying facedown in the grass about thirty or so feet south of the intersection between the east-west cut-through and the north-south dog walk, about seventy yards from Green's town house. The Arizona Watermelon Fruit Juice Cocktail fell out of his hoodie when the officer rolled him over to perform CPR. Whatever his intention was in buying it, neither the police nor his parents would ever know for sure.

On May 22, 2013, in the defendant's reply to a State's motion, the public learned a little more about Martin's drug use. According to the State's own toxicologist, Dr. Bruce Goldberger, the THC level in Martin's blood at the time of his death was "sufficient to cause some impairment." The State did not want this evidence admitted. The defendant's attorneys did. On the night of the shooting, Zimmerman told the dispatcher Martin looked "high."[11]

He probably was.

27

TAKING THE SHOW

ON THE ROAD

*A*FTER MARTIN'S DEATH became an international cause célèbre, everyone wanted a piece of his biological parents, Sybrina Fulton and Tracy Martin. For a variety of reasons, many of them understandable, even noble, they obliged. Exploiting their grief at every turn, however, were the old bulls of the BGI, Al Sharpton and Jesse Jackson, as well as their own attorneys, Benjamin Crump and Daryl Parks. If Martin's parents had a useful lesson to share, the audience rarely heard it. Their handlers saw to it they stayed on the BGI message.

The night of April 26, 2012, found the road show at West Angeles Church in Los Angeles, with Jackson and Sharpton leading the proceedings. "We need a movement from Brooklyn to Pasadena," the Reverend Al Sharpton told an angry crowd, lamenting not only the death of Martin, but also the shooting death of a black college student from nearby Pasadena, named Kendrec McDade. "This is not about coming out and watching a rally," Sharpton continued. "This is about making a permanent movement until we change the laws and the structure and the inequality and the unfairness and the disproportionate distribution of justice."[1]

Even Sharpton would be hard-pressed to know what laws would have to be changed to prevent a death as anomalous as McDade's. The incident began on a March night a month after Martin's death with the robbery of a computer from the car of a man named Oscar Carrillo.

Angry and eager for immediate police response, Carillo called 9-1-1 and told the dispatcher that the two thieves, nineteen-year-old McDade and his seventeen-year-old companion, had robbed him at gunpoint. "Both have a gun, man," Carrillo said. "They run away from me." A security video showed otherwise: the seventeen-year-old stole the computer from Carillo's car while McDade served as a lookout at the rear of the vehicle. Carillo later admitted lying about the pair having guns, and he was prosecuted for doing so.

As the Los Angeles County district attorney reported, McDade fled the scene on foot. Upon seeing him run, one officer, Mathew Griffin, sped past him in a patrol car and blocked the street while the other officer, Jeffrey Newlen, pursued him on foot. As he approached the police car, McDade veered from his route and ran directly toward Griffin, seated in the patrol car. "He left the sidewalk and he's running at me," Griffin told investigators. "This—this scares the crap out of me. I don't know why he is running at me. He's still clutching his waistband. I think he's got a gun. I'm stuck in the car. I got nowhere to go."[2] Afraid for his life, Griffin fired four times through his open window, then ducked to avoid the return fire he expected. Newlen heard the shots and fired at the wounded McDade, thinking he was the shooter.

Under pressure from "the community," the Pasadena Police Department revealed the officers' names and their race. Both were white. This upped the ante all around. Although the officers were cleared of wrongdoing, the parents, who were no longer together, filed a wrongful death and federal civil rights lawsuit against the Pasadena Police Department, claiming their son was wrongfully shot and then left on the street to die. A year later, the father demanded an additional ten thousand dollars in compensation, claiming the Pasadena police roughed him up during a separate stolen-property investigation.[3] Sharpton had no objection to shaking a little coin loose himself. "As a first step," the *Pasadena Star-News* reported, "Sharpton asked the rally attendees to donate everything they could to the Trayvon Martin Foundation."[4]

There were any number of useful lessons Sharpton and Jackson could have pulled from the unlikely shootings of Kendrec and Martin—don't wander around after dark without purpose, don't steal, don't run from authorities, don't think yourself invulnerable, or, for the parents, stay married, keep a close eye on your children, work together to protect them. Instead, the out-of-towners played the race card that night in Los Angeles much as local leaders had been playing it since McDade was shot and killed.

After touring some Southern cities, including Birmingham, where Martin was named an honorary citizen, the road show headed to London, as in England. The ground had been well prepared by solidarity protests throughout the spring. One well-organized rally had taken place outside the American embassy on March 31, just a week or so after the first major American rallies. Organizing the event was a group with the intriguing acronym "BARAC," short for "Black Activists Rising Against Cuts." The poster for the rally repeated the same sophism that was widely believed in progressive circles worldwide: "It beggars belief that in a country that calls itself the greatest democracy in the world, a man can gun down an innocent child and take refuge in a law that allows a ludicrous claim of self defence."[5]

This time, Jackson and Sharpton stayed home, but Crump and Parks were there to keep Martin's parents on message. In Birmingham, for instance, Sybrina wanted to talk about "conflict resolution," but that humble theme did not exactly resonate on the world stage. "The issue is profiling," Daryl Parks told the Society of Black Lawyers in London. "Profiling of any type of person is wrong, wrong, wrong."[6]

The British media embraced the road show uncritically. Like most of its counterparts, the mainstream *Independent* sifted all nuance out of its coverage. "Trayvon was shot in the chest by armed neighbourhood volunteer George Zimmerman as he walked through a leafy gated community in Stanford, Florida," the paper reported on the occasion of the Team Trayvon visit, "because his killer assumed he was 'up to no good.'"[7] This was standard fare in the UK and in Europe. The case was that simple.

As they did at just about every stop, team members found common cause with other seeming victims of white injustice. The Martin family reportedly went to Britain at the request of an activist named Doreen Lawrence. Originally from Jamaica, Lawrence lost her teenage son Stephen in 1993 when a member or members of a thuggish white juvenile gang stabbed him to death. In a long and complicated case, the gang members, none older than the "child" Martin, were initially acquitted due to lack of evidence. Inspired by Doreen Lawrence, the British civil rights community and the media rallied to the cause. The *Daily Mail* led the crusade with headlines like "MURDERS: The Mail accuses these men of killing. If we are wrong let them sue us." A public inquiry followed five years after the killing and recommended that Britain's historic double jeopardy protection be suspended so the boys, now young men, could be tried anew for the same crime.

This Britain did with the passage of the Criminal Justice Act of 2003. The media, with the impressively self-satisfied *Daily Mail* in the lead, cheered its enactment and the hounding of the presumed killers, two of whom were later convicted.[8]

From the British perspective, Trayvon Martin suffered much the same fate as Stephen Lawrence: murder at the hand of a white racist who was also being coddled by racist police. Often manic in their political correctness, the British media made their American counterparts seem a model of prudence and restraint. What all the hype disguised in Britain, however, was what it disguised in America: the Lawrence stabbing, like the Martin shooting, was a statistical anomaly. In both countries, whites suffered much more from black violence than blacks did from whites, and young black men suffered even more from black violence than did young whites.

A June 2010 *Daily Mail* article by Rebecca Camber conceded as much. "The majority of violent inner-city crime is committed by black men, police figures suggest," wrote Camber in her opening. "But the statistics also show that black men are twice as likely to be victims of such crimes." According to figures released by Scotland Yard under Freedom of Information Act laws, black men committed more than two-thirds of shootings and more than half of robberies and street crimes in 2009–2010. What made these figures even more troubling was that only 12 percent of London's 7.5 million people were black. To counter these statistics, Camber cited a predictable liberal alibi, "Critics say the figures merely show the continuing prevalence of racism in the Metropolitan Police."[9]

Indeed, if there were a real commonality between crime and Britain and the United States, it would be the cultural dominance in both counties of the aforementioned "critics." These were the people, black and white, who preached the gospel of black victimization. They welcomed the Trayvon road show to Britain because the traveling players sang from the same hymn book and made the grudge seem universal.

Later that May, the road show headed to Chicago, then in the throes of extraordinary street violence and desperately in need of some explanation beyond the obvious, namely, the welfare-fueled collapse of the black family. Chicago was Jesse Jackson territory, and Sharpton kept his distance. The take-away message at the road show's Chicago news conference was not racial profiling, conflict resolution, or what Sharpton memorably called "the disproportionate distribution of justice." The focus was on "senseless gun violence." It's time to "stop the killing," said Jackson, and in his own backyard there was plenty of it.[10] In 2012 Chicago recorded 20 percent more murders than New York City despite having only one-third of the population. Rather than face up to the causes of the violence, let alone the fact that blacks were proportionately eight times more likely to commit murder than whites, Jackson zeroed in on the extraordinary death of Trayvon Martin. He linked the Martin case to two even more unusual killings in the Chicago area, those of Rekia Boyd and Stephon Watts, both of whose families were represented onstage with Jackson, Crump, and the Martins.

In March 2012, a few weeks after Martin's death, a white off-duty Chicago detective named Dante Servin shot and killed Rekia. Her only crime was being in the wrong place at the wrong time. Servin was shooting at a man named Antonio Cross, and a stray bullet caught Rekia in the head. She was one of eight Chicagoans killed by police in 2012 and the only innocent bystander among the eight. More than five hundred Chicagoans were murdered that year by people other than police. A year after the shooting, Boyd's family would receive a $4.5 million settlement. The other five hundred were not so fortunate.[11]

A few weeks before Martin was killed, Calumet City police drove to the Watts home for at least the eleventh time in two years to help his parents subdue Stephon, a fifteen-year-old with Asperger's syndrome. The two officers found him in the basement, wielding a kitchen knife. After Stephon backed the officers into a corner, he "lashed out" and struck one in the arm. The officers each fired once, killing Stephon.[12] Although the Cook County state's attorney cleared the officers of wrongdoing, Stephon's mother filed a lawsuit against them and Calumet City.

The death of all these people—Trayvon, Rekia, Kendrec, Stephon, and Stephen—had only one thing in common: white people killed them. This made the cases newsworthy and thus exploitable. A lawsuit followed every death. No change in law or philosophy or community sentiment could have saved all of these five dead young people or even any two of them.

The ambiguity of it all left the well-intended Sybrina Fulton flailing to find some meaningful way to pull a message out of her grief. "He's not here to speak for himself," she said of Trayvon in Chicago, "so we as his parents have decided instead of sitting back and not doing anything, this is what we have decided to do, to help our community and to help other parents." Unfortunately, the advice she offered was counterproductive. As the *Chicago Sun-Times* reported, she spoke of the Justice for Trayvon Foundation, "which helps teens identify signs of racial profiling."[13] Of all the threats facing young black men today, profiling is the least of them. To present profiling as an evil, as Sybrina and others routinely do, puts black men at more risk, not less. It inspires some of these young men to project that evil onto those responsible for keeping watch. And attacking the watchman, as Martin learned the hard way, could be fatal.

Not surprisingly, Bob Zimmerman, George's father, looked at crime stories from an altogether different perspective than Trayvon's parents. He wondered, for instance, how a year after Martin's death, three young black Floridians, one of them a female, could lethally bludgeon a white woman with a hammer forty times and then set the woman's bed afire with her in it and get no media attention beyond the Pensacola area.[14] Even closer to home, Bob wondered how the national media could ignore another hammer attack just a month after the Martin shooting and just six miles away. The two perpetrators were black teens. The victim was a fifty-year-old white male. The two attacked the man in his car, then dragged him into the woods, bludgeoned him, and left him near death. Finally, they stole his car.

The *Orlando Sentinel* had to cover the case, of course, and even asked the public to help police catch the suspects. More than a little unhelpfully, the editors chose to leave the race of the attackers out of their description. There were no cries of racism, no marches, and, of course, no calls to restrict hammers.[15]

28

STRAIGHTENING THE STORY

*W*ITNESS 8, Trayvon Martin's mystery girlfriend, had to have cost Bernie de la Rionda more than a few nights' sleep. Despite her importance to his case, he had no sure way of knowing whether she was the same girl that Crump introduced to the world as "Dee Dee" or, for that matter, whether she was the witness she claimed to be. So he summoned her to Jacksonville for a come-to-Jesus meeting in August 2012, four months after his initial interview with her in April. The same FDLE agent who escorted de la Rionda to the April interview in Miami escorted Witness 8 to the Fort Lauderdale airport for her August trip to Jacksonville. In that the subsequent get-together went unrecorded, it was not until March 13, 2013, when he deposed this witness, that Mark O'Mara learned the details of what was said in the Jacksonville meeting. The very threat of a deposition, however, inspired the prosecution to prepare O'Mara for what he was about to learn.

Two weeks later, on March 25, O'Mara shared some of that newfound knowledge with the court. In this motion, he asked the court to sanction the prosecution for discovery violations regarding the elusive witness. As State attested, and O'Mara affirmed, Witness 8 was the same Dee Dee that Crump had interviewed in March, the one who was allegedly too ill to attend Martin's wake. O'Mara quoted Crump's March 2012 interview with Dee Dee on this subject. "And that's when you realized that the day of his wake that you were the last person talking to him and it just made you physically sick?" Crump had asked her, and the witness had responded yes. She said much the same to de la Rionda in their April meeting.

As early as August 23, 2012, O'Mara asked the prosecution about the witness's hospital records via e-mail, but he got no response. He sent a letter on September 19 inquiring again, but he got no response to that correspondence either. O'Mara also spoke to the prosecutors about these records repeatedly but without results. On February 21, 2013, he filed a motion to subpoena the medical records. Finally, two weeks later, assistant state attorney John Guy explained that there would be no need to move forward with a subpoena, as "no hospitalization records existed for Witness 8."[1] There were no records for the simple reason that Witness 8 had not gone to the hospital.

In deposing Witness 8 in March 2013, O'Mara confirmed that she confessed the hospital scam to de la Rionda during her August 2012 Jacksonville rendezvous. O'Mara accused the state attorney's office of being "fully aware" of her lie since that meeting. The reason she gave for lying made some sense. Sybrina Fulton was sitting next to her during her interview with the State in April, and she "felt the need to deceive as to the reason for not going to the wake or funeral." O'Mara also chastised the State for its decision to conduct the April 2012 interview in the living room of the Fulton home in Sybrina's presence. "Mr. de la Rionda had to know the potential influence that could occur," said O'Mara, adding that this arrangement put "the legitimacy and veracity of the entire statement at issue."

The State had some practice in keeping critical information about this witness away from the defense. As O'Mara noted in his motion, on several occasions Crump presented the witness to the public as a minor. On March 21, 2012, for instance, he told Matt Lauer on the *Today Show*, "She is a 16-year-old teenager who just lost a friend very special to her."[2] His colleagues on Team Trayvon repeated the same canard. When HLN's Nancy Grace asked Daryl Parks why this witness had still not talked to the police five weeks after Martin's death, he answered, "She's a minor. So it's a very delicate situation."[3] ABC's Matt Gutman, who might as well have been part of the team, was echoing the "minor" line as well. More curious still, he told Lawrence O'Donnell on his MSNBC show, "We've been talking to [Witness 8] for days now. This is not the first time that I've heard her speak."[4] He said this on March 28, 2012, four days before the State was able to locate her. By this time, Gutman had abandoned all journalistic distance: Team Trayvon was no longer a "they," but a "we."

For his part, de la Rionda played along with the charade, or at least he seemed to. If he truly believed her to be a minor, he would have made sure a parent or guardian accompanied her to the April deposition, but he did not. In any case, it was only in November 2012 that the defense learned, through the witness's affidavit, that she was eighteen when Crump interviewed her in March 2012.

"It became apparent that Mr. de la Rionda knew that Witness 8 was an 18 year old adult in April of 2012 when he interviewed Witness 8," O'Mara wrote in a footnote. "However, the State redacted that information from the Defense until months later." As to why this lie was permitted to fester so long, O'Mara did not speculate, but the Treepers did. One Treeper believed the age was concocted by Crump to limit the media's access to Dee Dee. For his part, Sundance was not at all convinced that the girl Crump interviewed on the phone was the same young woman that de la Rionda interviewed in Sybrina Fulton's living room a few weeks later.

Slowly, the media were beginning to face facts. "Chief witness in Trayvon Martin case lied under oath," read the CNN headline after O'Mara went public with his concerns.[5] If a few journalists were beginning to sense just how badly they had been played, the true believers in the Martin camp refused to hear a contrary word. "One service most ERs and many pharmacies offer is free [blood pressure] screening," wrote a commenter deeply in denial. "You simply go in, they take your pressure and unless it is dangerously high, you go home. No record is kept. This would undoubtedly be the kind of treatment DeeDee received the day of Trayvon's funeral."[6] After a year of relentless propaganda, some minds were beyond changing.

Not surprisingly, the state attorney's office rejected O'Mara's motion. What was a surprise, though, was the mocking tone of its response. Yes, Witness 8 lied, but the lie was immaterial. George Zimmerman also lied. Wittingly or not, O'Mara enabled his lies. Zimmerman's brother Robert also made inflammatory statements. "Targeting the prosecutors" was inevitable given O'Mara's incompetence. "No misconduct has occurred," wrote de la Rionda in conclusion, "nor should sanctions be awarded to compensate counsel. Indeed, the instant Motion appeared to be the product of

> [A] walking shadow, a poor player
> That struts and frets his hour upon the stage
> And then is heard no more: it is a tale . . .
> Full of sound and fury,
> Signifying nothing."[7]

Lest the court not get the reference, de la Rionda added, "William Shakespeare (1564–1616), 'Macbeth,' Act 5 scene 5." In his reply to the State, O'Mara questioned the "scurrilous and unfounded personal attacks" by the prosecutors and asked that the State's pleading be stricken.[8] If he had wanted to show off, O'Mara might have added his own line from Macbeth:

Confusion now hath made his masterpiece.[9]

29

REMEMBERING LEO FRANK

ON APRIL 30, 2013, Zimmerman and his attorneys faced off against prosecutor Bernie de la Rionda in a preliminary hearing that addressed, among other issues, whether there would be a pretrial Stand Your Ground immunity hearing. One of the revelations that came out of this hearing was that the *Treehouse*, a blogging outpost thoroughly ignored by the major media and not even ranked among the top two hundred conservative blogs, had cast its shadow on the prosecution's case.

Pleased by the grudging recognition, the Treepers and their friends commented in real time as they watched the hearings. Chip Bennett was first to notice: "BDLR [Bernie de la Rionda] mentions The Conservative Treehouse—Drink!" HughStone followed: "Bernie is about to cry. THE TREEHOUSE mentioned again!!!!!!!!!!!!!!!!" "He is behaving like a child that isn't getting his way," commented Rebelious [*sic*] Angel after de la Rionda's third reference to the *Treehouse*. "Obviously the Conservative Treehouse has done a better job at shining the light on the truth and it's got BDLR upset."[1]

The prosecutors' many references to the *Treehouse* did not make the news. What did was Zimmerman's unexpected decision to waive his right to a Stand Your Ground hearing. The experts consulted by the *New York Times* listed a series of "strategic and practical" reasons as to why Zimmerman would have made this unanticipated move. In such a hearing, said the experts, the burden to prove innocence is on the defendant. Then, too, the hearing would provide prosecutors a preview of his defense, and state attorney Angela Corey had shown her willingness to challenge vigorously the Stand Your Ground defense. The *New York Times* only hinted at another motive in suggesting that a ruling of immunity by a judge, not a jury, "would most likely provoke a strong public reaction in the highly charged case."[2]

Strong public reaction? Yes, and Zimmerman knew that better than anyone. He showed up at the late April hearing as much as one hundred pounds heavier than he was a year earlier. The media had rendered the mid-Florida ether so poisonous that Zimmerman felt compelled to spend that year in hiding, in legitimate fear for his life. He could not just pop down to the gym or go for a run around the neighborhood. On one rare excursion he made to a store, it was to buy a bulletproof vest.[3] As he fully understood, only a very public exoneration by a jury of his peers could begin to give him his life back. There would be no shortcuts, even if the law provided one.

There was no guarantee either that Zimmerman would get justice from a jury. Supreme Court justice Oliver Wendell Holmes anticipated the anxiety that a Florida jury might face in his sad commentary on the Leo Frank case. A century earlier, Frank, a Jewish entrepreneur from New York, was tried in an Atlanta court for killing a young woman in his employ. The case outraged the citizens of Georgia, and that outrage no doubt intimidated the members of the jury.[4] According to Holmes, they "responded to the passions of the mob" and found Frank guilty. "Mob law," said Holmes for the ages, "does not become due process of law by securing the assent of a terrified jury." The jury had cause to be terrified. After the Georgia governor commuted the death penalty for Frank, a well-organized, high-profile group of citizens kidnapped Frank from prison and brutally lynched him. "Lynch law is a good sign," said former Georgia congressman Thomas Watson at the time. "It shows that a sense of justice lives among the people."[5]

What has continued to live among the people is the urge to lynch, and Twitter provided the cyber platform for the wannabe lynchers. The day after Zimmerman was first released on bail, the day he began his year in hiding, there was a flurry of death threats on Twitter along the lines of "They done let Zimmerman free lets kill that MF" or "I think imma personally kill George Zimmerman . . . anyone's welcome to join." And these two were the more printable threats against that "mexican muther f**ker george Zimmerman."[6]

The State of Florida arrested George Zimmerman exactly fifty years after the release of the film *To Kill A Mockingbird*. The tweeters likely watched the movie in class at one point and were tasked to learn its lessons. These were the timeless lessons of the American civil rights movement: the obligation to respect other races; the need for civil discourse; the power of nonviolence; the imperative of due process; the glory of equal justice before the law. When they watched the film as students, these tweeters surely identified with the accused, Tom Robinson. They grew up, unfortunately, to become the mob that lynched him.

30

THE UNRAVELING OF TRAYVON

O N MAY 23, 2013, George Zimmerman's attorneys released new evidence in advance of the upcoming trial. Crump, of course, dismissed it as "irrelevant." He was wrong. It was damning. The text messages and photos from Martin's cell phone told a story profoundly different from the one the State of Florida and the media had been peddling for more than a year, but one altogether truer and sadder.

As the texts made clear, Team Trayvon knew what they were doing when they moved to seal Martin's school records even before the story went public. Martin's problems went well beyond "just regular teenage stuff." The exchange between Martin and a female friend on November 21, 2012, three months before his death, spoke to where his life was heading. After he told her he was "tired and sore" from a fight, she asked him why he fought. ("Bae" is shorthand for "babe.")

> **MARTIN:** Cause man dat nigga snitched on me
>
> **FRIEND:** Bae y you always fightinqq man, you got suspended?
>
> **MARTIN:** Naw we thumped afta skool in a duckd off spot
>
> **FRIEND:** Ohh, Well Damee
>
> **MARTIN:** I lost da 1st round :(but won da 2nd nd 3rd····

FRIEND: Ohhh So It Wass 3 Rounds? Damn well at least yu wonn lol but yuu needa stop fighting bae Forreal

MARTIN: Nay im not done with fool . . . he gone hav 2 see me again

FRIEND: Nooo... Stop, yuu waint gonn bee satisfied till yuh suspended again, huh?

MARTIN: Naw but he aint breed nuff 4 me, only his nose[1]

As his social media accounts showed, Martin was a student of mixed martial arts. The fight followed the MMA format. A day later, he told a friend that his opponent "got mo hits cause in da 1st round he had me on da ground nd I couldn't do ntn." As his girlfriend complained, Martin was "always" fighting. He was also something of a sadist. His opponent, after all, did not bleed enough. Why might this be relevant?

Witness 6, the closest of the eyewitnesses to the shooting, told the Sanford police that there was a "black man in a black hoodie on top of either a white guy . . . or an Hispanic guy in a red sweater on the ground yelling out help," and that the black man on top was "throwing down blows on the guy MMA [mixed martial arts] style."[2]

On November 22, the day after the MMA-style fight, Martin told a friend that his mother "just kicked [him] out" and that he had to move in with his father. When the friend asked why, Martin answered, "Da police caught me outta skool." Said the friend, "U a hoodlum." "Naw," said Martin. "I'm a gangsta." Incredibly, his death would transform this wannabe gangster into the cherubic preteen he appeared to be five years earlier or, in the words of Florida state attorney Angela Corey, a "precious victim."

On December 21, 2011, Martin told a friend, "Dam I just got in trouble 4 sum shit I aint even do." His mother, Sybrina Fulton, was dismayed. "Pack up your clothes now," she texted him. "I love u but I think u being w/ ur Dad is best." Martin lived with his stepmother most of his life and his mother only intermittently. He spent even less time with his father, who was then living with a sister in the Miami area. He appears to have been bouncing between their places and his uncle Stephen's house at the time.

On December 22 Martin confided to a girlfriend, "I got in trouble." She asked, "What did you do now[?]" As was typical, Martin took no responsibility. "I aint do ntn . . . call me." The friend had other priorities:

"I'm about to get my nails done so you gotta wait a few." On the day before Christmas Martin's mother texted him: "I'm concerned about u but I'm praying for u and I want U to pray for yourself EVERYDAY, ok." She was texting the son she used to know. The Trayvon who was about to turn seventeen, she knew next to nothing about.

On January 6, 2012, Martin got into trouble at school again. When asked why, he told a friend, "Caus I was watcn a fight nd a teacher say I hit em." Said the friend, "Idk how u be getting in trouble an shit." By that time, Martin's mother had thrown him out of the house for "fightn," and he had moved in with his aunt and uncle, not his father. This did not prevent Sybrina from telling de la Rionda in April 2012 that Trayvon "was a very good son."[3]

For all her troubles, Fulton fared better than Renette Emile, the mother of Martin's schoolmate Kit Darrant. A few months after Fulton threw her son out of the house, Emile had a bitter fight with her son. Darrant responded by strangling his mother and stabbing her more than a hundred times. "He was like a normal person. He makes people laugh. He's sweet," one friend said of Darrant, who had also been busted on a marijuana charge.[4]

The multiple texts about "weed" and the photos of marijuana plants confirmed Martin's interest in drugs. On February 21, five days before the shooting, "Weedhead"—as a friend called Martin—took the bus to Orlando to stay with his father's girlfriend, Brandy Green. He was free to travel because his school had suspended him again, this time for possession of marijuana and a pipe. The bust did little to sober him up. "I hid m weed," he confided to a girl friend, afraid that he might have been searched before the trip. He texted later that day, "I got weed nd I get money Friday."[5]

Curiously, when Tracy Martin had been interviewed by the State in April 2012, he corrected himself to get the date of Trayvon's departure right, but told de la Rionda that he "dropped the victim off with his girl-friend" and that she "met him half way between Miami and Sanford."[6] This would have meant a four-hour commitment on the part of both Martin and Green. This was not an error on Martin's part, nor was it an attempt to deceive Sybrina. She knew Trayvon took a bus, and she was with Tracy when the State took his testimony. So was Benjamin Crump. Martin also told the investigator that he had last seen his son on Saturday night. Brandy Green testified that Martin had last seen Trayvon on Sunday morning, the day of his death. There was no obvious reason why Team Trayvon collaborated to mislead the State beyond perhaps the felt need to make the parents, now public figures, seem more responsible and their son less at risk.

Trayvon Martin's cell phone photos pointed to an even more dangerous new hobby, namely, guns. Indeed, one of his photos showed a hand, likely Martin's own, on a pistol. Of note, de la Rionda asked Tracy in the April 2012 interview about his son's interest in guns. De la Rionda may have known even then what images the cell phone contained. When asked, Tracy claimed his son was "not familiar with guns." He was wrong. Guns excited Trayvon. "U got heat??" he enthused upon learning that a friend had access to a gun. On the bus trip to Orlando, Martin was negotiating to buy a handgun with a friend. "U wanna share a .380?" he asked.

That message was sandwiched between one by each of his parents. Tracy Martin texted his son, "Show much respect to [Green] and adjust to my Lady & [her son]. Show them you a good kid and you want positive things aroud you." His mother texted him as well, "R u comfortable on the bus?? Go to sleep n u will be there soon."[7] The texts from Martin's parents were the saddest messages of them all. They had all but lost control of their son but chose not to see how far out of control he had spun. Like so many divorced parents, they were torn between punishing him and appeasing him.

Upon leaving Miami, Martin seemed to be growing angrier. On February 21 he texted a girlfriend who was pouting about another girl, presumably in Sanford. Wrote Martin, "f**k u cuz I neva text ha 2 day I made dat shit up so u leav me df alone bout it." Two days later a friend tried to warn Martin off his bad behavior. "I ain't ya parent," he texted him, "but gshit thro it away." Martin was not in the mood to be lectured to. "Y u gotta knock my hustle??" he shot back. Although Martin's texts from February 26 had yet to be made public, a motion filed by the defendants on May 23, 2013, suggested his exchanges that day with Witness 8 were "hostile and angry." According to the motion, Martin's "emotional state" was such that on the evening of February 26, he "chose to hide and then confront George Zimmerman rather than simply go home." Had Zimmerman not finally reached for his gun, Martin might have rendered him unconscious, or even killed him. To that point, Zimmerman had obviously not managed to "breed nuff" (bleed enough) to pacify Martin.

If the police had arrested Martin for assault, he would have denied responsibility. He always did, but the evidence would have trumped his denial. The Miami school records, the social media messages, the texts, the THC in his blood, the bruises on his knuckles, and the photos in his phone all pointed to a viciously climactic moment in an increasingly disordered life. Martin's death spared the many responsible parties, the media included, the need to assess that disorder. In transforming an aspiring gangster into a precious victim, they could avoid all talk of hit-and-miss fatherhood, divorce, parental neglect, cultural breakdown, an exploitative civil rights movement, a corrupt school system, or what George Bush famously called "the soft bigotry of low expectations."[8] Instead, the culpable parties were encouraged to project their guilt onto preapproved targets: racist police, weak-willed prosecutors, the NRA, neo-Nazis, the gun culture and its reckless laws, and the living, breathing avatar of all things white and right-wing—George Zimmerman.

Team Trayvon attorney Natalie Jackson summed up the team spirit concisely in a tweet, "George Zimmerman's Defense Team Releases Texts and Photos to Fit Their Racist Narrative."[9] In her world, there was no other motive.

31

EXCLUDING THE UNPLEASANT

*J*UDGE DEBRA S. NELSON, like her predecessor on the case, Judge Kenneth Lester, had a hard time concealing her distaste for George Zimmerman and his defense team. Nelson got her turn on the bench after the Fifth District Court of Appeal ruled in August 2012 that Lester had to step down. Zimmerman's attorneys had filed a twenty-eight-page motion challenging his neutrality and his insinuations that Zimmerman was somehow "manipulating the system," and the court agreed. Lester was not the first judge to leave the case. Earlier, Judge Jessica Recksiedler had recused herself for potential conflict of interest.[1] As seen from the *Treehouse*, Nelson, pushing sixty and with thirteen years on the bench, did not seem much of an improvement over her predecessors. According to the *Orlando Sentinel*, Nelson was a prosecution-friendly hardnose with a John Lennon poster on her office wall. The *Sentinel* reporter did not hint at any contradiction.[2]

Dour and charmless, Nelson consistently ruled against the Zimmerman defense team, and she did so without a hint of the social graces that judges often employ to ease the sting of denial. In March 2013, for instance, she twice ruled against the defense's request to depose Martin family attorney Benjamin Crump. At question was Crump's phone interview with Dee Dee, the sixteen-year-old who morphed into the eighteen-year-old Witness 8. Crump and/or the witness lied not only about her age, but also about her hospitalization after learning of Martin's death.

By 2013 the court recognized these to be lies. There was little doubt about Crump's role in enabling these lies, if not actually manufacturing them. After much legal back-and-forth, Crump agreed to be deposed, or at least appeared to agree, but his own attorney intervened and refused to produce his client absent a ruling from the judge. Zimmerman's attorneys asked Nelson to compel Crump's deposition. Crump's attorney denied that his client's role in the affair was either relevant or crucial, and Nelson assented. In her final three-sentence ruling, she offered no explanation as to why she did. Motion denied. Move on.[3]

On May 28, 2013, Nelson ruled hard and heavy on the defense's attempt to introduce to the court the unsanctified Trayvon Martin, the one revealed in his texts and social media pages. Among other rulings, she deemed Martin's texts in the months leading up to his death inadmissible unless the prosecution inadvertently opened the door to their use. The text messages and photos from Martin's cell phone showed a troubled young man whose life was increasingly consumed with drugs, guns, and MMA-style fighting. They were damning.

Nelson did rule that Martin's history of fighting and his school records could be brought up during trial. The problem, of course, was that the best evidence of that history—the text messages—had been all but excluded. This information also had to be kept out of opening statements. Excluded, too, was any reference to social media or text messages that corroborated Martin's undeniable drug use. In fact, no information gleaned from Martin's social media accounts could be mentioned in an opening statement, and it could be used in trial only if it passed tests for authenticity and hearsay, and only then if the prosecution unwitting allowed its admission. Nelson said she might permit expert testimony on the chemical elements of marijuana found in Martin's system, but the State experts would surely try to undermine the defense experts and bore the jury to sleep in the process.

"Without question, today was a very important day in this case," Martin family attorney Daryl Parks told the media. "What was rather clear: All of the bad information put out by the defense team will not be evidence in this case."[4] If "bad" meant "damaging," then there was no denying Parks's insight. Nelson's rulings gladdened the hearts of the prosecution and put the possibility of conviction within reach.

Yet there was something altogether Pyrrhic about this victory. The prosecutors had moved to have the evidence of Trayvon's behavior excluded only because the blogosphere, the *Treehouse* in particular, had forced it into the open. Once the prosecution acknowledged the existence of the evidence, the defense was able to speak about it publicly, and its legal validation seemed to sober the media up. "Marijuana, fights, guns: Zimmerman loses key pretrial battles," read a CNN headline above a series of photos of Martin "recycling" his own marijuana smoke.[5] Indeed, many of the same media outlets that inundated the public with photos of an innocent twelve-year-old just a year earlier were showing on the eve of the trial the pot-smoking, gun-holding, grille-flashing young man who confronted Zimmerman. Team Trayvon and the more overtly leftist media accused the defense of attempting to poison the jury pool, but as O'Mara acknowledged, that had been done a long time ago by the accusers. O'Mara was, if anything, trying to detoxify that pool.

By May 28 the shift in public opinion was becoming obvious. In a *Miami Herald* poll in which nearly twenty thousand people voted, 95 percent of the voters disagreed with Judge Nelson's decision to exclude "Martin's tough-talking" messages. On conservative websites, the commentary ran overwhelmingly in Zimmerman's favor. On liberal sites it was becoming more and more balanced. As one commenter astutely observed upon watching the debate on the liberal *Huffington Post*, "there is no middle . . . your [sic] either team Trayvon . . . or Team Zimmerman." Those on the Team Zimmerman side tended to argue with facts, those on the Team Trayvon side with emotion. "This is crazy," said one typical Trayvon-friendly commenter. "They're trying to dig up anything they can. Give this boy and family their justice."[6] In his world, "justice" meant Zimmerman's head.

Only the Florida media and the UK *Daily Mail* followed up on O'Mara's most salient strike in the May 28 hearing. He produced in court a whistle-blower who openly admitted that de la Rionda had concealed evidence that, by law, should have been turned over to the defense. The man's name was Wesley White, an attorney who had worked as a prosecutor in the state attorney's office in Duval County. He quit that office in December 2012 citing differences of opinion with Angela Corey.

White revealed to the court that in Martin's cell phone were photos of a firearm in someone's hand, of drugs, and of an underage girl, presumably unclothed. Not surprisingly, de la Rionda objected to this testimony as hearsay, but White surprised him by naming his source, Ben Kruidbos, the IT director for the Fourth Judicial Circuit. White testified that he had learned of this mischief more than a month earlier and reached out to O'Mara. "I was saddened by it," White said of de la Rionda's potential evidence violations, "but I'm not surprised."[7]

At an impromptu press conference after the hearing, O'Mara claimed that Kruidbos would know what the state attorney's office had *not* turned over to the defense. The court's inquiry into the matter, said O'Mara, "could lead to some very dire consequences for those who made presentations to the judge that were not accurate."[8] This was news. The *Drudge Report* posted the story on this subject in red.

On June 3, a week before the trial was scheduled to start, the *New York Times* published a video "RetroReport" on the twenty-fifth anniversary of the Tawana Brawley hoax. The report made no mention of any parallels to the Trayvon Martin case, but they were there for anyone to see: the false claims, the marches, the demagogic Al Sharpton, the willfully gullible national media, the besieged state officials. "The press had its agenda, no offense. The advisors had their agenda, no offense," special prosecutor John Ryan told the *Times*. "Quite frankly, we had to deal where it was those of us in the armory against the rest of the world." For his part, Sharpton remained largely unrepentant. Although he admitted his rhetoric may have gone too far, he took refuge in the righteousness of his calling. "At least give me credit for a life that was geared to social justice even if you think I was wrong on some cases." Tellingly, the *Times* gave the final word to former *Village Voice* reporter Wayne Barrett, who openly questioned why the media paid any attention to Sharpton at all. "One would think," said Barrett, "if he sold you such a terrible bill of goods on such a giant story that dominated news cycles for such a long period of time and proved to be a total hoax that you might not show up at his next press conference with your camera crew."[9]

On that same June 3, the Fifth District Court of Appeal in Daytona Beach served up another dose of troubling news for the prosecution. The court ruled unanimously that Zimmerman's attorneys were entitled to depose Crump in regard to his interview of Witness 8 and the circumstances surrounding the interview. The appellate judges dismissed Nelson's contention that Crump was an "opposing counsel" given that he was not acting as a lawyer for the State or the defendant. As to "work product privilege," Crump abandoned any pretense of that when he interviewed his witness in the presence of "two media representatives," one of whom promptly shared excerpts on national television. "The trial court erred in denying Zimmerman an opportunity to depose Crump," said the Court of Appeal bluntly.[10] The ruling had to sting. It also put Nelson on notice that she was not trying this case in a legal vacuum. Although skeptical of the process and wary about the outcome, Sundance had to admit, "This is a HUGE VICTORY for George Zimmerman."[11]

Zimmerman scored one more legal win just before the trial got rolling. In the so-called Frye hearing to determine whether certain scientific evidence was admissible, the State presented evidence from two audio experts, Dr. Thomas Owen and a Dr. Alan Reich. They had hoped to tell the jury how their scientific analysis proved the screams for help on the crucial 9-1-1 tape were Martin's.

Some months earlier the *Orlando Sentinel* had contracted with Owen, a court-qualified expert witness and something of an authority on biometric voice analysis. Owen used software called "Easy Voice Biometrics" to determine whether or not it was Zimmerman who cried out for help on that fateful night in February. "I took all of the screams and put those together, and cut out everything else," Owen told the *Sentinel*. The software, however, registered only a 48 percent match, well below the 90 percent threshold needed to prove that the cries were Zimmerman's. "As a result of that, you can say with reasonable scientific certainty that it's not Zimmerman," said Owen. Lacking a sample of Martin's voice, he did not attempt to determine whether the voice was that of the dead teen, but if it were not Zimmerman screaming, who else could it have been?[12]

The state attorney's office contracted with Reich, a self-described "forensic acoustic consultant," to process and analyze two recordings, one Zimmerman's original call to the dispatcher and Witness 11's 9-1-1 call. A month before the trial began, he turned in a final report with an embarrassing richness of typos and misspellings—"investigatiaon," "signlas," "lazer," "wishpered," "howver"—and these are just a few of the many.

The report was also chockablock full with arcane pseudoscientific patois that no jury would ever have been able to understand, to wit, "Audio CD and 9-1-1 data-logging recording both have 16-bit amplitude resolution, which divides the vertical amplitude scae (*sic*) of the digital signal into $2^{16} = 65,526$ amplitude gradations."[13]

Where others had heard a single individual yelling, "Help" or "Help me" for forty seconds, Reich heard a "loud, purposeful, mostly 'turn-taking' linguistic dialogue." This dialogue included a "seeminly [*sic*] religious proclamation" by Zimmerman, "These shall be." According to Reich, this occurred simultaneously with Martin's "loud, high-pitched, distressed, and tremulous 'I'm begging you.'" Lest he be thought a total charlatan, Reich conceded that these statements are "challenging for the untrained listener to detect."[14]

At the hearing, which took place immediately before the trial, defense attorney O'Mara argued that trying to compare known speech samples with short bursts of screaming captured on the distant background of a 9-1-1 call while the caller and the dispatcher are speaking over the screams in the foreground was pointless. He presented testimony from four acknowledged experts in the field to make his case.

On June 7, in the middle of this hearing, ABC claimed "exclusive" possession of a potentially significant recording, specifically, about six seconds of Martin's voice as part of the cache found on his cell phone. The irrepressible Matt Gutman insisted that this recording would help solve "one of the biggest mysteries of this case so far," in particular, who was doing the screaming on the 9-1-1 recording. In fact, the source of the screams was a mystery only to the willfully deaf, like Gutman. He added that the prosecutors were sure that that new evidence "proves that Martin was crying for help before he was killed," but by this time, the State had to know that it was Zimmerman.[15]

By insisting on expert testimony, the prosecutors were doing what defense attorneys do when they have a weak case, namely, muddying the waters and hoping to plant the seed of reasonable doubt. For a defense attorney this is standard practice. For a prosecutor, this was unethical, perhaps even criminal. *All* evidence pointed to Zimmerman as the man who screamed, "Help" or "Help me" at least fourteen times. Again, as Witness 6 told the police immediately after the shooting, he saw a "black man in a black hoodie on top of either a white guy . . . or an Hispanic guy in a red sweater on the ground yelling out help."[16]

For a number of reasons, including perhaps the fear of a reversal on appeal, Judge Nelson proved a tough sell. The defense had the better case, and she knew it. Of all the expert witnesses, Nelson acknowledged that defense witness Dr. Peter French impressed her most. He had testified that if law enforcement had given him the recordings at the outset of the case, he would have "rejected the assignment as it would have been fruitless to undertake the task." Defense witness Dr. Hirotake Nakasone found it "disturbing" that anyone would even attempt such an analysis given the current state of the technology and the limited quality of the audio. On the twenty-second day of June, just two days after the jury was seated, Nelson ruled that "the opinion testimony of Mr. Owen and Dr. Reich are hereby excluded from trial."[17] In so doing, she spared the prosecution the embarrassment of presenting its trumped-up science in court as evidence but left observers wondering just what evidence the State could possibly present.

Part 2

THE TRIAL

32

FILTERING THE POOL

*T*HE CITY OF SANFORD CAME TO LIFE in Florida's Pleistocene era—mid-nineteenth century—and even at the beginning ethnic strife dictated its reality. Early settlers clustered around an army base called Fort Mellon, a forward staging area in the Seminole Wars of the 1830s. When the Seminoles were dispatched to points westward or skyward, more settlers headed south, some with their slaves in tow. In 1870 an ambitious entrepreneur saw the potential in "Mellonville's" location on the south shore of Lake Monroe, close to the geographical center of Florida, and purchased a good chunk of land west of town. By 1877 this entrepreneur, the less-than-modest Henry Shelton Sanford, had gotten a new city named after himself, and he and his fellow citizens promptly annexed Mellonville. The embryonic metro attracted the South Florida Railroad and was soon enough flourishing with its new train station, grand hotel, and an unrivaled distinction as Celery City in honor of the town's most fruitful crop.

In the years since, much of the prosperity that has blessed central Florida has bypassed Sanford. If Orlando has the glitz of Oz's Emerald City, Sanford has the grit of Dorothy's Kansas. The city claims to have plans afoot to "beautify" the road that leads into Sanford from Orlando, but at trial time it looked like the highway that time forgot, lined as it was by a weary mix of auto repair shops, vacant lots, bail bond operations, cheap motels, and fast food joints with no hope of ever being franchised. Thrown in the mix were the inevitable Chinese restaurant or two, an Islamic center, and, directly across from the newish Seminole County Justice Center, a vestigial amusement park. At first glance, the media trucks at the Justice Center looked like an extension of "Fun World." Looks deceived. Although the media occasionally beclowned themselves in their reporting, nothing about the case they covered was amusing.

To park, the visitor had to stop at four different informal checkpoints, all amiably staffed by sheriff's deputies. Guarding the courthouse itself, in addition to a half dozen or so uniformed personnel outside, were three groups of three deputies, each group manning a screening device. At the entrance to the smallish, understated, fifth-floor courtroom where George Zimmerman was being tried for second-degree murder was still another screening device and another deputy. The security may have seemed excessive, but the Zimmerman family did not think so. If the New Black Panther Party had rescinded its fatwa on "child killer" George Zimmerman, no one told them or the media.

On the first night of jury selection, June 10, Black Entertainment Television ran a well-produced but entirely unhelpful special, the message of which was implicit in its title: "Justice for Trayvon: Our Son Is Your Son."[1] Without intending to, the show revealed the dangers inherent in race-based television. It had an undeniable "us versus them" quality about it, the "them" being white America. The producers chose not to mention Zimmerman's ethnicity, his civil rights activism, or the many and terrifying threats against his life. They did, however, see fit to highlight a few trivial slights to Martin's memory and some unkind tweets to his celebrity supporters. To its humble credit, "Justice for Trayvon" closed with an appeal for peace should Zimmerman be acquitted, but it would have done much better to educate its audience as to the reasons why he might be.

The protestors who showed up at the courthouse during the first week of jury selection did not much resemble the throngs that unnerved Sanford officials in March 2012. They were fewer in number and, on average, considerably whiter. Seminole County NAACP president Turner Clayton Jr. had his excuses ready. "The so-called 'demonstration area' that has been designated you will not see us protesting in that particular area cause no one tells us where to go, how long to stay, what to do, and what to say," said Clayton.[2] The paucity of the crowd at a church rally on the opening day of the trial, however, suggested another reason for the NAACP's reluctance to jam at the courthouse. They were afraid not enough people would show. Of the protestors who did make it to the courthouse, many wore hoodies—something of a commitment on a June day in Florida—and some proudly carried the banners of the Revolutionary Communist Party, USA. "The Whole Damn System Is Guilty," read one of the posters. "Revolution—Nothing Less," said another. Zimmerman had always been a pawn in a larger game. These protestors just made it obvious.

Jury selection, a tedious affair even in a celebrated trial, served as an ad hoc focus group on American media habits. Defense attorney Don West summed up the thrust of it with a totally unexpected knock-knock joke at the outset of the defense's opening statement. "Knock-knock," said West. "Who's there?" he continued. "George Zimmerman. George Zimmerman who? All right, good, you're on the jury."[3] What impressed observers on either side of the divide was just how many people—many of them well educated and employed—could have known so little about the most divisive criminal case in the nation and the most disruptive in the history of Seminole County. Several potential jurors, most of them female, admitted to having no real source of news other than what they picked up on Facebook or at the water cooler.

The court pulled its jury pool from the county at large, which skews whiter—82 percent—and more affluent than the city of Sanford. The majority of county residents, as testament, did not vote for Barack Obama in either of his two presidential elections. The percent of the population recorded as "African American" was roughly 10 percent. At the end of day seven of jury selection Judge Debra Nelson announced that the Court and the attorneys had screened the jury pool down to a final forty candidates.[4] Kudos to the blog *Legal Insurrection (LI)* for the good work its editors did in tracking jury selection.

The would-be jurors proved to be a diverse lot with a wide range of opinions. During his voir dire (preliminary examination to determine a juror's competency), potential juror B35, a black male, unsettled those who think in stereotypes by referring to Sean Hannity and Bill O'Reilly as "Sean" and "Bill." He watched both of their shows on Fox News. Prospective juror B12, a female, recalled seeing a picture of Trayvon Martin as "a kid" and not much more. B29, also a female, may have inspired the knock-knock joke. "I don't like watching the news, period," she told West. "I don't read any newspapers, don't watch the news." She had "no idea" about the case. B37, a female, was not at all unique in expressing her distrust of the media. She was just more colorful. As the admitted owner of three dogs, four cats, a parrot, a crow with one wing, and two lizards, she credibly argued that the best use of a newspaper was to line "the parrot's cage." Andrew Branca, the author of *The Law of Self Defense* and writing for *Legal Insurrection*, described B54, a middle-aged male, as "by far [the] most informed juror so far."[5] He didn't have a prayer of making the final cut. Neither did B86, a woman who told the court, and I quote, "Trayvon Martin is expelled from school and if it hadn't been out there wouldn't have happened."[6]

Easily the most entertaining of the prospective jurors was E7, later outed as Jerry Counelis, an underemployed painter and musician in his fifties. When originally questioned, Counelis told the court that he chose not to discuss the case because he was wary of "making enemies," having seen the people around him "get so heated" in their conversations.[7] As to his own opinion, he believed that people were "perfectly within their rights to defend themselves,"[8] but he had yet to come to any conclusions about the case. Well, not exactly. When Judge Nelson asked him if he had ever contributed to the Facebook site "Coffee Party Progressives," he admitted he had.[9] His postings, in fact, suggested that Counelis was something of a mole trying to burrow his way into the courtroom.

"'Justice' IS coming," promised Counelis on Facebook.[10] He railed about "a corrupt City Police" that started "stonewalling" in the very minutes after the Martin shooting lest they be held liable for collaborating with an armed menace like Zimmerman. "But with the noise WE made," he added, "it couldn't be covered up."[11] Counelis injected the only bit of drama that first week when he returned to the courthouse the day after being dismissed, complaining that his anonymity had been breached and threatening to sue. Sheriff's deputies, who finally got to see some action, escorted him away.

It is a truism among attorneys that securing a favorable jury is less about selecting friendly jurors than de-selecting unfriendly ones. The defense scored a minor win when attorney Mark O'Mara questioned what gender-neutral/race-neutral criteria prosecutors had used in striking four consecutive white women. Unimpressed by their answer, Judge Nelson placed two of them on the jury: B76, a middle-aged woman who knew that Zimmerman had been injured and didn't trust the media; and E6, a mother and wife of gun owners, who had little knowledge of the case. At the end of the process, the six surviving candidates were all female. Although none were said to be black, the one Latina among the six, B29, the woman who had "no idea" about the case, appeared to be of African descent. "What I do think we have," said O'Mara afterwards, "and I'm very happy with this, is six jurors who have told us that they'll be fair and impartial."[12]

As time would tell, O'Mara had reason to be pleased. In the pro-Martin camp, however, the first faint rumbles were heard that the State may not have been playing to win. Among the rumblers was Al Sharpton. "I would hope that we get fairness," he said on the day the jury was selected. "I think, though, we must deal with what the obvious is in terms of what the county demographics are, what is on the jury." The juror that concerned him most was B-37, she with the three dogs, four cats, a parrot, a crow with one wing, two lizards, and a "concealed weapons permit."[13]

33

F-BOMBING THE BOURGEOISIE

*I*N A CRIMINAL TRIAL like *State of Florida v. George Zimmerman*, the prosecution goes first with its direct examination, a major advantage. The State presents those witnesses that it thinks will solidify its case. The defense cross-examines them hoping to limit the damage. The prosecution redirects, and the defense recrosses. In this trial, Judge Debra Nelson presided.

Representing the State as lead attorney was Bernie de la Rionda, "the bald dude" as his star witness would later call him. Backing up de la Rionda was John Guy, a toothsome young assistant state attorney straight out of central casting. Both had considerable experience trying murder cases, de la Rionda in particular. When the FBI presented de la Rionda with the Director's Community Leadership Award in 2010, the presenter evoked de la Rionda's "legendary" reputation as a prosecutor. That reputation would be sorely tested. Orchestrating the affair for the State was state attorney Angela Corey, who frequently took her place in the front row of the courtroom.[1]

Defense attorney Mark O'Mara was better known for his commentary on HLN during the Casey Anthony trial than for any case he had tried on his own. A native New Yorker in his late fifties, O'Mara seemed younger than his age and as far removed from his roots in Queens as de la Rionda was from his in Cuba. Unlike many defense attorneys who have handled high-profile cases, O'Mara was still doing divorce work at the time he took on Zimmerman as a client. In selecting Don West as cocounsel, O'Mara rescued the folksy, quietly humorous death penalty specialist from the federal public defender's office in Orlando. The two were friends before the trial. They meshed well.[2] In the movie version, casting widely over time, Jimmy Stewart plays O'Mara. Robert Duvall plays West. A young Kevin Costner plays Guy. The short bald character actor with the glasses and mustache whose name you can never quite remember plays de la Rionda, although Paul Giamatti might do in a pinch. And Kathy Bates plays the dual role of the flashy Angela Corey and the frumpy Judge Nelson.

At the outset of the trial, most media commentators presented the case to their audiences as though it were a perfectly legitimate exercise of state power, one whose outcome was too close to call. Florida's generous sunshine laws should have armed them all with enough information to be skeptical of the State's case, but either out of some unspoken journalistic ethic or their own biases, most chose not to know any more than they wanted to. The *Washington Post*'s Jonathan Capehart fell comfortably into this category.

Capehart predicted two "pivotal moments" in the trial to come. One would be the testimony of Witness 8, the State's star witness. The other would be the defense's resolve to keep Zimmerman off the stand. Said Capehart in conclusion, still stuck on the imagery first introduced by Martin family publicists, "From the precious little DNA evidence to back up his story to Trayvon's hands [sic], Zimmerman could be his own worst enemy in explaining how he killed a teenager armed with only a bag of Skittles and iced tea."[3]

Meanwhile, on the eve of the trial itself, the Treepers were doing the work that the *Washington Post* used to do, and still occasionally does when an issue fits its agenda. "The hourglass sand has been disappearing rapidly as of late—[a]ll building toward this date," wrote Sundance. "After spending thousands of hours, and thousands of miles, on this journey I can say with relative confidence the 'TRUTH' about Trayvon in Miami-Dade is far worse than even the most die-hard insider would grasp."[4] As Sundance related, the *Treehouse* had begun emergency legal motions to shed light on the issues at hand, particularly the efforts of the Miami-Dade School District and its allies in state government to bury what should have been Martin's criminal record.

"For the past several months," Sundance reported, "we have been engaged in a Truth Search against multiple self-interested parties all with a vested interest in keeping the Truth hidden." Sundance believed the State of Florida was fully aware of what secrets the vault files from the M-DSPD internal affairs investigation held. Sundance knew that at least one member of the FDLE Miami-Dade field office was given this information as a result of a phone call from Angela Corey's office, and that person in turn sent it to the prosecutors in Jacksonville. Sundance knew, too, that the parties at risk made a coordinated decision to stonewall the release of all relevant information. Was Sundance confident that the *Treehouse* could secure the needed information in time or that Judge Nelson would even allow it? No, he was not, but, as he admitted, "We are at that point where, for the first time, I'm willing to engage the Defense Team directly."[5] The clock was ticking.

"Good morning," said John Guy to the six-woman jury on day one, minute one, of the trial.[6] From that benign moment on, Guy's opening statement was pure shock and awe, what the French might call épater la bourgeoisie or "shocking the middle class."

"F**king punks. These a**holes always get away," said Guy, dramatically repeating what George Zimmerman was alleged to have said that fateful night in February 2012. "Those were the words in that grown man's mouth as he followed a seventeen-year-old boy." Although Zimmerman most likely said, "It's fu**ing cold," the defense attorneys had to be a little relieved that Guy did not lead with "fu**ing coons," the words CNN once insisted Zimmerman had said. The defense did not bother to challenge the State's interpretation in any case—Zimmerman had confirmed the "punks" line to the Sanford police and on the *Hannity Show*—and the media did not comment on the word switch. The State so liked the "f**king punks" phrase that Guy repeated it several times and, in the process, assured that going forward the cable networks would broadcast the trial with a time delay.

Beyond the shock and awe, Guy had little else to say. To prove second-degree murder, prosecutors had to convince the jury that Zimmerman killed Martin with a "depraved mind," one moved by ill will, hatred, or spite. Despite that burden, Guy took only thirty minutes, an unusually brief exposition for a trial of this visibility. Guy compensated for a lack of tangible evidence with dramatic incantations of words like "profiled" and "chased" and "semi-automatic" as though these very words proved a hateful intent on Zimmerman's part. In his most dishonest moment, Guy addressed the repeated cries for help heard on the 9-1-1 tape. "You will hear screaming in the background," said Guy disingenuously. "Trayvon Martin was silenced immediately when the bullet fired passed through his heart."

Although he dared not say that Martin was doing the screaming—he would leave that job to Martin's mother—Guy implied as much and, so saying, further inflamed the low-information portion of a preheated national viewing audience. Even more inflammatory, Guy claimed Zimmerman did not shoot Trayvon Martin because he had to. "He shot him for the worst of all reasons," said Guy, "because he wanted to." To make this case, the prosecution interpreted every slight variation in Zimmerman's various retellings of the incident as one more thread in his "tangled web of lies."

"[Zimmerman] told the police that it was just after he hung up with Sean Noffke, the nonemergency dispatcher, that Trayvon Martin approached him, confronted him, said a couple of words to him, and then punched him and knocked him to the ground just moments after that," said Guy to the jury. "Ladies and gentlemen, that did not happen." As to what did happen, the prosecution left that to the defense to describe. This soon became a pattern.

"There are no winners here," said Don West once he got beyond the knock-knock joke. "George Zimmerman is not guilty of murder. He shot Trayvon Martin in self-defense after being viciously attacked." In the three hours that followed, the low-key West detailed with maps and photographs just how the attack took place. For the first time, millions of people across the nation heard that Martin, the cute little boy in the red Hollister shirt, may have assaulted George Zimmerman, the brooding thug of their imaginations. It was the day's real shocker. To the end, many would refuse to accept this scenario even as a possibility.

34

FERRETING OUT THE

FALSEHOODS

*A*T THE *TREEHOUSE,* the Treepers and their allies were, in real time, or something very close to it, reviewing the testimony of various witnesses for accuracy and honesty and noting any discrepancies they discovered. They called it "crowdsourcing."[1]

"So here's where EVERYONE comes in," posted Sundance on the opening day of the trial. Given their exhaustive research to date, the Treepers were aware of "hundreds of lies told by potential witnesses for the prosecution," some of them in legal affidavits and sworn statements. Those who made false statements in the past, Sundance continued, would either have to lie under oath or give a conflicting account. With all their other burdens, the defense attorneys might miss the lie the moment it occurred. To compensate, the Treepers would "crowd source the witnesses as they take the stand."[2]

For the eight administrators of the site, this meant spending every spare moment monitoring the many information streams that the Treepers sprung. To make this strategy pay off, the "admins" had to keep contributors focused and to discreetly triage their comments. If a certain insight might help the prosecutors—they were visiting the site too—the admins would quietly divert it into a private thread.

By trial time, this obscure little blog had become information central in *Florida v. Zimmerman.* Florida had on its side the State bureaucracies, the US Justice Department, the president of the United States, the BGI, the entertainment industry, and the mainstream media. Zimmerman had on his side two folksy local lawyers and their aides, an army of bloggers, and, most important, the truth. Despite the pressures, the Treepers had retained their integrity. Truth was still the coin of their realm. They cozied up to no one, not even defense attorneys Mark O'Mara and Don West, whom they criticized as warranted. If the attorneys wanted information, they came to the *Treehouse*. The Treepers did not go to them. This was an unprecedented battle formation in the history of American jurisprudence, and the major media did not even notice. Their talking heads prattled on about trivia utterly irrelevant to the jurors in Sanford—Don West's knock-knock joke consumed them for a day—while the bloggers unearthed new information and processed it swiftly.

By trial time the Treepers had plenty of help. DiWataman had his own obsessive-compulsive site. The *Smoking Gun* kept digging up provocative dirt. *TalkLeft*'s Jeralyn Merritt, the Colorado attorney who made her bones in the Duke lacrosse case, offered much useful analysis as well as a reminder that some liberals still cared about justice. Cornell law professor William Jacobson of the smart and popular *Legal Insurrection* blog featured Andrew Branca throughout the trial. An attorney and author of the book *The Law of Self Defense*, Branca knew the subject as well as anyone anywhere, and the *Treehouse* linked to his material regularly. Zimmerman's attorneys helped the information flow as well. On their *George Zimmerman Legal Case* site, they promptly posted all legal documents and provided much of the raw material for the bloggers. Mining the legal data, the social media sites, and the local reporting for evidence, several of the more sophisticated bloggers found evidence threads that eluded the attorneys. Some, like Sundance, went the extra mile, pounding the pavement like reporters of old and filing FOIA requests when the pavement wouldn't yield.

The strategy showed its value on the second day of the trial. The witness in question, Selene Bahadoor, lived in a townhome that overlooked the site of the shooting. A young, black professional with an attractive presence, Bahadoor told de la Rionda how the sound of a "no" or an "uhh" first alerted her to the drama about to follow. She then heard urgent footsteps moving from her left to her right, meaning away from the Green town house and toward the intersection of the dog walk and the cut-through, the T, as it came to be known. Her testimony suggested the possibility of one person pursuing another.[3] If credible, it would have given the State the opportunity to create a scenario plausible enough to support a second-degree murder verdict.

The State's story line might have played out as follows: In his unaccounted-for minutes, Martin made it back to Green's townhome. Both Green and Tracy Martin had said as much. "He was sitting on the porch and this man killed him," Green told a reporter the day after the shooting. In his unaccounted-for minutes, according to this scenario, Zimmerman tracked Martin to that porch, prompting Martin to flee back toward the T with Zimmerman in pursuit, thus the left-to-right footsteps that Bahadoor heard. At the T, Zimmerman challenged Martin, and Martin responded as a scared child might. Embarrassed at his thrashing, Zimmerman murdered Martin with ill will, spite, and/or malice. The State hinted at these details but never quite told this story. They did not do so because of what happened in the cross-examination.

O'Mara sensed something amiss with Bahadoor's testimony and zoomed in. In her sworn deposition and other previous statements to the authorities, O'Mara did not remember any mention of a pursuit of any kind. He handed her one prior statement of hers after another and asked her to point out any reference to a left-to-right motion. She could find none. "When was the first time that you told anyone about this 'left-to-right' motion you've described to us today?" O'Mara asked her. "Is it in fact today, here in court, the first time you've ever told anyone about it?" Said Bahadoor, "It could be." What O'Mara implied but did not say is that the prosecution had coached her to say this in her pretrial preparation just a few days prior, a judicial no-no.

This much O'Mara discerned on his own. What followed had the scent of blogosphere about it, much as did the outing of Jerry Counelis. After establishing that Bahadoor's credibility was suspect, O'Mara probed as to why that might be so, asking Bahadoor if she had any particular sympathy for the Martin family. "I have sympathy for both families," she answered dismissively. This proved to be a perfect setup line for O'Mara: "But you 'liked' the Facebook page for the Martin family, but not the Facebook page for the Zimmerman family." Bahadoor claimed disingenuously that the opportunity never presented itself to like the latter.

In his redirect, de la Rionda tried to rehabilitate Bahadoor. In a strategy born of desperation, he led her to say that she had not mentioned the left-to-right movement previously because no one had asked her about it. He reminded the jury, too, that she had been a reluctant witness all along. He suggested that she was not eager to be famous or to go on television. In fact, she had not even volunteered information to the police in the hours after the shooting. Bahadoor followed de la Rionda's lead without resistance. On recross, O'Mara quickly dispelled the illusion of a reticent, impartial witness, "Isn't it true that you've actually been on national TV about this case?" he asked.

"No," said Bahadoor, "I did a video, but they never aired it." O'Mara pressed on: "But you wanted to be on TV. A television journalist interviewed you on camera for half an hour; you talked all about the case with them." Bahadoor claimed that she chose not to let the video air, that she had only considered appearing on video to bring attention to the shooting. "Because you thought that George Zimmerman killed Trayvon Martin improperly and should be prosecuted," said O'Mara.

"I never said that," Bahadoor shot back. "But you signed this petition, did you not?" said O'Mara as he held up the super Irish Kevin Cunningham's petition "Prosecute the killer of our son, 17-year-old Trayvon Martin." Bahadoor was one of the two million to sign it, and she could not deny that she had. This was not quite a Perry Mason moment, but it was close. O'Mara had just stripped Bahadoor of whatever value she might have had as a prosecution witness.

O'Mara did not discuss the source of his information, but he had two comely young women working with him, one black and one white, affectionately nicknamed Cobra and Viper by the *Treehouse*. "I'm always watching them research and relay info to O'Mara & West. Today the blonde said something to George at the end of the day during all the sidebar impeaching stuff & it looked for the first time like he was genuinely relieved and had to hide a smile," commented one Treeper. Added another, "I want to know what they're so busy reading back there on their puters . . . . Every time I catch a glimpse of a computer screen in the courtroom, I'm looking for the signature brick edging, lol."[4] That brick edging was the *Treehouse*'s distinctive background graphic, and it had indeed been spotted on a relevant "puter" more than once.

The Bahadoor smackdown was a decisive early turning point in the trial. "Her testimony and credibility," said *Legal Insurrection*'s Andrew Branca, were "utterly, indeed humiliatingly, crushed before the jury."[5] In fact, it was Bahadoor's sister who, on March 26, 2012, according to investigator T. C. O'Steen, "heard running outside and looked out her bedroom window. She looked out and saw shadows running from left to right. She heard someone say 'yo' or 'no.'"[6] De la Rionda could be forgiven for confusing the two. He wasn't there to interview Bahadoor, but John Guy was. Although cynics in the Martin camp might suspect Guy of ulterior motives, if they had spent their energy "crowdsourcing," instead of griping on cable talk shows, they might have been able to compensate.

35

ECHOING THE AGITPROP

*B*AHADOOR WAS NOT THE ONLY WITNESS to yield to the siren song of the media. She had enough neighborhood company to launch a Twin Lakes association for the easily spun. Two of her compatriots followed her to the stand on day three of the trial. Their testimony provided direct proof, if any were needed, of the corrupting influence of months and months of media disinformation. Although neither saw much of anything that rainy night in February 2012, the media managed to convince both of them, in defiance of the evidence, that George Zimmerman was the aggressor and Trayvon Martin the boy calling for help.

The media's effect on Jeannee Manalo would have been comical were there not so much at stake. The foreign-born Manalo lived with her husband on the west side of the dog walk, very near the site of the encounter. She gave her first interview to the Florida Department of Law Enforcement (FDLE) on March 20, 2012, three weeks after the shooting. She admittedly did not see much. She looked out from her town house window and "saw two shadow" [*sic*]. She added. "One was on top of the other. I don't know which one."[1] Nor at the time could she distinguish which of the two was bigger.

By the time of the trial, however, Manalo had concluded that the one on top, "just hitting down," had to be Zimmerman, as "the top was bigger than the bottom." The photos of Martin in the media convinced her he was the smaller of the two. O'Mara produced some of the photos she might have seen: the iconic photo of a youthful Martin in his red Hollister shirt, two photos of a preteen football player, and the photo of Martin in his hoodie. Manalo innocently confirmed these images as the source of her perception. In reality, of course, Martin was at least four inches taller than Zimmerman and, at 158 pounds, all but fully developed. Skimming the media as she did, Manalo had no idea Martin was that big.

Jayne Surdyka, a fiftyish blonde, lived alone in a townhome just north of the east-west cut-through where it intersected the dog walk, the T. She told the court that she initially heard a confrontation between two males, one with a dominant, aggressive voice and the other with a softer, meeker tone. "It was someone being very aggressive and angry at someone," she told the court. Although her view was obscured by the rain and the darkness, and she, too, just saw shadows, the sounds of violence sufficiently alarmed her to call 9-1-1. The State played all sixteen hysterical minutes of the call. Aggravating the hysteria was Surdyka's profound sense of isolation. Even after the police arrived, the very patient male dispatcher proved unable to calm her. When he recommended she go stay with family or friends, Surdyka, a former schoolteacher, confessed to having neither.

At the time of the shooting, Surdyka knew nothing about Martin or Zimmerman and had not talked to either one of them. From the imagery she gleaned in the media, she presumed that Zimmerman was the aggressor. "I truly believe the second yell for help was a yelp," said Surdyka. "It was excruciating. I really felt it was a boy's voice." Before the trial, she had never seen a photo of a bloody Zimmerman, a testament in itself to the breadth of media bias and the myopia of even college-educated professionals. It was clear to anyone watching that Surdyka's ignorance helped preserve her misperceptions.

Defense attorney Don West led Surdyka to concede that seventeen-year-old boys often have deep and mature voices, a fact that should have been obvious to her as a teacher. Since the defense was not allowed to reference Martin's social media pages, West was unable to enter into evidence the Martin memorial page on which a girlfriend had written that she loved "his deep voice."[2] Yet even if he had been able to, it would not likely have shaken Surdyka's confidence in her initial observations.

Indeed, despite all evidence to the contrary, she even continued to insist that she heard three shots.

As was true with Bahadoor, Surdyka's search for meaning—she occasionally and falsely listed herself as a "former Olympian"—led her to a new role as scorned eyewitness. Too rattled to even speak to the police on the night of the shooting, Surdyka was soon enough appearing on national television complaining about the lack of police follow-through. Near the end of West's cross-examination, he asked her about appearing on TV, and Surdyka denied it. "Really?" asked West.

SURDYKA: Well, just the one time on *Anderson Cooper*, but only on condition that I not be named or identified.

WEST: Weren't you also on television another time?

SURDYKA: Well, yes, I was videotaped by another journalist.

WEST: And that was played on TV several times?

SURDYKA: I only saw it once.

WEST: So you were taped, and you saw yourself on TV, that second time?

SURDYKA: Yes.

The State called still another female eyewitness to testify, a blonde Columbian named Selma Mora Lamilla. As Lamilla admitted through an interpreter, she and her roommate did not see anything until after the shot was fired. When she did look out, she saw Zimmerman on top of Martin. This revelation may have roused the ill-informed, but it only confirmed what Zimmerman said about the sequence of events. After the shot was fired, he told the Sanford police, "I slid out from underneath him and got on top of the suspect holding his hands away from his body." He never claimed otherwise.

Those paying close attention found it curious that the State called Lamilla to testify but not her outspoken, English-speaking roommate, Mary Cutcher. In the six-week-long hysteria between Martin's shooting and Zimmerman's arrest, Cutcher, a thirtyish blonde, was easily the most visible of the eyewitnesses. Her message was one that the media wanted to hear: the police were ignoring eyewitnesses whose testimony challenged Zimmerman's innocence. At the height of the post-shooting furor, Cutcher told David Weigel of *Slate* that after giving her initial testimony, she called the Sanford police several times and did not hear back. When the police did respond to her calls they had little interest in what she had to say. "We were told, 'you guys just need to calm down,'" Cutcher told Weigel. "They never followed up after that."[3]

To spread this message, Cutcher appeared on local TV, on CNN's *Anderson Cooper* show, on *Dateline NBC*, at press conferences with Benjamin Crump, and at rallies with the Martin family. "I don't know this family. I'm only trying to help," Cutcher said at a March 2012 press conference. "I think that they [the Sanford police] are trying to cover up something that they made a mistake and, honestly, I feel like they're taking the light off them and trying to discredit my statement."[4] The media then sought out more reticent witnesses like Surdyka, Lamilla, and Chahadoor to echo Cutcher's theme.

Although Cutcher admittedly did not see the struggle that led up to the shooting, she, like Surdyka, fully bought into the Trayvon-as-child narrative that the family's advisers had crafted from day one. "It sounded young. It didn't sound like a grown man, is my point," Cutcher told NBC's Lester Holt of the screaming she heard that night. "It sounded to me like someone was in distress and it wasn't like a crying, sobbing boo-hoo; it was a definite whine."[5] The online version of that *Dateline* piece was headlined, "Witnesses describe Trayvon Martin's final moments; Parents say 'He was headed on the right path.'"[6]

No, Trayvon was not on the right path, nor were the media. Ignored by the press in what Weigel described as Cutcher's "media tour" were the words Cutcher told the 9-1-1 operator on the night in question, namely that there was "a black guy standing up over him [the shooting victim]."[7] This call was available to the media as early as March 16, 2012. By not listening, they could take Cutcher seriously. The State could not afford to. With a sharp-edged question or two, the defense would have cut a swath through the fog of Cutcher's memory that would have embarrassed the State even more than it did Cutcher.

36

PROFILING THE PROFILER

*D*AY THREE SERVED UP THE MOST target-rich environment for crowdsourcing that the trial would present. Center
stage that afternoon was the elusive Dee Dee, Witness 8, the
real-life Rachel Jeantel, the plus-size, American–born daughter
of Haitian and Dominican parents. Nineteen at the time of the trial,
Jeantel defied easy description. On her first afternoon on the stand, she
was sassy, defiant, and often incomprehensible. On the second day, she
was sluggish, depressive, and still very nearly incomprehensible. Before she
was through, she would test the patience of the prosecution, the defense,
the judge, the jury, and especially the court reporter.

During her first afternoon of testimony, de la Rionda prodded Jeantel
through the familiar story she had been coached imperfectly to tell: she
was on the phone with Martin; a man in a truck was observing him; she
encouraged Martin to run home; he tried to; the man followed him and
kept getting closer. Finally, a breathless Martin turned to Zimmerman and
said, "Why you following me for?" to which Zimmerman responded, "What
are you doing around here?" He then bumped or pushed Martin. The fatal
altercation began. Martin cried out, "Get off, get off." The phone went dead.

The uncoached highlight of the day, arguably of the trial, occurred
when de la Rionda asked Jeantel how Martin first described Zimmerman.
According to Jeantel, he sized Zimmerman up as "a creepy ass cracka," a

slur she liked enough to repeat. In so saying, she introduced a phrase into the American lexicon that may outlast the memory of Trayvon Martin. She also reversed the understanding of just who profiled whom. This was a point Don West did not hesitate to make in his cross-examination. In fact, he repeated the "creepy ass cracka" line at least twice as often as Jeantel did. As he stressed to Jeantel and jurors, "[the incident] was racial because Trayvon Martin put race in this."[1]

In fact, however, West may have misunderstood the meaning of the phrase. The *Urban Dictionary* defines an "ass cracker" as "one who engages in anal sex." In other words, Martin may have thought Zimmerman a homosexual, even a "rapist" according to Jeantel. This was a point that Jeantel repeated in posttrial interviews; so, curiously, would de la Rionda. Given the unintelligibility of Jeantel's speech, West seemed to have missed it.

In his cross-examination, West established for the jury the many lies that Jeantel and her handlers had been telling, some from her first introduction to the larger world in March 2012. The media already knew about them. The jury did not. No, Jeantel was not sixteen and a minor as Crump first insisted. She was eighteen at the time of the shooting. And no, she had not been hospitalized on hearing of Martin's death. That was pure fabrication. The prosecution had trouble as well with the age of its first witness, Brandy Green's son, Chad Joseph. During his opening statement, John Guy insisted Chad was twelve at the time of the shooting. In the media accounts at the time, he was alternately said to be thirteen or fourteen. Sixteen months later, at the trial, Chad identified himself as a fifteen-year-old.

West touched on many of the inconsistencies in Jeantel's storytelling over time: the unaccounted-for twenty-five minutes between Martin's leaving the 7-Eleven and arriving at the Retreat at Twin Lakes; the unaccounted-for four minutes between the time Martin ran for Green's town house and the time Zimmerman allegedly confronted him; her conveniently recovered memory of Martin yelling, "Get off, get off" after his phone was knocked free. But West scored major points on one seeming discrepancy: the change in Zimmerman's response to Martin's first question.

Following West's circuitous interrogation was not easy, but here is the gist of it. In her phone interview with Crump, Jeantel recounted that when Martin asked Zimmerman, "Why are you following me?" Zimmerman responded nonthreateningly, "What are you talking about?" However, in her interview with de la Rionda two weeks later, as West pointed out, she claimed that Zimmerman answered Martin with the confrontational response, "What are you doin' around here?" This shift mattered.

Jeantel's revised statement, argued *LI*'s Branca, "was much more in line with what the State need[ed] to support the arrest and prosecution of Zimmerman. Indeed, Jeantel's newly revealed testimony formed the very backbone of the State's affidavit of probable cause."[2] Although Branca was reporting close to real time, he understood the importance of what West was doing.

This was sharp-eyed work on West's part. As he understood, and as everyone else in the media missed, Crump had finessed Jeantel's testimony *during* his much-interrupted, overly edited phone conversation with Jeantel. After Jeantel had Zimmerman say, "What are you doin' around here?" Crump intervened: "I'm a, I'm a hold for a second. I just want to ask the part about . . . the alt . . . when you say you heard the other person yeah, you know like you told Mr. Tracy and Ms. Sybrina this when you say he loud, 'It was like what you doing in here and stuff.'"

In that original Crump interview, Jeantel got the hint and immediately changed Zimmerman's response to the one Crump wanted: "And the man come said, 'What you doing around here?' And then the man, Trayvon come ask him, 'Why you following me for?' And the man said, 'What you doing around here?'" In the edited transcript ABC and others produced, Crump's deception was lost. West caught it. So did Branca.

De la Rionda did not refute West. Like West, de la Rionda had to suspect that much of Jeantel's testimony had been fabricated with Crump's help, including her alleged overhearing of Martin's final exchange with Zimmerman. One wonders whether he had gotten lost trying to follow Jeantel's mumbled responses or whether he had grown queasy about his own role in her fabrications. Once again, though, the skeptics in his own camp had to question whether he was actually playing to win.

Had Jeantel been sharper, West might have enjoyed picking her testimony apart, but she was so sadly slow that at one point she had to confess her inability to read back a letter that she herself had dictated. When this American-born high school senior told the court, "I don't read cursive," she made more than a few people question the public education enterprise, particularly in Miami-Dade. She also turned herself from an object of scorn to one of pity. West had to tread carefully.

That he did, shifting the blame for the prevarications from Jeantel to the people who had put her in that awkward position. With great patience, West reconstructed her reluctant interview with de la Rionda in April 2012. As Jeantel told the story, a two-car caravan drove to the house where she was staying and escorted her back to Sybrina Fulton's living room. In the cars were Crump, Fulton, and de la Rionda, among others. During her sworn interview with de la Rionda, Jeantel sat next to Fulton on the couch while Fulton's attorneys hovered nearby. As Branca saw it, "A more coercive environment for the taking of a witness's statement is hard to imagine."[4] West offered Jeantel the excuse that she'd altered her testimony lest it upset Fulton, who was sitting next to her, weeping. Jeantel took the bait. She made it as clear as she could in her butchered English that she had changed some details to spare Fulton any further pain. It was hard to tell whether Jeantel meant what she said, but for the prosecution, there was no taking that admission back.

Jeantel dismayed more than a few commentators who had been expecting a genuine star witness, but not the painfully predictable Sunny Hostin, CNN's "legal analyst." Her summary of Jeantel's testimony to Anderson Cooper showed just how single-minded at least some major players in the media remained:

> I thought that she was a credible witness. I thought it was raw, I thought it was un-coached. I thought that she spoke like a teenager, and what I thought was very important is everything she says, Anderson, is corroborated. She says she was on the phone. Well, there are phone records. She said the amount of time that she was on the phone with Trayvon Martin. Well, there are records of that. She is at least the third or fourth witness that contradicts directly what George Zimmerman told police, his version of events. And so I think when you look at it in context, it's very, very helpful to the prosecution.[5]

This was madness. Beyond the mere fact of the phone call, nothing was corroborated. Jeantel's testimony was much more helpful to the defense than the prosecution. Martin's humblest fans in the blogosphere saw Jeantel's testimony more clearly than Hostin did. For some, that day marked a turning point—the first time they sensed that Zimmerman just might be acquitted. Rather than digging up facts as the Treepers did, they took to Twitter to express their outrage. What follows were some of the more printable threats:[6]

If they don't kill Zimmerman Ima kill me a cracka.

I'll kill him. George Zimmerman goin walk.

I swear ill kill Zimmerman my damn self

Bruh ill kill George Zimmerman ass

Watching the Zimmerman trial. If he don't get life ill kill him myself.

Ima kill a white person in self defense if Zimmerman go free lol on everything.

If George Zimmerman win I'm gonna kill a fat white boy dat look lik George Zimmerman I swear lol

If Zimmerman get off ima kill him myself since no one wanna take care of his Mexican burrito eatin ass.

As for the Treepers, Jeantel surprised them only in her oddball extravagance. They had been anticipating this train wreck since Benjamin Crump tied the sixteen-year-old "Dee Dee" to the tracks some fifteen months earlier. "Remove your snark hats, remove your emotional dropped jaw, and focus, focus, focus on what she said today," posted Sundance that first afternoon. He asked his fellow Treepers to compare what she said on the stand with her original interview with Ben Crump and ABC, her first written statement, and her first interview with the Florida Department of Law Enforcement. "After you have provided the context for the falsehood identified," wrote Sundance, "then outline the possible line of inquiry that West/O'Mara might take to expose the lie in court. Again, be intellectual in analysis—not emotional. Provide the substance and [h]ow the question would be appropriately framed."[7]

One point that West did not raise, but that Sundance did, was how de la Rionda could have interrogated a girl he thought to be a minor without the permission of a parent. As Jeantel made clear, the caravan picked her up at a friend's house. According to Jeantel's testimony, her mother was in Haiti at the time of Fulton's first approach and may have been two weeks later when this interview took place. More than one Treeper noticed something that the defense overlooked or chose not to pursue—Jeantel's off-handed observation that she and Martin feared that Zimmerman might be gay. Said Treeper "Fred12" in response, "So Trayvon was a homophobe?"[8]

The Treepers also noticed Jeantel's casual admission that not all of the texts sent from her phone were sent by her. If not she, they wondered, then who? Others were curious about Jeantel's odd description of where she and Martin rediscovered each other. "He came around my area," said Jeantel cryptically. She tracked the renewal of this relationship—they had not really seen each other in six years—to February 1, 2012, three weeks before Martin left for Sanford. They had only seen each other a few times, and although unattractive and admittedly not his girlfriend, she quickly developed a bond with Martin around their shared interests. For Martin, as Sundance noted, those interests included "Dope, Weed, Guns, and "gangsta-isms.""[9]

Unpaid and underappreciated, Sundance was doing the best reporting in America on the case. At the time of Jeantel's appearance, he was in the Miami area, digging into Martin's background, especially his relationship with the Miami-Dade School Police Department. One thing he could be sure of, however, was that certain people did not welcome the work he was doing. The school police, for instance, were "slow-walking" his FOIA requests through the system, but that was the least of his concerns. During the second day of Jeantel's testimony, Sundance called a contact in the media. He gave that person his full name, his address, and his social security number, "just in case something happens to me." He had reason to worry. That morning someone had surgically removed the valve stems from two of his tires, leaving them terminally flat. That same person had also taken a Miami-Dade Police business card, sliced off the name on the bottom, and written one word on the back—*STOP!!*[10]

37

THROWING DOWN, MMA-STYLE

*P*ROSECUTORS CALLED JONATHAN GOOD as a witness only because they had to. If the State had not called him, the defense surely would have. Good was Witness #6, a thirtyish college graduate who worked in finance, the man whose testimony the State knew from the beginning would subvert its case. Good lived in the Retreat at Twin Lakes. On the night of February 26, 2012, the altercation between Zimmerman and Martin ended up right on his doorstep. He was the only witness who had an outside light on. His testimony was worth more than all the other witnesses' combined.[1] Several other eyewitnesses had already testified, as artfully steered by the defense, that Good was the only eyewitness to step outside and address the combatants.

Of all the witnesses Good was also the most succinct and coherent. He kept his testimony clinical and dispassionate. He betrayed no obvious sympathy for Zimmerman or Martin. He answered de la Rionda's perfunctory questions—"Can you recall what [TV] program you were watching?"—as though they mattered. If it were not for the content, the observer would have thought him an excellent witness for the prosecution. Yet, as would prove true with many of the State's witnesses, the longer Good remained on the witness stand, the more problems he created for the prosecution. Observed Andrew Branca in *Legal Insurrection*, "The testimony of State witness Jonathan Good was remarkably, almost shockingly, destructive to the State's theory of the case."[2]

In his cross-examination, O'Mara raised one issue with Good that most trial observers overlooked: Martin had no apparent intention of stopping his assault on Zimmerman. In response to a question from O'Mara, Good recalled that he had said to the pair, "What's going on? Cut it out. Stop." O'Mara then asked, "[Martin] kept on doing what he was doing?" Again, without obvious emotion, Good affirmed that he had. The implication was that if Good's threat to call 9-1-1 could not slow Martin down, nothing Zimmerman could say would stop him, nothing he could do, nothing, that is, save shooting him.

Exploiting the rule of completeness, O'Mara took the opportunity to read back to Good what he told investigator Chris Serino immediately after the shooting: "So I open my door. It was a black man with a black hoodie on top of the other, either a white guy or now I found out I think it was a Hispanic guy with a red sweatshirt on the ground yelling out help! And I tried to tell them, get out of here, you know, stop or whatever, and then one guy on top in the black hoodie was pretty much just throwing down blows on the guy kind of MMA-style." To repeat, "MMA-style" means mixed martial arts. O'Mara continued:

O'MARA: OK. And do you stand by that today, that what you saw was a Ground-and-Pound event?

GOOD: It looked like that position was a Ground-and-Pound type of position, but I couldn't tell 100 percent that there were actually fists hitting faces.

O'MARA: But you did see [reading] "the guy in the top in the black hoodie pretty much just throwing down blows on the guy kind of MMA-style."

GOOD: Meaning arm motions going down on the person on the bottom. Correct.

In confirming the accuracy of his early statements, Good validated Zimmerman's version of the event and established beyond any reasonable doubt that it was Zimmerman who was yelling out for help. The media had no excuse for not anticipating Good's testimony. Good had talked to an Orlando TV station the day after the shooting. "The guy on bottom who I believe had a red sweater on was yelling to me, 'Help, help,'" Good told the reporter. "I told them to stop and I was calling 9-1-1." For reasons of their own, the media chose to keep alive the increasingly pointless debate as to who was the source of those screams.

Guy and de la Rionda had first spoken to Good in March 2012, just days after they had taken over the case. With full indifference to prosecutorial ethics, the memorandum summarizing this interview stressed only the actions that Good did not hear or see. "When he opened the door, he only placed one foot onto the patio. He did not go all the way outside. He definitely did not go out onto the grass," wrote T. C. O'Steen. "Good advised that during the struggle between the two guys, he never heard anything that sounded like a fist hitting another nor did he ever hear any sounds of someone's head or other body part hitting the concrete hard."[3] In the early days at least, the prosecutors did not want to hear any facts that might have cleared Zimmerman. The media obliged them. At the trial, however, they and the media finally had to face the flimsiness of the case they had collectively sold America.

38

SCORING FOR THE

OPPOSITION

WHEN CAPTAIN ALEXIS CARTER, US Army judge advocate general, entered the courtroom on day eight of the trial, he gave Zimmerman supporters in the larger audience pause. Well-dressed and good-looking, this African American army officer had come to court as a witness for the prosecution. As he explained his credentials and his role as Zimmerman's criminal justice teacher at Seminole State College, those watching had to sense that whatever he said about Zimmerman would have weight commensurate with his stature. Richard Mantei, the youthful, overeager third attorney on the prosecution team, walked Carter through his coursework for one particular purpose. Mantei wanted to establish that when Zimmerman told Sean Hannity in a televised interview that he had not known about Florida's Stand Your Ground law until after the shooting, he was lying. To make this point, Mantei asserted that Zimmerman was an A student, and Carter confirmed him to be "one of the better students in the class."[1]

Whatever good Carter did for the prosecution was undone by the time Don West finished introducing his client. "You see George over here?" said West as Zimmerman stood and nodded. Carter gave him a friendly wave. "How ya doing, George?" he said, eliciting in the process a shy smile out of the otherwise stone-faced defendant. In his opening statement Don West had said, "There are no monsters here." With a wave and a smile,

Captain Carter confirmed the truth of West's contention.

From that moment on, almost everything Carter said damaged the prosecution's case. To the growing frustration of Mantei, Carter and West engaged in a good-natured discussion of Florida's self-defense law that served ultimately to justify Zimmerman's action on the night of February 26. *LI*'s Branca described it, in fact, as "a legal seminar for the jury."[2] Said West to Carter at one point, "I know you're taking us to school," but it was the cagey West who was taking the jury to school as he worked his way around prosecutorial objections and finessed Carter through the practical application of the law of self-defense.

"You don't have to wait until you're almost dead before you can defend yourself?" West asked Carter at one point. "No, I would advise you probably don't do that," said Carter with enough good humor to cause the audience to laugh and Zimmerman to smile. When West opined that you never know for sure when that ultimate moment will be, Carter answered, "No, unfortunately, you don't."

Carter was not the only prosecution witness to score what soccer fans call an "own goal," meaning a goal for the other team. Others before him had done much the same, at least four of them consequentially. Among them was Sean Noffke, whose reasoned advice on George Zimmerman's nonemergency call made him America's most famous police dispatcher. Assistant state attorney John Guy had the congenial thirtysomething Noffke explain the mechanics of taking and responding to a call. In his subsequent questions Guy hoped to get Noffke to concede that Zimmerman had exceeded the role of a neighborhood watch coordinator and that he did so with something like vengeance, given that the "f**king punks" were always getting away.

In addition, Guy planted the seed that after Zimmerman finished the call with the dispatcher, he set out to hunt Martin down. The suggestion was that by first agreeing to meet the police at the community mailboxes, then at his truck, and then just through phone contact, Zimmerman would have had the freedom to roam and stalk. But Guy recognized the weak point in his own line of attack and exposed it before the defense had the opportunity. In fact, Noffke did not order Zimmerman to cease following Martin because he lacked the authority to do so. He was not a police officer. And as a dispatcher, liability concerns prevented him from giving commands of any sort. He could only make suggestions. This essentially put a lie to the myth that Zimmerman had "disobeyed" the Sanford police.

At the beginning of jury selection, an Associated Press (AP) reporter wrote, "Zimmerman called 911, got out of his vehicle and followed Martin behind the townhomes despite being told not to by a police dispatcher."[3] As Noffke's testimony made clear, the AP made at least three errors in one sentence: Zimmerman called the nonemergency number, not 9-1-1; he exited the truck and started following Martin *before* the dispatcher said otherwise; finally, the dispatcher could not and did not tell Zimmerman to do anything. The *Washington Post*'s Jonathan Capehart, to his credit, conceded that Noffke absolved Zimmerman of disobeying a direct order. Ironically, however, in an article titled "Five Myths About . . . the killing of Trayvon Martin," Capehart perpetuated the myth that Zimmerman was still in his truck when Noffke suggested he not follow Martin.[4]

This was not a minor oversight on Capehart's part. As O'Mara drove the point home in cross-examination, Noffke may have inspired Zimmerman to maintain visual contact with Martin. O'Mara reviewed the critical moment on the dispatcher tape for Noffke and the jurors. After Zimmerman told Noffke that Martin was running, Noffke asked, "He's running? Which way is he running?" It was just as this question was asked that Zimmerman started walking in haste. O'Mara then asked if Zimmerman might have taken his question as a suggestion to keep an eye on Martin. Said Noffke, "I understand how someone could have misinterpreted the intent of that." Through O'Mara's questioning, Noffke also undermined the State's implication that Zimmerman was enraged and keen on vengeance.

If anything, State witness Wendy Dorival, an African American who served as volunteer program coordinator for the Sanford Police Department, proved even more helpful to Zimmerman's cause. It was Dorival who worked with Zimmerman to launch the neighborhood watch program in his community. In calling her to the stand, the State had hoped that she would confirm the much-bruited notion that Zimmerman was an overzealous cop wannabe who disregarded the limits of his authority in "profiling" Martin and "following" him. It didn't quite work out that way.

On cross-examination by the defense, Dorival spoke repeatedly of the many burglaries in the community. She told specifically of how she had met with a female neighbor of Zimmerman's who had endured a home invasion and was "still shaken up by it." On the questions of gun ownership and concealed carry, Dorival remained fully agnostic. Those were not subjects she ever brought up at neighborhood watch meetings.

Dorival spoke highly of Zimmerman throughout her testimony. "He seemed like he really wanted to make changes in his community, to make it better," Dorival said. His professionalism and dedication to his community impressed her enough that she asked him to join the Sanford PD's Citizens on Patrol program, a program that trained residents to patrol their neighborhoods. Zimmerman politely declined her offer. After the Sherman Ware incident a year earlier, Zimmerman had denounced the Sanford police for operating "in the gray" and the chief for his "illegal cover-up and corruption." Neither job endeared this alleged wannabe cop to the local constabulary.

Just as importantly, Dorival repeated the point frequently that she and her colleagues "always encourage [neighborhood watch people] to call." Asked West, "You err on the side of making the call?" Dorival answered yes. "When something about them doesn't seem quite right?" asked West again, referring to people acting suspiciously. "Yes," said Dorival. The neighborhood watch coordinator, she explained, is the "eyes and ears" of the community.

On day six of the trial, the prosecution called Doris Singleton to the stand. She was the Sanford police officer who first interviewed Zimmerman in depth on the night of the shooting. For no apparent reason, de la Rionda played the interview in full. The jurors heard Singleton explain the Miranda rules and Zimmerman waive his right to an attorney. They also heard Zimmerman, always respectful, recount in chilling detail the savagery of Martin's attack, his own cries for help, his fruitless appeal to a neighbor, and his quick submission to the police when they arrived.

As Singleton explained, Zimmerman did not know that Martin was dead until she told him. He was dismayed. After noticing Singleton was wearing a cross, he questioned if she was Catholic. She asked why that might matter, and he responded, "In the Catholic religion, it's always wrong to kill someone." She responded, "If what you're telling me is true, I don't think that what God meant was that you couldn't save your own life." If the prosecutors had hoped that Singleton would paint Zimmerman as a person of depraved mind who killed Martin out of ill will, spite, or hatred, she did not at all oblige them. In fact, as the replay of the interview showed, she had offered him something like a spiritual acquittal.

The Sanford PD's lead investigator on the Zimmerman case, Chris Serino, followed Singleton to the stand. Of all the officers who testified, none undermined the prosecution's line of attack more substantially than he did. Serino had a score to settle. An ever-tightening vise of political pressure had badly damaged his law enforcement career. He told the FBI early on that three Sanford police officers—two of them black, the third married to an African American—pressured him to file charges against Zimmerman almost immediately after the incident. He refused to do so without probable cause. Serino implied that these officers were also leaking information about the case, and those leaks were fueling the growing firestorm.

Sanford police chief Bill Lee resisted the storm as long as he was able, telling a crowd of reporters and black activists outside Sanford City Hall, "Mr. Zimmerman has made the argument of self-defense. Until we can establish probable cause to dispute that we don't have the grounds to arrest him." Serino told the FBI the same thing, namely that he "did not believe he had enough evidence at the time to file charges."[5] The only new "evidence" to emerge after the pressure mounted was the concocted testimony of Rachel Jeantel. That testimony proved sufficient, however, for the State to arrest Zimmerman and put Serino on the stand to testify, presumably *against* the beleaguered neighborhood watch coordinator.

Those who knew the history of this gruff, tough-looking cop sensed that he would rather have been a thousand other places than a Seminole County courtroom on the first day of July 2012. Still, despite the pressure, he stuck to the facts. Usually, the lead investigator is the one who nails the coffin shut in a murder trial. Serino, however, spent much of his time on the witness stand prying the nails loose. As he told the jury, with a little helpful prodding by O'Mara, Zimmerman never failed to cooperate fully with the police during several weeks of interviews. Those interviews were part of an investigation that eventually involved several people within the Sanford PD, including the chief, as well as others from the local state attorney's office. When O'Mara asked Serino if Zimmerman had said anything to contradict the diverse evidence he had gathered, Serino firmly answered, "No, sir."

O'Mara then asked Serino to explain the details of what is often called the "challenge interview," an intense cross-examination by investigators of a suspect to try to reveal any false testimony. In the Zimmerman case, this interview took place three days after the shooting. In a challenge interview, the police officer occasionally bluffs about evidence that he may not have. As O'Mara explained, Serino did just that, telling Zimmerman that one of Martin's hobbies was videotaping "everything he does." As a result, claimed Serino, Martin had a "very impressive" library of images trapped in his phone. O'Mara played the recording of a crucial exchange in that interview. The jurors heard Serino saying, "There's a possibility that whatever happened between you and him is caught on videotape" and Zimmerman replying, "I prayed to God that someone videotaped it." At the time, of course, Zimmerman did not know Serino was bluffing.

Much to the prosecutors' chagrin, Serino told the court that he could find no reason to doubt George Zimmerman's account of what transpired that fateful night in February. "Do *you* think George Zimmerman was telling you the truth?" O'Mara asked him. "Yes," admitted Serino as the Monday afternoon session wrapped up. So compelling was this admission that the Tuesday proceedings began with the prosecution demanding that it be stricken from the record. It was, but as *TalkLeft*'s Jeralyn Merritt observed, "You can't put toothpaste back in the tube."[6] Juror B37 confirmed as much. Two nights after the jury returned its verdict, she told Anderson Cooper that Serino's testimony "made a big impression on me." When Cooper asked why, she answered, "He deals with, you know, murder, robberies; he's in it all the time. And I think he has a knack to pick out who's lying and who's not lying."[7]

B37 spoke to Cooper artlessly and honestly before she understood the negative consequences of doing so. Her presentation was sensitive to the Martin family and, at the end, very emotional. It represents the most detailed and candid discussion of what went on in the jury room and will be treated as such from here on out.

39

SOURCING THE SCREAMS

ON MARCH 16, 2012, Sanford city manager Norton Bonaparte Jr., a middle-aged mustachioed African American, convened Trayvon Martin's parents and their attorneys in the Sanford mayor's office and played for them the 9-1-1 calls from the night Trayvon was shot. In reporting on what followed, ABC's Matt Gutman posted a piece headlined "Trayvon Martin Neighborhood Watch Shooting: 9-1-1 Tapes Send Mom Crying from Room."[1] Gutman was not on the scene. He relied fully on the word of Team Trayvon as to what happened. "You hear a shot, a clear shot, then you hear a 17-year-old boy begging for his life," said attorney Natalie Jackson. "Then you hear a second shot." It quickly became an article of faith among Trayvon supporters, the media included, that the forty seconds of screams heard on the one 9-1-1 call were those of young Martin. His mother, Sybrina Fulton, emerged as the high priestess of this orthodoxy. In drawing up its affidavit of probable cause to charge George Zimmerman with the second-degree murder of Trayvon Martin, the State of Florida relied on her identification of "the voice crying for help" as her son's.

During the trial, the 9-1-1 call that captured the screams came to be called the "Lauer 9-1-1 call" after the witness who made the call, Jenna Lauer. On the Friday that the State wrapped up its case, prosecutors put Fulton on the stand to discuss that call.[2] Although normally well turned out, Fulton looked positively matronly with her spectacles, her demure black dress, and her hair in a bun. As expected, and as highly anticipated by those wanting to see Zimmerman convicted, Fulton was not backing off her claims about the Lauer tape.

"Ma'am, that scream or yell, do you recognize that?" asked de la Rionda. "Yes," she said. When de la Rionda asked whose voice she thought it was, Fulton answered firmly and defiantly, "Trayvon Benjamin Martin." In cross-examination, defense attorney Mark O'Mara asked Fulton two questions, the impact of which was understood only by those following the case closely: Did she anticipate what she was about to hear when she first heard the Lauer tape? And did she discuss the tape in advance with any member of the family? She denied doing either.

Taking the stand Friday morning after Fulton was her son and Martin's older half brother, Jahvaris Fulton. Jahvaris also claimed to recognize the voice on the Lauer tape as Trayvon Martin's. O'Mara pointed out in cross-examination, however, that Jahvaris had told a reporter two weeks after listening to the tape in the Sanford mayor's office that he could not be sure whose voice he heard. "I guess I didn't want to believe that it was him; that's why during that interview I said I wasn't sure," said Jahvaris. To anyone with an open mind, his recovered memory seemed all too predictable.

The Fultons were the prosecution's last two witnesses. Right after the close of the State's case, O'Mara made a motion for a judgment of acquittal—a request to the judge to end the case from the bench. He argued eloquently that given the absence of any direct evidence of Zimmerman's guilt, the case should not go to the jury. "The motion was well-reasoned, and strongly founded on Florida's case law," said Ralph Branca at *LI*. "It was also doomed to fail before a Judge who has consistently denied reasonable defense motions out of hand, while rubber-stamping motions by the State that [bore] not the slightest relevancy to the facts of this case."[3] And fail it did.

Although it was late on a Friday afternoon, Judge Nelson ordered the defense to present its witnesses. This actually played well for the defense. On the same day that Sybrina Fulton testified, Zimmerman's mother, Gladys, took the stand as an emotional counterbalance. Gladys was the first of eight witnesses to testify that it was Zimmerman's voice calling for help on the Lauer 9-1-1 call. Jorge Meza, Gladys's brother, followed his sister. Both had dark complexions and spoke accented English. They were every bit as sympathetic as Martin's parents and even more convincing in their testimony.

Following the family members to the stand on Monday were four Zimmerman friends, all of whom said that the voice they heard on the Lauer tape was unquestionably Zimmerman's. Perhaps more importantly, they provided quiet testament to Zimmerman's character. Of the friends, the fourth was the most compelling. John Donnelly had been a medic in Vietnam. In his emotional testimony, he explained that when he heard a friend crying for help on the battlefield, he knew who it was without even seeing him. In a similar vein, Donnelly claimed that he had no trouble linking Zimmerman's speaking voice to his screaming voice. Juror B37 found Donnelly to be the most credible of all the witnesses. "I thought he was awe inspiring, the experiences that he had had over in the war," she said.[4] When Donnelly finished, the court broke for lunch. Martin supporters in Twitterdom had no patience for the testimony of these good people and no sense of the irony of their own impatience:[5]

> Hearing them refer to this overfed, overzealous child-killer as "Georgie" is kind of making me nauseous

> George Zimmerman's best friend & wife? We are supposed to believe them? TUH. How insulting.

> How utterly shameful that TM's parents are forced to listen to him scream again and again to facilitate these defense liars

It was after lunch that the hammer came down on the prosecution's case. The man delivering the blow was Investigator Serino. Under O'Mara's guidance, Serino told how he played the 9-1-1 tapes, including the Lauer tape, for Tracy Martin. He played them two days after the shooting and more than two weeks before Martin's ex-wife would hear the Lauer tape. When Serino asked Martin if his son were the one heard screaming, Martin said no. Sanford police officer Doris Singleton testified next. She witnessed the exchange and confirmed what Serino had said. "He was telling Chris it was not his son's voice," said Singleton. The testimony of the two officers, both of whom were sympathetic to the Martin family, undercut Fulton's testimony that she was unaware of the Lauer call until she heard it in her ex-husband's presence.

In a bold move, the defense called Tracy Martin to the stand after the two police officers. He had been listening with obvious discomfort to the Sanford police officers from his seat in the family row. As might be expected, he denied that he ever said that the voice was not Trayvon's. As Martin recounted, when Serino asked him, "Do you recognize the voice?" he rolled away from the desk on his chair, shook his head, and said, "I can't tell." Martin also denied ever telling his ex-wife that he had heard the tape before their collective listening session. A week before that session, however, he and Fulton had filed a complaint demanding the tapes' release.[6] O'Mara did not challenge him on that complaint, but he did on why he changed his mind about the source of the screams. Martin claimed to have listened to the tape twenty times in the mayor's office, finally recognizing, "It was Trayvon's voice." He was not at all convincing.

"I think they said anything a mother and a father would say," said Juror B37 of Martin's parents. "Just like George Zimmerman's mom and father." She told Anderson Cooper that she and four of her fellow jurors believed Zimmerman was the one screaming. The sixth juror wasn't sure. The source of that scream mattered hugely. "I think it was pretty important," said B37. "Because it was a long cry and scream for help, that whoever was calling for help was in fear of their life."[7]

Any disinterested observer would have had to agree with *LI*'s Andrew Branca that the biggest news of the defense's first day "was the utter implosion of the State's 'scream' narrative into which they had invested the heart and soul of their theory of the case."[8] Irresponsible to the bitter end, the folks at ABC did not quite see it that way. Diane Sawyer led the network's coverage of the story with the maudlin and deceptive opening, "Today a father did everything in his power to convince a jury that the cry for help on that audio tape was not Zimmerman. That was his son. Matt Gutman was there." Of course Matt Gutman was there, apparently unrepentant about past malpractice. The footage used to support his reporting featured a mournful Martin "listening to his [son's] life being taken."[9] That "listening" phrase was used in the headline of the accompanying online piece.

"George Zimmerman's fate could hinge on those screams," said Gutman on air in Sanford, as though there remained any doubt as to their source. Sixteen months earlier, Benjamin Crump had ventured a theory as to why Martin might have been yelling for help. "You can conclude who is the person crying out for help presumably when they see a gun," he said. Revelations about Martin's character since then, particularly his fondness for guns, had rendered that theory absurd, but in the interim the mainstream media had not ventured any other explanation. Nor had the prosecution offered any during its two weeks of presenting evidence. Given so obvious an information gap, Zimmerman supporters in the blogosphere ventured to fill it in:[10]

> GZ punched himself in the nose, threw himself onto the sidewalk, slamming the back of his own head into the concrete, and finally pulled a terrified and screaming TM onto himself while simultaneously shooting him through the heart.

> Trayvon was the one screaming. When you are breaking someone's nose and banging his head against the ground, it hurts your hands and your wrists.

> Powerful George "Hulk Hogan" Zimmerman had little Trayvon by his little wrists and was slamming the poor little guy's fists into his nose. Obviously a clever move on Zimmerman's part to set up his dastardly racist crime. Fortunately the judge and DA were too smart to fall for it.

Not content to elevate the Martin-as-screamer scenario, Gutman concluded his reporting as dishonestly as he had begun, with Zimmerman's own comment on first hearing the Lauer tape, "That doesn't even sound like me." True to form, ABC's producers did not include Serino's clarification of that innocent remark. On the encouraging side, however, ABC's legal analyst, Dan Abrams, publicly backed off his earlier comments. "Now that the prosecution's case against Zimmerman is in," said Abrams a day before Gutman's report, "as a legal matter, I just don't see how a jury convicts him of second degree murder or even manslaughter in the shooting death of Trayvon Martin."[11] The media were catching on, but not enough of them, and not soon enough.

At the end of the day on which Tracy Martin testified, former Sanford police chief Bill Lee took the stand. He told the jurors about the mechanics of how the Martin family and their attorneys got to hear the

Lauer tape. As he explained, the group listened together in a room with no law enforcement present. This, Lee said, was a conspicuous violation of the best practices for identifying anything. He had recommended that the tape be played for each family member individually "so their identification would not be influenced by others." For a variety of reasons, none of them good, that did not happen.

After testifying, Lee did his first TV interview in more than a year, this time a fair-minded one with CNN's George Howell. Lee spoke regretfully of the pressure that had been brought to bear upon him in March 2012. During the course of the interview, Howell alluded to "outside" pressures but did not identify them. A principal source of that pressure, city manager Norton Bonaparte, asked Lee "several times" during that period, "Can an arrest be made now?" Bonaparte was not the only one prodding him. "It was related to me that they just wanted an arrest," said Lee. "They didn't care if it was dismissed later." Lee did not specify who the "they" was, but Crump and Parks had to be among them. Lee paid for his resistance. Bonaparte fired him before his first anniversary on the job. "I upheld my oath to abide by the laws of the State of Florida and the Constitution," said Lee in retrospect, "and I'm happy that at the end of the day I can walk away with my integrity."[12]

The same day as the Howell interview, day twelve of the trial, the conservative watchdog group Judicial Watch released the results of its investigation into Justice Department activities in Florida in March and April 2012. For more than a year the *Treehouse* had been calling attention to the provocative role played by the stealthy and powerful Community Relations Service (CRS) within the Department of Justice. Judicial Watch was able to document at least some of its involvement. Although CRS is officially tasked with identifying and easing racial tensions, the information secured by Judicial Watch showed that the agency "actively worked to foment unrest."[13] Former CRS director Ondray Harris confirmed that its career employees were often guilty of "acting as advocates instead of mediators."[14]

In their own words, CRS employees traveled to Florida on the taxpayer dime to "work marches, demonstrations, and rallies, . . . provide technical assistance to the City of Sanford, event organizers, and law enforcement agencies for the march and rally on March 31, . . . [and] provide technical assistance, conciliation, and onsite mediation during demonstrations planned in Sanford."[15] Harris, himself an African American, had particular problems with regional director Tommy Battles, who was coordinating the CRS Sanford efforts in 2012. He is "black, and very pro-black," said Harris. "I felt such views compromised implementing the CRS mandate."[16] Obama and his Department of Justice apparently felt otherwise. They played favorites along racial lines in the Zimmerman case from day one, never ceased, and never apologized.

Also leaning on Chief Lee, according to Judicial Watch, was a "collective of young people of color" known as the "Dream Defenders."[17] After marching from Daytona to Sanford before Zimmerman was arrested in April 2012, the group barricaded the entrance to the Sanford police station and demanded that Lee be fired for failing to file murder charges in the case. Backed by the Service Employees International Union (SEIU), the White House's favorite union, the Dream Defenders purportedly "organize to end the criminalization of black and brown youth." Apparently, Zimmerman was either not brown enough or young enough to secure their blessing.

40

RESCUING SCIENCE

O N THE SECOND FULL DAY of the defense's presentation, day eleven of the trial, Mark O'Mara called Dr. Vincent Di Maio to the stand. The defense's goal was to align George Zimmerman's account of the shooting with the medical evidence. In the process, Di Maio helped revive the reputation of the forensic pathology profession after the woeful performance of the two medical examiners who had testified earlier on behalf of the State: Dr. Valerie Rao and Dr. Shiping Bao.[1]

First up had been Dr. Valerie Rao. Educated in India, Rao had little to recommend herself other than the fact that she worked in the same judicial district as state attorney Angela Corey. In her eagerness to downplay the damage done to Zimmerman's skull, Rao gave all the appearance of throwing the game for her hometown team. At one point, for instance, she interpreted a couple of obvious goose eggs as natural configurations of Zimmerman's head. On another occasion, when asked by John Guy to assess Zimmerman's injuries, she answered, "They were very insignificant." In fact, she repeated the words "insignificant," "minor," and "only"—as in "only three impacts of his head on cement"—as if her side scored a point every time she did so.

In cross-examination, O'Mara quickly established that Rao owed her position to Corey. He then clarified her prior working relationship with the prosecutors. More to the point, he got Rao to admit she really had no idea how many blows to the head Zimmerman sustained. Better still, her presence on the stand allowed O'Mara to trot out once again the many gruesome photos of Zimmerman's bloodied skull.

Dr. Shiping Bao, the pathologist who oversaw the autopsy of Trayvon Martin, set back the cause of the international pathologist even further. In heavily accented English, Bao waded erratically through his notes to establish little except that it took Martin from one to ten minutes to die. Freelancing emotionally, Bao attempted to describe the suffering that Martin would have endured before the defense successfully cut off his testimony with an objection. At the end, Bao left the jury more confused about the nature of Martin's death than they were before he began. Again, though, the jurors saw many photos of Zimmerman's badly bruised head.

By contrast, Di Maio's accent was pure New York. Accent can matter as much to a jury as it can to a frustrated cable customer asking why his HBO is cutting out. More than accent, though, Di Maio had credentials—nearly an hour's worth—much of it dealing with gunshot wounds. His experience informed his presentation style, which was both colorful and concise. Di Maio clearly explained something neither Rao nor Bao could, specifically what comes out of a gun when it is fired and why it matters.

Di Maio observed that the fatal shot left a two-inch-by-two-inch area of gunpowder "tattooing" around the wound on Martin's chest. From this observation, he was able to determine that Zimmerman fired his Kel-Tech PF9 at a distance of two to four inches from Martin. Had Zimmerman pressed the gun's muzzle against Martin's chest, as the State insinuated, the unburnt gunpowder would have been found in the wound, not on the skin around it. This determination mattered for one particular reason. The two-to-four-inch gap between the shirt and the chest strongly suggested that Martin was leaning over Zimmerman when the shot was fired—just as Zimmerman claimed. If Martin were standing or sitting up, as the prosecution desperately tried to establish, the wet shirt would have clung to his body.

Di Maio also addressed the issue of evidence collection and preservation. Being as charitable as he could, he pointed out that by storing the wet clothes in plastic bags, not paper bags, as best practices dictate, Bao's office may have degraded any DNA found on the clothes. Equally problematic, according to Di Maio, was the Sanford PD's failure to bag Martin's hands. This oversight might have allowed the rain to wash Zimmerman's DNA off Martin's knuckles. Di Maio went on to explain that Bao failed to examine Martin's fingers for internal bruising despite the obvious abrasions on them. In sum, whatever DNA points the State might have scored with Bao's testimony, and they could not have been many, Di Maio wiped them from the scoreboard. Juror B37 confirmed as much.

Under West's guidance, Di Maio clarified a minor inconsistency that the State had been trying to pound into a "lie." In his original statement to the Sanford police, Zimmerman said that after shooting Martin and pushing him off, he climbed on Martin's back, "holding his hands away from his body." Not knowing the seriousness of Martin's wound, Zimmerman told a neighbor who had stepped out, "I need you to help me restrain this guy." When the Sanford police arrived minutes later, they found Martin's hands pulled under his body. Given the weakness of its case, the State hoped to present this as still another example of Zimmerman's mendacity. As Di Maio vividly explained, however, Martin should have been able to control his movements for a minimum of ten to fifteen seconds even if his heart had been ripped out of his body. He shared a colorful anecdote about a man who had taken a point-blank shotgun blast that "completely shredded his heart" and yet was still able to turn and run sixty-five feet. These were details that seemed to capture the jury.

Di Maio also addressed Zimmerman's head wounds, the severity of which Rao had tried to minimize. Di Maio observed that intracranial bleeding is not always obvious and can sometimes cause death hours after the injury that caused it. He discussed, too, a consequence of a blow to the head known as *diffuse axonal injury*, a major cause of unconsciousness, coma, and persistent vegetative state. The police, he argued, should have taken Zimmerman to the hospital whether he wanted to go or not. This testimony had weight because Florida statute allows for deadly force if the person threatened "believes that such force is necessary to prevent imminent death or great bodily harm to himself or herself." According to Di Maio, Zimmerman had good reason to fear serious harm, even death, given his circumstances. His testimony badly undermined the State's attempt to trivialize Zimmerman's wounds. Just as crucially, it made the jurors question the reliability of the State's DNA evidence.

There wasn't much the State could say to put Di Maio on the defensive. At one point de la Rionda mocked his assertion that a heartless man could talk for ten to fifteen seconds by miming a heartless man for fifteen seconds. In response, Di Maio explained to the prosecutor those fifteen seconds matter enough to SWAT teams that they shoot for the head not for the heart. On another occasion, in an obvious attempt to tweak the sympathy of the jury's animal lovers, de la Rionda drew attention to Di Maio's direct testimony that he used live animals in his study of gunshot patterns. As de la Rionda flinched in dismay, Di Maio assured him that he ran all experiments using a federally approved methodology in a federally approved facility. In this round, like so many others, the State did not fare much better than Di Maio's animals.

41

FIXING THE FIGHT

*T*O THE GREAT BENEFIT OF PEOPLE like Nancy Grace, the State of Florida permits just about everything that happens in court to be televised. This includes what is known as a "proffer." In a proffer, one of the parties argues as to why certain evidence should not be ruled inflammatory, insufficiently authenticated, or hearsay, and why it should be presented to the jury in open court. To preserve the right to appeal on the basis of excluded evidence, the given party must make such a proffer. In a four-minute piece after an evening session on day eleven of the trial, ABC's Matt Gutman devoted twelve seconds to the trial's most contentious proffer, the one addressing the texts and pictures captured on Trayvon Martin's phone.

This particular proffer deserved much more time. "The defense said they showed Martin liked to fight," said Gutman. Lest the viewer dwell on this note, Gutman's producer promptly cut to prosecutor John Guy saying, "We don't know who typed these messages."[1] As sketchy as its coverage was, ABC gave this subject—potentially the most critical in the trial—more attention than did most of their major media rivals.

Like virtually all of his media peers, Gutman concentrated on the theme of "lawyers attacking lawyers." He fully ignored the testimony of the man at the center of the proffer, Richard Connor. An attorney as well as a certified computer forensic expert, Connor explained to the court the content of what Martin had communicated on his cell phone and the efforts of Martin—or someone else—to protect those communications from scrutiny. That protection included a special application that allowed the user to delete messages in such a way as to avoid easy retrieval. Even using a sophisticated recovery tool, Connor had to work hard to retrieve those data. As he discovered, there was a good reason to bury them. What the data revealed was Martin's unhealthy interest in guns, drugs, and fighting. Defense attorney Don West had Connor testify before Judge Nelson to show that this information was more than just "reputational." Rather, it spoke directly to Martin's physical abilities and his knowledge of fighting. "This is absolutely compelling evidence and it's highly relevant," argued West. The fact that the jury was not present for Connor's testimony gave the media the excuse to ignore it, but their collective neglect did not make the story the data told any less true or real.[2]

The blogosphere had been aware of Martin's unwholesome interests for a year or more. Just before the trial, the defense posted much of the data from Martin's cell phone on its legal website, and the major media felt obliged to discuss the issue, however briefly. With Connor's testimony, the media had the opportunity, indeed the responsibility, to share these revelations with a more attentive public. Had they done so, they would have helped dispel the widespread illusion about Martin's innocence and helped prepare the nation, black America in particular, for the eventual outcome of the trial. To share Connor's testimony, however, would have meant unspinning the web of disinformation that ABC and others had been busy weaving since the beginning. That wasn't about to happen.

With West's guidance, Connor laid it all out for those who cared to listen. In the week before he died, Martin had had at least four online conversations about purchasing a .22 caliber revolver. Connor identified the several people with whom he had had these exchanges. Among them was someone nicknamed Fruit. As the *Treehouse* discovered in its exploration of the relevant social media, "Fruit" was Tracy Martin's nickname.[3] Whether he was the Fruit discussing a gun purchase with Trayvon remains uncertain. One would hope it was someone else named Fruit. In the cache recovered by Connor was a photo of a hand gripping a pistol. Whoever took the photo used Martin's cell phone. It appears to have been a self-portrait.

Although Martin's enthusiasm for guns spoke to the unfortunate turn his life had taken, the defense team had more interest in the data related to MMA-style fighting. In a semicomical turn, West had Connor read word for word from Martin's November 2011 conversation with a girl named Lavondria. It bears repeating. After Martin told Lavondria he was "tired and sore" from a fight, she asked him why he continued fighting. "Bae" is shorthand for "babe." Here is what Connor related:

MARTIN: Cause man dat nigga snitched on me

LAVONDRIA: Bae y you always fightinqq man, you got suspended?

MARTIN: Naw we thumped afta skool in a duckd off spot

LAVONDRIA: Ohh, Well Damee

MARTIN: I lost da 1st round :(but won da 2nd nd 3rd . . . .

LAVONDRIA: Ohhh So It Wass 3 Rounds? Damn well at least yu wonn lol but yuu needa stop fighting bae Forreal

MARTIN: Nay im not done with fool..... he gone hav 2 see me again

LAVONDRIA: Nooo... Stop, yuu waint gonn bee satisfied till yuh suspended again, huh?

MARTIN: Naw but he aint breed nuff 4 me, only his nose

West had Connor establish, over several objections by the prosecution, that Martin had engaged in an MMA-style fight and clearly knew how to get a distinct advantage by establishing the dominant position. This became evident in a second conversation with someone named Michael "Suave" French. A day after his dialogue with Lavondria, Martin told French that his opponent "got mo hits cause in da 1st round he had me on da ground nd I couldn't do ntn." Two weeks after the shooting, this same Michael French told a local Miami TV Station that Martin "was smart and funny and he always kept to himself, too, so I know he wouldn't start anything." When asked why Martin was shot, French had his stock response ready, "It was a predominantly white neighborhood. So he looked suspicious. So that's probably why."[4] The *Treehouse* found and posted a photo of French and Martin flashing gang signs.[5]

Even more damning perhaps, Connor read from a Facebook post by Martin's younger half brother, Demetrius Martin. Last seen in the media crying as he remembered his brother during a "March for Peace" rally, Demetrius asked Trayvon when he was "going to teach me to fight." This all mattered, West insisted. Martin had a clear knowledge of fighting, some hard-earned experience, a knack for making noses bleed, and, as one of the photos showed, a buff enough physique to prevail when engaged. The prosecution, West argued, had a previous witness testify to Zimmerman's interest in mixed martial arts. The defense had countered with Zimmerman's trainer, who described his client as being a one on a one-to-ten scale of ability. The subject was in play. Fairness, West argued, dictated that the defense be able to make its best case. Not to admit this highly probative evidence, said West forcefully, would violate Zimmerman's rights to due process under both the Florida and the United States Constitutions.

Prosecutor John Guy thought—or at least argued—otherwise. "We don't know who typed these messages," he claimed. He insisted, too, that the cryptic text language defied interpretation, that the word "fight" might be code for something else, and that the photo of a pumped-up Martin could have been taken after a workout. Throughout Guy's argument, West looked like he wanted to strangle him. He and O'Mara had been in court for nearly fourteen hours, one more exhausting day on the forced march of a schedule dictated by Judge Nelson.

In his rebuttal, West was unsparing. As he explained, the reason he had to present this critical proffer so late in the game was because the State had concealed the evidence. "We were misled, Judge," said West. He was not exaggerating. Attorney Wesley White testified in a May 28, 2013, hearing that Ben Kruidbos, the IT director for Angela Corey's Fourth Judicial Circuit, had alerted him that prosecutors were playing games with the evidence. Specifically, they failed to turn over to the defense the photos and pictures contained in Martin's cell phone as required by evidence-sharing laws. Kruidbos confirmed this at a June 6 pretrial hearing. Corey fired Kruidbos a month later for violating "numerous State Attorney's Office (SAO) policies and procedures" and engaging "in deliberate misconduct."[6] Kruidbos, in turn, has sued the State. As to White, he had already left her employ. The media scarcely raised an eyebrow about any of this.

At the *Treehouse*, Sundance advanced a credible theory as to what data went missing and why. Connor, he argued, was "outlining a very specific educated thesis that the phone was scrubbed of damning evidence after death." Deleted were the many references to Martin's indulgence in fighting, guns, and drugs. "The STATE prosecutorial team intentionally deleted the data," Sundance speculated, "then delivered a partial file with the non-deleted data, then at the last minute before trial delivered the full data set, but omitted the deleted data from the written report summarizing the entire 'bin' file."[7] To be sure, this was never made explicit in court, but clearly someone buried the data that spoke to Martin's character. Given the recklessness of the life he was living, it seems unlikely that Martin would have gone to this trouble.

Judge Nelson appeared to have already made up her mind. "I do have an authentication issue about it," she said of the data contained in Martin's phone. "Anybody could have picked up that phone and sent these text messages." An exasperated West tried to explain that the phone had double passcode protection that even the FDLE could not crack. What is more, West continued, an earlier deposition with Jeantel confirmed that Martin had discussed fighting with her during this same period. It was hardly out of character. Nor would it have been difficult to confirm Martin's authorship of the messages if the defense had had time to check with his phone mates, all of whose identifying information Connor easily deduced.

"It's simply unfair for Mr. Zimmerman not to be able to put on his defense because of the State's tactics," said West with barely controlled fury. "It is a strategy obviously because they had it in January and kept us from it." West excoriated the prosecution for "playing games with us" and "lying to the court" before asking rhetorically, "and now it's our fault?" Nelson was not listening—literally. "I'm not getting into this. Court is in recess." So saying, she turned her back on West while he was talking and left the courthouse. For the media, the walkout was the story, and Nelson was its heroine. A word search for "Richard Connor" turns up precious little. A word search in the major media for "Lavondria" or "Michael Suave French" or "Demetrius Martin" turns up nothing at all.

"It appears that Judge Nelson is on the verge of reversible error if she excludes the text messages on authentication grounds," wrote *LI*'s William Jacobson immediately after the hearing. He cited a Florida case that a reader had forwarded, *State v. Lumarque*. This case considered the admissibility of photos and text messages found on the defendant's cell phone. "This fact, testified by the State's forensics expert, is sufficient to authenticate these exhibits," ruled the appeals court. "As much as the State wants to keep out the text messages," argued Jacobson, "reversible error due to an improper authentication ruling is not the way to go."[8] Sundance had a more generous take. "Nelson essentially ruled against admissibility based on 'authentication,'" he argued. "She could have kept it out under other legal reasoning, but no, she chose the one without the slightest chance of being upheld by a District Court of Appeals." He thought this ruling an "intentional" gift to Zimmerman, "his personal Platinum Express DCA Acquittal Card."[9]

If she read *Legal Insurrection*, Nelson did not pay it much mind. The next morning, without explanation, she ruled that Connor could not testify. The State still had a chance. Had Nelson allowed Connor's testimony in open court, the prosecutors would have had to close with some story other than the delusional saga they were telling.

42

MAKING CRIME REAL

*A*LTHOUGH SHE WAS ON THE STAND for only eighteen minutes, the next-to-last witness for the defense may well have been the most effective. Her name was Olivia Bertalan. When her name was called, even the most dedicated trial observers were wondering who the demure, twentysomething blonde was. To that point, save for an appearance a year earlier on Nancy Grace, Bertalan had stayed in the shadows.[1]

Bertalan served one primary purpose for the defense. She put a human face on crime. As O'Mara helped her explain, she had been at her Retreat at Twin Lakes home in August 2011 with her nine-month-old son when her life changed forever. "Two young African American guys" started ringing her doorbell and then probed the house for a point of entry. With her husband Michael at work, she told the Court, "I called my mom because I didn't know what to do." Bertalan was upstairs with her son when she heard the two young thugs try to break in. "I started crying, and I called the police," she said.

The dispatcher told the frightened young woman to retreat to a secure place and "grab any weapon" she could find. The best Bertalan could do was to lock herself and her son in his bedroom while wielding a pair of rusty scissors—as effective an argument for gun ownership as ever heard on national TV. At least one of the men came upstairs. "He was shaking the doorknob trying to get in," said Bertalan, still obviously rattled by the experience. Fortunately, the police arrived before he could break through. The two men grabbed what they could grab and hustled out the back. As Bertalan discovered, they took her laptop and her camera, and almost succeeded in disconnecting her television. "Is that the reason you moved?" O'Mara asked. "Yes, it was," she answered.

At that point, O'Mara rested. John Guy would have done well to let the witness stand down, but he chose to cross-examine her. "You had some contact with George Zimmerman after that event, did you not?" he asked. O'Mara objected. He had not so much as mentioned Zimmerman's name. Guy's question was outside the scope of his direct examination. Before Guy could continue, the jury had to clear the room. Guy continued his questioning of Bertalan in the form of a proffer. Once O'Mara saw how harmless his line of inquiry was, he withdrew his objection, and the jury returned.

Thrown off his game a bit, Guy asked Bertalan whether Zimmerman visited her the day of the incident. He had. "You described for him the people that had victimized you," Guy asked. She had. He then led her through a series of questions to establish the suspects' sex, ages, and especially race. "African American," said Bertalan to the last question. Guy then asked her whether she talked to Zimmerman as many as twenty times about the incident. She had. Among the subjects she and Zimmerman discussed, Guy suggested, was that one of the suspects lived within the community, near the back gate, and was then arrested and released prior to February 2012. She agreed that he had been. Although he could not express it directly, Guy was trying to insinuate that Zimmerman was obsessed with crime and especially with black criminals. Implied too was that when Zimmerman saw Martin heading in the direction of the back gate, he might have suspected him to be one of the punks who broke into his neighbor's home.

O'Mara must have sensed the ham in Guy and suspected perhaps that he could not resist the urge to cross-examine. Whatever his motive, O'Mara saved much of his better material for his redirect. "We were terrified when this happened," said Bertalan, referring to the "home invasion," a phrase O'Mara introduced and would repeat in one form or another four times. Yes, Zimmerman did come over. "I was just appreciative he was offering his hand," said Bertalan. He even put a lock on her sliding glass door. There was nothing strange or weird about his attention, Bertalan confirmed. He was not "too involved."

O'Mara offered some clarity to the case. The young man who "invaded" Bertalan's home, Emmanuel Burgess, as it turned out, lived on the same street as Zimmerman and Bertalan, Retreat View Circle, near the back gate. At the time of the home invasion, Burgess was less than a year older than Martin was when killed, but Burgess did not have an overly helpful school district to spare him the consequences of his behavior. Burgess had been arrested several times, and, as O'Mara stated for the record, the Sanford police rearrested Burgess for a separate burglary two weeks before Martin arrived in Sanford.[2] Zimmerman knew this. So should have Guy. Contrary to Guy's insinuation, Zimmerman did not confuse Martin with Burgess. Bertalan's testimony had an impact on the jury. She was young, sensitive, sincere, and, yes, white. The jurors could see themselves in her. They remembered the details of her ordeal. She spoke not only to the emotional consequences of crime, but also to the chivalrous appeal of a protector like Zimmerman.

"The prosecution tried to paint George Zimmerman as a wannabe cop, overeager. Did you buy that?" Anderson Cooper asked Juror B37 after the trial. "I think he's overeager to help people like the lady who got broken in and robbed while her baby and her were upstairs," the juror corrected Cooper. "He came over and he offered her a lock for her backsliding glass door. He offered her his phone number, his wife's phone number. He told her that she could come over if she felt stressed or she needed anybody, come over to their house, sit down, have dinner. Not anybody—I mean, you have to have a heart to do that and care and help people."[3] B37 remembered the details. In the final analysis, Bertalan may have had more impact per minute than any other witness.

Bob Zimmerman followed Bertalan to the stand and testified that it was his son George's voice calling for help on the tape. At that point, Bob's presence mattered more than his testimony. By putting both the senior Zimmerman and his wife, Gladys, on the witness list, the State effectively, if underhandedly, kept them out of the courtroom during the trial. Martin's parents, meanwhile, were allowed to sit stoically in the courtroom every day. The late testimony offered at least a little bit of balance and, unlike Tracy Martin, Bob Zimmerman had no doubt whose voice he heard on the tape. Also unlike Tracy Martin, Bob Zimmerman listened to the tape by himself in the presence of law enforcement.

After Bob Zimmerman testified, the defense rested. Before the case moved to closing arguments, the prosecution dropped something of a bombshell on the defense. In addition to the charges of second-degree murder and manslaughter, the latter of which everyone expected, the State wanted the jury to consider the charge of third-degree murder. In order to press this charge the State had to prove that the killing took place during the act of another felony. Incredibly, the felony the State offered was "child abuse." This last-minute request pushed Don West to the very edge of self-control. "Just when I thought this case couldn't get any more bizarre!" he said in exasperation. The State, he claimed, had been lying in wait, collecting child abuse case law on crimes involving two-year-olds and the like for months, only to spring the new charge on the defense that very morning. So impassioned was West, and so precise in his accusation, that prosecutors Guy and Mantei looked down sheepishly while he spoke. "This is outrageous," he said. "It is outrageous that the State would seek to do this at this time in this case. It is just hard for me to believe that the Court would take this seriously." In her response, Judge Nelson took it seriously indeed—or at least seemed to—but with a night to sleep on it, and consider the potential blowback from the legal community, she chose to protect her reputation and rule out the third-degree murder charge. The show moved on.

43

CONCOCTING A CLOSE

*T*O HIS CREDIT, Bernie de la Rionda was consistent. He made stuff up at the beginning of the trial, and he was making stuff up at the end. A few minutes into his closing argument, for instance, he recounted the testimony of former Zimmerman neighbor Jonathan Manalo, the man who took the revealing photos of Zimmerman's wounds right after the shooting.[1]

As de la Rionda told the story, Manalo was on the phone with Zimmerman's wife, telling her about the shooting, when Zimmerman blurted out casually, "Just tell her I killed him." Killed him? Zimmerman said no such thing. Neither did Manalo. A few days earlier, Manalo had testified that Zimmerman, then in handcuffs, asked him to call his wife and tell her what had just happened. When Manalo began to explain to Shellie that Zimmerman was involved in a shooting, "He cut me off and said, 'Just tell her I shot someone'." There was nothing casual about it. Zimmerman was in shock. He wanted Shellie to know he was okay. As de la Rionda knew, neither Zimmerman nor Manalo used the word "kill."

Zimmerman did not even know Martin was dead. Minutes earlier, in his closing statement, de la Rionda had ripped into Zimmerman for not performing CPR on the man he had just shot. If Zimmerman knew he had killed Martin, why would he have done CPR? "Lie" may be a strong word, but that is precisely what de la Rionda did when he used the word "kill." He would accuse Zimmerman of lying at least a score of times, but that accusation in itself was knowingly false.

In fact, de la Rionda had begun his close with a lie, though a subtler one. "A teenager is dead," said the prosecutor in his dramatic opening line. "He is dead through no fault of his own. He is dead because another man made assumptions." Through no fault of his own? Although de la Rionda would lead the jury to believe otherwise, he knew Martin had circled back to the T, sucker punched a man four inches shorter, and proceeded to wail on him MMA-style, over the protest of neighbor Jonathan Good. An unprovoked assault suggests at least some culpability on Martin's part.

De la Rionda continued dissembling, if a bit less blatantly. "Unfortunately, because his assumptions were wrong," de la Rionda said of Zimmerman, "Trayvon Benjamin Martin no longer walks on this earth." No, in fact, Zimmerman's assumptions were largely right. Martin was high. His toxicology report proved that. As de la Rionda knew, Martin had left the 7-Eleven roughly thirty-five minutes before Zimmerman spotted him wandering in the rain and looking at houses. The site was just a ten-minute walk from the 7-Eleven. In the unaccounted-for twenty-five minutes, given Martin's history with stolen jewelry, he may well have been "up to no good." The fact that Martin launched a savage and unprovoked attack shortly thereafter also suggested that Zimmerman's assumptions were more right than he knew.

In suppressing all exculpatory facts, de la Rionda dishonored the ethics of his office. Fifty years earlier, in *Brady v. Maryland*, the US Supreme Court established that a prosecutor's responsibility was "to seek justice fairly, not merely win convictions by any means." De la Rionda was not seeking justice fairly or otherwise. He was hell-bent on convicting a man he knew to be innocent. His deceptions were often petty, even comical. Early in his close, for instance, he identified Martin as a "young man." This was true enough, but a clear mistake from the prosecutors' perspective. He quickly recognized his error and promptly reminded the jurors that Martin was a "seventeen year-old man" and barely seventeen at that. Within a few minutes, he was calling Martin a "young boy." Later, he called him an "innocent young boy." Perversely, the media came down on Juror B37 in the wake of her *Anderson Cooper* appearance for referring to Martin during her voir dire as a "boy of color." An attorney contacted by

Slate had no problem with the phrase "of color" but chided B37 for "not remembering the freight of 'boy.'" The prosecution, on the other hand, could and did say "boy" with impunity.

In another petty deception, de la Rionda refused to tell the jury the name of the drink Martin was carrying. Toward the end of his closing statement, he posted a slide on a screen. The banner on the top of the slide read, "Which Owner would be more inclined to yell for help?" The slide was divided in two. On the left was an object Zimmerman owned, a Kel-Tec PF-9 9mm handgun. On the right was an object Martin owned, a can of Arizona Watermelon Fruit Juice Cocktail.

So absurd was de la Rionda's presentation, and the whole case, for that matter, that the prosecutors turned the can sideways so the label could not be read. Throughout the trial, prosecutors called the drink "iced tea" lest the word "watermelon" be said in court. "Fu**ing" was okay. The prosecutors said it more times than the average rapper, but "watermelon," apparently because of its racial connotations, was not. Then too, as the State knew, a sweet soft drink like a watermelon cooler and some Skittles got the user two-thirds of the way to that intoxicating elixir known as "fire ass lean." Better the jury not even suspect this. Of course, keeping the texts and social messages out of the trial assured they would not.

Concealing the label was the least of de la Rionda's tricks. This slide had several others built in, including the phrase "more inclined to yell for help." The prosecutors did not dare say that Martin was the one yelling. They just kept suggesting it. Beneath the gun on that same slide was the question, "Who followed?" Under the can was the question, "Who ran?" As to who ran, Martin had four minutes to run the hundred or so yards to the house he was visiting. When he attacked Zimmerman, he was still seventy or so yards from that town house. He wasn't running anywhere. The prosecutors knew this and glossed over it. The defense knew it and exploited it.

If the prosecutors' job had been to sow the seeds of reasonable doubt, one could forgive them their many deceits, but that was not their job. That was the defense's. Lacking a story line that made any sense, de la Rionda mostly just poked holes, often deceptively, in Zimmerman's several unforced accounts to the authorities. One of Zimmerman's "numerous lies" allegedly occurred when Chris Serino told him, "There's a possibility that whatever happened between you and him is caught on videotape."

Zimmerman responded, "I prayed to God that someone videotaped it." According to de la Rionda, this statement had no weight because the clever Zimmerman knew the cameras at the front gate were not functioning. Serino, however, had not referred to those cameras but to the camera on Martin's cell phone and the "very impressive" library of images captured therein. It was this reference that prompted Zimmerman's response, and de la Rionda knew it.

The full flavor of de la Rionda's hodgepodge prevarications is best captured by reading an extended excerpt. In this one, de la Rionda played a clip from Zimmerman's interview with Sanford police officer Doris Singleton and followed it with an explanatory comment of his own to the jury:

ZIMMERMAN:	And when I walked back towards him, I saw him coming at me.
DE LA RIONDA:	Did you hear that? "When I walked back towards him" — he switches mid-sentence. I saw him coming towards me. He acknowledges at that point that he is the aggressor. He's the one that's going and pursuing the victim. But he catches himself when he says that, and then he goes, Oh, he walked towards me.
ZIMMERMAN:	And I went to get my phone. I don't remember if I had time to pull it out or not.
DE LA RIONDA:	And he claims he went for the phone, see, because he's got to then explain why he, being a 5-7, 204-pound perfectly healthy 28-year-old man, is overpowered by this 5-11, 158-pound kid. And he being the one that's tracking him or following him. He's on guard. He's got two flashlights. He's got a gun. This kid is the one that's scared because this guy's following him. He's got to explain why this kid got the upper hand. 'Oh, I was going for my phone and I just got distracted.' Was he going for his phone or was he going for his gun? Were they in the same place?

In the most overwrought stretch of this excerpt, de la Rionda used the word "lie" or one its derivatives in six consecutive sentences:

DE LA RIONDA: He's got a gun. He's got the equalizer. He's going to take care of it. He's a wannabe cop. The defendant is lying. Or is he lying about that? Lies. Or is it just another lie? One lie after another after another. And he was caught in numerous lies. He profiled him as a criminal. It doesn't allow, quite frankly, even the police to take the law into their own hands. But this defendant didn't give Trayvon Martin a chance. But then he followed him. He tracked him. Because in his mind, in the defendant's mind, this was a criminal. He automatically assumed that Trayvon Martin was a criminal. This innocent 17-year-old kid was profiled as a criminal.

"What the jury got was not a compelling narrative of guilt," wrote *LI*'s Andrew Branca at the time, "but a rambling monologue of isolated bits of circumstantial evidence, much of which was consistent with—and even supportive of—the defense's 'self-defense' theory of the case."[2] The jury ended up agreeing with Branca.

The reporters covering the trial had their doubts about de la Rionda's close, but the headlines did not reflect them. "Zimmerman Prosecution's Emotional Closing Argument: Lead prosecutor Bernie De La Rionda gave an animated, sometimes theatrical statement," said ABC.[3] "George Zimmerman Trial: The Prosecution's Dramatic Arguments," said the *Daily Beast*.[4] "George Zimmerman trial: Zimmerman was a 'wannabe cop' who profiled Trayvon Martin, prosecutor says in closing argument," said CBS News.[5] Beneath the headlines, though, was the suspicion that de la Rionda did not deliver the goods. Jose Baez, the defense attorney who represented Casey Anthony, told Matt Gutman, "I think Trayvon Martin deserved more."[6] If Baez had been paying close attention, he would have known that there was no more to give.

44

STATING THE OBVIOUS

*T*OWARD THE END of his largely subdued, three-hour closing statement, defense attorney Mark O'Mara raised an intriguing theoretical point.[1] What if Rachel Jeantel's story were accurate? What if Zimmerman did verbally challenge Martin? If so, what should the appropriate response have been? According to Dennis Root, the use-of-force expert who testified for the defense, Martin ought to have responded with a counter verbal challenge. Instead, he responded with a brutal punch to the nose, a mounting of the victim, and a sustained beating while the victim screamed for help and neighbors threatened to call 9-1-1. Indeed, O'Mara continued, if Zimmerman had shot Martin through the hip and Martin survived, there was little doubt that State prosecutors would have tried Martin for aggravated assault.

O'Mara could take this speculative riff no further. As he asked the jurors earlier, "What do you know about Trayvon Martin?" His answer to his own question was "not much." With the text and the social media excluded, all the jurors knew about Martin was how he behaved in those eight critical minutes when his and Zimmerman's paths crossed.

For those who had been following the case closely, O'Mara's "what if" question had a deeper resonance. If only injured, Martin would not have attracted any national attention. The governor of Florida would not have intervened. The local media would have shown only recent photos. No one on either side of the case would have dared to call Martin a "boy" or a "child." A Seminole County prosecutor would have tried the case, not against Zimmerman—there was never enough evidence—but against Martin. The jurors would have learned of Martin's history as a brawler, and they would have convicted him. Given the rules under which the defense worked, however, this was not a story that O'Mara was allowed to tell.

The story O'Mara *could* tell was hard enough. He had to prove what he called a "double negative," namely, that the State did *not* prove beyond a reasonable doubt that Zimmerman did *not* kill Trayvon Martin in self-defense. Semantically at least, it would have been easier to prove Zimmerman's innocence. In fact, as O'Mara artfully and patiently explained, the State offered no credible evidence at all that Zimmerman killed Martin for any reason other than self-defense.

O'Mara referred to this as a "Bizarro" case after the antihero in the *Superman* comics who, like the State of Florida, did everything backwards. From the beginning, the prosecutors were the ones raising the specter of reasonable doubt. Theirs was the language mired in subjunctives. "How many 'could have beens' have you heard from the State in this case?" O'Mara asked. That was not the way the game was supposed to be played. He knew because he used to be a prosecutor. "Good prosecutors," said O'Mara with a bite, presented a case with certainty or something close to it. The State did no such thing. In presenting its evidence, such as it was, the State never raised its case out of the sea of uncertainty. "If you have a reasonable doubt as to whether George Zimmerman was justified in the use of deadly force, he's not guilty," O'Mara told the jurors.

O'Mara spent roughly half an hour leading the jury through the burden of proof that the State faced before turning to the evidence. He demolished the "wannabe cop" theme by reminding the jurors just how noble a profession law enforcement was, a point he and the testifying officers had reinforced throughout the trial. Besides, he told them, Zimmerman turned down the chance to participate in its Citizens on Patrol program. And no witness had accused Zimmerman of playing cop or patrolling the neighborhood. On that fateful Sunday night he spotted Martin, Zimmerman was driving to Target as he always did on Sundays. He had reason to be suspicious. A crime wave had swept the Retreat at Twin Lakes. The jurors would find a pile of police reports amid the evidence they would receive. And as O'Mara said, without making a major point of it, virtually all the culprits were young black males.

Zimmerman did not respond to this crime wave, O'Mara continued, with anything like the hatred the State attributed to him. Here, O'Mara cleverly used Olivia Bertalan's "home invasion" as a point of reference. Despite the horror of it, Zimmerman had responded calmly and helpfully. He did not rage or threaten revenge. The prosecutors offered no evidence from any source that he had ever done so, and if they did have such evidence, O'Mara challenged John Guy to present it in his rebuttal. As to the night of February 26, Zimmerman did not stalk Martin angrily, gun in hand. He simply did what he believed the dispatcher asked him to do—track the direction in which Martin was heading. The fact that both Guy and de la Rionda had shouted out profanities—O'Mara pointedly avoided the words themselves—did not mean that Zimmerman had.

Given the centrality of the "fu**ing punks" phrase to the State's case, the knowing observer would have liked O'Mara to remind the Court just how the word "punks" evolved from indecipherable garble to "coons" to "cold" to "punks." But O'Mara avoided digressions. He did not address the unaccounted-for twenty-five minutes in Martin's journey from the 7-Eleven, or his likely exchange outside the 7-Eleven with "Curly." He stayed true to his assignment, which was subverting the State's case on the encounter itself.

O'Mara also gave a pass to the racist and/or homophobic "creepy ass cracka" slur uttered by Martin and repeated by Rachel Jeantel. For strategic reasons, he handled Jeantel very gently. In this regard, he read the jury correctly. "She just didn't want to be there, and she was embarrassed by being there because of her education and her communication skills," said B37 of Jeantel. "I just felt sadness for her."

On the subject of the hatred, ill will, and spite required to show a "depraved mind," O'Mara returned to Zimmerman's nonemergency call. If the State dwelled on the dispatcher's suggestion, "We don't need you to do that," O'Mara focused the jurors on that same dispatcher's request to Zimmerman: "Just let me know if this guy does anything else." Once Martin began running, the dispatcher asked, "Which way is he running?" Zimmerman's calm response to these questions showed not only an absence of hatred or anger but also a willingness to honor the dispatcher's request for information. He could not tell him where Martin had gone from his truck. It may have been imprudent for Zimmerman to follow Martin, even at a distance, but it was not at all illegal. As to the most critical of the dispatcher's requests, the request not to follow Martin, Zimmerman responded passively. "Is that when George Zimmerman snaps?" asked O'Mara. "No. He simply says, 'Okay.'"

Zimmerman agreed not to follow Martin, said O'Mara. He then asked what evidence the State presented to prove Zimmerman continued to pursue Martin. "Let [the prosecutors] show you in the record of this case that they had evidence that he ran after Trayvon, walked after him, after he said, 'Okay,' because if it's there, I missed it," said O'Mara. All evidence, physical and eyewitness, put the point of the initial encounter at the T juncture where the east-west cut-through met the north-south dog walk. "We know the altercation started exactly where George Zimmerman said it started," observed O'Mara emphatically. He proceeded to show an animation as to what did happen and where it happened. The prosecution offered no counteranimation. To do so would have highlighted the holes in its imagined scenario.

As O'Mara noted, the State had made a fuss about the allegedly mysterious two-minute gap between the end of Zimmerman's phone call with the dispatcher and the beginning of the confrontation with Martin. In fact, these two minutes presented a mystery only to those who chose not to believe Zimmerman when he said that he walked across the east-west cut-through to get an address reference on Retreat View Circle. De la Rionda thought he had demolished this account by showing a photo of the Lauer residence on Twin Trees Lane with a clearly lit address. According to de la Rionda, Zimmerman would have seen the address on Twin Trees even before he reached the cut-through. He might have, said O'Mara, if the light were on, but the prosecution had offered no evidence of any kind that the Lauers had their outside light on at 7:15 on the night of February 26, 2012. The photos shown in court were taken later. One suspects that the residents were more inclined to keep their lights on *after* the shooting.

The real mystery, said O'Mara, was where Martin had gone in the four minutes from when he started running to when he confronted Zimmerman. In the day's best bit of theater, O'Mara set a clock on the podium and sat in silence while four minutes counted down. Those minutes passed slowly. In four minutes, said O'Mara, some men could run a mile, but the athletic Martin was apparently unable or unwilling to run a couple hundred feet to the house where he was staying. More problematic, O'Mara added, was the State's failure to explain where Martin might have gone during that time.

After a lunch break, O'Mara continued to pound away at the State's evidence or lack thereof. He walked the jurors through a photographic tour of all the witnesses, both the State's and the defense's, and recalled what they had to contribute. Where, he asked, was the evidence that Zimmerman attacked Martin or did anything to justify Martin's attack? There was none. As to the notion that Martin was unarmed, O'Mara lugged a large chunk of concrete over to the jury box to show its lethal potential. He called the State's contention that concrete could not be a weapon "disgusting," a rare and oddly placed display of anger on O'Mara's part.

As he wound down, O'Mara predicted that in his rebuttal John Guy would call Zimmerman a liar and a murderer, but unless the State disproved self-defense beyond a reasonable doubt, there could be no conviction. He asked the jurors to examine the definition of reasonable doubt. "You look at that definition," concluded O'Mara. "You go back to that room and say let's talk first about self-defense. If I think George may have acted in self-defense, we are done." That simple.

John Guy lived down to O'Mara's expectations. Unchastened by O'Mara's warning, he referred to Zimmerman as a liar even more often than he referred to Martin as a child. Were one to title his rebuttal, "The Liar and the Child" would work just fine. "That child had every right to be where he was," said Guy. "That child had every right to be afraid of a strange man following him." Conceding now that Martin beat the snot out of Zimmerman, he added, "Did that child not have the right to defend himself from that strange man?"

On style points, there was no faulting Guy. He looked good, spoke well, and showed a theatrical knack for calling attention to key words. "The last thing [Martin] did on this earth was to try to get home," said Guy. No, that was false, one of many falsehoods Guy told in the close. As Guy and his colleagues knew, Martin had no home. His mother had kicked him out. His father was in no position to take him in. Still, he could have easily gotten to the house where he was staying if he had chosen to, but he chose otherwise. The *last* thing Martin did was brutally attack a man he did not know for reasons that will remain forever unknown.

Guy did not see it that way. He repeated his libelous canard from the opening that Zimmerman stalked Martin and "shot him because he wanted to." He continued, "What is that when a grown man, frustrated, angry, with hate in his heart, gets out of his car with a loaded gun, follows a child, a stranger, with a gun and shoots him through his heart? What is that?" What *that* was, the savvy observer understood, was fiction. Said Harvard law professor Alan Dershowitz later that same day, "To ask the jury to believe that is to ask the jury to convict based on complete and utter speculation and that's not the way the law operates." Dershowitz recommended, in fact, that the prosecutors be charged with "prosecutorial misconduct" for even suggesting Zimmerman somehow planned the shooting of Martin.[2] ABC News was less judgmental. The headline for Matt Gutman's online piece that day read simply, "George Zimmerman 'Had Hate in His Heart' Prosecutor Tells Jury."[3] ABC, though, was hardly through with its mischief. In fact, the diehards in its newsroom were just warming up.

45

SAVING THE SYSTEM

"**M**EMBERS OF THE JURY,** I thank you for your attention during this trial," said Judge Nelson to the six female jurors chosen to decide George Zimmerman's fate on Friday afternoon, day fourteen of the trial. "Please pay attention to the instructions I am about to give you."[1]

The instructions were complicated. As the jurors had heard during the trial, and as Nelson repeated, they could find Zimmerman guilty of second-degree murder if the evidence demonstrated a "depraved mind without regard for human life." As testament to that depravity, Zimmerman would have had to act "from ill will, hatred, spite or an evil intent." The homicide would be justifiable, however, "if necessarily done while resisting an attempt to murder or commit a felony upon George Zimmerman." The homicide, if deemed justifiable, would also rule out the lesser charge of manslaughter.

For the jurors the instruction that would concern them most was the definition of the justifiable use of deadly force. "A person is justified in using deadly force," they were told, "if he reasonably believes that such force is necessary to prevent imminent death or great bodily harm to himself." Judge Nelson continued:

In deciding whether George Zimmerman was justified in the use of deadly force, you must judge him by the circumstances by which he was surrounded at the time the force was used. The danger facing George Zimmerman need not have been actual; however, to justify the use of deadly force, the appearance of danger must have been so real that a reasonably cautious and prudent person under the same circumstances would have believed that the danger could be avoided only through the use of that force. Based upon appearances, George Zimmerman must have actually believed that the danger was real.

If George Zimmerman was not engaged in an unlawful activity and was attacked in any place where he had a right to be, he had no duty to retreat and had the right to stand his ground and meet force with force, including deadly force if he reasonably believed that it was necessary to do so to prevent death or great bodily harm to himself or another or to prevent the commission of a forcible felony.

In considering the issue of self-defense, you may take into account the relative physical abilities and capacities of George Zimmerman and Trayvon Martin.

If in your consideration of the issue of self-defense you have a reasonable doubt on the question of whether George Zimmerman was justified in the use of deadly force, you should find George Zimmerman not guilty.

However, if from the evidence you are convinced beyond a reasonable doubt that George Zimmerman was not justified in the use of deadly force, you should find him guilty if all the elements of the charge have been proved.[2]

Restricted from talking about the case, the jurors to that point talked among themselves about everyday things, their children, their spouses, their pets, their favorite reality TV shows. In addition to her two grown daughters, B37 was the one with all the pets. No fan of the media, she found the best use of the newspaper was to line the parrot cage. Of note, too, she was the only juror to have once had a concealed carry permit.

Retired and unmarried, B51 was one of the few admitted newspaper readers among the forty would-be juror finalists. As such she had a better understanding of the facts of the case than her fellow jurors. She also seemed to have a better grasp on the law and its application. She even thanked Mark O'Mara for explaining the legal concepts involved and the roles of the jurors.

B76 was one of the two jurors that the State tried to strike. A middle-aged mother of two grown children, she had formerly helped her husband run his construction business but now spent much of her time rescuing pets. B76 did not trust the media and knew little about the case save for the basics. Still, she wondered what a "kid" was doing out at night buying candy. This had to have alarmed the prosecutors.

"I don't put much stock to what's in the news," said E6, a ponytailed blonde. "It's so speculative."[3] That comment may have been enough to provoke the State to try to strike her too. The fact that her thirteen-year-old son, one of her two children, had a hunting rifle and that her husband owned several pistols could not have reassured the prosecutors.

The sixtyish E40 was living in Iowa at the time of the Martin shooting and paid little attention to the story. The mother of one grown son, she had moved to Seminole County only seven months prior to the trial. She worked as a safety officer and did not own any guns, although she had a brother-in-law who did. Of all the jurors, she endured the shortest voir dire, which may have been due to the lateness of the day she took the stand.

Juror B29 was the outlier of the group. Although the media routinely reported that the Zimmerman jury was all white or at least devoid of African Americans, juror B29, a Puerto Rican in her mid-thirties, was clearly of African descent. The mother of eight, she and her family had moved to Florida just months before the trial. Like several of the jurors and eyewitnesses, her cursory attention to the news of the incident led her to believe that Martin was only twelve or thirteen years old at the time of his death. She preferred reality TV to the news. *The Real Housewives of New Jersey* was her favorite show.

Once they left the courthouse each day, the six jurors pushed the trial from their minds to the degree they could and made the best use possible of their communal down time. Given that their private hotel rooms were stripped of all electronics, and they could only make one supervised phone call a day, no one begrudged them their diversions, not at least until they returned their verdict. During the twenty-two days of sequestration, they went shopping together, bowled a few games, got manicures, took side trips, even attended a couple preapproved movies—*The Lone Ranger* and *World War Z*, to be precise.[4]

As soon as the trial was over, the jurors were free to speak about their experiences. The two jurors who went public in the immediate aftermath of the trial—B29 and B37—disagreed somewhat on the evidence but told fairly consistent stories about the process. Once the word got out that B37 had signed on with a literary agent, however, she suffered what the *Washington Post* called "a social media smackdown." An anger-fueled petition on *Change.org* coerced her agent to drop the deal and to apologize publicly for taking it on. "I believe I made a grave error in judgment in wanting to represent this story," the agent told the *Los Angeles Times* despite the fact that she typically represents people involved in high-profile criminal cases.[5]

The backlash persuaded four other jurors to distance themselves from B37. "The opinions of Juror B37, expressed on the Anderson Cooper show were her own, and not in any way representative of the jurors listed below," they wrote on court stationery.[6] They did not, however, specify in what way they might have disagreed. Juror B37 felt obliged to back away from her own comments in a statement two days after her appearance. "My prayers are with all those who have the influence and power to modify the laws that left me with no verdict option other than 'not guilty' in order to remain within the instructions," she wrote to CNN. "No other family should be forced to endure what the Martin family has endured."[7] For all the backtracking, however, her original comments continued to ring true.

After the instructions were read, the jurors retired to the jury room with little idea of what to do next. Likely from seeing this done on TV, they chose a foreman, or foreperson, in this case. This they had to figure out on their own. There were no instructions. Then they took an initial vote. Three of the jurors, including B37, voted not guilty. Two voted for manslaughter. B29 alone voted to convict Zimmerman of second-degree murder. At this point, the jurors started reviewing the evidence. They listened multiple times to the 9-1-1 calls, the reenactment video, and various other recordings in evidence. "That's why it took us so long," said B37. "We're looking through the evidence, and then at the end we just—we got done, and then we just started looking at the law." The jurors broke for the evening Friday at six and resumed Saturday morning at nine.[8]

The jurors deliberated throughout the day. At about 6:00 p.m. Saturday evening, as protestors gathered anxiously outside the courthouse, the jurors asked for clarification on the manslaughter charge. Legal commentators speculated that this meant the jurors had removed second-degree murder from consideration, and in this, they were correct. "We actually had gotten it down to manslaughter, because the second degree, it wasn't at second degree anymore," said B37.[9] At that point, the jurors had reduced their options to not guilty or manslaughter, and they received little clarification from the court in moving forward. Aware of their responsibility, they continued deliberating into the night.

"There was a couple of [jurors] that wanted to find [Zimmerman] guilty of something," said B37. Most resolved of those jurors was B29. "I was the juror that was going to give them the hung jury. I fought to the end," she said.[10] What changed her mind was not bullying by the other jurors, but the law itself. As the jurors came to see, all that really mattered was whether Zimmerman felt that he was at legitimate risk of death or great bodily harm when Martin was slamming his head into the concrete. Everything else that preceded that moment faded into irrelevancy. "That's how we read the law. That's how we got to the point of everybody being not guilty," B37 told Anderson Cooper.

"So that was the belief of the jury, that you had to zero in on those final minutes/seconds, about the threat that George Zimmerman believed he faced?" asked Cooper. "That's exactly what had happened," said B37. "And after hours and hours and hours of deliberating over the law and reading it over and over and over again, we decided there's just no way—[no] other place to go."[11] Although inclined to find Zimmerman guilty of something, B29 conceded, "As the law was read to me, if you have no proof that he killed him intentionally, you can't say he's guilty."[12] This was not exactly the way the law was read to her, but it wasn't too wide of the mark.

Having reached a consensus, the jurors voted. "After we had put our vote in," said B37, "and the bailiff had taken our vote, that's when everybody started to cry." She continued, "It was just hard, thinking that somebody lost their life, and there's nothing else that could be done about it. I mean, it's what happened. It's sad. It's a tragedy this happened, but it happened. And I think both were responsible for the situation they had gotten themselves into. I think both of them could have walked away. It just didn't happen."[13] As B29 and B37 each admitted separately, the issue of race, the issue that made the trial a national sensation, never entered the equation for them. For the jurors, it was not about black and white. It was about life and death.

The court reconvened shortly before 10 p.m. Florida time on July

13, 2013. The jurors returned to the courtroom and took their customary seats, arranged by their designated number. As the Zimmermans held their breath—Martin's parents had chosen not to return to the courtroom—and the world waited, the foreperson stood and read. "In the circuit court of the eighteenth judicial circuit in and for Seminole County, Florida, *State of Florida v. George Zimmerman*, verdict: we the jury find George Zimmerman not guilty. So say we all, foreperson."[14] Even at the moment he heard the phrase "not guilty" Zimmerman stared ahead as impassively as he had throughout the trial. There was not a sound of exultation or despair from either side. Sensing they were about to enter only a new circle of hell, Bob and Gladys Zimmerman did not so much as smile.[15]

"Does either side want to poll the jury?" said Nelson, who seemed oddly pleased with the verdict. "We would your honor," said de la Rionda. "Okay, ladies and gentlemen, I mean, ladies, I'm sorry," said Nelson with a smile. "As your jury number is being called please answer whether this is your verdict."

"Juror B29 is this your verdict?" asked the female bailiff. "Yes," said the deeply conflicted mother of eight. Zimmerman's face began to relax just a little as each juror in turn affirmed that she, too, had voted not guilty. Nelson promptly ordered the GPS device on his ankle to be removed, his bond to be returned, and told him that he had "no more business with the Court." Zimmerman shook hands with his attorneys and smiled only after the court had adjourned.[16] After fifteen months, he was finally a free man—no electronic monitoring, no curfews, no prohibitions—but for the time being at least, he would keep his thoughts to himself. "I still see sadness in his eyes," said his brother Robert soon afterwards. "He was definitely not the same person I had seen a few days before the incident."[17]

Immediately afterwards, although "ecstatic with the results," Mark O'Mara did not try to conceal his disgust with the case the State brought against his client. "George Zimmerman was never guilty of anything but protecting himself in self-defense," O'Mara said. He reminded the assembled reporters that Zimmerman's first words when the police arrived were, "I screamed out for help but nobody came." O'Mara heaped scorn on the State's notion that Zimmerman was "some wannabe cop savant" who plotted an alibi from the moment of the shooting. "He believes in a system he really wanted to be part of," said O'Mara of Zimmerman.

"And then he gets prosecutors who charged with him a crime they could never, ever prove."[18]

The admittedly "blunt" Don West did not hesitate to call the prosecution of George Zimmerman a "disgrace." On a more positive note, he added, "I'm thrilled that this jury kept this tragedy from becoming a travesty." West also explained the rationale behind the much-maligned knock-knock joke. "There needed to be a disconnect from an act that was hard to follow," he said in reference to Guy's histrionic opening. "But I knew, Mr. O'Mara knew, and you all found out, it was indeed just an act."[19] By the way, of all the commentators on the case, Sundance may have been the only one to divine West's knock-knock strategy. "Have you ever personally talked with George's defense team? I mean, your theory about the purpose of West's knock-knock joke was 100% accurate," a Treeper asked Sundance after West confirmed it. Sundance had not. "It was a classic [cognitive] reset," said Sundance, "and it worked."[20]

Shortly after the verdict, Bob Zimmerman sent an e-mail to Sundance and his colleagues at the *Treehouse*. "I have thanked Mark Omara [sic] and Don West. Now I would like to extend our heartfelt appreciation to you, our friends at CTH," read the missive. "Currently, our family is happy knowing our son no longer faces a malicious, unethical prosecution. Further, to whatever extent possible, I will attempt to hold every individual fully responsible for their actions. Again, Thank You."[21]

The normally restrained Sundance confessed, like O'Mara, to being ecstatic upon hearing the verdict.[22] The Treepers, the best-informed group of people on this subject anywhere, shared his enthusiasm. The first post on the *Treehouse* verdict thread came in at 10 p.m., and it read simply, "Woohoo!!!" Three minutes later, Chip Bennett posted, "Thank you, Jesus! God Bless you, George Zimmerman. May God's peace and protection be upon you and your entire family."[23]

The prayers drifted skyward. The champagne corks popped. The tears flowed:

StellaP: There is some laundry calling my name! But tonight—we dance!!!

Ytz4mee: And drink. Break open the "good" wine!

Auscitizenmom: I can't stop crying. I was hoping the verdict would come in tonight so I could sleep, but I wonder if I will. Thank you, God.

Ad Rem: Words can not express my joy for George, his family, and all his loyal and steadfast friends.

WeeWeed: Bless you and your family, George! It's been a long haul for you and your loved ones. We rejoice with you!

DiWataman: Thank you all for your work, thoughts and words of encouragement. Let us hope now a true accounting can begin and all of the schemers are dealt with legally and properly along with a restoration of those harmed in the process.[24]

As the verdict thread moved through the *Treehouse* that night and the Treepers observed the unrepentant response of the State and the agitated state of the BGI, the tone changed. The Treepers did not kid themselves. The court battle may have ended, but the battle in the court of public opinion would only get bloodier and stupider, and they knew it.

46

DENYING REALITY

*T*HE WORD THEY USE IN GERMAN is *Dolchstoss*. It means "stab in the back." The *Dolchstoss* legend gained currency after the German defeat in World War I. When the German advance on the western front collapsed in 1918, many in the military refused to believe that they lost on the battlefield. They found it much more comforting to believe that the politicians back home subverted their valiant efforts through their double dealing. The myth endured for years; still does in some quarters.

Although there had been griping about the prosecution before the verdict, a new *Dolchstoss* legend quickly coalesced around the State's defeat on the Zimmerman front. Talk of betrayal began mere hours after the verdict came down. Asked one blogger at the *Democratic Underground*, "Did the prosecution lose on purpose?"[1] Asked another, "Did the prosecution in the Zimmerman trial 'throw the case'?"[2] New Orleans columnist Jarvis DeBerry and the attorneys he consulted came away with the impression that "the prosecution didn't want to win a conviction."[3] "Listening to the lead prosecutor's final argument in the Zimmerman case, it's hard to believe he really wanted a conviction," agreed William Boardman at *Reader Supported News*.[4] Queried Floyd Blue of the *Daily Kos* in his headline, "Who Among Us Honestly Believes the Zimmerman Prosecution Tried to Win?"[5]

More substantially, Steven Rosenfeld promised in the headline of his civil liberties column on *AlterNet* "10 Reasons Lawyers Say Florida's Law Enforcement Threw Away George Zimmerman's Case." The lawyers he surveyed came down particularly hard on the State's seemingly lax jury selection, its failure to demand a change in venue, its haphazard witness preparation, and the selection. of Angela Corey to lead the prosecution team. Among other attorneys, Rosenfeld cited outspoken New York–based attorney Warren Ingber on the case. "I find it personally difficult to believe it was not thrown," said Ingber. "I am far from alone in this assessment, and it reveals even harder truth why this case was a miscarriage of justice." Ingber argued that Governor Rick Scott and Angela Corey, both Republicans, got a "cost-free" bargain out of defeat. They gave the illusion of taking the case seriously, but with an acquittal they spared themselves the burden of a retrial or an appeal.[6]

The article evoked nearly a thousand comments, almost all of them in agreement, many of them inflammatory. "Reason 11: KILLER Z's ex magistrate dad, court-clerk mom, & FL cop uncle—most likely pulled some strings—to initially get their boy released from custody [for 45 days] & then to pulled some more strings to influence the prosecution to botch the case," concluded Nixak.77. "I said this a year ago, that even if they charge that turd, the state will help him walk. I hate being right," said Gene Starwind. "In a just world, the DOJ should be taking all this into account, and arresting as many as possible who conspired to let the murderer walk free," added AlphaNumeric111. "Florida needs a federal takeover as soon as possible[. T]hey're too stupid, too cruel, and too criminal for self rule," wrote bickle2.

Angela Corey gave life to the *Dolchstoss* legend with her oddly chipper performance at the postverdict press conference. "What we promised to do was get this case in front of a jury and give George Zimmerman and Trayvon Martin each their day in court," Corey said, all but affirming Ingber's theory that the State was more interested in staging a trial than winning a conviction. This was a theme that Corey repeated throughout the press conference. "We felt that everyone had a right to know everything about this case," she contended, and in that goal the State largely succeeded. It was less her words, however, than her tone that irked, if not outraged, the Martin faithful. She did not seem remotely upset about losing the case.[7] The *Twitchy* headline captured the bewilderment of the pro-Martin camp: "Viewers wonder: Why is Florida state attorney Angela Corey smiling so big?"[8]

"FL State Atty Angela Corey happy & smiling way too much. Does she not know prosecution lost???" tweeted former CNN anchor Rick Sanchez. "Head Prosecutor Angela Corey is she for real? Proud of the job they did? No remorse in their loss. I'm APPALLED," comedian Steve Harvey weighed in. "Angela Corey and the entire prosecution team are idiots. For someone who just lost a major case she sure is smiling a lot," chimed in Aquarian Rick Stro. "Florida State Attorney Angela Corey smiling this much right now is really upsetting," added Adam Burton, like Stro, an engaged citizen watching the press conference and tweeting.

Although much of the *Dolchstoss* commentary was empty-headed and virtually all of it off the mark, the question that the commenters raised was a legitimate one: Did the State do all it could to convict George Zimmerman? The answer was not a simple one. Yes, on the surface at least, the State went above and beyond the call of duty. Prosecutors collaborated with Team Trayvon in creating a story line that was in large part false. They enabled Jeantel's largely fictitious account of her final phone calls with Martin. They conspired to keep Martin's damaging phone and social media data first out of the hands of the defense and then out of the trial. They blustered and lied shamelessly throughout the trial itself. Indeed, they fought hard enough and dirty enough to merit a disbarment recommendation by Alan Dershowitz. And yet, the four of them, Corey included, had to feel conflicted about their assignments. They knew too much not to be uneasy.

Unlike the defense, however, the prosecutors had no *Conservative Treehouse* or *Legal Insurrection* or *TalkLeft* to reassure them or to help shore up their line of attack. In this regard, the pro-Martin pundits were hardly in a position to complain about a *Dolchstoss*. In the sixteen months between the emergence of the case and the verdict, they did almost no useful research. At the one critical juncture when the prosecution did drop the ball, either through neglect or intent, they did not even notice.

This prosecutorial oversight deserves a quick review, and that was the discrediting of Selene Bahadoor's testimony. Contrary to what de la Rionda had Bahadoor say, it was Bahadoor's sister who in her very first interview said that she "heard running outside . . . and saw shadows running from left to right." Had prosecutors been able to present this account as credible, they would have at least had a story to tell. Yes, Martin made it back to Green's townhome. Zimmerman found him there, chased him back to the T, and confronted him aggressively.

If de la Rionda seemed genuinely disappointed with the verdict, John Guy was another story. It was he who had interviewed Bahadoor's sister in March 2012. He should have remembered what she told him and prevented de la Rionda from embarrassing himself. At the postverdict press conference, he seemed unbowed. His one prepared statement was ambiguous to a fault: "We have from the beginning just prayed for the truth to come out and for peace to be the result, and that continues to be our prayers and we believe they have been answered."[9] One could argue that his prayers were answered. The truth did come out, but it was not the kind of truth that was going to result in any kind of peace.

47

LEARNING NOTHING

I N THE ARCHIVES OF LEGAL FICTION, two characters best embody liberal self-perception. One is attorney Atticus Finch of *To Kill A Mockingbird* fame. The other is Juror #8, the character played by Henry Fonda in the 1957 movie *Twelve Angry Men*. In his screenplay notes, Reginald Rose describes #8 as "a man who sees all sides of every question and constantly seeks the truth. A man of strength tempered with compassion. Above all, he is a man who wants justice to be done and will fight to see that it is." Not one for nuance, Rose describes #8's nemesis, Juror #3, played by Lee J. Cobb in the film, as "a humorless man who is intolerant of opinions other than his own and accustomed to forcing his wishes and views upon others." Set as the film was in the mid-fifties, Juror #3 serves as the inevitable Joe McCarthy proxy. In the drama that follows, he allies himself with Juror #10, "a bigot who places no values on any human life save his own."[1] Such was the conservative profile in the liberal mind nearly sixty years ago. Not much has changed.

The plot of *Twelve Angry Men* unfolds fully in the jury room. The jurors have convened to discuss the case. As fate would have it, the defendant is a young, five-foot-seven-inch, Hispanic man accused of killing a much taller man. Sound familiar? In this case, however, the victim was the father and the weapon was a knife. In the initial go-round, only #8 votes not guilty. The other jurors are stunned. "I just think he's guilty," says Juror #2. "I thought it was obvious. I mean, nobody proved otherwise." The Fonda character responds sagely, "Nobody has to prove otherwise. The burden of proof is on the prosecution. The defendant doesn't have to open his mouth. That's in the Constitution. The Fifth Amendment."

When one of the jurors points out that the accused cannot even remember what movie he was alleged to have seen on the evening of the murder, #8 answers, "Do you think you'd be able to remember details after an upsetting experience such as being struck in the face by your father." This being Hollywood, the good liberal juror persuades the others one by one to his point of view. "We may be wrong," #8 concedes. "We may be trying to return a guilty man to the community. No one can really know. But we have reasonable doubt, and this is a safeguard that has enormous value in our system." Finally, even #10 and #3 yield to his wisdom, and the jurors vote to acquit.

That was then. This is now. If the Zimmerman jurors honored the Constitution, the prosecutors, politicians, and pundits showed in their posttrial comments a stunning indifference to the traditional protections built into our legal system. As the jurors quickly discovered, liberalism isn't what it used to be. The finely wrought verdict that they had anguished their way to after three weeks of testimony and sixteen hours of deliberation was widely maligned, and their own efforts mocked.

Although the prosecutors made all the appropriate noise about "respecting" the jury's verdict, their extended comments showed little respect at all. After getting blistered for her too-cheerful press conference, Angela Corey started talking tough. Her one-word response to a question on the show *HLN After Dark* was as tough as it gets. When host Vinnie Politan asked her to sum up George Zimmerman, Corey paused thoughtfully and said "murderer."[2] Alan Dershowitz and other legal commentators rocked back in disbelief. "Clearly [Zimmerman] is somebody who was acquitted by a jury on the grounds of self-defense," said Dershowitz, "and she shouldn't be going around second-guessing the jury verdict and calling him a murderer. He probably has a defamation action against her."[3]

Corey and de la Rionda seemed to actually believe the story line the prosecutors had been feeding the jury. "What we said," explained Corey, "is you can't take a concealed weapon and encourage or incite a fistfight, which is what [Zimmerman] did by stalking a teenager who didn't know who he was, and then whip your gun out and shoot." De la Rionda added new imaginative detail. "My theory is that he pulled [the gun] out early," said the defeated prosecutor. "He was going to make sure [Martin] didn't get away. He wanted to be a cop." The pair implicitly faulted the female jurors for failing to see through Zimmerman's many presumed fabulations. "Those lies were put in front of the jury, one after the other," said Corey, who had obviously learned nothing about memory or about mercy from Juror #8.[4]

For every Alan Dershowitz monitoring the case, there was a Richard Thompson Ford. In a July 16 *New Republic* article, this Stanford professor of law and author of several books on race and crime mined several new veins of misinformation. Ford made the larger point that underemployment in the black community and an overworked court system conspired to put more African Americans in prison than there ought to be. This, in turn, led people like Zimmerman to project criminality even onto a "kid" like Martin, "who had avoided a run-in with the law."[5]

That was not exactly true. Martin had had multiple run-ins with the law. What spared him formal entry into the justice system was the preferential treatment afforded to black male offenders by the Miami-Dade Schools Police Department. Unfortunately, this kid-glove treatment kept the adults in Martin's life ignorant of the depth of the young man's problems. That ignorance, in turn, left Martin wandering high and unsupervised on a rainy February night in Sanford, 250 miles from whichever house in the Miami area he then called home.

In Sanford, Martin ran into Zimmerman. Ford initially described him as "an edgy basket case with a gun who had called 911 46 times in 15 months, once to report the suspicious activities of a *seven year old* black boy."[6] Although quick to denounce stereotypes, Ford here flirted with libel in his crude profile of this "vigilante." Virtually every assertion in his sentence was wrong. Zimmerman had called not 9-1-1 but the nonemergency number. He made the calls over a period of eight years, not fifteen months, and many were made at the request of beleaguered neighbors. He once reported that a seven-year-old had been left unattended, not that he was involved in suspicious activities. As to what it was about this highly respected, happily married, well-employed young man that made him an edgy basket case, Ford never bothered to explain.

He did not need to. Much of the *New Republic* audience, perhaps most, shared his preconceptions. The editors apparently did too. When various legal scholars alerted them to the article's defamatory errors, they amended them only grudgingly and slowly and even then refused to give up on the "edgy basket case" slur.[7]

Liberal attorneys like Ford may identify with Atticus Finch, but Atticus Finch would not identify with them. Atticus ignored public opinion. He stared down the mobs intent on extralegal justice. He protected his "mockingbird" as well as he could. Attorney Ford did none of the above. Nor, to say the least, did attorney Benjamin Crump. Said Crump, insulting those who know the past, "Trayvon Martin will forever remain in the annals of history next to Medgar Evers and Emmett Till, as symbols for the fight for equal justice for all."[8] Till, a fourteen-year-old Chicago boy, was brutally lynched for allegedly flirting with a white woman in 1955 Mississippi. The courageous civil rights leader Evers took a bullet in the back from a racist assassin in 1963 Mississippi. Martin took a bullet to the chest while gratuitously bashing in the head of a Hispanic man he did not know in a multiethnic 2012 Florida community.

The old bulls responded much as one would expect them to. Initially, they just asked for an arrest and then just a trial. Neither proved sufficient. "I do not accept the [Zimmerman verdict]," Jackson told the world in pure *Dolchstoss* spirit. He compared the trial to that of Emmett Till's murderers. "Not one black lawyer on either side, not one black on the jury, not one male on the jury, and so something about it was stacked from the very beginning," said Jackson, fully ignoring the demographics of Seminole County and the State's blundering effort to squash Zimmerman.[9] Jackson apparently preferred the dynamics of the 1995 O. J. Simpson trial. In that case, a 75 percent black jury, pulled from a jury pool only 28 percent black, acquitted the transparently guilty Simpson of a brutal double homicide after just four hours of deliberation.[10] If Jackson did not accept the Simpson verdict, there is no record of his protest.

Al Sharpton called the Zimmerman verdict an "atrocity" and laid the blame on the jurors. "What this jury has done," said Sharpton, "is establish a precedent that when you are young and fit a certain profile, you can be committing no crime . . . and be killed and someone can claim self-defense." Conceding the role mob pressure played in the arrest of Zimmerman, Sharpton added, "We had to march to even get a trial and even at trial, when he's exposed over and over again as a liar, he is acquitted."[11]

Although admittedly "outraged and heartbroken" by the verdict, the NAACP's Ben Jealous proved to be slightly more prudent in his response than Sharpton or Jackson. As egged on by CNN's Candy Crowley, Jealous boasted that the NAACP was in talks with the Justice Department about filing civil rights charges against Zimmerman. "When you look at comments made by young black men who lived in that neighborhood about how they felt, especially targeted by him," said Jealous of some hitherto unknown young black men, "there is reason to be concerned that race was a factor in why he targeted young Trayvon."[12]

The media showed some restraint, but many could not resist the urge to join the mob. The day after the verdict, the *New York Post* summed up newsroom sentiments in the quippy headline "TRAY-VESTY."[13] The *Guardian* headline announced "George Zimmerman Skirts Justice with All-White Jury."[14] The preposterous comparison to Emmett Till got a ton of play. "Trayvon Martin Is Our Emmett Till; Our Jury Selection Process Is No Better Now Than It Was In 1955," read the misbegotten headline of a *Daily Kos* article that denounced the "all-white jury."[15] "When will it all end?" The *New York Daily News* asked below a list of deceased young black men that began with Emmett Till and ended with Trayvon Martin.[16] A month before the trial began, Lil Wayne, the rapper candidate Obama gave a shout-out to during the 2008 campaign, apologized to the Till family for the lyric, "Beat that pussy up like Emmett Till."[17] In the wake of the postverdict comparisons, he was not the only one who should have been apologizing to Till's family.

48

MISLEADING AMERICA

"*J*UROR SAYS ZIMMERMAN 'GOT AWAY WITH MURDER.'"
So read the headline in the *New York Times* twelve days after the
trial ended.[1] The *Washington Post, Los Angeles Times, USA Today,*
and *Chicago Tribune* ran comparable, if not identical, headlines.
What none of those publications mentioned—and kudos to *Slate*'s William Saletan for breaking the story[2]—was that the juror in question
intended to say no such thing.

ABC News gets the credit again for its continued commitment to
misleading America. In this case, its producers recruited the one woman
of color on George Zimmerman's "all-white" jury and twisted her words
to incite the public. In an "exclusive" interview, *Good Morning America*'s
Robin Roberts said to juror B29, "Some people have said, point-blank,
'George Zimmerman got away with murder.' How do you respond to
those people who say that?" In the edited video ABC floated to get the
media's attention, "Maddy" answered unhesitatingly, "George Zimmerman got away with murder. But you can't get away from God."[3]

Given the bait, the media bit big-time and generated their own misleading headlines. In the accompanying *Times* article by Lizette Alvarez—
the reporter who gave the world "White Hispanic"—there was not even
a mention of the prompt by Roberts. In fact, though, Roberts not only
prompted Maddy, but she also set her up for a seriously deceptive edit.

In the unedited version, after Roberts asked her the leading question, Maddy paused, started her response over, and clearly played back the gist of Roberts's question—"George Zimmerman got away with murder"—as the stated premise to her own answer, "But you can't get away from God." In other words, that was how she would answer that question if asked. She never volunteered that Zimmerman got away with murder, nor did she openly agree with the premise. In fact, she stood by her decision to acquit Zimmerman and said the case should not have gone to trial.

In her introduction to Maddy's interview, Roberts made several factual mistakes to complement the network's manipulation of the video. In the way of example, Roberts said of Zimmerman, "He called police. They suggested he stay in his car." The dispatcher, of course, never asked Zimmerman to stay in his truck and did not even recommend he go back to it once aware he had left it. Nor was the dispatcher a police officer. Mistakes this fundamental made skeptics wonder whether they were, in fact, mistakes. Intentionally or otherwise, ABC News had been stoking black paranoia for more than a year and continued unapologetically after the verdict.

That paranoia exploded in angry postverdict demonstrations across the country and the occasional small-scale riot. A *Washington Post–ABC News* poll showed that 86 percent of African Americans disagreed with the verdict, almost all of them "strongly," against only 9 percent who approved. By contrast, whites approved of the verdict by 51 to 31 percent.[4] Of note, the better educated the individual was, the more likely he or she was to approve of the verdict. Of note, too, the media effort to whiten Zimmerman helped suppress his support among Hispanics, who disapproved of the verdict by slightly more than a two-to-one margin.

The sequestration of the jury quite possibly saved Zimmerman from conviction. To repeat the words of Justice Holmes, "Mob law does not become due process of law by securing the assent of a terrified jury."[5] The jurors, especially Maddy, had little idea of the terror that awaited them after the verdict. It was only "as the negative news reports about their verdict erupted," said Robin Roberts uncritically, that Maddy "crumbled."[6]

"I literally fell on my knees and I broke down," confessed Maddy. "My husband was holding me. I was screaming and crying, and I kept saying to myself I feel like I killed him." In her interview with Roberts, Maddy tried to explain the jury process to those watching. "I feel that if maybe if [the media] would [explain] the law, and a lot of people would read it, they would understand the choices that they gave us," said Maddy. She pleaded in vain. Her exculpatory appearance on ABC News did little to quiet the critics. "I do feel like she caved," said black radio host Mo Ivory on CNN. "Part of me is very upset with her, and I think that the apologies after were empty apologies."[7] In the blogosphere both sides attacked her, despite the fact that she was, in Mark O'Mara's words, a "model juror." Said O'Mara accurately, "Based on her comments, Juror B29 accepted a tremendous burden, set her feelings aside, and cast a verdict based on the evidence presented in court and on the law she was provided."[8]

Although more than 60 percent of college graduates thought the Zimmerman verdict just, that number did not include any Democrat running for office.[9] This pronounced deviation from the norm was most evident in New York City, where a highly contested mayoral primary loomed less than two months down the road. Bill de Blasio, the city's public advocate, called the not-guilty verdict "a slap in the face to justice." City Council speaker Christine Quinn called it "a shocking insult to his family and everyone seeking justice for Trayvon." Said controller John Liu, "Today's decision is shocking and highlights the sad reality that the day of equal justice for Trayvon and millions of other young men of color has yet to arrive." The only black mayoral candidate, Bill Thompson, said, "Trayvon Martin was killed because he was black. There was no justice done today in Florida." And finally, in one of the few times the words "tweet" and "Anthony Weiner" were not part of someone's punch line, mayoral hopeful Weiner tweeted, "Keep Trayvon's family in our prayers. Deeply unsatisfying verdict. Trial by jury is our only choice in a democracy."[10]

At the national level, the pandering was no less obvious. Democratic Senate majority leader Harry Reid said on NBC's *Meet the Press*, "This isn't over with, and I think that's good."[11] By "not over with" he meant that Eric Holder's Justice Department would continue to hound Zimmerman despite his having been cleared more than a year earlier by the FBI. By "good," there was no telling what he meant. Democratic presidential aspirant Hillary Clinton also welcomed "the next steps from the Justice Department" and added some empty words about "the need for a national dialogue," a dialogue that her party would never initiate in any meaningful way.[12]

No prominent Democrat defended the verdict or raised hard questions about the factors that put Martin in harm's way that tragic night in Sanford, Florida. Those factors did not include Stand Your Ground, guns, or racial profiling. They did include sporadic parenting, indifferent schooling, and an inner-city culture that openly celebrated violence, drugs, and lawlessness. To discuss these issues candidly was to risk the Democratic stranglehold on a profoundly troubled and dependent population. As to Republican politicos, Angela Corey excepted, they did what they normally do when tough racial issues surface—hide.

It took a retired NBA star to risk his public standing by stating what should have been obvious to everyone. "I think Trayvon Martin—God rest his soul—I think he did flip the switch and started beating the hell out of Mr. Zimmerman," said the outspoken Charles Barkley. "I agree with the verdict."[13] Unfortunately for America, the president did not show nearly the courage that Barkley did.

49

DOUBLING DOWN

ID GEORGE ZIMMERMAN "profile" Trayvon Martin? Of course he did, and he did not hesitate to share that fact with the Sanford police. In his initial call to the nonemergency dispatcher and in his subsequent interviews, he explained the variables, all of them relevant, that led him to suspect Trayvon Martin may have been "up to no good."

- It was raining, and Martin was wandering about, not jogging or walking swiftly to a destination. Zimmerman's observation was validated by the unaccounted-for twenty-five minutes in Martin's return from the 7-Eleven.

- Martin was looking at houses. The area had been plagued by burglaries and home invasions, particularly along its unfenced western flank, where Zimmerman first spotted Martin.

- Martin looked high. The THC in his blood indicated he was. As Martin's recent history suggested, he got high a lot.

- Martin looked like he was "up to no good." Given his recent apprehension for possession of stolen jewelry and a burglary tool, Zimmerman may have been right.

- Martin was male. This was perhaps the most significant variable. Males had committed all known property crime in the area.

- Martin was in his "late teens." So were a disproportionate percentage of the criminal suspects.

- Martin was tall. He was a full-grown young man, not a child.

- When asked, Zimmerman speculated that Martin "looked black." Forty seconds later, he confirmed that Martin was black. Zimmerman had dubbed him "suspicious" before he knew his race. In that all recent arrests had been of young black men, however, Martin's race likely factored into Zimmerman's thinking. How could it not?

- The fact that Martin wore a hoodie seemed the least significant of all variables. Zimmerman mentioned this only when asked—"Yeah, a dark hoodie, like a gray hoodie, and either jeans or sweat pants and white tennis shoes"—and made no point of the hoodie afterwards. It was, after all, raining.

In the past, Zimmerman had shied from confronting suspects—there is no better word—and refrained this time as well. When the dispatcher asked in which direction Martin was running, Zimmerman followed at a prudent distance and stopped following when the dispatcher so requested. Martin's behavior had sufficiently alarmed him that he affirmed his request for an officer to come to the scene. Zimmerman never left the east-west cut-through. Martin came back to confront him. There is no doubt of that. He came back for a reason, and it was not a good one. Still, had the police arrived two minutes earlier, the names George Zimmerman and Trayvon Martin would have meant little to anyone but their families and friends.

Needing to make some sense of the shooting, or to exploit it, Zimmerman's accusers focused on two issues, race and guns, more specifically, racial profiling and Stand Your Ground laws. It is hard to pinpoint exactly when the phrase "racial profiling" first entered everyday vocabulary, let alone acquired a taint. In the year 1996, the Supreme Court ruled in the *United States v. Armstrong et al.* that the plaintiffs "failed to show that the Government declined to prosecute similarly situated suspects of other races."[1] Although the word "profiling" was not used in the decision, the

Court rejected the idea that a racial quota of some sort should be applied to prosecutions. In the year 2000, however, a lawsuit in New Jersey prompted the State to release ninety-one thousand pages of police records on turnpike traffic stops, and critics made of these records what they would.

After the events of September 11, 2001, activists extended the concept of racial profiling to include Muslims or people suspected of being Muslims. In 2003, President George W. Bush signed an executive order prohibiting employees in seventy different federal agencies from using race, color, or ethnicity to profile potential suspects.[2] By 2010, profiling had become taboo in progressive circles, even if done by private citizens. Black NPR commentator Juan Williams learned this the hard way after sharing with Fox News's Bill O'Reilly a sentiment felt by virtually all cognizant Americans of any stripe.

"Look, Bill, I'm not a bigot," said Williams ingenuously. "You know the kind of books I've written about the civil rights movement in this country. But when I get on the plane, I got to tell you, if I see people who are in Muslim garb and I think, you know, they are identifying themselves first and foremost as Muslims, I get worried. I get nervous."[3] That comment cost William his position with NPR. Fortunately for Jesse Jackson, he made his remarks about profiling the white people who walked behind him before such comments were verboten.

Disallowed from using the phrase "racial profiling" in *Florida v. George Zimmerman*, prosecutors stuck to the word "profiling" but wielded it like the archetypal man with a hammer to whom everything looked like a nail. Zimmerman, said Bernie de la Rionda in his close, "profiled [Martin] as a criminal. He assumed certain things, that Trayvon Martin was up to no good, and that is what led up to his death." Not exactly. In his prior forty-six calls to the nonemergency dispatcher—"See something, say something"—Zimmerman profiled any number of suspicious individuals, and none of them died. To demonize the broad-based profiling Zimmerman did, that all police officers do, is to drive common sense from the public square, but that is exactly what Zimmerman's many accusers have tried to do.

One of those accusers has been US attorney general Eric Holder. In a speech to the NAACP convention in Orlando three days after the verdict, Holder urged the nation to "confront the underlying attitudes, the mistaken beliefs and the unfortunate stereotypes that serve too often as the basis for police action and private judgments." He recounted how he himself had been stopped by the police, twice on the infamous New Jersey Turnpike and once while running at night through the streets of Georgetown, presumably for no offense other than his color.

"So Trayvon's death last spring caused me to sit down to have a conversation with my own fifteen-year-old son, like my dad did with me," said Holder. "This was a father-son tradition I hoped would not need to be handed down." Although conceding opportunities had improved for blacks—what with him being AG and Obama president, that would be hard to deny—he felt the obligation to make his son "aware of the world that he must still confront."[4]

In a thoughtful *National Review Online* article, classics scholar Victor Davis Hanson explained what that world was actually like. "I fear that for every lecture of the sort that Holder is forced to give his son, millions of non-African Americans are offering their own versions of ensuring safety to their progeny," said Hanson. What Hanson's liberal father told him was not about race in any theoretical sense, nor about any potential threat from the old, the very young, or the female. Instead, he told him "about the tendency of males of one particular age and race to commit an inordinate amount of violent crime." Hanson's awareness of crime statistics and his personal experience living in the San Francisco Bay Area moved him, however reluctantly, to pass this same message on to his own son. He suspected that Holder, too, worries more about the threat to his son from other black youths than from the police or neighborhood watch captains. Given the realities of life in urban America, Hanson argued that Holder's speech "might as well have been given on Mars." It would convince no one "that stereotyping of young African American males and Stand Your Ground laws are the two key racial problems facing America."[5]

Yes, Holder also denounced Stand Your Ground laws. Although these laws were not relevant to Zimmerman's trial, Holder's attack on them gave the NAACP attendees the illusion that he was doing something to address the Martin shooting. To be sure, this was not what black activists wanted. What they really wanted was his Justice Department to try Zimmerman for some rights violation or another. Indeed, the Detroit City Council took time off from going bankrupt to pass a unanimous resolution demanding a federal investigation of Zimmerman.[6] Holder knew this wasn't going to happen and, unlike his audience, he knew why. The FBI had already cleared Zimmerman of any thought crimes, past or present. Given his history, if Zimmerman were a "racist," every nonblack in America was. Holder knew, too, that activists in Orlando and elsewhere wanted to hear none of this. So he spared them.

"In things racial," Holder told Justice Department employees during a controversial Black History Month speech in February 2009, "we have always been and we, I believe, continue to be in too many ways essentially a nation of cowards."[7] Four years later, in Orlando, Holder had the opportunity to prove himself something other. He did not take it. And yet, in that first week after the verdict came down, Holder was the one administration official scoring points with the Democratic base. He did so simply by aligning his interests with black concerns, even if ineffectually.

"On Trayvon Martin and other racial issues, Holder speaks out in ways Obama does not," shouted the headline of an article by Perry Bacon Jr., the political editor of NBC's influential blog, the *Grio*. Bacon spanked Obama for avoiding the Martin issue and traced his reticence to the Henry Louis Gates controversy in Cambridge four years earlier. "He has not delivered a version of his eloquent 2008 campaign speech on race while in office," Bacon complained.[8] Princeton professor Cornel West complained even louder. "He's still too tied," said West in dissecting Obama's postverdict silence. "He's too uncritical. He's too deferential. He's too subservient as it were, and as long as that's in place we're going to find ourselves unable to tell the fundamental truth." No fan of Obama's foreign policy, West described the president as a "global George Zimmerman."[9] The White House was listening. The criticism had begun to sting.

Six days after the verdict came down, Obama made an unexpected appearance at a routine White House press conference specifically to address the "Trayvon Martin ruling." He did not really want to be there. Said Tavis Smiley on *Meet the Press*, "A week of protests outside the White House, pressure building on him inside the White House, pushed him to that podium."[10] As a first priority, Obama sent his thoughts and prayers to the family of Trayvon Martin. As to George Zimmerman and his extended family, still in hiding after a year and a half of death threats, Obama offered not a word of hope or encouragement. Nor did he rebuke those whose threats had forced the Zimmermans into an internal exile. In fact, Obama mentioned Zimmerman only once, and that late in the press conference.[11]

Expanding on his remarks from more than a year prior, Obama once again identified himself with Martin, now even more intimately. "Trayvon Martin could have been me thirty-five years ago," said Obama. Although at seventeen Obama was living in Hawaii with his white family and attending an exclusive prep school, their color apparently was bond enough. Like all men of color, said Obama, he knew what it was like to be followed in a department store or have women clutch their purses upon seeing him enter an elevator.[12] Even if true, Obama neglected to mention the motive behind this seemingly bad behavior. Like Hanson's father, like Obama's own grandmother, even liberal-minded nonblacks know that black males commit more than their share of crime, far more. According to best evidence, blacks commit interracial muggings, robberies, and rapes at thirty-five times the rate of whites.[13]

Obama did acknowledge that young men black men "are dispropor-tionately both victims and perpetrators of violence," but he abandoned this thread prematurely. Although he had the opportunity to shake up the debate, to show that he was not one of Holder's cowards, he instead pulled his ultimate punch, not in what he said, but in what he did not say. He let the idea stand that Martin was one of the victims of violence, but not one of the perpetrators. If the president had called attention to the fractures in Martin's domestic life, his suppressed criminal record, his all-but-unseen descent into drugs and violence, and especially his reckless attack on Zimmerman, Obama might have lent a dollop of moral seriousness to his remarks. But he did not. Instead, he tacitly encouraged his audience to project their anger and anxiety onto racial scapegoat George Zimmerman. Jesse "I want to cut his nuts out" Jackson had scared Obama off the track of serious cultural reform five years earlier. He never got back on.

Fearful of going deep, Obama spent most of the talk on shallow side issues like the limits of federal intervention, racial profiling, and Stand Your Ground laws. He capped the talk off with a cheerful bromide about America becoming, racially at least, "a more perfect union."[14] If that last sentiment had been true, one could forgive his swap of form for substance here, but it was not. A comprehensive poll taken by NBC News and the Wall Street Journal during the days immediately before and after his talk showed that Obama failed in the one area in which even the opposition hoped he would succeed: bridging the racial divide. In the month of his inauguration, 79 percent of whites and 63 percent of blacks held a favorable view of race relations in America. By July 2013, those figures had fallen to 52 percent among whites and 38 percent among blacks, a calamitous decline, rarely addressed, never explained.[15]

"I am my brother's keeper," said Barack Obama in his breakthrough speech at the 2004 Democratic National Convention. "I am my sister's keeper—that makes this country work."[16] George Zimmerman believed that, too, really believed it. His friends called him Tugboat, the one who always came to the rescue. He helped a black homeless man find justice. He helped guide two black teens through life. He helped a terrified mother secure her house. He helped his wary neighbors secure their community. Even after the verdict, when he had reason to run and hide, he helped pull a family from their overturned SUV. And although he supported Obama, and lobbied for Obama, and voted for Obama at least once, in the final analysis he did not look enough like Obama to be his son.

And that made all the difference. ■

Notes

CHAPTER 1: BRAVING THE TANK

1. Sundance, in a series of phone interviews with the author, at least monthly from February to July 2013.
2. Information and quotes in this section were obtained from Sharon, StellaP, Ytz4mee, DiWataman, and Chip Bennett, in phone interviews with the author and Treepers interview by the author, between February 16 and March 1, 2013.
3. Sundance, "We Ain't Backing Down—Get That Through Your Thick Skulls . . . This Ain't about Trayvon v. Zimmerman—Never Was," *The Last Refuge* (blog), April 13, 2012, http://theconservativetreehouse.com/2012/04/13/we-aint-backing-down-get-that-through-your-thick-skulls-this-aint-about-trayvon-v-zimmerman-never-was/.

CHAPTER 2: GATHERING THE FACTS

1. George Michael Zimmerman, "Narrative Report," Sanford Police Department, February 26, 2012, cached at Trayvon.axiomamnesia.com.
2. The preceding quote and the account that follows are from the audio of the Zimmerman call, cached at http://trayvon.axiomamnesia.com/trayvon-martin-911-calls-audio/.
3. Prairie Drifter, "Trayvon Martin 4: Trayvon Lies in Wait (timeline analysis)," *Gullibility Planet* (blog), April 12, 2012, http://gullibilityplanet.blogspot.com/2012/04/trayvon-martin-4-trayvon-lies-in-wait.html.
4. Transcript can be seen at Jack Cashill, "Getting the Facts Straight," *American Thinker*, June 4, 2013, http://www.americanthinker.com/2013/06/getting_the_facts_straight_in_the_zimmerman_case.html; axiomamnesia.com. An additional transcript can be seen at http://transcripts.cnn.com/TRANSCRIPTS/1307/01/cnr.07.html.
5. Timothy Smith, "Offense Report," Sanford Police Department, February 26, 2012, cached at Trayvon.axiomamnesia.com.
6. T. C. O'Steen, State Attorney's Office, Investigative Division, memorandum re: Officer Tim Smith Interview, March 23, 2012, http://www.clickorlando.com/blob/view/-/15490330/data/1/-/kligxm/-/Zimmerman-documents.pdf, 23.
7. Jordan Broderick, "Offense Report," Sanford Police Department, February 26, 2012, cached at Trayvon.axiomamnesia.com.
8. Jonathan Mead, "Offense Report," Sanford Police Department, February 26, 2012, cached at Trayvon.axiomamnesia.com.
9. Dale Gilbreath, State Attorney's Office, Investigative Division, memorandum re: Witness Interview – Mead, April 2, 2012, http://www.clickorlando.com/blob/view/-/15490330/data/1/-/kligxm/-/Zimmerman-documents.pdf, 11.
10. Richard Ayala, "Offense Report," Sanford Police Department, February 26, 2012, cached at Trayvon.axionamnesia.com.

11. Stanford Police Department Offense Report No. 201250001136, Event No. 20120571671, 2/26/12, http://www.axiomamnesia.com/TrayvonMartinFiles/Trayvon-Martin-George -Zimmerman-FULL-case-report-documents.pdf, 7.

12. Ibid., 6.

13. O'Steen, State Attorney's Office, Investigative Division, memorandum re: Officer Tim Smith Interview.

14. Transcript, "Doris Singleton Interviews of George Zimmerman," February 26, 2012, http:// www.talkleft.com/zimm/singletontranscript1.pdf.

15. "Complete Transcript, Serino Interview," February 27, 2012, https://www.txantimedia.com.

16. Daniel Trotta, "Trayvon Martin: Before the world heard the cries," Reuters, April 3, 2012, http://www.reuters.com/article/2012/04/03/us-usa-florida-shooting-trayvon -idUSBRE8320UK20120403.

17. T. C. O'Steen, State Attorney's Office, Investigative Division, memorandum, March 27, 2012, http://www.clickorlando.com/blob/view/-/15490330/data/1/-/kligxm/-/Zimmerman -documents.pdf.

18. George E. Curry, "Trayvon Martin's parents re-live a 'nightmare,'" *Madison Times*, March 28, 2012: http://www.themadisontimes.com.

19. Kerry Sanders and James Novogrod, "In audio of police call, Trayvon Martin's father worries about his son," NBC News, June 20, 2012, http://usnews.nbcnews.com /_news/2012/06/20/12321970-in-audio-of-police-call-trayvon-martins-father-worries-about -his-son?lite.

20. Stanford Police Department Offense Report No. 201250001136.

21. Ibid.

22. "Trayvon Martin shot and killed in neighborhood altercation," Fox 35 News, February 27, 2012, http://www.myfoxorlando.com/story/17374352/trayvon-martin-shot-and-killed-in -neighborhood-altercation.

23. The following details were gleaned from MattWarner531, "George Zimmerman Re-enactment," published June 21, 2012, http://www.youtube.com/watch?v=VakGZgJxTi4.

24. Ibid.

25. "Trayvon Martin shot and killed in neighborhood altercation."

26. Arelis R. Hernández, "George Zimmerman answers lie detector questions," *Orlando Sentinel*, June 21, 2012, http://articles.orlandosentinel.com/2012-06-21/news/os-george-zimmerman -lie-detector-video-20120621_1_questions-gated-community-ervin.

27. See comments by rumpole2 and video at "George Zimmerman/Trayvon Martin Discussion #2, *RT (Random Topics)*, posted January 28, 2013, http://randomtopics.org/viewtopic .php?f=48&t=584&p=20744.

CHAPTER 3: BRACING FOR THE STORM

1. "911 tapes to be released this afternoon. Re: Trayvon Martin shooting," article attributed to the *Orlando Sentinel*, as posted on *Democratic Underground*, http://www.democraticunderground .com/1002432286; last edited March 16, 2012.

2. Rene Stutzman and Bianca Prieto, "Trayvon Martin shooting: Screams, shots heard on 911 call," *Orlando Sentinel*, March 17, 2012, http://articles.orlandosentinel.com/2012-03-17 /news/os-trayvon-martin-shooting-911-call-20120316_1_deadly-shooting-shot-man-reports.

3. T. C. O'Steen, State Attorney's Office, Investigative Division, Tracy Benjamin Martin Interview, http://www.talkleft.com/zimm/tracyapril2high.pdf. Martin also told O'Steen that he drove his son halfway to Sanford on his final trip and that Brandy Green took him the remaining half. In fact, Trayvon took the bus.

4. Trotta, "Trayvon Martin."
5. Marc Caputo, "Attorneys use bootcamp playbook to press Trayvon Martin case," *Tampa Bay Times*, March 23, 2012, http://www.tampabay.com/news/politics/national/attorneys-use -bootcamp-playbook-to-press-trayvon-martin-case/1221545.
6. Bruce B. Blackwell, esq., "Response in Opposition to Defendant's Motion to Compel," February 20, 2013, http://www.gzdocs.com/documents/0213/blackwell.pdf.
7. Caputo, "Attorneys use bootcamp playbook to press Trayvon Martin case."
8. "Witness #9 Files," cached at Trayvon.axionamnesia.com.
9. Chris Serino, "FBI Report," transcribed April 5, 2012, http://www.talkleft.com/zimm /serinofbireporthigh.pdf.
10. George Zimmerman, "Detective Serino's Interview with George Zimmerman," February 29, 2012, http://trayvon.axiomamnesia.com.
11. "Complete Transcript, Serino Interview, 2/29/2012, Tape 1," txandimedia, https://www .txantimedia.com/?p=1025.
12. Ibid.
13. Ibid.
14. Ibid.
15. Susan Jacobson, "Boy, 17, shot to death in Sanford during 'altercation,' police say," *Orlando Sentinel*, February 29, 2012, http://articles.orlandosentinel.com/2012-02-29/news/os-fatal -shooting-sanford-townhomes-20120226_1_gated-community-death-sunday-night-shot.
16. Trotta, "Trayvon Martin."
17. Alexia Cooper and Erica L. Smith, "Homicide Trends in the United States, 1980–2008," US Department of Justice, November 2011, http://bjs.gov/content/pub/pdf/htus8008.pdf.

CHAPTER 4: MOBILIZING THE PLAYERS

1. Trotta, "Trayvon Martin."
2. Sundance, "How and Why the Media Got It So Wrong—The Zimmerman Case—Packaged and Sold by Ryan Julison, Benjamin Crump, Natalie Jackson," *The Last Refuge* (blog), posted June 30, 2013, http://theconservativetreehouse.com/2013/06/30/how-and-why-the-media -got-it-so-wrong-the-zimmerman-case-packaged-and-sold-by-ryan-julison-benjamin-crump -natalie-jackson/.
3. Ryan Julison, Julison Communications Facebook page, accessed July 15, 2013, https://www .facebook.com/permalink.php?story_fbid=185970194846926&id=282453708439557.
4. Lee Stranahan, "USDA Continues to Lie About Pigford Fraud Despite Lawyer Statements," *Huffington Post*, December 20, 2010, http://www.huffingtonpost.com/lee-stranahan/usda -continues-to-lie-abo_b_799208.html.
5. "Left, Right, and Pigford: Introducing Lee Stranahan—Biggovernment.Com's 'Progressive' Pigford Film Documentarian," *Breitbart*, December 19, 2010, http://www.breitbart .com/Big-Journalism/2010/12/19/Left--Right--and-Pigford--Introducing-Lee-Stranahan ---BigGovernmentcom---s----Progressive----Pigford-Film-Documentarian.
6. Sharon LaFraniere, "U.S. Opens Spigot after Farmers Claim Discrimination," *New York Times*, April 25, 2013, http://www.nytimes.com/2013/04/26/us/farm-loan-bias-claims-often -unsupported-cost-us-millions.html?pagewanted=all&_r=1&.
7. Sundance, "Ryan Julison Takes Down Company Website and Scrubs Facebook Page to Hide the Racial Media Pitch in the Trayvon Martin Case . . ." *The Last Refuge* (blog), May 4, 2012, http://theconservativetreehouse.com/2012/05/04/ryan-julison-takes-down-company -website-and-scrubs-facebook-page-to-hide-the-racial-media-pitch-in-the-trayvon-martin -case.

8. Barbara Liston, "Family of Florida boy killed by Neighborhood Watch seeks arrest," Reuters, March 7, 2012, http://www.reuters.com/article/2012/03/08/us-crime-florida-neighborhoodwatch-idUSBRE82709M20120308.

9. Ibid.

10. Ibid.

11. *The Young Turks*, "Trayvon Martin Shot, Killed by Neighborhood Watch," You Tube, published March 8, 2012. http://www.youtube.com/watch?v=1CcVCoU-elc.

12. Trotta, "Trayvon Martin."

13. Scott McDonnell, "George Zimmerman rips Sanford police in audio from 2011 meeting," Bay News 9, May 23, 2012, baynews9.com/content/news/articles/cfn/2012/5/23/zimmerman_new_audio.html.

14. Jack Cashill, "Trayvon, George, and the Homeless Man," *American Thinker*, May 31, 2013, http://www.americanthinker.com/2013/05/trayvon_george_and_the_homeless_man.html.

15. Dan Barry et al., "Race, Tragedy and Outrage Collide after a Shot in Florida," *New York Times*, April 1, 2012, http://www.nytimes.com/2012/04/02/us/trayvon-martin-shooting-prompts-a-review-of-ideals.html?_r=5&hp=&pagewanted=all&&pagewanted.

16. George Zimmerman, MySpace pages (page 8 of 12), accessed May 2, 2012, on http://www.clickorlando.com/blob/view/-/15490330/data/1/-/kligxml/-/Zimmerman-documents.pdf, 224.

17. Rene Stutzman, "Shellie and George Zimmerman: Family finances were a problem," *Orlando Sentinel*, June 13, 2012, http://articles.orlandosentinel.com/2012-06-13/news/os-shellie-zimmerman-profile-20120613_1_therealgeorgezimmerman-com-family-finances-george-zimmerman.

18. Barry et al., "Race, Tragedy and Outrage Collide after a Shot in Florida."

19. Mark Osterman and Sondra Osterman, *Defending Our Friend: The Most Hated Man in America* (Mustang OK: Tate, 2013), 24.

20. Rene Stutzman, "Zimmerman's family: George handed out fliers, protesting police coddling of white suspect," *Orlando Sentinel*, April 5, 2012, http://articles.orlandosentinel.com/2012-04-05/news/os-george-zimmerman-fliers-20120405_1_sherman-ware-justin-collison-robert-zimmerman.

21. Letter from Zimmerman family member to Turner Clayton of the NAACP, March 26, 2012, http://www.gzdocs.com/documents/0513/discovery_3/naacp_letter.pdf.

22. Frances Robles, "Friends, lawyers wage campaign for Zimmerman in Trayvon Martin shooting," *Miami Herald*, April 7, 2012, http://www.palmbeachpost.com/news/news/crime-law/friends-lawyers-wage-campaign-for-zimmerman-in-tra/nN2yb/.

23. Osterman and Osterman, *Defending Our Friend*, 20.

24. Name redacted, FBI interview, April 3, 2012. http://www.clickorlando.com/blob/view/-/15490330/data/1/-/kligxml/-/Zimmerman-documents.pdf.

25. Quoted by Nandi in "Family of Florida boy killed by Neighborhood Watch seeks arrest" (accessed August 13, 2013) at http://www.blackvisions.org/Boards/index.php?topic=10541.135;wap2.

26. "George Zimmerman's Exclusive Full Interview with Sean Hannity," July 18, 2012, posted on YouTube on July 19, 2012, by ThePhantomNetwork, http://www.youtube.com/watch?v=kaua8aAUpOs.

27. Chris Francescani, "George Zimmerman: Prelude to a shooting," Reuters, April 25, 2012, http://www.reuters.com/article/2012/04/25/us-usa-florida-shooting-zimmerman-idUSBRE83O18H20120425.

28. Bob Zimmerman, in an interview with the author, in Sanford, Florida, June 17, 2013.

29. Richard Pérez-Peña, "Survivor Recounts Horror of Attack in Newark Schoolyard," *New York Times*, April 29, 2010, http://www.nytimes.com/2010/04/30/nyregion/30newark.html?_r=0.

30. Steven Malanga, "The Rainbow Coalition Evaporates," *City Journal*, Winter 2008, http://www.city-journal.org/2008/18_1_blacks_and_immigration.html.

31. David Horowitz, *Radical Son* (New York: Simon & Schuster, 1997), 246–48.

32. Janet Murguía, "A Complete Investigation Is Vital for Justice in Trayvon Martin Case," *Huffington Post*, March 22, 2012, http://www.huffingtonpost.com/janet-murguia/trayvon-martins-death-rem_b_1371407.html?ref=latino-voice.

33. Caroline May, "Latino organizations dismiss George Zimmerman, question his ethnicity," *Daily Caller*, March 29, 2012, http://dailycaller.com/2012/03/29/latino-organizations-dismiss-george-zimmerman-question-his-ethnicity/.

CHAPTER 5: MANAGING THE HYSTERIA

1. "Poynter's News University, Journalism's E-Learning Leader, Registers Its 250,000th User," posted April 15, 2013, on the Poynter. About Us web page, under "About Poynter and Poynter News University," http://about.poynter.org/about-us/press-room/poynter%E2%80%99s-news-university-journalism%E2%80%99s-e-learning-leader-registers-its-250000th-.

2. Andrew Beaujon, "CBS credits Mark Strassmann with breaking Trayvon Martin story," Poynter website, April 17, 2012, http://www.poynter.org/latest-news/mediawire/170572/cbs-credits-atlanta-correspondent-mark-strassmann-with-breaking-trayvon-martin-story/.

3. Brian Stelter, "In Slain Teenager's Case, a Long Route to National Attention," *New York Times*, March 25, 2012, http://www.nytimes.com/2012/03/26/business/media/for-martins-case-a-long-route-to-national-attention.html?pagewanted=all.

4. Beaujon, "CBS credits Mark Strassmann."

5. Daralene Jones, "Lawsuit Filed in Neighborhood Watch Shooting," ABC Eyewitness News 9, March 9, 2012, http://abcnews.go.com/US/video/lawsuit-filed-neighborhood-watch-shooting-15888368.

6. Ibid.

7. Christian Yazdanpanah, "How Marketers Brought George Zimmerman to Jail," *Relationship Era*, April 13, 2012, http://www.relationshipera.com/how-marketers-brought-george-zimmerman-to-jail/.

8. Ryan Julison, Julison Communications Facebook page, accessed July 15, 2013, https://www.facebook.com/permalink.php?story_fbid=378039282214609&id=282453708439557.

9. Yunji de Nies, "Orlando Watch Shooting Probe Reveals Questionable Police Conduct" ABC News Atlanta, March 13, 2012, http://abcnews.go.com/US/neighborhood-watch-shooting-trayvon-martin-probe-reveals-questionable/story?id=15907136#.UeWWS43FUud.

CHAPTER 6: MANNING THE GATES

1. Chris Francescani, "George Zimmerman: Prelude to a shooting," Reuters, April 25, 2012, http://www.reuters.com/article/2012/04/25/us-usa-florida-shooting-zimmerman-idUSBRE83O18H20120425?feedType=RSS&feedName=domesticNews&utm_source=dlvr.it&utm_medium=twitter&dlvrit=60573.

2. Osterman and Osterman, *Defending Our Friend*.

3. Lane DeGregory, "Trayvon Martin's killing shatters safety within Retreat at Twin Lakes in Sanford," *Tampa Bay Times*, March 24, 2012, http://www.tampabay.com/news/humaninterest/trayvon-martins-killing-shatters-safety-within-retreat-at-twin-lakes-in/1221799.

4. Ibid.

5. SA Matthew R. Oliver, "Federal Bureau of Investigation Report," Orlando, FL, May 2, 2012, http://www.gzdocs.com/documents/1112/discovery9/sa_oliver_taaffee.pdf.

6. "Sanford Crime Rate Report (Florida)," *City Rating*, http://www.cityrating.com/crime -statistics/florida/sanford.html#.UeWceo3FUud.

7. Oliver, "Federal Bureau of Investigation Report."

8. SA John M. Weyrauch and SA Johnny Lavender, "Federal Bureau of Investigation Report," Sanford, FL, April 5, 2012, http://www.gzdocs.com/documents/1112/discovery9 /sa_weyrauch_w47.pdf.

9. SA James Majeski and SA John M. Weyrauch, "Federal Bureau of Investigation Report," Maitland, FL (telephonic), April 9, 2012, http://www.gzdocs.com/documents/1112 /discovery9/sa_majeski_w46.pdf.

10. Dale Crosby, "Florida Department of Law Enforcement Investigative Report," March 19, 2012, http://www.clickorlando.com/blob/view/-/15490330/data/1/-/kligxm/-/Zimmerman -documents.pdf.

11. George Zimmerman, e-mail to Sanford Police Chief Bill Lee on September 18, 2011, http:// www.gzdocs.com/documents/0513/defense_discovery/general/2011-09-20_triplettj_email _re-dorivalw.pdf.

12. Barry et al., "Race, Tragedy and Outrage Collide after a Shot in Florida."

13. DeGregory, "Trayvon Martin's killing shatters safety within Retreat at Twin Lakes in Sanford."

14. "Retreat at Twin Lakes News," February 12, 2012, https://twitter.com/RTL_News /status/168735685455519745.

15. George Zimmerman, e-mail, February 7, 2012, 2012.http://www.gzdocs.com /documents/0513/discovery_3/feb_7_email.pdf.

16. George Zimmerman, e-mail, February 20, 2012, http://www.gzdocs.com/documents/0513 /discovery_3/feb_20_email.pdf.

17. Dale Gilbreath, State Attorney's Office, Investigative Division, memorandum re: Witness Interview – Mead, April 2, 2012, http://www.clickorlando.com/blob/view/-/15490330 /data/1/-/kligxm/-/Zimmerman-documents.pdf, 11.

18. Oliver, "Federal Bureau of Investigation Report."

19. Andrew Cohen, "Trayvon Martin's Killer Was Looking for Trouble—and Found It," *The Atlantic*, March 21, 2012, http://www.theatlantic.com/national/archive/2012/03/trayvon -martins-killer-was-looking-for-trouble-and-found-it/254815/.

20. Dan Gross, "'Stand Your Ground' Laws Promote Vigilante Mentality," *US News & World Report*, Debate Club (blog), March 28, 2012, http://www.usnews.com/debate-club/are-stand -your-ground-laws-a-good-idea/stand-your-ground-laws-promote-vigilante-mentality.

CHAPTER 7: WASHING ONE'S HANDS

1. "Trayvon Martin Case Moves to State Attorney's Office," WESH.com Orlando, March 13, 2012, www.wesh.com/trayvon-martin-extended-coverage/Trayvon-Martin-Case-Moves-To -State-Attorney-s-Office/-/14266478/13118970/-/view/print/-/5845d2z/-/index.html.

2. Elizabeth C. Alexander and Matthew R. Oliver, Federal Bureau of Investigation, Chris Serino, FBI Report, March 3, 2012, http://www.talkleft.com/zimm/serinofbireporthigh.pdf, 2.

3. Amy Pavuk and Jeff Weiner, "Jose Baez representing Sanford officer in George Zimmerman case," *Orlando Sentinel*, November 20, 2012, articles.orlandosentinel.com/2012-11-20/news /os-george-zimmerman-jose-baez-officer-20121120_1_jose-baez-george-zimmerman-case -trayvon-martin.

4. Stanford Police Department Offense Report No. 201250001136, Event No. 20120571671, 2/26/12, http://www.axiomamnesia.com/TrayvonMartinFiles/Trayvon-Martin-George -Zimmerman-FULL-case-report-documents.pdf.

5. "Rep. Frederica Wilson: Trayvon hunted down like a rabid dog, shot in the street and racially profiled," *The Right Scoop* (blog), March 28, 2012, http://therightscoop.com/rep-frederica -wilson-trayvon-hunted-down-like-a-rabid-dog-shot-in-the-street-and-racially-profiled/.

6. Rene Stutzman, "Trayvon Martin shooting case goes to State Attorney's Office today," *Orlando Sentinel*, March 13, 2012, http://articles.orlandosentinel.com/2012-03-13/news/os-trayvon -martin-shooting-case-20120312_1_patrol-car-gated-community-police-department.

7. Bianca Prieto, "Police turn over Travyon Martin shooting case to State Attorney," *Orlando Sentinel*, March 13, 2012, http://www.orlandosentinel.com/news/local/breakingnews /os-trayvon-martin-shooting-state-attorney-20120313,0,6200217.story.

8. Tom Wolfe, *Radical Chic & Mau-Mauing the Flak Catchers* (New York: Farrar, Straus & Giroux, 1970).

9. Rebecca Dana, "ABC's Gulf Hunks," *Sexy Beast* (*Daily Beast* blog), July 13, 2010, http:// www.thedailybeast.com/articles/2010/07/13/bps-gulf-oil-spill-the-hunks.html.

10. Wikipedia, s.v. "Journalist's Creed," accessed August 13, 2013, http://en.wikipedia.org/wiki /Journalist's_Creed.

11. John Nolte, "ABC News Correspondent: Trayvon Shot 'Because He Was Black'," *Breitbart*, April 3, 2012, http://www.breitbart.com/Big-Journalism/2012/04/03/ABC-News-Trayvon -Shot-Because-Black.

12. Matt Gutman, "Trayvon Martin Neighborhood Watch Shooting: 911 Tapes Send Mom Crying from Room," ABC News, March 16, 2012, http://abcnews.go.com/US/treyvon -martin-neighborhood-watch-shooting-911-tapes-send/story?id=15937881#.UecG043FUud.

13. Ibid.

14. Witness #6, in an interview with Sanford Police on February 26, 2012; audio posted on the *Axiom Amnesia* blog, http://trayvon.axiomamnesia.com/people/witnesses/witness-6-files -trayvon-martin-george-zimmerman-case/.

15. Witness #13, in an interview with Sanford Police on February 26, 2012; audio posted on the *Axiom Amnesia* blog, http://trayvon.axiomamnesia.com/people/witnesses/witness-13-files -trayvon-martin-george-zimmerman-case/.

16. "Trayvon Martin shot and killed in neighborhood altercation."

17. "Witness #5 (Mary Cutcher) Files: Trayvon Martin / George Zimmerman Case," *Axiom Amnesia*, accessed August 13, 2013, http://trayvon.axiomamnesia.com/people/witnesses /witness-5-files-trayvon-martin-george-zimmerman-case/.

18. Ibid.

19. See Sundance, "Pass #3—Stone Turnin'—'Flip Them Stones and Watch Em Scatter,'" *The Last Refuge* (*Conservative Treehouse* blog), June 23, 2013, http://theconservativetreehouse .com/2013/06/23/pass-3-stone-turnin-flip-them-stones-and-watch-em-scatter/.

20. Matt Gutman and Seni Tienabeso via *Good Morning America*, "Trayvon Martin Killing: 911 Tape Reveals Possible Racial Slur by Neighborhood Watchman," ABC News, March 20, 2012, http://abcnews.go.com/US/neighborhood-watch-killing-911-tape-reveals-racial-slur /story?id=15966309.

21. Lizette Alvarez, "Justice Department Investigation Is Sought in Florida Teenager's Shooting Death," *New York Times*, March 16, 2012, http://www.nytimes.com/2012/03/17/us/justice -department-investigation-is-sought-in-florida-teenagers-shooting-death.html?_r=2&.

22. Lizette Alvarez, "City Criticizes Police Chief after Shooting," *New York Times*, March 22, 2012, http://www.nytimes.com/2012/03/22/us/police-chief-draws-fire-in-trayvon-martin -shooting.html?_r=0.

23. Robert Zimmerman, *Florida v. Zimmerman: Uncovering the Malicious Prosecution of My Son, George* (Seattle: Amazon Digital Services, 2013), 44.

CHAPTER 8: HOGGING THE STAGE

1. *Politics Nation with Al Sharpton*, transcript, March 19, 2012, http://www.talkleft.com/zimm /sharptonmar19b.pdf.

2. James Barron, "Cuomo Won't Remove Abrams in Brawley Case," *New York Times*, February 23, 1988, http://www.nytimes.com/1988/02/23/nyregion/cuomo-won-t-remove-abrams-in -brawley-case.html.

3. Ibid.

4. William Saletan, Ben Jacobs, and Avi Zenilman, "The Worst of Al Sharpton," *Slate*, September 8, 2003, http://www.slate.com/articles/news_and_politics/ballot_box/2003/09 /the_worst_of_al_sharpton.html.

5. *Politics Nation*, transcript, March 19, 2012.

6. Ibid.

7. Trymaine Lee, "Trayvon Martin Case: 911 Audio Released of Teen Shot by Neighborhood Watch Captain," *Huffington Post*, March 16, 2012, http://www.huffingtonpost .com/2012/03/16/trayvon-martin-911-audio-_n_1354909.html.

8. Florida Department of Law Enforcement, March 19, 2012, interview with Bob Zimmerman by Investigator Jim Merck, http://trayvon.axiomamnesia.com/people/witnesses/audio -interviews-statements-george-zimmermans-father/.

9. "Key evidence revealed in Martin shooting," May 18, 2012, http://www.today.com/video /today/47473516.

10. Bob Zimmerman, interview with author in Sanford, Florida, June 17, 2013.

11. Dr. Drew On Call, "Zimmerman's brother speaks to Dr. Drew," HLN TV, June 24, 2013, http://www.hlntv.com/video/2013/06/20/goerge-zimmermans-brother-speaks-dr-drew.

12. "Statement by the NBPA in Response to the Death of Trayvon Martin" NBPA Press Release, March 23, 2012, http://www.nbpa.org/press-release/nbpa-press-release-march-23-2012.

13. John Perazzo, "The New Black Panthers' Bounty on George Zimmerman," *FrontPage Magazine*, March 29, 2012, http://frontpagemag.com/2012/john-perazzo/trayvon-martin -and-collective-racial-guilt/.

14. AP News, "Black militia group wants to arrest Trayvon Martin shooter," reprinted on the website of MSNBC's *The Grio*, March 19, 2012, http://thegrio.com/2012/03/19/black -militia-group-wants-to-arrest-trayvon-martin-shooter/.

15. Ralph Parekh, "McCann Staffer Behind Million-Hoodie March to Protest Trayvon Martin Slaying," *Ad Age*, March 23, 2012, http://adage.com/article/agency-news/mccann-staffer -million-hoodie-march/233694/.

16. Crimesider staff, "'Million Hoodie March' held in NYC in memory of Trayvon Martin," CBS News, March 22, 2012, http://www.cbsnews.com/8301-504083_162-57402318-504083 /million-hoodie-march-held-in-nyc-in-memory-of-trayvon-martin/.

CHAPTER 9: CHASING THE TRUTH

1. Ytz4mee, phone interview with author, February 26, 2013.

2. Sundance, "Look, I'm as concerned at Trayvon Martin's shooting as anyone, but "A Million Hoodie March"? Really? C'mon . . . ," *The Last Refuge* (blog), March 23, 2012, http://theconservativetreehouse.com/2012/03/23/look-im-as-concerned-at-trayvon-martins -shooting-as-anyone-but-a-million-hoodie-march-really-cmon/.

3. Ytz4m33, in ibid., comment posted March 23, 2012.

4. The reference is to Bianca Prieto and Robert Nolin, "Tensions still simmer in Trayvon Martin shooting case," *Orlando Sentinel*, March 17, 2012, http://articles.orlandosentinel .com/2012-03-17/news/os-trayvon-martin-shooting-tension-20120317_1_shooting-death -english-teacher-uncle.

5. barnslayer, commenting on Sundance, "Look, I'm as concerned at Trayvon Martin's shooting as anyone," March 23, 2012.

6. Patriot Dreamer, on ibid., March 23, 2012, in reference to the article at http://www.orlandosentinel.com/news/local/os-trayvon-martin-shooting-zimmerman-letter-20120315,0,1716605.story.

7. Stuart Taylor and KC Johnson, *Until Proven Innocent: Political Correctness and the Shameful Injustices of the Duke Lacrosse Rape Case*, Nook version (New York: Thomas Dunne Books, 2008), 119–22.

8. *Meet the Press*, September 6, 2009, available at http://www.youtube.com/watch?v=BUf1H77jQXI.

9. "Van Jones," DiscoverTheNetworks.org, http://www.discoverthenetworks.org/individualProfile.asp?indid=2406.

10. Aaron Klein, "Van Jones: 'Resist' against Police," *WND*, September 4, 2009, http://www.wnd.com/2009/09/108900/.

11. *Meet the Press*, September 6, 2009.

12. Sharon, in phone interview with author, February 28, 2013.

13. DiWataman, in phone interview with author, March 12, 2013.

14. Sundance, in phone interview with author, February 20, 2013.

15. Zimmerman, *Florida v. Zimmerman*, 30.

16. Osterman and Osterman, *Defending Our Friend*, 39.

CHAPTER 10: RUNNING OF THE BULLS

1. Al Sharpton at a rally in Sanford, Florida, March 22, 2012, as reported on MSNBC's blog *The Last Word*, www.nbcnews.com/id/45755883/ns/msnbc-the_last_word/vp/46830071#46830071.

2. Invitation, Democrats Abroad Belgium, http://myemail.constantcontact.com/DAB-and-LABM-present--A-dinner-debate-with-Reverend-Jesse-Jackson--19-March-2012.html?soid=1108816220780&aid=TtmouT_M0Ok.

3. Richard S. Dunham, "Clinton Retreats to Safer Ground in New York," *Business Week*, January 14, 1999, www.businessweek.com/bwdaily/dnflash/jan1999/nf90114e.htm.

4. Geoff Metcalf, "UNMASKING JESSE JACKSON," *WND*, March 31, 2002, http://www.wnd.com/2002/03/13339/.

5. Eric Hoffer, *The Temper of Our Time* (Titusville, NJ: Hopewell Publications, 2008).

6. "Jesse Jackson: One Leader Among Many," *Time* magazine, March 12, 2002, http://www.time.com/time/magazine/article/0,9171,216924,00.html.

7. Jay Leno on the *Tonight Show* as reported by Lowell Ponte in "Fessee, William, Martin & John," *FrontPage Magazine*, January 24, 2001, http://archive.frontpagemag.com/readArticle.aspx?ARTID=21847.

8. "Jesse Jackson Admits Affair, Illegitimate Child," ABC News, January 18, 2001, http://abcnews.go.com/Politics/story?id=122032&page=1.

9. Wayne Barrett, "What Al Did to Jesse," *Village Voice*, November 30, 2004, http://www.villagevoice.com/2004-11-30/news/what-al-did-to-jesse/full/.

10. Craig Franklin, "Media myths about the Jena 6," *Christian Science Monitor*, October 24, 2007, http://www.csmonitor.com/2007/1024/p09s01-coop.html.

11. Ben Jealous, in an interview by Amy Goodman and Juan Gonzalez on *Democracy Now*, March 22, 2012, http://www.democracynow.org/2012/3/22/naacps_ben_jealous_justice_for_trayvon.

12. Ibid.

13. Rene Lynch, "Trayvon Martin case: 'Blacks are under attack,' says Jesse Jackson," *Los Angeles Times*, March 23, 2012, http://articles.latimes.com/2012/mar/23/nation/la-na-nn-trayvon-martin-case-jesse-jackson-20120323.

14. "Jackson, Sharpton to Lead March for Trayvon Martin," WESH.com, March 26, 2012. http://www.wesh.com/trayvon-martin-extended-coverage/Jackson-Sharpton-To-Lead-March-For-Trayvon-Martin/-/14266478/13118498/-/kg8o4v/-/index.html.

15. Paul Glastris and Jeannye Thornton, "A New Civil Rights Frontier," *U.S. News & World Report*, July 19, 2013, http://www.usnews.com/usnews/news/articles/940117/archive_012245.htm.

16. Ibid.

17. Jeffrey Goldberg, "The Color of Suspicion," *New York Times* magazine, June 20, 1999, http://www.nytimes.com/1999/06/20/magazine/the-color-of-suspicion.html?pagewanted=all&src=pm.

18. Glastris and Thornton, "A New Civil Rights Frontier."

CHAPTER 11: OBLIGING THE MOB

1. Rene Stultzman and Jeff Weiner, "Sanford police chief steps down temporarily amid criticism for handling of Trayvon Martin case," *Orlando Sentinel*, March 22, 2012. http://articles.orlandosentinel.com/2012-03-22/news/os-trayvon-martin-sanford-chief-20120322_1_evidence-backs-shooting-death-police-academy.

2. Madison Gray, "Trayvon Martin Killing: Prosecutor Orders Probe as Calls for Justice Rise," *Time*, March 21, 2012, newsfeed.time.com/2012/03/21/trayvon-martin-killing-prosecutor-orders-probe-as-calls-for-justice-rise/print/.

3. Trymaine Lee, "Trayvon Martin Case: State Attorney Quits Investigation as State Studies 'Stand Your Ground' Law," *Huffington Post*, March 23, 2012, www.huffingtonpost.com/2012/03/22/trayvon-martin-state-attorney_n_1374206.html.

4. Attorney General Pam Bondi, in a press conference discussing the Trayvon Martin case, March 20, 2012, http://www.fsunews.com/VideoNetwork/1520870466001/Attorney-General-Pam-Bondi-discusses-the-Trayvon-Martin-case.

5. "Key Players: Bernie de la Rionda," WKMG Local 6, March 26, 2013, www.clickorlando.com/news/Key-Players-Bernie-de-la-Rionda/-/1637132/19394606/-/view/print/-/pih62rz/-/index.html.

6. Julie Stewart, "Florida Gun Law Gives Disabled Vet the 'TSA Treatment'," *Huffington Post*, June 8, 2012, www.huffingtonpost.com/julie-stewart/florida-gun-law-gives-dis_b_1575803.html?view=print&comm_ref=false.

7. "Florida woman sentenced to 20 years in controversial warning shot case," CNN, May 11, 2012, www.cnn.com/2012/05/11/justice/florida-stand-ground-sentencing.

8. Roland S. Martin, "Mandatory Minimums the Problem in the Marissa," *Roland Martin Reports* blog, May 11, 2012, rolandmartinreports.com/blog/2012/05/roland-s-martin-mandatory-minimums-the-problem-in-the-marissa-alexander-case/.

9. "Florida woman sentenced to 20 years in controversial warning shot case."

10. Congresswoman Corrine Brown reporting on her House Web page, April 11, 2012, http://corrinebrown.house.gov/index.php?option=com_content&view=article&id=645:congresswoman-corrine-brown-extremely-relieved-that-george-zimmerman-will-face-criminal-charges-in-death-of-trayvon-martin-&catid=3:press-releases&Itemid=35.

11. Roland Martin, "Is Trayvon Martin's death the catalyst of a new movement?" CNN, April 15, 2012, http://www.cnn.com/2012/04/14/opinion/roland-martin-florida-case.

12. Rick Scott, news release, March 22, 2012, http://www.flgov.com/2012/03/22/governor-rick-scott-announces-new-state-attorney-and-task-force-in-response-to-trayvon-martin-incident/.

CHAPTER 12: BEGETTING A SON

1. Julie Bosman, "Obama Sharply Assails Absent Black Fathers," *New York Times*, June 16, 2008, http://www.nytimes.com/2008/06/16/us/politics/15cnd-obama.html?_r=0.
2. Senator Barack Obama in a Father's Day speech at the Apostolic Church of God, June 15, 2008, http://www.c-spanvideo.org/program/205980-1.
3. Ibid.
4. Susan Duclos, "Is Jesse Jackson a Hypocrite for Using the Word 'Nigger'?" *Digital Journal*, July 16, 2008, http://digitaljournal.com/article/257506#ixzz2OUMB6TLb.
5. "Jesse Jackson Used N-Word In Obama Remarks," CBS News, June 18, 2009, http://www.cbsnews.com/2100-250_162-4266693.html.
6. Suzanne Goldenberg, "US election 2008: 'I want to cut his nuts out'—Jackson gaffe turns focus on Obama's move to the right," *Guardian*, July 10, 2008, http://www.guardian.co.uk/world/2008/jul/11/barackobama.uselections2008.
7. Ibid.
8. Barack Obama, *Dreams from My Father: A Story of Race and Inheritance* (New York: Crown, 2007), xvi.
9. Ibid., 93.
10. Barack Obama, in a speech at the Brown Chapel A.M.E. church to commemorate the forty-second anniversary of Bloody Sunday, March 4, 2007, *Chicago Sun-Times* blog *Voices*, http://voices.suntimes.com/early-and-often/sweet/obamas-selma-speech-text-as-de/.
11. Yvette Carnell, "Why Obama Shouldn't Personally Intervene in the Trayvon Martin Case," *Your Black World* (blog), March 24, 2012, http://www.yourblackworld.net/2012/03/uncategorized/yvette-carnell-why-obama-shouldnt-personally-intervene-in-the-trayvon-martin-case/.
12. Emanuel Cleaver, in a formal statement, reported by Arelis R. Hernández and Rene Stutzman in "Sanford officials, Rep. Corrine Brown meet with Justice officials in Washington," *Orlando Sentinel*, March 20, 2012, http://articles.orlandosentinel.com/2012-03-20/news/os-trayvon-martin-doj-investigation-20120320_1_shooting-sanford-church-sanford-officials.
13. Barack Obama in a press conference in the White House Rose Garden on March 23, 2012, as reported by Stacia Deshishku, "President Obama statement on Trayvon Martin case," *The 1600 Report* (White House blog), http://whitehouse.blogs.cnn.com/2012/03/23/president-obama-statement-on-trayvon-martin-case/.
14. Ibid.
15. Sundance, "Gag-A-Maggot Opportunism—President Obama Says 'If I had a son, he'd look like Trayvon'," *The Last Refuge* (blog), March 23, 2012, http://theconservativetreehouse.com/2012/03/23/gag-a-maggot-opportunism-president-obama-says-if-i-had-a-son-hed-look-like-trayvon/.
16. Tracy Jan, "Harvard professor Gates arrested at Cambridge home," *Boston Globe*, July 20, 2009, http://www.boston.com/news/local/breaking_news/2009/07/harvard.html.
17. Lynn Sweet, "Obama tells Lynn Sweet police acted "stupidly" in arresting Gates," *Chicago Sun-Times*, July 22, 2009, http://blogs.suntimes.com/sweet/2009/07/obama_tells_lynn_sweet_police.html.
18. "Friends and police rally behind Sgt. James Crowley, who arrested Harvard professor," *Metro West Daily News*, July 24, 2009, http://www.metrowestdailynews.com/news/x905592581/Friends-and-police-rally-behind-Sgt-James-Crowley-who-arrested-Harvard-professor#axzz2VjaVvCCE.
19. Newt Gingrich, speaking on the *Sean Hannity Show* as reported by Matthew Shelley, in the article "Gingrich Calls Obama Comments on Trayvon Martin Shooting 'Disgraceful'," *National Journal*, March 23, 2012, http://www.nationaljournal.com/2012-presidential-campaign/gingrich-calls-obama-comments-on-trayvon-martin-shooting-disgraceful-20120323.

20. Heather Mac Donald, "Why Manipulate the Tragedy of Trayvon Martin?" *National Review*, March 25, 2012, http://www.nationalreview.com/corner/294357/why-manipulate-tragedy -trayvon-martin-heather-mac-donald.
21. Robert VerBruggen, "Standing Your Ground and Vigilantism," *National Review Online*, March 21, 2012, http://drupal6.nationalreview.com/articles/294006/standing-your-ground -and-vigilantism-robert-verbruggen.
22. Rich Lowry, "Shocker! Sharpton is right for once," *New York Post*, March 24, 2012, http:// nypost.newspaperdirect.com/epaper/viewer.aspx.
23. Osterman and Osterman, *Defending Our Friend*, 43.
24. Ibid., 55–56.

CHAPTER 13: REMOVING THE SCALES

1. Karen Franklin and Ari Odzer, "Father Wants Man Who Shot His Son Arrested," NBC Miami, March 9, 2012, http://www.nbcmiami.com/news/local/Father-Wants-Man-Who -Shot-His-Son-Arrested-142067953.html.
2. Monique Madan, Charles Rabin, and Frances Robles, "Sanford shooting victim's parents want to keep national attention on case," *Miami Herald*, March 16, 2012, http://articles.sun -sentinel.com/2012-03-16/news/mh-trayvon-martin-0317-20120316_1_sanford-shooting -dispute-police-version-press-conference.
3. Prieto and Nolin, "Tensions still simmer in Trayvon Martin shooting case."
4. Audra D. S. Burch and Larua Isensee, "Trayvon Martin: a typical teen who loved video games, looked forward to prom," *Miami Herald*, March 22, 2012, http://www.miamiherald .com/2012/03/22/v-fullstory/2708960/trayvon-martin-a-typical-teen.html.
5. John H. Richardson, "Trayvon," *Esquire*, November 13, 2012, http://www.esquire.com /features/americans-2012/trayvon-martin-1212-2.
6. "Two Neighbors Testify in George Zimmerman Trial; Interview with Trayvon's Stepmother," *Anderson Cooper 360°*, June 28, 2013, http://transcripts.cnn.com/TRANSCRIPTS/1306/28 /acd.01.html.
7. Ibid.
8. Tracy Martin's Facebook page 2010, reported in *Sundance* post "Trayvon Martin—Perhaps the Inconsistencies from Tracy and Sybrina are more easily explained . . ." at *The Last Refuge* (blog), June 23, 2012, http://theconservativetreehouse.com/2012/06/23/trayvon-martin -perhaps-the-inconsistencies-from-tracy-and-sybrina-are-more-easily-explained/.
9. Richardson, "Trayvon."
10. Frances Robles, "Multiple suspensions paint complicated portrait of Trayvon Martin," March 26, 2012, http://www.miamiherald.com/2012/03/26/2714778/thousands-expected -at-trayvon.html.
11. Ibid.
12. Ibid.
13. David Carr, "TV Corrects Itself, Just Not on the Air," *New York Times*, April 22, 2012, http://www.nytimes.com/2012/04/23/business/media/tv-news-corrects-itself-just-not-on -the-air.html?pagewanted=all&_r=0.
14. Barry et al., "Race, Tragedy and Outrage Collide after a Shot in Florida."
15. "Complete Transcript, Serino Interview, 2/29/2012, Tape 1," txandimedia, https://www .txantimedia.com/?p=1025.
16. "Pot traces behind Trayvon Martin suspension," CBS News/AP, March 26, 2012, http://www .cbsnews.com/8301-201_162-57404664/pot-traces-behind-trayvon-martin-suspension/.

17. Elizabeth Belsom Johnson and Rachel E. Fugate, "Access to Juvenile Records and Proceedings," Florida Bar Association, updated November 2004, https://www.floridabar.org /DIVCOM/PI/RHandbook01.nsf/1119bd38ae090a748525676f0053b606/dc411ea998456 04a852569cb004c9bf9!OpenDocument.

18. Sundance, "Part I—Revealing the Trayvon Martin Coverup—M-DSPD and Former Police Chief Hurley," *The Last Refuge* (blog), April 12, 2013, http://theconservativetreehouse .com/2013/04/12/part-i-revealing-the-trayvon-martin-coverup-m-dspd-and-former-police -chief-hurley/.

19. Sworn Statement of Commander Deanna Fox-Williams, May 1, 2012, 62, http://www .scribd.com/doc/135692728/Affidavit-From-Commander-Deanna-Fox-Williams.

20. Sworn Statement of Sergeant William Tagle, May 3, 2012, 51, http://www.scribd.com /doc/135564937/Sergeant-William-Tagle-Internal-Affairs-Investigative-Report.

21. Steve Litz and Edward B. Colby, "Miami-Dade Schools Police Chief Reassigned, District Says," NBC 6, May 22, 2012, http://www.nbcmiami.com/news/local/Miami-Dade-Schools -Police-Chief-Reassigned-District-Says-152359695.html.

22. Sworn Statement of Sergeant Tagle, 87.

23. Sworn Statement of Commander Fox-Williams, 58.

24. Police Chief Charles J. Hurley in a Department of Juvenile Justice press release, as reported in the *Tampa Bay Times*, February 3, 2012, http://www.tampabay.com/blogs/gradebook /content/djj-fewer-delinquents-florida-schools.

25. Sworn Statement of Sergeant Tagle, 51.

26. White House Press Release, "President Obama Signs New Initiative to Improve Educational Outcomes for African Americans," July 26, 2012, http://www.whitehouse.gov/the-press -office/2012/07/26/president-obama-signs-new-initiative-improve-educational-outcomes -africa.

27. "Thousands gather at Miami rally for Trayvon Martin," *Times Leader*, February 16, 2013, www.timesleader.com/apps/pbcs.dll/article?avis=TL&date=20120401&category=news&lope nr=304019515&Ref=AR.

28. Marc Caputo, "Jesse Jackson's false sermon on Trayvon Martin," *Miami Herald* blog, April 30, 2012, http://miamiherald.typepad.com/nakedpolitics/2012/04/jesse-jacksons-false -sermon-on-trayvon-martin.html.

29. Carr, "TV Corrects Itself, Just Not on the Air."

30. Sundance, in interviews with the author by phone and e-mail, May 5–6, 2013.

31. "Was Trayvon Martin a Drug Dealer?" posted by Dan-Linehan on *Wagist* (blog), March 25, 2012, http://www.wagist.com/2012/dan-linehan/was-trayvon-martin-a-drug-dealer.

32. "Zimmerman Defense Receives Trayvon Martin's School Records," January 16, 2013, http:// www.gzlegalcase.com/index.php/press-releases/80-zimmerman-defense-receives-trayvon -martin-s-school-records.

CHAPTER 14: PICKING THE WRONG FIGHT

1. "Did Trayvon Martin Referee School Fights?" posted by Dan Linehan on *Wagist* (blog) April 1, 2012, http://www.wagist.com/2012/dan-linehan/did-trayvon-martin-referee-school-fights.

2. Dylan Stableford, "Trayvon Martin shooting: New details emerge from Twitter account, witness testimony," *The Cutline* (Yahoo! News blog), March 26, 2012, http://news .yahoo.com/blogs/cutline/trayvon-martin-shooting-details-emerge-facebook-twitter -accounts-180103647.html.

3. Linehan, "Did Trayvon Martin Referee School Fights?"

4. David Martosko, "The *Daily Caller* obtains Trayvon Martin's tweets," *Daily Caller*, March 26, 2012, http://dailycaller.com/2012/03/26/the-daily-caller-obtains-trayvon-martins-tweets/.

5. Rene Stutzman, "Police: Zimmerman says Trayvon decked him with one blow then began hammering his head," *Orlando Sentinel*, March 26, 2012, http://articles.orlandosentinel .com/2012-03-26/news/os-trayvon-martin-zimmerman-account-20120326_1_miami -schools-punch-unarmed-black-teenager.

6. David Martosko, "Second Trayvon Martin Twitter feed identified," *Daily Caller*, March 29, 2012, http://dailycaller.com/2012/03/29/second-trayvon-martin-twitter-feed-identified/.

7. "Bloggers Cherry-Pick from Social Media to Cast Trayvon Martin as a Menace," posted by Robert Mackey on the *Lede*, a *New York Times* blog, March 29, 2012, http://thelede.blogs .nytimes.com/2012/03/29/bloggers-cherry-pick-from-social-media-to-cast-trayvon-martin -as-a-menace/.

8. "Gawker Will Be Conducting an Experiment, Please Enjoy Your Free Cute Cats Singing and Sideboobs," posted by AJ Daulerio to *Gawker*, January 23, 2012, http://gawker .com/5878065/gawker-will-be-conducting-an-experiment-please-enjoy-your-free-cute-cats -singing-and-sideboobs.

9. "White Supremacist Hacks Trayvon Martin's Email Account, Leaks Messages Online," posted by Adrian Chen to *Gawker* on March 29, 2012, http://gawker.com/5897485/white -supremacist-hacks-trayvon-martins-email-account-leaks-messages-online.

10. Arelis Hernandez and Jon Busdeker, "Trayvon marchers: 'We want an arrest. Shot in the chest'," *Orlando Sentinel*, March 31, 2012, http://articles.orlandosentinel.com/2012-03-31 /news/os-trayvon-martin-naacp-march-sanford-20120331_1_trayvon-marchers-arrest-chest.

11. "Trayvon Martin compared to Jesus Christ, reference scrubbed from news reports," *Examiner*, April 1, 2012. http://www.examiner.com/article/trayvon-martin-compared-to-jesus-christ -reference-scrubbed-from-news-reports.

12. Sundance, "Trayvon Martin was apparently a 17 year old undisciplined punk thug, drug dealing, thief and wannabe gangsta . . . ," *The Last Refuge* (blog), March 27, 2012, http:// theconservativetreehouse.com/2012/03/27/trayvon-martin-was-apparently-a-17-year-old -undisciplined-punk-thug-drug-dealing-thief-and-wannabe-gangsta/.

13. "Update: Trayvon Martin—the Latest," *The Last Refuge* (blog), March 31, 2012, http:// theconservativetreehouse.com/2012/03/31/update-trayvon-martin-the-latest-media -narrative-continues-to-crumble-under-the-weight-of-their-false-narrative-of-events/.

CHAPTER 15: NETWORKS BEHAVING BADLY

1. Alicia Shepard, "The iconic photos of Trayvon Martin & George Zimmerman & why you may not see the others," *Poynter*, March 30, 2012, http://www.poynter.org/latest-news/top -stories/168391/the-iconic-photos-of-trayvon-martin-george-zimmerman-why-you-may-not -see-the-others/.

2. Tom Burton, "Behind the photos of the Trayvon Martin case," *Orlando Sentinel*, June 19, 2012, http://www.orlandosentinel.com/videogallery/69125947/News/Behind-the-photos-of -the-Trayvon-Martin-case.

3. Shepard, "The iconic photos of Trayvon Martin & George Zimmerman."

4. Andrew Beaujon, "NBC Miami reporter fired for edited Zimmerman tape," *Poynter*, April 25, 2012, http://www.poynter.org/latest-news/mediawire/171717/report-producer-fired-over -zimmerman-tape-editing-is-jeff-burnside-of-wtvj-in-miami/.

5. "Part I Identifying the Specific Litigants for Civil Action—Who is Jeff Burnside?" *Conservative Treehouse*, August 5, 2012. The Facebook postings from March 22–24 are screen captured here. http://theconservativetreehouse.com/2012/08/05/part-1-identifying -the-specific-litigants-for-civil-action-who-is-jeff-burnside/.

6. The times and transcripts for these clips are nicely deconstructed by attorney Jeralyn Merritt,

"NBC's Bad Edit Pre-dated Today Show and Still Appears on NBC News Sites," *TalkLeft*, April 9, 2012, http://www.talkleft.com/story/2012/4/9/43020/94141/media/NBC-s-Bad-Edit-Pre-dated-Today-Show-And-Still-Appears-on-NBC-News-Sites.

7. Transcript, *Today Show*, NBC, March 27, 2012, http://www.talkleft.com/media/todayronallenmarch27.pdf.

8. Frederica Wilson, March 28, video available at http://www.youtube.com/watch?v=mmg1aY6_AJI.

9. Brent Bozell, speaking on the *Sean Hannity Show* on Fox News, March 29, 2012, http://www.mrctv.org/videos/bozell-hannity-media-mash-nbc-deliberately-skewed-travyvon-martin-story-selective-editing.

10. *George Zimmerman v. NBC* Universal Media et al., available at http://www.washingtonpost.com/r/2010-2019/WashingtonPost/2012/12/06/Editorial-Opinion/Graphics/Zimmerman-NBC-suit.pdf.

11. Erik Wemple, "NBC to do 'internal investigation' on Zimmerman segment," *Washington Post Opinions* blog, March 31, 2012, http://www.washingtonpost.com/blogs/erik-wemple/post/nbc-to-do-internal-investigation-on-zimmerman-segment/2012/03/31/gIQAc4HhnS_blog.html?hpid=z4.

12. Jim Treacher, "NBC: We deeply regret our error that made George Zimmerman sound like a racist, and now you should leave us alone," *Daily Caller*, April 3, 2012, http://dailycaller.com/2012/04/03/nbc-we-deeply-regret-our-error-that-made-george-zimmerman-sound-like-a-racist-and-now-you-should-leave-us-alone/.

13. Brian Stelter, "NBC Fires Producer of Misleading Zimmerman Tape," *New York Times*, April 6, 2012, http://mediadecoder.blogs.nytimes.com/2012/04/06/nbc-fires-producer-of-misleading-zimmerman-tape/?ref=brianstelter.

14. Beaujon, "NBC Miami reporter fired for edited Zimmerman tape."

15. Francis Robles, "NBC6 fires local reporter Jeff Burnside in editing of Zimmerman police call," *Miami Herald*, April 25, 2012, http://www.miamiherald.com/2012/04/25/2767769/nbc6-fires-local-reporter-in-editing.html.

16. *The Young Turks*, Current TV, March 20, 2012, available at http://www.mediaite.com/tv/currents-the-young-turks-airs-alleged-'fcking-cns'-trayvon-martin-911-call-uncensored/.

17. Anderson Cooper, *Anderson Cooper 360°*, CNN, March 21, 2012, available at http://www.mediaite.com/tv/cnn-isolates-audio-on-alleged-'fcking-cns'-trayvon-martin-911-call/.

18. Tommy Christopher, "CNN Isolates Audio on Alleged 'F*cking C**ns' Trayvon Martin 911 Call," *Mediaite*, March 22, 2012, http://www.mediaite.com/tv/cnn-isolates-audio-on-alleged-'fcking-cns'-trayvon-martin-911-call/.

19. Jon Stewart, "C.N.I.: Cable News Investigators & Dick Cheney's Heart," *Daily Show with Jon Stewart*, March 26, 2012, http://www.thedailyshow.com/watch/mon-march-26-2012/c-n-i---cable-news-investigators---dick-cheney-s-heart.

20. Gary Tuchman on CNN's *Anderson Cooper 360°* covering Zimmerman's 911 call, CNN, April 4, 2012: http://www.youtube.com/watch?v=JJLA9vr97qw.

21. Zimmerman, *Florida v. Zimmerman*, 39.

22. This information came to light when the FBI interviewed an anonymous Zimmerman coworker on April 4, 2012. http://www.clickorlando.com/blob/view/-/15490330/data/1/-/kligxm/-/Zimmerman-documents.pdf.

23. Tuchman on CNN's *Anderson Cooper 360°*.

24. Transcript, "What Happened to Trayvon Martin," *Nancy Grace Show*, March 26, 2012, http://transcripts.cnn.com/TRANSCRIPTS/1203/26/ng.01.html.

CHAPTER 16: DEFENDING THE DEFENSELESS

1. Graham Winch, "Neighbor: Zimmerman stopped possible crime," HLN, April 6, 2012, http://www.hlntv.com/article/2012/04/03/zimmermans-neighbor-perfect-storm-caused-shooting.
2. Oliver, "Federal Bureau of Investigation Report."
3. Michelle Washington, "A beating at Church and Brambleton," *Virginian-Pilot*, May 1, 2012, http://hamptonroads.com.nyud.net/2012/05/beating-church-and-brambleton.
4. Kunbi Tinuoye, "Joe Oliver: Who is Zimmerman's black friend and chief defender?" *Grio*, March 29, 2012, http://thegrio.com/2012/03/29/joe-oliver-who-is-zimmermans-black-friend-and-chief-defender/.
5. Joy-Ann Reid, "George Zimmerman supporter Frank Taaffe arrested for DUI," *Grio*, July 30, 2012, http://thegrio.com/2012/07/30/george-zimmerman-supporter-frank-taaffe-arrested-for-dui/.

CHAPTER 17: DECONSTRUCTING THE DECEIT

1. Matt Gutman, "Trayvon Martin Video Shows No Blood or Bruises on George Zimmerman," ABC News, March 28, 2012, http://abcnews.go.com/US/trayvon-martin-case-exclusive-surveillance-video-george-zimmerman/story?id=16022897#.UbdYF5VO7Hg.
2. Ibid.
3. Sundance, "Reported Damning Zimmerman Video Actually Shows More Support for Zimmerman's Case . . . ," *The Last Refuge* (blog), March 29, 2012, http://theconservativetreehouse.com/2012/03/29/reported-damning-zimmerman-video-actually-shows-more-support-for-zimmermans-case/.
4. Ibid.
5. Mark Strassmann, "Martin funeral director: No signs of fight on body," CBS Evening News, March 29, 2012, http://www.cbsnews.com/8301-18563_162-57406725/martin-funeral-director-no-signs-of-fight-on-body.
6. Ibid.
7. Ibid.
8. Lisa J. Huriash, "Sustaining the Dream," *Sun-Sentinel*, January 16, 2001, http://articles.sun-sentinel.com/2001-01-16/news/0101160016_1_jeb-bush-voting-blacks.
9. Office of the Medical Examiner, Volusia and Seminole Counties "Medical Examiner Report," February 27, 2012, http://i2.cdn.turner.com/cnn/2012/images/05/17/trayvon.martin.autopsy.pdf?hpt=hp_t2.
10. Louis Peitzman, "New Evidence Contradicts Zimmerman's Claim of a Violent Fight with Trayvon Martin," *Gawker*, March 31, 2012, http://gawker.com/5898036/new-evidence-contradicts-zimmermans-claim-of-a-violent-fight-with-trayvon-martin.

CHAPTER 18: AWAITING THE NAZIS

1. Michael Miller, "Armed Neo-Nazis Now Claim to Be Patrolling Sanford, Say They Are "Prepared" for Post-Trayvon Martin Violence UPDATED," *Miami NewTimes* (blog), April 8, 2012, http://blogs.miaminewtimes.com/riptide/2012/04/heavily_armed_neo-nazis_patrol.php/.
2. The headlines that follow are all listed in William Jacobson, "Sanford (FL) Police deny any indication of Neo-Nazis patrolling," *Legal Insurrection*, April 7, 2012, http://legalinsurrection.com/2012/04/sanford-fl-police-deny-any-indication-of-neo-nazis-patrolling/.

3. Charles Johnson, "This Should Help: Armed Neo-Nazis Patrolling Sanford, Ready for Race War," *Little Green Footballs* (blog), April 6, 2012, http://littlegreenfootballs.com /article/40178_This_Should_Help-_Armed_Neo-Nazis_Patrolling_Sanford_Ready_for _Race_War.

4. Matthew Lysiak and Jonathan Lemire, "Neo-Nazis pledge to descend on Sanford, Fla., where Trayvon martin was killed, to protect 'white citizens'," *New York Daily News*, April 7, 2012, http://www.nydailynews.com/news/national/neo-nazis-patrolling-streets-sanford-fla-trayvon -martin-shot-killed-report-article-1.1057851.

5. Jacobson, "Sanford (FL) Police deny any indication of Neo-Nazis patrolling."

6. Southern Poverty Law Center, "Intelligence Files," Jeff Schoep, http://www.splcenter.org /get-informed/intelligence-files/profiles/jeff-schoep#.UYfNBJiCTZ8.

7. Miller, "Armed Neo-Nazis Now Claim to Be Patrolling Sanford."

8. Danielle Cadet, "Trayvon Martin Case: Armed Neo-Nazis Patrolling Sanford (UPDATE)," *Black Voices* (*Huffpost* blog), upd. April 9, 2012, http://www.huffingtonpost.com/2012/04/06 /trayvon-martin-case-armed_n_1409099.html.

9. "Intelligence Files: Jeff Schoep," SPLC website, http://splcenter.org/get-informed /intelligence-files/profiles/jeff-schoep, accessed August 14, 2013.

CHAPTER 19: GRABBING FOR THE GUNS

1. George Zornick, "At Capitol Hill Hearing on Trayvon, Strong Words on Gun Control," *The Nation* (blog), March 28, 2012, http://www.thenation.com/blog/167095/capitol-hill -hearing-trayvon-strong-words-gun-control#.

2. "Concealed Carry State Statistics," legallyarmed.com, updated July 2, 2013, http:// legallyarmed.com/ccw_statistics.htm.

3. Zornick, "At Capitol Hill Hearing on Trayvon, Strong Words on Gun Control."

4. "Nationwide Murder Rates, 1996–2011," deathpenaltyinfo.org, http://www.deathpenaltyinfo .org/murder-rates-nationally-and-state#MRalpha.

5. "Texas study: Concealed carry permit holders commit less than 1% of the crimes," *Beaufort Observer*, December 22, 2012, http://www.beaufortobserver.net/Articles-NEWS -and-COMMENTARY-c-2012-12-22-264494.112112-Texas-study-Concealed-carry -permit-holders-commit-less-than-1-of-the-crimes.html.

6. David Adams and Kevin Gray, "Trayvon Martin killing puts spotlight on 'Gunshine' state," Reuters, April 13, 2012, http://articles.chicagotribune.com/2012-04-13/news/sns-rt-us -florida-gunsbre83c1iv-20120413_1_gun-laws-gun-ordinances-brady-campaign.

7. Alvarez, "Justice Department Investigation Is Sought in Florida Teenager's Shooting Death."

8. Josh Horwitz, "Arming Zimmerman," *Huffington Post*, March 20, 2012, http://www .huffingtonpost.com/josh-horwitz/arming-zimmerman_b_1367648.html.

9. John Lott, "Stand Your Ground makes sense," *New York Daily News*, April 25, 2012, http:// www.nydailynews.com/opinion/stand-ground-sense-article-1.1066823.

10. Zimmerman defense team press release, "A Response to Jonathan Capehart's Editorials in Regards to the Zimmerman Case, February 21, 2013, http://gzlegalcase.com/index.php /press-releases/98-a-response-to-jonathan-capehart-s-editorials-in-regards-to-the -zimmerman-case.

11. Erika Bolstad, "Congressional Black Caucus, in honor of Trayvon Martin, calls for Florida to repeal 'Stand Your Ground' law," *Miami Herald* blog, April 4, 2012, http://miamiherald .typepad.com/nakedpolitics/2012/04/congressional-black-caucus-in-honor-of-trayvon -martin-calls-for-florida-to-repeal-stand-your-ground-.html.

12. Zimmerman, *Florida v. Zimmerman*, 46.

13. Toluse Olorunnipa, "Florida task force says no major changes needed to Stand Your Ground law, *Miami Herald*, February 22, 2013, http://www.miamiherald.com/2013/02/22/3248131 /florida-task-force-says-no-major.html.

CHAPTER 20: CHANNELING ORWELL

1. Matt Gutman, Olivia Katrandjian, and Seni Tienabeso, "Trayvon Martin Family Seeks FBI Investigation of Killing by Neighborhood Watchman," ABC News, March 18, 2012, http://abcnews.go.com/US/trayvon-martin-family-seeks-fbi-investigation-killing /story?id=15949879#.UYU-l5iCTZ8.
2. Matt Gutman, Jason Ryan, and Dean Schabner, "FBI, Justice Department to Investigate Killing of Trayvon Martin by Neighborhood Watchman," ABC News, March 19, 2012, http://abcnews.go.com/US/fbi-justice-department-investigate-trayvon-martin-killing /story?id=15955985#.UYVACpiCTZ8.
3. SA Elizabeth C. Alexander and SA Matthew R. Oliver, "Federal Bureau of Investigation transcript," Sanford, FL, April 3, 2012, http://www.talkleft.com/zimm/serinofbireporthigh .pdf.
4. Letter from Sgt. Randy Smith to M-DSPD Detective Hadley, February 29, 2012, posted on the *The Last Refuge* (blog), http://theconservativetreehouse.files.wordpress.com/2013/04/foia -preview.jpg.
5. "Miami-Dade Schools Police Department Affidavit," Steven Hadley, May 15, 2012, 77, http://www.scribd.com/doc/135684004/Steven-N-Hadley-Sr-affidavit-and-investigation.
6. "Miami-Dade Schools Police Department Affidavit," Randy Smith, April 13, 2012, 5, http:// www.scribd.com/doc/150463116/Randy-Smith-Sanford-Police-Department.
7. Frances Robles, "Detective in Zimmerman case said he was pressured to file charges," *Miami Herald*, July 12, 2012, http://www.miamiherald.com/2012/07/12/2892510/detective-in -zimmerman-case-said.html.
8. Elizabeth Harrington, "Eric Holder Praises Left-Wing Activist Al Sharpton, Says Facts, Law Will Guide Trayvon Martin Investigation," CNS News, April 11, 2012, http://cnsnews .com/news/article/eric-holder-praises-left-wing-activist-al-sharpton-says-facts-law-will-guide -trayvon.
9. Corey Dade, "The Rev. Al Sharpton, in Six True-False Statements," NPR News, January 19, 2013, http://www.npr.org/2013/01/19/169734710/the-rev-al-sharpton-in-six-true-false -statements.
10. Matthew Fleischer, "On Trayvon Martin and the 20th Anniversary of the L.A. Riots," *Take Part*, April 27, 2012, http://www.takepart.com/article/2012/04/27/trayvon-martin-and-la -riots.
11. "Rodney King: 'I am grieving' for Trayvon Martin," *Los Angeles Times*, April 11, 2012, http:// latimesblogs.latimes.com/lanow/2012/04/rodney-king-speaks-out-on-trayvon-martin.html.

CHAPTER 21: HOWLING FOR GEORGE'S HEAD

1. DavidKC, "Sanford, Florida's Long, Troubled History of Racism & Racial Injustice," *Daily Kos* (blog), April 1, 2012, http://www.dailykos.com/story/2012/04/01/1079682/-Sanford -Florida-s-Troubled-History-of-Racial-Injustice-Prejudice#.
2. Michael Cohen, commenting to the *Opinion Zone* article, "Should George Zimmerman be charged with killing Trayvon Martin?" *Palm Beach Post Opinion Zone* blog, March 21, 2012, http://blogs.palmbeachpost.com/opinionzone/2012/03/21/should-george-zimmerman-be -charged-with-killing-trayvon-martin/.

3. *Nancy Grace Show*, "New Developments in Trayvon Martin Case," March 27, 2012, http://edition.cnn.com/TRANSCRIPTS/1203/27/ng.01.html.
4. Erika Bolstad, "Trayvon Martin slaying sparks racial profiling discussions on Capitol Hill," *McClatchy Newspapers*, March 28, 2012, http://www.mcclatchydc.com/2012/03/27/v-print/143314/trayvon-martin-slaying-sparks.html.
5. Matt Gutman, "Trayvon Martin Investigator Wanted Manslaughter Charge," ABC News, March 27, 2012, http://abcnews.go.com/US/trayvon-martin-investigator-wanted-charge-george-zimmerman-manslaughter/story?id=16011674#.UZY1-ZiCTZ8.
6. Alexander and Oliver, "Federal Bureau of Investigation transcript."
7. Robles, "Detective in Zimmerman case said he was pressured to file charges."
8. Justia Trademarks, serial number 85575974, March 21, 2012, trademarks.justia.com/855/75/i-am-trayvon-85575974.html.
9. Sundance, "Trayvon Martin—The Heart of the Agenda—Exposing The REAL Family Motive in the words of their attorney . . . ," *The Last Refuge* (blog), April 5, 2012, theconservativetreehouse.com/2012/04/05/trayvon-martin-the-heart-of-the-agenda-exposing-the-real-family-motive-in-the-words-of-their-attorney/.
10. Florida Senate 2011 Florida Statues, Title XLVI, Chapter 776, Section 032, www.flsenate.gov/Laws/Statutes/2011/776.032.
11. Rene Stutzman, "Trayvon Martin's parents settle wrongful-death claim," *Orlando Sentinel*, April 5, 2013, articles.orlandosentinel.com/2013-04-05/news/os-trayvon-martin-settlement-20130405_1_trayvon-martin-benjamin-crump-george-zimmerman.
12. David Knowles, "Trayvon Martin's family settles wrongful death lawsuit with Sanford, Florida, homeowner's association," *New York Daily News*, April 5, 2013, http://www.nydailynews.com/news/national/trayvon-martin-death-civil-case-housing-complex-settled-1-million-article-1.1308943.

CHAPTER 22: LOOKING FOR DEE DEE

1. Phone interview with author, March 18, 2013.
2. Juan Ortega, "Trayvon Martin was on phone with his girlfriend moments before he was slain, attorney says," *Sun Sentinel*, March 20, 2012, articles.sun-sentinel.com/2012-03-20/news/fl-trayvon-fort-lauderdale-presser-20120320_1_miami-girl-press-conference-girlfriend.
3. Natalie Jackson, interviewed by *Democracy Now*, March 30, 2012, www.democracynow.org/2012/3/30/trayvon_martin_family_attorney_on_mounting.
4. Rene Stutzman and Amy Pavuk, "Lawyer for Trayvon's family: Wolfinger and police chief met the night teen was killed," *Orlando Sentinel*, April 2, 2012, articles.orlandosentinel.com/2012-04-02/news/os-trayvon-martin-federal-review-justice-letter-20120402_1_chief-bill-lee-federal-review-federal-agency.
5. Kyra Phillips, CNN anchor, commenting prior to the press conference in which Attorney Crump revealed Witness # 8, March 20, 2012, transcripts.cnn.com/TRANSCRIPTS/1203/20/cnr.03.html.
6. Sunny Hostin, CNN Legal Analyst, interviewed by CNN anchor Kyra Phillips, March 20, 2012, transcripts.cnn.com/TRANSCRIPTS/1203/20/cnr.03.html.
7. Benjamin Crump press conference, covered live by CNN, March 20, 2012, transcripts.cnn.com/TRANSCRIPTS/1203/20/cnr.03.html.
8. Ibid.
9. Ibid.
10. Matt Gutman and Seni Tienabeso, "Trayvon Martin's Last Phone Call Triggers Demand for Arrest 'Right Now'," ABC News, March 20, 2012, http://abcnews.go.com/US/trayvon-martin-arrest-now-abc-reveals-crucial-phone/story?id=15959017#.Ube-25VO7Hg.

11. Benjamin Crump press conference.
12. "Trayvon Martin shot and killed in neighborhood altercation."

CHAPTER 23: LOOKING FOR CAUSE

1. Pam Bondi, interviewed by Piers Morgan on *Piers Morgan Tonight*, March 27, 2012, http://transcripts.cnn.com/TRANSCRIPTS/1203/27/pmt.01.html.
2. Bernie de la Rionda interview with Rachel "Dee Dee" Jeantel, or Witness #8, April 2, 2012, posted as Florida State Attorney's Office—April 2, 2012 Track 2 on *Axiom Amnesia* (blog), http://trayvon.axiomamnesia.com/people/witnesses/witness-8-files-trayvon-martin-george-zimmerman-case/.
3. Ibid.
4. T. C. O'Steen, State Attorney's Office Investigative Division Memorandum, March 27, 2012.
5. de la Rionda interview with Rachel "Dee Dee" Jeantel.
6. Ibid.
7. Ibid.
8. Tracy Martin in an interview by Arelis R. Hernández, *Orlando Sentinel*, March 22, 2012, https://www.youtube.com/watch?v=x34vSJrIqe0#at=63.
9. Affidavit of Probable Cause—Second Degree Murder from the Office of the State Attorney, by investigators T. C. O'Steen and Dale Gilbreath, April 11, 2012, http://media.trb.com/media/acrobat/2012-04/69353440.pdf.
10. Ibid.
11. Florida State Attorney Angela Corey at a press conference to announce the charge of second-degree murder against George Zimmerman, April 11, 2012, http://www.youtube.com/watch?v=4UskHmQ5DHw.
12. Osterman and Osterman, *Defending Our Friend*, 65.
13. Kirk Veazey, "Florida Department of Law Enforcement Investigative Report," April 12, 2012, http://www.clickorlando.com/blob/view/-/15490330/data/1/-/kligxm/-/Zimmerman-documents.pdf.
14. Ad Rem, "UPDATE #33 – Trayvon Martin Shooting – "The Bloom Is Off The Ruse" . . . The Gang Connections," *The Last Refuge* (blog), July 14, 2012, http://theconservativetreehouse.com/2012/07/14/update-33-trayvon-martin-shooting-the-bloom-is-off-the-ruse-the-gang-connections/.
15. Angela Corey press conference, April 11, 2012.
16. Ibid.
17. Sundance, "Prosecutor Charges Zimmerman with 2nd Degree Murder," *The Last Refuge* (blog), April 11, 2012, http://theconservativetreehouse.com/2012/04/11/prosecutor-charges-zimmerman-with-2nd-degree-murder/.
18. Tom Wolfe, *Bonfire of the Vanities* (New York: Farrar, Straus & Giroux, 1987).
19. "Experts argue appropriateness of murder charge in Martin case," CNN, April 12, 2012, http://www.cnn.com/2012/04/12/justice/florida-shooting-charge.
20. Jonathan Capehart, "Pursuing justice: George Zimmerman arrested, charged with second-degree murder," *Washington Post*, April 11, 2012, http://www.washingtonpost.com/blogs/post-partisan/post/pursuing-justice-george-zimmerman-arrested-charged-with-second-degree-murder/2012/04/11/gIQA2DSGBT_blog.html?wprss=post-partisan.
21. Sundance, "Trayvon Martin Case – Mission Accomplished – The fuse for the racial powder keg has been lit by prosecutor Angela Corey. . . ," *The Last Refuge* (blog), April 11, 2012, http://theconservativetreehouse.com/2012/04/11/trayvon-martin-case-mission-accomplished-the-fuse-for-the-racial-powder-keg-has-been-lit-by-prosecutor-angela-corey/.

CHAPTER 24: DUELING WITH DERSHOWITZ

1. "Affidavit says Zimmerman 'profiled' Martin," CNN, April 13, 2012, www.cnn .com/2012/04/12/justice/florida-teen-shooting.
2. Conversation between George and Shellie Zimmerman on April 12, 2012, the audio and transcripts of which are posted at *Axiom Amnesia*, trayvon.axiomamnesia.com/audio /george-zimmerman-jailhouse-calls/george-zimmerman-shellie-zimmerman-jailhouse-calls -transcripts-included-audio/.
3. Alan Dershowitz, interviewed by guest host Michael Smerconish on *Hardball with Chris Matthews* on April 13, 2012, http://www.nbcnews.com/id/3036697/ns/msnbc-hardball _with_chris_matthews/vp/47034974#47034974.
4. Sanford Police Department, "Capias Request," March 13, 2012, http://www.axiomamnesia .com/TrayvonMartinFiles/Trayvon-Martin-George-Zimmerman-FULL-case-report -documents.pdf.
5. Mark Geragos, interviewed by guest host Michael Smerconish on *Hardball with Chris Matthews*, April 13, 2012, www.nbcnews.com/id/47064491/ns/msnbc-hardball_with_chris _matthews/t/hardball-chris-matthews-friday-april/#.UZKXkpiCTZ8.
6. Matt Gutman, Seni Tienabeso, and Ben Forer, "George Zimmerman Tells Trayvon Martin's Parents 'I Am Sorry'," ABC News, April 20, 2012, abcnews.go.com/US/george-zimmerman -tells-trayvon-martins-parents/story?id=16177849#.UZUeepiCTZ8.
7. Investigator Gilbreath answering attorney O'Mara's questions during the bond hearing, transcripts posted at CNN, transcripts.cnn.com/TRANSCRIPTS/1204/20/cnr.02.html.
8. Ibid.
9. Alan Dershowitz, "Zimmerman Prosecutor Threatening to Sue Harvard for My Criticism," *Newsmax*, June 5, 2012, http://www.newsmax.com/AlanDershowitz/Zimmerman-Trayvon -Angela-Corey/2012/06/05/id/441305.
10. Ibid.
11. Zimmerman, *Florida v. Zimmerman*, 78.
12. Sundance, "'Parseltongue'—If He Wins, He Loses—If He Loses, He Loses Less . . . ," Conservative Treehouse, June 16, 2013, http://theconservativetreehouse.com/2013/06/16 /parseltongue-if-he-wins-he-loses-if-he-loses-he-loses-less/.

CHAPTER 25: SHOOTING ONE'S FOOT

1. Frances Robles, "Judge: Zimmerman was going to jump bail with other people's money," *Miami Herald*, July 5, 2012, http://www.miamiherald.com/2012/07/05/v-print/2882584 /zimmerman-bond-ruling-expected.html.
2. Sundance, "*The State vs Zimmerman*," *The Last Refuge* (blog), June 1, 2012, http:// theconservativetreehouse.com/2012/06/01/the-state-vs-zimmerman/.
3. "Details Regarding the Request for a Second Bond Hearing for George Zimmerman," George Zimmerman Legal Case, June 4, 2012, http://gzlegalcase.com/index.php/press-releases/24 -details-regarding-the-request-for-a-second-bond-hearing-for-george-zimmerman.
4. Conversations between George and Shellie Zimmerman, April 15–16, 2012, the audio and transcripts of which are posted at *Axiom Amnesia*, trayvon.axiomamnesia.com/audio /george-zimmerman-jailhouse-calls/george-zimmerman-shellie-zimmerman-jailhouse-calls -transcripts-included-audio/.
5. Dershowitz, "Zimmerman Prosecutor Threatening to Sue Harvard for My Criticism."

6. Jeff Weiner, "George Zimmerman's wife arrested, charged with perjury," *Orlando Sentinel*, June 12, 2012, articles.orlandosentinel.com/2012-06-12/news/os-george-zimmerman-wife -arrested-20120612_1_perjury-charge-prosecutors-deputies.

7. Rene Stutzman, "Judge: Corey has authority to prosecute Shellie Zimmerman," *Orlando Sentinel*, February 19, 2013, http://articles.orlandosentinel.com/2013-02-19/news/os-shellie -zimmerman-dismissal-hearing-20130219_1_shellie-zimmerman-george-zimmerman -special-prosecutor-angela-corey.

8. Eighteenth Judicial Circuit Court, *State of Florida v. George Zimmerman*, CASE NO. 12 -CF-1083-A, Order Setting Bail in *State of Florida v. George Zimmerman*, July 5, 2012, http:// www.flcourts18.org/PDF/Press_Releases/SKMBT_363-V12070510360.pdf.

9. Frances Robles and Scott Hiaason, "FBI records: agents found no evidence that Zimmerman was racist," *Miami Herald*, July 12, 2012, http://www.mcclatchydc.com/2012/07/12/155918 /more-evidence-released-in-trayvon.html#.UgYqp5VO7Hh.

10. All of these interviews were done in the first week of April 2012 and are cached at http://www .clickorlando.com/blob/view/-/15490330/data/1/-/kligxml-/Zimmerman-documents.pdf.

11. *The View*, ABC, June 7, 2013, available at http://www.youtube.com/watch?v =DFrwWwuWQbw.

CHAPTER 26: LOOKING FOR SOME LEAN

1. "The 'Whole' Story of Trayvon Martin at 7 Eleven" posted to YouTube by DiWataman, May 27, 2012, http://www.youtube.com/watch?v=o286bRPGfqI.

2. Barbara Liston, "Family of Florida boy killed by Neighborhood Watch seeks arrest," Reuters, March 7, 2012, http://mobile.reuters.com/article/idUSBRE82709M20120308?irpc=932.

3. Sami K. Martin, "Boy Killed by Neighborhood Watch Shooter Disobeyed 911," *Christian Post*, March 9, 2012, http://m.christianpost.com/news/boy-killed-by-neighborhood-watch -shooter-disobeyed-911-71140/.

4. *Geraldo at Large*, Fox News, April 2, 2012, http://archive.org/details/FOXNEWSW _20120402_080000_Geraldo_at_Large.

5. MJ Lee, "Geraldo Rivera: My own son ashamed of me," *Politico*, March 23, 2012, http:// www.politico.com/news/stories/0312/74403.html#ixzz2TaH7FWNT.

6. "The 'Whole' Story of Trayvon Martin at 7 Eleven" posted to YouTube.

7. Dale Gilbreath, State Attorney's Office Memorandum, May 10, 2012. http://www .clickorlando.com/blob/view/-/15490330/data/1/-/kligxml-/Zimmerman-documents.pdf.

8. O'Steen, State Attorney's Office Investigative Division Memorandum, March 27, 2012.

9. Sundance, "Update #26 Part 2 – Trayvon Martin Shooting – A year of drug use culminates in predictable violence," *The Last Refuge* (blog), May 24, 2012, theconservativetreehouse .com/2012/05/24/update-26-part-2-trayvon-martin-shooting-a-year-of-drug-use-culminates -in-predictable-violence/.

10. This video is the full-length interview that the *Miami Herald* conducted with the family of Trayvon Martin, March 19, 2012, http://www.youtube.com/watch?feature=player _embedded&v=71Ytt7zTB6A.

11. Eighteenth Judicial Circuit Court, *State of Florida v. George Zimmerman*, CASE NO. 12 -CF-1083-A, Defendant's Reply to State's Motion for Protective Order/Motion in Lemine Regarding Toxology, May 4, 2013, http://www.gzdocs.com/documents/0513/052113 _reply_limine_toxicology.pdf.

CHAPTER 27: TAKING THE SHOW ON THE ROAD

1. Lauren Gold, "Rally honors late Kendrec McDade, Trayvon Martin," *Pasadena Star-News*, April 26, 2012, http://www.pasadenastarnews.com/news/ci_20493388/rally-honors-late -kendrec-mcdade-trayvon-martin.

2. "Pasadena police shooting of Kendrec McDade was justified, D.A. says," *L.A. Now*, December 17, 2012, http://latimesblogs.latimes.com/lanow/2012/12/kendrec-mcdade-pasadena-police -shooting-justified.html.

3. Joe Piasecki, "Kendrec McDade's father files new allegation against Pasadena police," *Los Angeles Times*, May 14, 2013, http://www.latimes.com/local/lanow/la-me-ln-father-police -shooting-20130514,0,4167963.story.

4. Gold, "Rally honors late Kendrec McDade."

5. Comedian Kevin Day, quoted in a Justice for Trayvon Martin press release, March 29, 2012, http://blackactivistsrisingagainstcuts.blogspot.com/2012/03/press-release-justice-for-trayvon .html.

6. Jerome Tayler, "Trayvon Martin's parents call for an end to racial profiling in Britain," *Independent*, May 11, 2012, http://www.independent.co.uk/news/uk/home-news/trayvon -martins-parents-call-for-an-end-to-racial-profiling-in-britain-7737747.html.

7. Ibid.

8. Stephen Wright, "The Mail's victory: How Stephen Lawrence's killers were finally brought to justice years after our front page sensationally branded the evil pair murderers," *Daily Mail*, January 3, 2012, http://www.dailymail.co.uk/news/article-2080159/Stephen-Lawrence-case -How-killers-finally-brought-justice.html.

9. Rebecca Camber, "Black men 'to blame for most violent city crime' . . . but they're also the victims," *Daily Mail*, June 27, 2010, http://www.dailymail.co.uk/news/article-1290047 /Metropolitan-Police-crime-statistics-reveal-violent-criminals-black--victims.html.

10. Tina Sfondeles, "Trayvon Martin's parents in town to condemn violence," *Chicago Sun-Times*, May 26, 2012, http://www.suntimes.com/news/crime/12789483-418/trayvon -martins-parents-in-town-to-condemn-violence.html.

11. "Rekia Boyd family awarded $4.5 million settlement," ABC7 News, March 13, 2013, http:// abclocal.go.com/wls/story?section=news/local&id=9026410.

12. Becky Schlikerman and Liam Ford, "Teen with autism shot to death by police, *Chicago Tribune*, February 02, 2012, http://articles.chicagotribune.com/2012-02-02/news/ct-met -calumet-city-shooting-20120202_1_tasers-kitchen-knife-officers.

13. Sfondeles, "Trayvon Martin's parents in town to condemn violence."

14. Zimmerman, *Florida v. Zimmerman*, 46–48; Cory Pippin, "Three charged with homicide, robbery after fatal fire," Fox 10 News, April 7, 2013, http://www.fox10tv.com/dpp/news /crime/three-charged-with-homicide-robbery-after-pensacola-fatal-fire.

15. Kyle Rogers, "Two teens arrested for gruesome hammer attack near Sanford, FL," *Examiner*, April 2, 2012, http://www.examiner.com/article/two-teens-arrested-for-gruesome-hammer -attack-near-sanford-fl.

CHAPTER 28: STRAIGHTENING THE STORY

1. Eighteenth Judicial Circuit Court, *State of Florida v. George Zimmerman*, CASE NO. 12 -CF-1083-A, Motion for Reconsideration and Clarification of the Courts Order, May 4, 2013, http://www.gzdocs.com/documents/0313/motion_for_reconsideration.pdf.

2. Scott Stump, "Trayvon Martin's parents: Trust friend's phone call," *Today Show*, March 21, 2012, http://www.today.com/id/46805726/ns/today-today_news/t/trayvon-martins-parents -trust-friends-phone-call/#.UfFgno3FUud.

3. *Nancy Grace Show*, HLN, April 2, 2012, http://transcripts.cnn.com/TRANSCRIPTS/1204/02
    /ng.01.html.
4. ABC's Matt Gutman: Lawrence O'Donnell, *The Last Word*, March 28, 2012, excerpted
    at http://www.talkleft.com/story/2012/10/23/195459/60/crimenews/George-Zimmerman
    -The-Witness-8-Interviews.
5. Vivian Kuo and Josh Levs, "Chief witness in Trayvon Martin case lied under oath," CNN
    .com, March 7, 2013, http://www.cnn.com/2013/03/06/us/florida-trayvon-martin-case.
6. Nancy Benefiel commenting on the equally delusional article "US media pushes false
    narrative that DD (Witness 8) lied in Zimmerman case," *Frederick Leatherman Law Blog*,
    Wednesday, March 6, 2013, http://frederickleatherman.com/2013/03/06/us-media-pushes
    -false-narrative-that-dd-witness-8-lied-in-zimmerman-case/.
7. Eighteenth Judicial Circuit Court, *State of Florida v. George Zimmerman*, CASE NO. 12
    -CF-1083-A, State's Response to Defendant's Motion for Sanctions Against State Attorney's
    Office for Discovery Violations, March 28, 2013, http://www.gzdocs.com/documents/0313
    /response_to_sanctions.pdf.
8. Eighteenth Judicial Circuit Court, *State of Florida v. George Zimmerman*, Reply to State's
    Response to Defendant's Motion for Sanctions Against State Attorney's Office for Discovery
    Violations, April 26, 2013, http://www.gzdocs.com/documents/0413/042513_reply_to
    _sanctions.pdf.
9. William Shakespeare, *Macbeth*, act 2, scene 3.

CHAPTER 29: REMEMBERING LEO FRANK

1. Comments to Sundance's "State v. George Zimmerman Hearing – April 30th 9:00am – Open
    Discussion Thread," *The Last Refuge* (blog), April 30, 2013, http://theconservativetreehouse
    .com/2013/04/30/state-v-george-zimmerman-hearing-april-30th-900am-open-discussion
    -thread/.
2. Lizette Alvarez, "Zimmerman Forgoes Pretrial Hearing, Taking Issue of Immunity to a
    Jury," *New York Times*, April 30, 2013, http://www.nytimes.com/2013/05/01/us/george
    -zimmerman-waives-right-to-pretrial-hearing.html?_r=0.
3. Melanie Eversley, "George Zimmerman ordered bulletproof vest while on bond," *USA Today*,
    August 9, 2013. http://www.freep.com/article/20130809/NEWS07/308090067/George
    -Zimmerman-ordered-bulletproof-vest-while-on-bond.
4. David Turner, "The United States and the Holocaust, 1: Background to Passivity," *the
    Jerusalem Post*, March 7, 2012, http://blogs.jpost.com/content/united-states-and-holocaust
    -1-background-passivity.
5. Leonard Dinnerstein, *The Leo Frank Case*, rev. ed. (Athens, GA: University of Georgia Press,
    2008), 113.
6. "Twitter lynch mob: George Zimmerman is out on bail? Let's kill him!" *Twitchy.com*, April
    23, 2012, http://twitchy.com/2012/04/23/twitter-lynch-mob-now-that-george-zimmerman
    -is-out-on-bail-lets-kill-him/.

CHAPTER 30: THE UNRAVELING OF TRAYVON

1. Extraction Report, SMS Messages, http://www.gzdocs.com/documents/0513/discovery_3
    /extraction_reports/report1.pdf.
2. Witness #6 in an interview with Sanford Police on Feburary 26, 2012; audio posted on *Axiom
    Amnesia* (blog), http://trayvon.axiomamnesia.com/people/witnesses/witness-6-files-trayvon
    -martin-george-zimmerman-case/.

3. O'Steen, State Attorney's Office Investigative Division Memorandum, March 26, 2012, http://www.clickorlando.com/blob/view/-/15490330/data/1/-/kligxm/-/Zimmerman -documents.pdf.

4. David Ovalle, "Records detail allegations against teen in murder of North Miami-Dade mom," *Miami Herald*, July 9, 2012, http://www.miamiherald.com/2012/07/09/2888656 _p2/records-show-details-of-allegations.html.

5. Extraction Report, SMS Messages.

6. O'Steen, State Attorney's Office Investigative Division Memorandum, April 2, 2012, http:// www.clickorlando.com/blob/view/-/15490330/data/1/-/kligxm/-/Zimmerman-documents .pdf.

7. Extraction Report, SMS Messages.

8. George Bush, acceptance speech before the NAACP, 2000.

9. https://twitter.com/NatJackEsq/statuses/337980842183897088.

CHAPTER 31: EXCLUDING THE UNPLEASANT

1. "Appeals court grants George Zimmerman new judge," WFTV 9, August 29, 2012, http://www.wftv.com/news/news/local/appeal-court-rules-zimmermans-favor-judge-lester-s /nRN6p/.

2. Rene Stutzman, "George Zimmerman's new judge: Debra S. Nelson," *Orlando Sentinel*, August 31, 2012, http://articles.orlandosentinel.com/2012-08-31/news/os-george-zimmerman-new -judge-20120830_1_george-zimmerman-trayvon-martin-mark-o-mara.

3. Rene Stutzman, "Judge: Crump need not answer questions from George Zimmerman's lawyers," *Orlando Sentinel*, March 28, 2013, http://articles.orlandosentinel.com/2013-03-28 /news/os-zimmerman-no-crump-depo-20130328_1_george-zimmerman-trayvon-martin -benjamin-crump.

4. Josh Levs. Graham Winch and Victor Blackwell, "Marijuana, fights, guns: Zimmerman loses key pretrial battles," CNN, May 29, 2013, http://www.cnn.com/2013/05/28/justice/florida -zimmerman-trial/index.html.

5. Ibid.

6. "Trayvon Martin's Texts & Photos Limited," *Huffpost Live*, May 28, 2013, http://live .huffingtonpost.com/r/segment/trayvon-martin-texts-and-photos-limited/51a4da322b8c2a3 c840002f6.

7. "Court employee in Zimmerman case dismissed after lawyer testifies that he withheld gun and drug photos on Trayvon Martin's cellphone," *MailOnline*, May 30, 2013, http://www .dailymail.co.uk/news/article-2333423/George-Zimmerman-trial-Court-employee-withheld -photos-Trayvon-Martins-phone-lawyer-claims.html.

8. Kyle Hightower, "Lawyer: Zimmerman Prosecutor Withheld Evidence," Associated Press, May 29, 2013, http://www.theledger.com/article/20130529/NEWS01/130529429?p=1&tc=pg.

9. "The Tawana Brawley Story," June 3, 2013, retroreport.org/the-tawana-brawley-story/.

10. Fifth District Court of Appeal of the State of Florida, Petition for Certiorari Review of Order from the Circuit Court for Seminole County, *State of Florida v. George Zimmerman*, June 3, 2013, http://www.5dca.org/Opinions/Opin2013/060313/5D13-1233.op.pdf.

11. Sundance, "Crump Will be Deposed—5ᵗʰ DCA Decision—O'Mara Wins—Judge Nelson reversed," *The Last Refuge* (blog), June 3, 2013, http://theconservativetreehouse .com/2013/06/03/crump-will-be-deposed-5th-dca-decision-omara-wins-judge-nelson -reversed/.

12. Jeff Weiner, "Trayvon Martin shooting: It's not George Zimmerman crying for help on 911 recording, 2 experts say," *Orlando Sentinel*, March 31, 2012, http://articles.orlandosentinel .com/2012-03-31/news/os-trayvon-martin-george-zimmerman-911-20120331_1_george -zimmerman-owen-forensic-services-llc-trayvon-martin.

13. Alan R. Reich, Ph.D, Acoustic Consultants Report, *George Zimmerman -vs- Trayvon Martin* blog, May 9, 2013, zimmerman-vs-martin.blogspot.com/2013/05/text-version-alan-r-reich -phd-acoustic.html.

14. Ibid.

15. Matt Gutman, *Good Morning America*, ABC News, June 7, 2013, http://archive.org/details /tv?time=20130606-20130614&q=george+zimmerman&fq=program:%22ABC+News+Goo d+Morning+America%22.

16. Witness #6 in an interview with Sanford Police on February 26, 2012, audio posted on *Axiom Amnesia*, http://trayvon.axiomamnesia.com/people/witnesses/witness-6-files-trayvon-martin -george-zimmerman-case/.

17. Eighteenth Judicial Circuit Court, *State of Florida v. George Zimmerman* CASE NO. 12 -CF-1083-A, Order Excluding the Opinion Testimony of Mr. Owen and Dr. Reich, June 22, 2013, http://www.scribd.com/doc/149371530/Florida-v-Zimmerman-Order-Excluding -Expert-Testimony.

CHAPTER 32: FILTERING THE POOL

1. "Justice for Trayvon: Our Son Is Your Son," BET, June 10, 2013, http://www.bet.com/video /news/national/2013/justice-for-trayvon.html.

2. Joel Schipper, "George Zimmerman trial: NAACP holds town hall meeting at church," 13 News, June 24, 2013, http://www.cfnews13.com/content/news/cfnews13/news/article.html /content/news/articles/cfn/2013/6/24/george_zimmerman_tri_0.html.

3. All trial references are from the video of the trial cached on the blog *Legal Insurrection* (*LI*), at http://legalinsurrection.com/tag/george-zimmerman/. The cited day in the text corresponds to *LI*'s designation. In other words, day one was the first day of the trial itself, June 24. The last day was day fourteen, Friday, July 12. Court was not in session on the weekends or on July 4.

4. Andrew Branca, "Zimmerman Jury Selection Profiles—"Top 40" Advanced to Next Round," *Legal Insurrection*, June 19, 2013, http://legalinsurrection.com/2013/06/zimmerman-jury -selection-profiles-of-the-top-40-wjpe-advanced-to-next-round/.

5. Ibid.

6. "Jury selected in George Zimmerman murder trial," *Click Orlando*, June 20, 2013, http://www.clickorlando.com/news/jury-seated-in-george-zimmerman-murder -trial/-/1637132/20648712/-/mg3494/-/index.html.

7. Andrew Branca, "Zimmerman Prosp. Juror E7: "no conclusions," but posted on pro-Trayvon, anti-Zimmerman site containing threat against Zimmerman," June 12, 2013, *LI*, http:// legalinsurrection.com/2013/06/zimmerman-props-juror_e7-no-conclusions-but-posted-on -kill-zimmerman-site/.

8. Sundance, "Update: Mole Juror Busted—The Manipulation and the Trayvon Scheme of Lies Continues . . . (Video Added)," *The Last Refuge* (blog), June 12, 2013, http:// theconservativetreehouse.com/2013/06/12/the-manipulation-and-the-trayvon-scheme-of -lies-continues/.

9. "Deputies escort dismissed George Zimmerman juror from courthouse," *Click Orlando*, June 14, 2013, http://www.clickorlando.com/news/deputies-escort-dismissed-george-zimmerman -juror-from-courthouse/-/1637132/20575140/-/oyd2jo/-/index.html.

10. C. R., "Trolling a Troll: Digging Dirt on Jerry P. Counelis," *Gucci Little Piggy* (blog), June 12, 2013, http://glpiggy.net/2013/06/12/trolling-a-troll-digging-dirt-on-jerry-p-counelis/.

11. Branca, "Zimmerman Prosp. Juror E7."

12. Andrew Branca, "Meet the Zimmerman Trial Jurors," *Legal Insurrection*, June 23, 2013, http://legalinsurrection.com/2013/06/meet-the-zimmerman-trial-jurors/.

13. *Politics Nation*, MSNBC, June 20, 2013.

CHAPTER 33: F-BOMBING THE BOURGEOISIE

1. Richard Dool, "George Zimmerman trial: Meet the attorneys," HLN, June 23, 2013.

2. Ibid.

3. Jonathan Capehart, "The George Zimmerman trial begins," *Washington Post*, June 24, 2013, http://www.washingtonpost.com/blogs/post-partisan/wp/2013/06/24/the-george-zimmerman-trial-begins-2/.

4. Sundance, "Zimmerman Case—Inside Baseball from an Exhausting Battle . . . That Continues," *The Last Refuge* (blog), June 22, 2013.

5. Ibid.

6. All trial references in this chapter are from the video of the trial cached on the blog *Legal Insurrection* (*LI*), at http://legalinsurrection.com/tag/george-zimmerman/.

CHAPTER 34: FERRETING OUT THE FALSEHOODS

1. Sundance, "During Trial—Crowdsourcing the Liars—State Witnesses First," *The Last Refuge* (blog), June 23, 2013, http://theconservativetreehouse.com/2013/06/23/during-trial-crowdsourcing-the-liars-the-state-witnesses-first/.

2. Ibid.

3. This and all other trial references in this chapter are from the video of the trial cached on the blog *Legal Insurrection* (*LI*), at http://legalinsurrection.com/tag/george-zimmerman/.

4. Sundance, "Heroine Recognition: Cobra and Viper," *The Last Refuge* (blog), June 27, 2013, http://theconservativetreehouse.com/2013/06/27/heroine-recognition-cobra-and-viper/.

5. Andrew Branca, "Zimmerman Trial Day 2 – Analysis of State's Witnesses" (live video), *Legal Insurrection*, June 25, 2013, http://legalinsurrection.com/2013/06/zimmerman-trial-day-2-analysis-of-states-witnesses/.

6. O'Steen, State Attorney's Office Investigative Division Memorandum, March 27, 2012.

CHAPTER 35: ECHOING THE AGITPROP

1. All trial references in this chapter are from the video of the trial cached on the blog *Legal Insurrection* (*LI*), at http://legalinsurrection.com/tag/george-zimmerman/.

2. Sundance, "Pass #3—'Flip Them Stones and Watch Em Scatter,'" *The Last Refuge* (blog), June 23, 2013.

3. David Weigel, "Where Were You When Trayvon Was Killed?" *Slate*, April 6, 2012, http://www.slate.com/articles/news_and_politics/crime/2012/04/witnesses_mary_cutcher_and_selma_mora_offer_their_account_of_what_happened_the_night_trayvon_martin_died_.html.

4. Hal Boedeker, "Trayvon Martin: Thank God for the Media," *Orlando Sentinel*, March 16, 2013.

5. Lester Holt, *Dateline* NBC, March 25, 2013.

6. Jessica Hopper, "Witnesses describe Trayvon Martin's final moments; Parents say 'He was headed on the right path,'" http://insidedateline.nbcnews.com/_news/2012/03/25/10843593 -witnesses-describe-trayvon-martins-final-moments-parents-say-he-was-headed-on-the-right -path?lite.

7. "Witness #5 (Mary Cutcher) Files," http://trayvon.axiomamnesia.com/people/witnesses /witness-5-files-trayvon-martin-george-zimmerman-case/.

CHAPTER 36: PROFILING THE PROFILER

1. All trial references in this chapter are from the video of the trial cached on the blog Legal Insurrection (LI), at http://legalinsurrection.com/tag/george-zimmerman/.

2. Andrew Branca, "Zimmerman Trial Day 4," *Legal Insurrection*, June 27, 2013, http:// legalinsurrection.com/2013/06/zimmerman-trial-day-end-of-day-analysis-video-of-states -witnesses/.

3. Jeantel's letter to Fulton is available at http://www.talkleft.com/story/2013/3/29/74056/4011 /crimenews/Zimmerman-Case-Attorney-Warfare-and-Witness-8.

4. Branca, "Zimmerman Trial Day 4."

5. *Anderson Cooper 360°*, June 26, 2013, http://transcripts.cnn.com/TRANSCRIPTS/1306/26 /acd.02.html.

6. Dave Urbanski, "'if zimmerman get off, ima go kill a white boy': trayvon martin supporters make shocking threats ahead of verdict," *The Blaze*, June 27, 2013, http://www.theblaze .com/stories/2013/06/27/if-zimmerman-get-off-ima-go-kill-a-white-boy-trayvon-martin -supporters-make-shocking-threats-ahead-of-verdict/.

7. Sundance, "Witness #8 – First Crowdsourcing Thread – Deconstructing The lies – - – *Update – Videos Added!: Bearing False and Improper Witness," *The Last Refuge* (blog), June 26, 2013, http://theconservativetreehouse.com/2013/06/26/witness-8-first-crowdsourcing -thread-deconstructing-the-lies/.

8. Fred12, commenting on Sundance, "Thread 3 – Day 23 (Week #5) Zimmerman Trial – Closing Arguments," *The Last Refuge* (blog), July 11, 2013, http://theconservativetreehouse .com/2013/07/11/thread-3-day-23-week-5-zimmerman-trial-closing-arguments/.

9. Sundance, "Witness #8 – Rachel Jeantel – Scheme Participation, Dot Connection . . . ," *The Last Refuge* (blog), June 27, 2013, http://theconservativetreehouse.com/2013/06/27/witness -8-rachel-jeantel-scheme-participation-dot-connection/.

10. phone interview with the author, June 27, 2013.

CHAPTER 37: THROWING DOWN, MMA–STYLE

1. All trial references in this chapter are from the video of the trial cached on the blog *Legal Insurrection* (LI), at http://legalinsurrection.com/tag/george-zimmerman/.

2. Andrew Branca, "Zimmerman Trial Day 5 – Analysis & Video – State's own witnesses undercut theory of guilt," *Legal Insurrection*, June 28, 2013, http://legalinsurrection .com/2013/06/zimmerman-trial-day-5-analysis-video-states-own-witnesses-undercut-theory -of-guilt/.

3. O'Steen, State Attorney's Office Investigative Division Memorandum, March 27, 2012.

CHAPTER 38: SCORING FOR THE OPPOSITION

1. All trial references in this chapter are from the video of the trial cached on the blog *Legal Insurrection* (*LI*), at http://legalinsurrection.com/tag/george-zimmerman/.

2. Andrew Branca, "Zimmerman Update Exclusive—Mid-Day 8—State Wins Evidentiary Battle, Loses Testimony War," *Legal Insurrection*, July 3, 2013, http://legalinsurrection.com/2013/07/zimmerman-update-exclusive-mid-day-state-wins-evidentiary-battle-loses-testimony-war/.

3. "George Zimmerman's attorney walks tight line in defense," Associated Press, June 9, 2013, http://www.foxnews.com/us/2013/06/09/george-zimmerman-trial-for-trayvon-martin-killing-set-to-start-his-lawyer-walks/.

4. Jonathan Capehart, "Five Myths About . . . the killing of Trayvon Martin," *Washington Post*, July 5, 2013.

5. "Trayvon Martin Case Moves to State Attorney's Office," WESH.com, March 13, 2012, http://www.wesh.com/trayvon-martin-extended-coverage/Trayvon-Martin-Case-Moves-To-State-Attorney-s-Office/-/14266478/13118970/-/1505qea/-/index.html.

6. Jeralyn Merritt, "Zimmerman Juror B37: It Was Self Defense," *TalkLeft*, July 16, 2013, http://www.talkleft.com/story/2013/7/16/92019/5240/crimenews/Zimmerman-Juror-B37-It-Was-Self-Defense.

7. *Anderson Cooper 360°*, CNN, July 15, 2013.

CHAPTER 39: SOURCING THE SCREAMS

1. Matt Gutman and Seni Tienabeso, "Trayvon Martin Neighborhood Watch Shooting: 9-1-1 Tapes Send Mom Crying from Room," ABC News, March 16, 2012, http://abcnews.go.com/US/treyvon-martin-neighborhood-watch-shooting-911-tapes-send/story?id=15937881.

2. All trial references in this chapter are from the video of the trial cached on the blog *Legal Insurrection* (*LI*), at http://legalinsurrection.com/tag/george-zimmerman/.

3. Andrew Branca, "Why Zimmerman's Motion for Acquittal Should Have Been Granted," *Legal Insurrection*, July 3, 2013, http://legalinsurrection.com/2013/07/why-zimmermans-motion-for-acquittal-should-have-been-granted/.

4. *Anderson Cooper 360°*, CNN, July 15, 2013.

5. Underground Forum: mixedmartialarts.com, July 9, 2013.

6. Seminole County Clerk of Courts, Case 2012CA001276, filed July 9, 2012.

7. *Anderson Cooper 360°*, CNN, July 15, 2013.

8. Andrew Branca, "Implosion: Police Testify Trayvon's Father Originally Denied Son Was Screaming," *Legal Insurrection*, July 8, 2013, http://legalinsurrection.com/2013/07/implosion-police-testify-trayvons-father-originally-denied-son-was-screaming/.

9. *Good Morning America*, ABC News, July 8, 2013.

10. Comments following Jack Cashill, "Ten Aha! Moments in the Zimmerman Trial to Date," *American Thinker*, July 9, 2013, http://www.americanthinker.com/2013/07/ten_aha_moments_in_the_zimmerman_trial_to_date.html.

11. Dan Abrams, "Analysis: George Zimmerman Probably Won't Be Convicted of Murder or Manslaughter—Here's Why," ABC News, July 7, 2013, http://abcnews.go.com/US/george-zimmerman-convicted-murder-manslaughter/story?id=19598422.

12. *The Situation Room with Wolf Blitzer*, CNN, July 10, 2013.

13. "Documents Obtained by Judicial Watch Detail Role of Justice Department in Organizing Trayvon Martin Protests," Judicial Watch, July 10, 2013, http://www.judicialwatch.org/press-room/press-releases/documents-obtained-by-judicial-watch-detail-role-of-justice-department-in-organizing-trayvon-martin-protests/.

14. Patrick Howley, "Former DOJ official: Civil rights unit sent to mediate anti-Zimmerman protests has history of advocacy," *Daily Caller*, July 21, 2013, http://dailycaller .com/2013/07/21/former-doj-official-civil-rights-unit-sent-to-mediate-anti-zimmerman -protests-has-history-of-advocacy/.
15. "Documents Obtained by Judicial Watch Detail Role of Justice Department in Organizing Trayvon Martin Protests."
16. Howley, "Former DOJ official."
17. "Documents Obtained by Judicial Watch Detail Role of Justice Department in Organizing Trayvon Martin Protests."

CHAPTER 40 RESCUING SCIENCE

1. All trial references are from the video of the trial cached at http://legalinsurrection.com/tag /george-zimmerman/.

CHAPTER 41: FIXING THE FIGHT

1. *Good Morning America*, July 10, 2013.
2. All trial references are from the video of the trial cached at http://legalinsurrection.com/tag /george-zimmerman/.
3. Sundance, "Richard Conner [sic] – The 'Expert' Who Panicked Nelson," *The Last Refuge* (blog), July 21, 2013, http://theconservativetreehouse.com/2013/07/21/richard-conner-the -expert-who-panicked-nelson-worth-re-watching-his-testimony/.
4. Karen Franklin and Ari Odzer, "Father Wants Man Who Shot His Son Arrested," 6 South Florida website, March 9, 2012, http://www.nbcmiami.com/on-air/as-seen-on/Father _Wants_Man_Who_Shot_His_Son_Arrested_Miami-142158853.html.
5. Sundance, "Richard Conner."
6. Tom Watkins and Nancy Leung, "Ben Kruidbos, IT Director fired: Headed information technology for the State Attorney's Office," News Channel 5 wptv.com, July 13, 2013, http://www.wptv.com/dpp/news/national/ben-kruidbos-it-director-fired-headed-information -technology-for-the-state-attorneys-office.
7. Sundance, "Richard Conner."
8. William Jacobson, "Zimmerman judge needs to read this case on authentification of text messages," *Legal Insurrection*, July 10, 2013, http://legalinsurrection.com/2013/07 /zimmerman-judge-needs-to-read-this-case-on-authentication-of-text-messages/.
9. Sundance, "Day 23 (Week #5) Zimmerman Trial—Closing Arguments," *The Last Refuge* (blog), July 11, 2013, http://theconservativetreehouse.com/2013/07/11/thread-3-day-23 -week-5-zimmerman-trial-closing-arguments/.

CHAPTER 42: MAKING CRIME REAL

1. All trial references are from the video of the trial cached at http://legalinsurrection.com/tag /george-zimmerman/.
2. "Emmanuel Burgess," http://florida.arrests.org/Arrests/Emmanuel_Burgess_7189120/.
3. *Anderson Cooper 360°*, CNN, July 15, 2013.

CHAPTER 43: CONCOCTING A CLOSE

1. Trial references in this chapter are from the video of the trial cached at http://legalinsurrection .com/tag/george-zimmerman/.
2. Andrew Branca, "State's Closing Argument: Two Hours of Raising Doubt," *Legal Insurrection*, July 11, 2013, http://legalinsurrection.com/2013/07/states-closing-argument -two-hours-of-raising-doubt/.
3. "Zimmerman Prosecution's Emotional Closing Argument: Lead prosecutor Bernie De La Rionda gave an animated, sometimes theatrical statement," ABC News, July 12, 2013, http:// abcnews.go.com/GMA/video/george-zimmerman-trial-trayvon-martin-death-prosecutions -emotional-19647095.
4. Jacqui Goddard, "George Zimmerman Trial: The Prosecution's Dramatic Closing Arguments," *Daily Beast*, July 11, 2013, http://www.thedailybeast.com/articles/2013/07/11 /george-zimmerman-trial-the-prosecution-s-dramatic-closing-arguments.html.
5. Erin Donaghue, "George Zimmerman trial: Zimmerman was a 'wannabe cop' who profiled Trayvon Martin, prosecutor says in closing argument," CBS News, July 11, 2013, http://www .cbsnews.com/8301-504083_162-57593345-504083/george-zimmerman-trial-zimmerman -was-a-wannabe-cop-who-profiled-trayvon-martin-prosecutor-says-in-closing-argument/.
6. *Good Morning America*, ABC, July 12, 2013.

CHAPTER 44: STATING THE OBVIOUS

1. Trial references in this chapter are from the video of the trial cached at http://legalinsurrection .com/tag/george-zimmerman/.
2. Bill Hoffman, "Dershowitz: Zimmerman Prosecutors 'Should Be Disbarred,'" *Newsmax*, July 12, 2013, http://www.newsmax.com/Newsfront/dershowitz-zimmerman-trayvon -martin/2013/07/12/id/514847.
3. Matt Gutman, "George Zimmerman 'Had Hate in His Heart' Prosecutor Tells Jury," ABC News, July 12, 2013, http://abcnews.go.com/US/george-zimmerman-jury-adjourns-verdict /story?id=19645098.

CHAPTER 45: SAVING THE SYSTEM

1. William Jacobson, "Zimmerman Final Jury Instruction," *Legal Insurrection*, July 12, 2013, http://legalinsurrection.com/2013/07/zimmerman-final-jury-instructions/.
2. Ibid.
3. Branca, "Zimmerman Jury Selection Profiles—"Top 40" Advanced to Next Round."
4. Barbara Liston, "Zimmerman Jurors Got Manicures, Watched Movies, Went Bowling," Reuters, July 17, 2013, http://www.huffingtonpost.com/2013/07/17/zimmerman-jurors -manicures-movies_n_3613841.html.
5. Michelle Singletary, "A swift public verdict on 'Zimmerman Juror B37,'" *Washington Post*, July 19, 2013, http://articles.washingtonpost.com/2013-07-19/business/40670268_1 _trayvon-martin-first-juror-george-zimmerman.
6. "4 Jurors from Zimmerman Trial Distance Themselves from Juror B37," Fox News, July 17, 2013, http://www.foxnews.com/us/2013/07/17/zimmerman-jurors-request-privacy-in -statement/.
7. Josh Levs. Dana Ford, and Holly Yan, "Exclusive: Juror pushes for new laws following Zimmerman trial," *CNN Justice* (blog), July 18, 2013, http://www.cnn.com/2013/07/17 /justice/zimmerman-verdict-aftermath.

8. *Anderson Cooper 360°*, CNN, July 15, 2013.

9. Ibid.

10. *Good Morning America*, ABC, July 25, 2013.

11. *Anderson Cooper 360°*, CNN, July 15, 2013.

12. *Good Morning America*, ABC, July 25, 2013.

13. Tracy Conner and Andrew Rafferty, "Zimmerman juror: He shouldn't have gotten out of that car," July 15, 2013, http://tv.msnbc.com/2013/07/15/zimmerman-juror-he-shouldnt-have-gotten-out-of-that-car/.

14. Greg Botelho and Holly Yan, "George Zimmerman found not guilty of murder in Trayvon Martin's death," *CNN Justice*, July 14, 2013, http://www.cnn.com/2013/07/13/justice/zimmerman-trial.

15. Ibid., see embedded video.

16. Ibid.

17. Billy Hallowell, "Zimmerman's Brother Opens Up To The Blaze: George Was Made Into A 'Mythological Monster,'" *The Blaze*, July 28, 2013, http://www.theblaze.com/stories/2013/07/28/zimmermans-brother-opens-up-to-theblaze-says-george-was-made-into-a-mythological-monster/.

18. "Zimmerman Attorneys React to Verdict," July 13, 2013, http://www.bing.com/videos.

19. Ibid.

20. Sundance, "Ask Sundance Questions—Your Opportunity to Ask Any Questions," *The Last Refuge* (blog), July 14, 2013, http://theconservativetreehouse.com/2013/07/14/ask-sundance-your-opportunity-to-ask-any-questions/.

21. Sundance, "From Robert Zimmerman—George's Dad," *The Last Refuge* (blog), July 14, 2013, http://theconservativetreehouse.com/2013/07/14/from-robert-zimmerman-georges-dad/.

22. Interview with author, July 13, 2013.

23. Sundance, "Zimmerman—NOT Guilty," *The Last Refuge* (blog), July 13, 2013, http://theconservativetreehouse.com/2013/07/13/zimmerman-not-guilty/.

24. Ibid.

CHAPTER 46: DENYING REALITY

1. Liberal Stalwart71, "I Ask Again: Did the prosecution lose on purpose?" *Democratic Underground*, July 13, 2013, http://www.democraticunderground.com/10023248087.

2. Renew Deal, "Did the prosecution in the Zimmerman trial 'throw the case?'" *Democratic Underground*, July 13, 2013, http://www.democraticunderground.com/10023241942.

3. Jarvis DeBerry, "Did George Zimmerman's prosecutors try to get him off?" *Nola.com*, July 15, 2013, http://www.nola.com/opinions/index.ssf/2013/07/did_george_zimmermans_prosecut.html.

4. William Boardman, "Zimmerman Prosecutor Worse Than Jury?" *Reader Supported News*, July 21, 2013, http://readersupportednews.org/opinion2/277-75/18516-focus-zimmerman-prosecutor-worse-than-jury.

5. Floyd Blue, "Who Among Us Honestly Believes the Zimmerman Prosecution Tried to Win?" *Daily Kos*, July 19, 2013, http://www.dailykos.com/story/2013/07/19/1224911/-Who-Among-Us-Honestly-Believes-the-Zimmerman-Prosecution-Tried-to-Win#.

6. Steven Rosenfeld, "10 Reasons Lawyers Say Florida's Law Enforcement Threw Away George Zimmerman's Case," *AlterNet*, August 7, 2013, http://www.alternet.org/civil-liberties/10-reasons-lawyers-say-floridas-law-enforcement-threw-ryan-zimmermans-case-away.

7. "Zimmerman Trial Prosecutors Post Verdict Press Conference," July 13, 2013, Mox News/YouTube, http://www.youtube.com/watch?v=BAJqBXS7eks.

8. "Viewers wonder: Why is Florida state attorney Angela Corey smiling so big?" *Twitchy*, July 13, 2013, http://twitchy.com/2013/07/13/viewers-wonder-why-is-florida-state-attorney -angela-corey-smiling-so-big/. The tweets that follow can be found at same source.

9. "Zimmerman Trial Prosecutors Post Verdict Press Conference," YouTube.

CHAPTER 47: LEARNING NOTHING

1. Reginald Rose, *Twelve Angry Men*, 1957, screenplay available at http://fischersoph.files .wordpress.com.

2. *HLN After Dark*, July 15, 2013.

3. Bill Hoffman, "Dershowitz: Zimmerman Has Defamation Case Against Florida Prosecutor," *Newsmax*, July 15, 2013, http://www.newsmax.com/Headline/Dershowitz-zimmerman -defamation-trayvon/2013/07/15/id/515150.

4. *HLN After Dark*, July 15, 2013.

5. Richard Thompson Ford, "The Law That Acquitted Zimmerman Isn't Racist. But that doesn't mean the outcome wasn't," *New Republic*, July 16, 2013, http://www.newrepublic .com/article/113873/zimmerman-trial-racist-laws.

6. Michelle Meyer, "How TNR Doesn't Correct the Record," *Attack Machine* (blog), posted by Big Baloney, July 25, 2013, http://attackmachine.com/2013/07/25/how-tnr-doesnt-correct -the-record/. See also ibid., paragraph that begins, "*This article has been corrected.*"

7. Ford, "The Law That Acquitted Zimmerman Isn't Racist"; Jonathan Adler, "How Not to Correct the Record—TNR Edition," *The Volokh Conspiracy*, July 25, 2013, http://www .volokh.com/2013/07/25/how-not-to-correct-the-record-tnr-edition/.

8. Benjamin Crump, press conference, July 13, 2013, video accessible at "Martin Family Lawyer Likens Trayvon to Medgar Evers and Emmett Till," http://www.realclearpolitics.com /video/2013/07/14/martin_family_lawyer_likens_trayvon_to_medgar_evers_and_emmett _till_.html.

9. "Jesse Jackson: 'I Do Not Accept' Zimmerman Verdict," KRWG TV FM, July 15, 2013, http://krwg.org/post/jesse-jackson-i-do-not-accept-zimmerman-verdict.

10. "The O. J. Simpson Trial: The Jury," Famous American Trials, The O. J. Simpson Trial, 1995, http://law2.umkc.edu.

11. "Sharpton reacts to Zimmerman verdict," MSNBC, July 13, 2013, accessible at *Huff Post Media*, http://www.huffingtonpost.com/2013/07/13/al-sharpton-george-zimmerman -verdict_n_3593001.html.

12. Ben Jealous interview, *CNN Press Room*, July 14, 2013, http://cnnpressroom.blogs.cnn.com.

13. *New York Post*, July 14, 2013. See Meg Storm, "Op-Ed: Exposing the real 'TRAY-VESTY,'" Glenn Beck website, July 15, 2013, http://www.glennbeck.com/2013/07/15/op-ed-exposing -the-real-tray-vesty/.

14. *Guardian Express*, July 13, 2003, http://guardianlv.com/2013/07/george-zimmerman-skirts -justice-with-all-white-jury-video/.

15. Kwik, "Trayvon Martin is Our Emmett Till; Our Jury Selection Process Is No Better Now That It Was In 1955," *Daily Kos*, July 25, 2013, http://www.dailykos.com /story/2013/07/25/1225369/-Trayvon-Martin-is-Our-Emmett-Till-Our-Jury-Selection -Process-Is-No-Better-Now-Than-It-Was-In-1955.

16. "When will it end? Deadly racial targeting of black men and teens is hardly ancient history," *New York Daily News*, July 14 2013, http://www.nydailynews.com/news/national/black-men -killed-white-men-ancient-history-article-1.1398806.

17. RJ Carrubarubia, "Lil Wayne Apologizes for 'Inappropriate' Emmett Till Lyric," *Rolling Stone*, May 1, 2013.

CHAPTER 48: MISLEADING AMERICA

1. Lizette Alvarez, "Juror Says Zimmerman 'Got Away With Murder,'" *New York Times*, July 25, 2013, http://www.nytimes.com/2013/07/26/us/juror-says-zimmerman-got-away-with-murder.html?_r=0.

2. William Saletan, "Did George Zimmerman Get Away with Murder?" *Slate*, July 26, 2013, http://www.slate.com/articles/news_and_politics/frame_game/2013/07/did_george_zimmerman_get_away_with_murder_no_juror_b29_is_being_framed.html.

3. "George Zimmerman Juror: 'In Our Hearts, We Felt He Was Guilty,'" *Nightline*, ABC News, July 25, 2013. Full interview shown on *Good Morning America*, July 26, 2013.

4. Jon Cohen, "Zimmerman verdict: 86 percent of African Americans disapprove," *Washington Post*, July 22, 2013.

5. Record of *Leo M. Frank v. C.Wheeler Mangum, Sheriff*, Supreme Court of United States, No. 775. Argued February 25 and 26, 1915. Decided April 19, 1915. See http://law2.umkc.edu/faculty/projects/ftrials/frank/frankvmagnumdissent.html.

6. "George Zimmerman Juror: 'In Our Hearts, We Felt He Was Guilty.'"

7. CNN *News Room*, July 26, 2013.

8. "Zimmerman's Attorney Says Juror B29 Was a 'Model Juror'," ABC News Radio, July 26, 2013.

9. Cohen, "Zimmerman verdict."

10. Joel Siegel, "George Zimmerman verdict: New York City mayoral candidates berate not guilty verdict," *New York Daily News*, July 14, 2013.

11. *Meet the Press*, NBC, July 14, 2013.

12. Emily Schultheis, "Hillary Clinton: George Zimmerman verdict brought 'deep heartache,'" *Politico*, July 16, 2013, http://www.politico.com/story/2013/07/hillary-clinton-trayvon-martin-george-zimmerman-verdict-94301.html.

13. Melissa Rohlin, "Charles Barkley agrees with George Zimmerman verdict," *Los Angeles Times*, July 19, 2013.

CHAPTER 49: DOUBLING DOWN

1. *United States v. Armstrong et al.*," Legal Information Institute, http://www.law.cornell.edu.

2. Tom Head, "Racial Profiling in the United States," Civil Liberties, *About.com*.

3. David Folkenflik, "NPR Ends Williams' Contract After Muslim Remarks," *NPR.org*, October 21, 2010, http://www.npr.org/templates/story/story.php?storyId=130712737.

4. Attorney General Eric Holder's remarks on Trayvon Martin at NAACP convention (full text)," *Washington Post*, July 16, 2013.

5. Victor Davis Hanson, "Facing Facts About Race," *National Review Online*, July 13, 2013, http://www.nationalreview.com/article/354122/facing-facts-about-race-victor-davis-hanson.

6. Joe Gullien, "Detroit council supports calls for federal investigation of possible civil rights charges against George Zimmerman," *Detroit Free Press*, July 13, 2013.

7. Ed Hornick, "Holder 'nation of cowards' remarks blasted, praised," *CNNPolitics.com*, February 19, 2009, http://www.cnn.com/2009/POLITICS/02/19/holder.folo/.

8. Perry Bacon, "On Trayvon Martin and other racial issues, Holder speaks out in ways Obama does not," *The Grio*, July 16, 2013, http://thegrio.com/2013/07/16/on-martin-and-other-racial-issues-holder-speaks-out-in-ways-obama-does-not/.

9. Lily Workneh, "Cornel West: MSNBC a 'rent-a-negro' network, Sharpton on 'Obama plantation.' *The Grio*, July 23, 2013, http://thegrio.com/2013/07/23/cornel-west-msnbc-a-rent-a-negro-network-sharpton-on-obama-plantation/.

10. *Meet the Press*, NBC, July 21, 2013.
11. "President Obama's remarks on Trayvon Martin (full transcript)," *Washington Post*, July 19, 2013.
12. Ibid.
13. Pat Buchanan, "Leading From Behind Al Sharpton," the Patrick J. Buchanan official website, March 23, 2013, http://buchanan.org/blog/leading-from-behind-al-sharpton-5722.
14. President Obama's remarks on Trayvon Martin (full transcript).
15. HART RESEARCH ASSOCIATES/PUBLIC OPINION STRATEGIES July 2013, http://msnbcmedia.msn.com.
16. "Barack Obama's Remarks at the Democratic Convention," July 27, 2004.

Index

RACIAL VIOLENCE IS BACK!

In this latest edition of *'White Girl Bleed a Lot'*, award-winning reporter Colin Flaherty breaks the code of silence on the explosion of racial violence in more than one-hundred cities since 2010 and makes an undeniable case for one of the largest and most underreported problems facing America today.

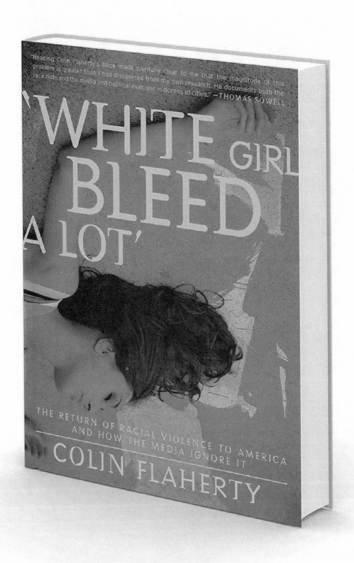

WND Books • a WND Company • Washington, DC • www.wndbooks.com

American society is gripped

by a bizarre and baffling condition that threatens the nation's very well being. But don't expect any surgeon general warnings, celebrity PSAs, or prescription drug commercials to even whisper of it. That's because this societal sickness is rooted in (peek over shoulders, lower voice)... race.

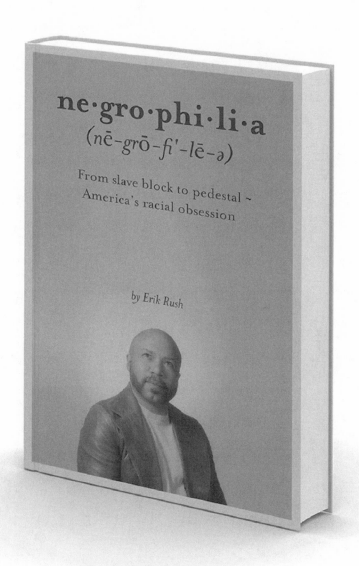

THE MOST DANGEROUS CITIZEN IS NOT ARMED BUT UNINFORMED.

Have you ever heard the phrase, "Forty acres and a mule"? Do you know how slavery actually began in America? Did you know the KKK lynched over a thousand white people? Do you know why? Have you ever wondered what African-Americans want, and why they vote Democratic?

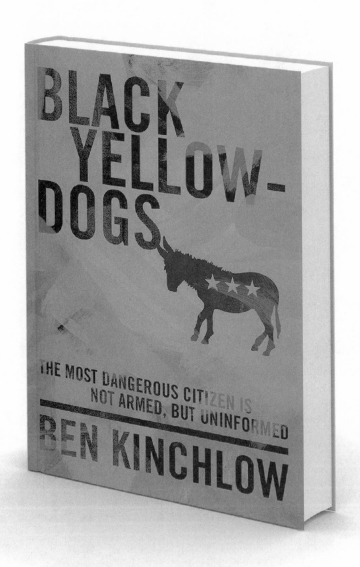

No publisher in the world has a higher percentage of *New York Times* bestsellers.

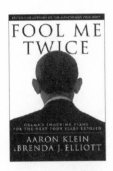

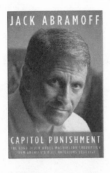

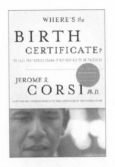

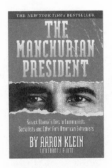

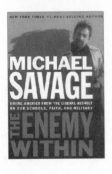

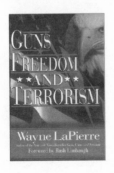

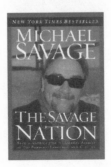

WND Books • a WND Company • Washington, DC • www.wndbooks.com